Pariah Politics

Pariah Politics

Understanding Western Radical Islamism and What Should be Done

SHAMIT SAGGAR
Foreword by Trevor Phillips

OXFORD
UNIVERSITY PRESS

OXFORD

UNIVERSITY PRESS

Great Clarendon Street, Oxford OX2 6DP

Oxford University Press is a department of the University of Oxford.
It furthers the University's objective of excellence in research, scholarship,
and education by publishing worldwide in

Oxford New York

Auckland Cape Town Dar es Salaam Hong Kong Karachi
Kuala Lumpur Madrid Melbourne Mexico City Nairobi
New Delhi Shanghai Taipei Toronto

With offices in

Argentina Austria Brazil Chile Czech Republic France Greece
Guatemala Hungary Italy Japan Poland Portugal Singapore
South Korea Switzerland Thailand Turkey Ukraine Vietnam

Oxford is a registered trade mark of Oxford University Press
in the UK and in certain other countries

Published in the United States
by Oxford University Press Inc., New York

British Library Cataloguing in Publication Data
Data available

Library of Congress Cataloging in Publication Data
Data available

Typeset by SPI Publisher Services, Pondicherry, India
Printed in Great Britain
on acid-free paper by the
MPG Books Group, Bodmin and King's Lynn

ISBN 978-0-19-955813-1
ISBN 978-0-19-958746-9 (pbk.)

1 3 5 7 9 10 8 6 4 2

In memory of my late mother, Kamla Saggar, née Bhakoo (1936–74), and my late uncle, Braham Dev Saggar (1931–89). In their own ways, both established a lasting base for intellectual curiosity, diligence, and deeper thinking in our family, now scattered across four continents. They are greatly missed.

Foreword by Trevor Phillips

"What do they know of cricket who only cricket know?" wrote the Caribbean intellectual, CLR James echoing Kipling's poignant question about England in his 1908 poem "The English Flag". Kipling's point was that no one could fully understand the swashbuckling expansionist spirit of his small island without understanding its place in the whole Empire. In his 1963 masterwork *Beyond The Boundary*, probably the greatest work of literature in English about any sport, James paraphrased Kipling in order to deliver an elegant exposition of the history and social landscape of post-war British colonialism, which still beguiles even those who are mystified by the popularity of the game.

But the old polymath was also making a different point—that the world-wide appeal of this complex, arcane, game could only be understood against the background of a landscape in which it had emerged as both a product of and a metaphor for the decline of Empire. Today we could observe that the huge earning power of the game in India parallels the extraordinary rise of that country as a global economic giant. In essence, the point is that there are some social phenomena which can only be properly understood within a wider geopolitical, social, and economic context; but that in reaching that understanding we illuminate the wider terrain in a way that reveals new insights about it.

In this magisterial study, Professor Shamit Saggar sets out the landscape surrounding an even more complex and critical phenomenon of our time: the emergence of British Muslims as a political and social force. However, he sets this in a geographical, demographic, social, and economic framework which demonstrates that the real challenge of this new force is less how best to deal with particular communities and their alleged tendency towards extremism, but more how to understand the maelstrom of change for which they have become a leading indicator in Western societies. The study of British Muslims in their context, he implicitly contends, can tell us a great deal about the whole of Western society.

I agree.

It is understandable that until recently most analyses of the challenge of integration focused largely on the ethnic differentness and cultural separateness of British Muslims. Most Asian Muslims are, relatively speaking, geographically and socially isolated. It is also true that the default template for considering diversity in Britain has always been racial. And the activist lobby groups, such as the Muslim Council of Britain, have self-consciously adopted the language of the race relations pressure groups (itself borrowed from America's Civil rights movement) to make their case. Thus, Islamophobia has become a convenient, though inaccurate, analogue for racism.

But we knew, even before 7/7, that this approach has obscured a proper understanding of British Muslims, and would not do. The demographic profile of British Muslims is decidedly supra-racial. Today, there are 1.8 million Muslims in the UK. Sixty per cent live in London and the South East. They are not a homogeneous group. British Muslims have backgrounds in dozens of nations. We have come to think of them as predominantly South Asian, but this is less and less true. Today, one third of Muslims are not Asians, half of Asians are not Muslims.

Then there is their political expression. The advent of organizations such as the Muslim Council of Britain, with their narrow focus on the defence of Muslim religious and cultural sensibilities should have been a warning that we were not dealing with "just another" ethnic immigrant community. So should have been the pietistic preoccupations of the more radical movements within the British Muslim communities.

Even without these signs that the description of British Muslims was wrong, there is another factor that should have made them different: security. The intimate relationship between the position of British Muslims and the wider geopolitical and security questions of a post–Cold War world has made any comparison with racial groupings seem eccentric. It may be that the poor life-chances and alienation that characterize the lives of many British Muslims are similar to those of some racial minorities; but I doubt if anyone in their right minds would draw parallels between the geopolitical significance of Britain's former Caribbean possessions, and that of, say, present-day Pakistan.

And there is always history. Though there have been different races in Europe from before Roman times, the significance of race as a determinant in social relations has only really emerged in the past three centuries, with the struggle over the slave trade. Not so with Islam. Our history with Islam is at least as deep, but profoundly different.

To listen to most of our media and read our newspapers, you would reasonably assume that Britain's first domestic encounter with Islam occurred sometime in the post-war period with the arrival in Northern towns of textile workers from Pakistan. You would be wrong of course.

Perhaps the earliest encounter between Britain and Islam that we can identify goes back to the eighth century. King Offa, the Anglo Saxon King of Mercia, minted some gold coins with Arabic inscriptions on them.

They can still be seen in the British Museum and they carry the inscription "There is no God but Allah". Nobody is sure why. Did Offa or someone in his court convert? Or did he need these coins to trade with Muslim countries? Or perhaps to honour a Muslim visitor. Who knows?

But we do know that of all the countries of Europe, Britain enjoyed the most extensive trade with Muslim lands throughout the first millennium after Christ.

Happily, today English schoolchildren are learning that there is more to Genghis Khan than the hordes.

We also know that we can tell a more complex story about the wars which we came to call the Crusades than was given in my childhood storybooks about Richard the Lionheart; and that Saladin was not just "a villain in a Hollywood movie", but one of the great line of Arab Muslim leaders who were not only warriors to match any that Europe's knightly tradition could produce, but also scholars and sages.

In fact, Muslim scholarship was well known among the learned in Britain by 1386. In the Prologue to Chaucer's Canterbury Tales, there is among the pilgrims wending their way to Canterbury, a "Doctour of Phisyk" whose learning included Razi, Avicenna (Ibn Sina), and Averroes (Ibn Rushd). Ibn Sina's canon of medicine was a standard text for medical students well into the seventeenth century.

Later, my own nomination for the greatest British genius of all time, Isaac Newton, drew freely on the work of Arab scholars in mathematics and astronomy, in order to revolutionize our understanding of the universe.

Increasingly we are discovering new links with the Muslim world. For example researchers at London University have recently uncovered letters indicating that when the first Queen Elizabeth was menaced by the Spanish Armada she turned to Turkish Muslims for help.

So maybe the reason that I am writing in English today rather than Spanish lies not with Sir Francis Drake's derring-do, but with the first Anglo–Turkish alliance. Perhaps that should count for something when Turkey's membership of the EU comes to be considered.

In the nineteenth century Muslims from Africa, the Indian sub-continent, and the Middle East not only traded with this country but also started to settle here. There are Muslim communities of which we hear little but which have been here far longer than we imagine.

For example, a few years back at a meeting in the North-East of England, it was a surprise to me, but no one else there, to see a contingent from the long-settled Yemeni community, probably the descendants of Yemeni sailors who arrived in Britain by way of the newly opened Suez Canal.

Similar Muslim communities can still be found in Cardiff, Liverpool, and towns such as Sheffield where Yemeni workers came to work in the steel industry. That particular community has also given us Prince Naseem Hamed of course, a role model for young British boxers of both Muslim and non-Muslim heritage.

During both First World War and Second World War, Muslims helped fight alongside British troops. Noor Inayat Khan was a spy for British Intelligence who died behind enemy lines in the Second World War.

The arrival of communities from the Indian subcontinent is well-documented. Today, there are few areas of the British economy where these Muslims and subsequent generations have not made their mark. Shopkeepers, teachers, doctors, dentists, barristers, broadcasters, factory workers, engineers, scientists—everywhere Muslims are making a substantial contribution in business, the public service, and the professions. Increasingly, they are becoming involved in the political life of the country, especially in local government and on official advisory bodies.

In the past 20 years, particularly since the fall of the Berlin Wall released the Soviet grip on many European Muslim states, further groups of Muslims arrived in Britain mainly as refugees. These included Afghans, Somalis, Kurds, Bosnians, and Algerians.

Today, all sorts of Muslims are making positive contributions to Britain. We know about many of the famous names, but perhaps we should not forget the many thousands of ordinary people who clean hospitals as well as the consultants who carry out heart surgery, and the bookkeepers, as well as the TV stars.

So it seems indisputable that Britain has benefited for centuries from its association with the Islamic world.

In spite of the current tensions both at home and abroad I think we still benefit and will continue to do so. That is why it is so important to understand how best to meet the challenge to the rest of us posed by the presence of a substantial Muslim minority. We need to ensure that we so configure our society that it provides a congenial home for this new strain of Britishness; and that we can be explicit with Muslims about the nature of the society into which they are expected to integrate.

This is not just a question for today, or for Muslims and non-Muslims. This century is likely to see more movement across the globe by more people than at any time in human history. To put it another way, more of us will be encountering more people different in many ways from ourselves than any of our ancestors. We already know that increasingly, the first great battle for twenty-first-century humankind will be to live sustainably with our planet. It is becoming clear that the second great struggle will be to live with each other "graciously" in the words of Sir Isaiah Berlin. We know it will be more difficult against a background of greater economic and social competition in a rapidly changing world. And we know that one aspect of identity politics is the growing assertiveness of those who profess faith of one kind or another—and of those who reject religion as oppressive and irrational.

The stage is set for a long period of potential conflict. But I believe that it does not need to be like that. In the words of a great twentieth-century songwriter, we can work it out. That task must start with a deeper understanding of both foreground and background; and of the role of public policy in preventing that conflict. This book is a distinguished contribution to that understanding.

Trevor Phillips

London

Preface to the paperback edition, July 2010

The paperback edition of *Pariah Politics* has been finalized as the House of Commons begins the 2010 summer recess. A new parliament has been elected at Westminster and with it a new and historic Coalition Government has taken residency in Whitehall. The political backdrop has changed significantly, in other words.

Three key developments have taken place since the publication of the first edition of this book: the election of the Obama administration in the US, the launch of the Iraq Inquiry in Britain (and the imminent end to US combat operations in Iraq), and the installation of a new Coalition Government in the UK. Each of these has made a great difference to the context and background of understanding and combating Islamist inspired terrorism. Together, the external environment has been all but transformed to the casual eye.

The new administration in Britain nevertheless inherits many of the security risks and worries that formed the basis of the first edition of this book in 2008. The scale and sophistication of terror plots has not abated although the prominence given the small trickle that has gone to trial has waned. The Government is the beneficiary of several years of experience of persuading and cajoling British Muslims to create greater clear water between legitimate dissent as against unwitting support for violence. Very many senior politicians in office recognize that whilst the moral oxygen for extremism and terror has not been removed, it has thankfully been correctly identified as its largest contributory factor.

But the Government also presides over great uncertainty about the so-called boomerang effects of counter terrorism policy. Many well intentioned measures have led to unanticipated spin offs that have caused anger and bitterness in Muslim communities and minds. The simplistic idea that security policy was needed to isolate and criminalize extremists bent on violence has given way to a new reality that sees security and community policies as mutually interdependent. CT strategy simply cannot afford to jettison community activism to challenge the blind eye of many towards jihadist confrontationists.

The real debate is based around getting a greater synchronicity between security and community based approaches to CT strategy, and searching for fresh opportunities to avoid essentialising the position of Muslims in Britain and other western societies.

The Coalition Government's most eye catching intervention has been to begin a fresh review of CT strategy and policy. At one level, this is deflating, coming less than 18 months after the last review under its predecessor resulted in minimal changes. However, three concerns drive the new review.

The first is the growing unease about the unintended consequences of the Prevent strand of the strategy. The new Home Secretary's comments chime with those critics of the strategy who claim that an intrusive policy of communities policing themselves – one of the necessary-evil conclusions of this book – carries the risk of alienating the very people who are needed to combat grassroots extremism. In fact, the review will find that there is no simple way around this conundrum. The best that can be achieved is to make more use of sensitive operational practices so that community-based intelligence is swiftly obtained with little lasting impact on community relationships. It is certainly right that unintended and unforeseen radicalization is reviewed in this way. But is it usually the result of a climate that takes a purist and naïve view of CT operations based on binary divisions between us and them. This book challenges this viewpoint, arguing that continuums of support or opposition to radical ideas and violence exist in British Muslim communities.

The second driver is cost, value and opportunity cost. In common with most of the rest of Government in 2010, the emphasis has switched to cutting the country's mammoth public deficit. Combating Islamist extremism and terror is not exempt from the new public sector culture of doing more with less. Britain is not alone here since much of Western Europe has begun curbing public spending across the board, even where real dangers remain. From any plausible angle, this constraint must be correct. The UK spend on CT (including the rapidly bloated budget of MI5) stood at more than £1.8 Billion at the time of the last Home Office review in 2009. There has been a nagging irritation in Westminster about the public accountability and transparency of such spending, so it must be a welcome development that basic value for money and efficacy questions are probed in relation to the cost of CT measures.

The final driver is a more complex one to understand in the round. It is that the calculus of risk (to national security and to public safety) is today well embedded in national political life. The bulk of politicians accept that radical Islamist politics has taken root in many British cities, and that Government has to be prepared in response. This necessitates a number of obligations on Government to sanction and take actions that can appear intrusive and heavy handed. The use of criminal sanctions to tackle photography of various public spaces is an obvious, high profile such intrusion. The difficulty for the new Coalition Government is that this grates with a number of important civil liberties instincts among the two parties' MPs and rank and file. An early illustration of this change has been the very public decision to abandon stop and search in operational policing precisely because this practice has been received in such hostile terms in all Asian communities.

The message, therefore, is one of continuity in some regards and important changes in others. A particular challenge that the new Government has set itself is to find ways to bear down on extremism and violent conspiracies whilst ensuring that the measures used are both proportionate to the risks and also able to carry public legitimacy.

A cynical retort to the new administration might be that it has been excessively influenced by the passage of time since the London attacks of summer 2005. Public vigilance undoubtedly has waned in this period and the arrival of the Chilcot Inquiry has at last enabled a popular connection between Iraq and domestic terror to be stated openly.[1] The legality – and not merely the legitimacy – of the 2003 invasion has been questioned at the highest levels of the new Government, conferring a new consensus that sees that misadventure as the sole cause of conflict with and among Britain's Muslims.

Of course radicalism and radicalization in Britain today cannot be put down to the Iraq episode alone, any more than it can be argued that Iraq was and remains irrelevant to the country's biggest domestic security threat since 1945. This is the honest reality that is found among ministers and officials. It embodies the sort of nuanced long view that underpins the argument of this book.

Navigating future risks

"CT 2.0" is nothing if it is not about taking a long view of how an apparently hopeless picture might be turned around over 15–20 years. Sir David Omand, a former national security coordinator-in-chief, has argued this position for a number of years, lamenting the fact that most political leaders have had little appetite to think or act beyond the short term. The difficulty, of course, is that government is a time-poor environment that cannot afford the luxury of the long view of CT or indeed many policy areas.

In the meantime revising the picture of the problem or problems cannot be neglected. For one thing, it is the iterative approach to security and community policy that has thrown new light on the relationship between these sometimes overlapping areas.

The evidence points to three insights for the future. The first is that Islamist extremism can no longer be contained as a simple political category. In reality the various soft and hard recruits to this amorphous cause span a multitude

---

[1] This is despite the fact that the opposite argument was put by the Deputy Head of MI5 in correspondence with the Permanent Secretary at the Home Office. See: 'Iraq: Possible terrorist response to a US attack', letter from Eliza Manningham-Buller to John Gieve, 22 March 2002, declassified and published by the Iraq Inquiry, July 2010.

of political and non-political motives. Organised crime has a strong representation, as does low level, street criminality. But the most sinister appears to be that of confused, isolated individuals seeking a personal connection with a much grander narrative of oppression and grievance than can be justified from their own circumstances. These are casual identifiers, some of whom will readily seize on chance opportunities to support and lead violence. The case of the so-called "lyrical terrorist" graphically shows that the nature of extremism has morphed into a variety of lifestyle attitudes and behaviours. These will be exceptionally hard to tackle in a proportionate manner.

Secondly, the differences and divisions with Western Islamic communities are likely to increase and with these both negative fallout and positive opportunities. On the minus side, community pressures to conform and retreat into a single, stand-alone religious identity will threaten many within and beyond these communities. On the more positive side, positioning complex differences as simplistic binary choices will ensure that new opportunities will emerge to underpin the interests and alliances of many western Muslims with others. Government has an effective role to play not by seeking opportunities to divide but rather by encouraging individuals and families to make greater use of personal autonomy and discretion. If this cannot be done without external support, there is a strong case to mandate government agencies in education, health and employment to assist those who face the greatest obstacles. The sensitivity in doing so should not be understated since many such obstacles are often created within and by others from communities.

Finally, the future will be shaped by the politics of reputation. This has been the consistent message of the book and remains central to those who are thinking about how to approach the challenge over the long term. Therefore measures to incentivize particular individuals and families to stand back from and repudiate violence will be critical. Creating effective mechanisms for doing so will not be easy. However, a simple, low key honesty about the community and societal benefits of repudiation will help. And a similar tone will be needed in quietly pointing to the costs to all Western Muslims of failing to do so.

These are certainly uncomfortable messages for some who are unaccustomed to making difficult choices. However, the evidence suggests that violence can be successfully tackled if the moral oxygen for it is stemmed and cut off at source. Elements of this are already taking place across Britain on a daily basis, usually with little or no fanfare. Reputations are slowly and effectively turned around in such a manner.

Reputations matter.

Preface

Origins and Preliminary Thoughts

The basic thoughts that underpin this book are scattered over a number of years and a range of academic, policy, and journalistic settings. At the point of publication, it is a useful exercise to try to look back and assess the building blocks in one's thinking and to specify particular ideas and exchanges that have allowed the project to proceed to fruition. There are three moments that stand out in the gestation of this book: one relates to its context in foreign affairs and international politics, the second touches on synchronizing the needs of the academic and policy communities, and the last speaks to the sheer enormity of the politics of religious extremism among Muslims in the West.

The international politics origins of this book lie in the mid-summer of 2001. In the first weekend of July, more than two months before the events on 9/11, a private conference on the theme of transatlantic relations took place in Normandy, France. The tone of the discussion and debate during this gathering was undeniably fraught and argumentative. I, personally, was on the brink of joining the Blair administration as a full-time official, assigned to develop long-term strategic thinking on integration and inclusion policy. The French and Americans used this opportunity to live up to caricatures of themselves in modern international affairs.

At the heart of this lay a dispute about the nature and trajectory of transatlantic relations in the post–Cold War world. A Europeanist perspective stemmed from a criticism that the American posture no longer suited the massive de-escalation of military risk on the European continent. A decade after the fall of the Berlin Wall, there was some merit in this perspective in that it raised more bluntly the serious question marks about the Truman Doctrine than had been aired while Europe remained territorially and ideologically divided. However, such a perspective served only to ignite a series of prejudices and latent instincts among members of the US delegation at the conference. A new Republican administration had recently taken the reigns in Washington and, while even precise estimations could not be given about its foreign policy priorities, it was clear that several disjointed neoconservative instincts drove basic reactions and assessments. European governments, it was said, tended towards a naive simplicity in thinking that serious challenges to Western security no longer existed. This outlook was the result of a longer-running idealism, often an irritant even during the Cold War, together with a fundamental failure to acknowledge the potential emerging geopolitical flux, a subset of which, it was asserted, might crystallize into genuine threats to Western nations. Significantly, the American counterblast conspicuously did not list the matter of Islam in the West, but instead was illustrated by reference to new twists in energy security, directionless turmoil in the Arab world, and the rise of China—and its potential allies—in industrial and strategic terms. Listening and participating in this exchange, it was obvious to me that aspects of militant Islam, within and beyond Western countries, could so easily have been added to this list.

The unifying lesson I took from this exchange was that international security concerns at the start of the new millennium continued to be the subject of traditional misrepresentation and misunderstanding among even Atlantic allies. Previously during the Cold War era, it was important to remember that striking differences in political, economic, and cultural perspectives had characterized the Atlantic alliance. However, equally striking was the common realization that the alliance had held together in the face of these differences not merely for common security reasons but also in part due to a desire to protect, and promote, common values of democracy and individual liberty. These may have appeared to have been grand Western claims at one level but they also meant that only the most naive would rule out the possibility of future challenges, possibly from within, to Western traditions of liberal democracy. Equally dubious was the claim that Western societies, despite considerable lines of ideological fragmentation, would want to respond to such a challenge in terms that drew upon post-Enlightenment ideas about the relationship between religion, the state, and the individual.

The period after the Cold War, I surmised, would not only involve new, non-state actors but also that the politics of ethnic and religious difference would play a disproportionate role in conditioning the cleavages around which conflicts would arise. This link between domestic demographic and social changes on one hand and international foreign and security policy concerns on the other has been one of the most intriguing to emerge in recent years. This book is designed to add to thinking along that particular intellectual nexus.

Second, this book also has its origins in my own ongoing task of promoting better insights and actions across academia and public policy. From the mid-1990s, I had found myself taking on an increasingly practical role in government and public affairs. Having published a major book in 2000 looking at electoral choice in an ethnically plural liberal democracy, it was clear from the research I had conducted that ethnicity alone did not account for the full degree of behavioural difference. Put another way, social scientists—and others—in Britain and similar countries had spent more than a generation looking at non-European immigration and ethnic diversity through the prism of race relations. This framework yielded less and less utility in helping to explain patterns of association and behaviour, whether this was measured in electoral, economic, or social terms. My job in Whitehall involved taking these insights and applying them for practical purposes for a long-term review of government policies towards the labour market achievements of ethnic minorities. An early conclusion in this exercise was that the old picture of white advantage juxtaposed against non-white disadvantage simply failed to match a large slice of reality. Britain's ethnic Indians, Hindus, Sikhs and Muslims and those drawn from East African origins, now excelled in schools, universities, and workplaces and made the poor attainment of Pakistanis and Bangladeshis appear even starker in comparison.

Much of this was widely appreciated in academic cloisters and yet hardly known at all in ministerial corridors. On one occasion, in spring 2002, a Cabinet minister I was briefing had been quick to grasp the implications for long-run government policy. He was also quick to seize the possibility that such differences in the real world experiences of British citizens of different ethnic and religious backgrounds might also been understood, if not explained, in overtly religious terms. The concerns of some public intellectuals about 'Islamophobia' had surfaced, somewhat hesitantly, during the latter half of the 1990s. Government-backed evidence, so the minister argued, that showed that non-Indian South Asians were a left-behind group, could and would rapidly translate into the politics of a Muslim underclass. Of course, my own thoughts had been, and still remain, that this scenario was by no means inevitable. And it probably meant something rather different once allowance was made for the equal and opposite rising tide of 'Westophobia'. The larger point was that, post-9/11, it would be a Herculean task, at best, to place the genie of confrontationalist religious identity and Muslim embitterment back into the bottle.[2]

This ministerial conclusion has contributed to the origins of this book in the sense that it places an even greater weight on the shoulders of those actively working at the academic–public policy interface. Despite the putative advantage of a better informed policy community than ever before, it remains the case that the task of disentangling religion from ethnicity, and both of these from social class, is as difficult as ever. One of the reasons for this has been the self-fulfilling prophetic nature of the 'Islamophobia' thesis. Patterns of disadvantage among immigrants and their offspring who happen to be

---

[2] Clarke, Richard A., *Against All Enemies: Inside America's War on Terror*, Free Press, 2004.

Muslims are arguably the result of a number of factors. However, to the extent that these gaps are understood and narrated in religious terms means that the perception of Muslim exclusion matters above all else. Therefore, and somewhat perversely, scholars and policymakers have some obligation to handle religion as not yet another dry variable but rather as a very special factor that operates all too frequently in shaping subjective experience and subconscious perceptions. This obligation, candidly speaking, is not something that comes naturally or easily to academic researchers who typically are self-taught to not play to any gallery, religious or otherwise. Moreover, in seeking to create sufficient policy space to address the most pressing aspects of religious prejudice and discrimination—for example in modernizing anti-blasphemy laws—it is all too likely that policymakers will go farther than is reasonably required or desired.

The origins of this book have, not surprisingly, also been influenced by the insoluble politics of Muslim communities in Western societies. The pessimism that surrounds these communities' interactions with Western societies and governments is something that I came to fully appreciate while living and working in the USA in 2003–4. Until then, I had conducted several pieces of academic research and written various policy documents on this topic but, to be frank, had been put off taking on anything more substantial by the posturing of numerous politicians, community leaders, and members of the media. All, it seemed, had a perverted interest in ensuring that the pariah reputation of Western Muslim communities remained fixed in the collective consciousness of publics and elites alike. This was not an attractive arena to enter, even for someone with a fresh and hopefully helpful perspective to share. In many ways, that arena has not become any more attractive in the three years since. For instance, in spring 2006, as I prepared to deliver a public lecture on an aspect of this topic, I found myself subject to concerns about personal security following unattributed threats. The Danish cartoons controversy had ensured fresh sensitivity in which even senior uniformed police officers could no longer be sure who would be dragged to the front of the crowd next.[3] The atmosphere created by a personal security team while giving a public lecture is not one that we should be proud of and is one that is often forgotten.

The period shortly after the Madrid bombings in early March 2004 caused me to reassess my reluctance. One powerful reason for this was the public call by one set of British Muslim leaders, the Muslim Council of Britain (MCB), in late March 2004 for cooperation with security and intelligence agencies in combating terror. My own reaction to this event cannot have been so different from many others. This was that, however valuable such a declaration may have been politically for governments, it sadly smacked of a timid leadership

---

[3] 'Press in conflict over Islam cartoons', *The Times*, 2 February 2006, p. 43.

getting their excuses in first. Preventing the next chapter of unannounced violence was less of an imperative, it appeared, than ensuring that politically astute disclaimers of responsibility were projected in the aftermath of an expected outrage. In other words, the basic driver had become the political self-interested instinct of a leadership to survive a raging storm.[4] And I had begun to put down some of my own initial thinking into print by that point.[5]

There was no shock or surprise in this as such, since similar episodes of duplicity had previously characterized religious and ethnic violence in Northern Ireland and elsewhere. However, the crude demonstration of political interests caused me to rethink whether it was possible to challenge the status quo. I have concluded—in this book and elsewhere—that it was, although the evidence to back this is likely to take several years to emerge and be fully accepted.

The political pessimism that has surrounded this issue has been further underlined by the prominence of Huntingtonian prophecies.[6] I have not sought to tackle such generalizations directly, but, by mid-2004, it was clear to me that a counter-argument could—and should—be assembled and deployed. I noted that influential arguments had already been published that pushed in the same general direction.[7] While participating at a private meeting organized by the US intelligence community in Oxford in July 2004, I noted numerous unchallenged claims about the inevitability of Muslim/non-Muslim conflict in Europe. A similar event in June 2005 repeated the same charges and also, bizarrely, ended up concluding that the prospects for Al-Qaeda–inspired terrorism in Britain were minimal. I found myself as one of only two or three dissenters in the room at this watershed moment, and increasingly alarmed and frustrated by the complacency of what I saw. In an ironic and tragic twist, events just weeks later revealed the degree of blinkered thinking (wishful or otherwise) at even the most senior security policy tables.[8]

The troubling thing about this discussion was partly its one-sidedness (hence my inclination here to rebalance things), and partly also its failure to observe some elementary lessons from thirty years' worth of immigrant and

---

[4] Friedman, T. L., *Longitudes and Latitudes: Exploring the World after September 11th*, 2002.

[5] Saggar, S., 'Shifting identities', in *The Next Decade: Understanding Change*, Final Report of the Pontingnano Tenth Anniversary Conference, 20–2 September 2002.

[6] Huntington, Samuel P., *The Clash of Civilizations and the Remaking of World Order* (London: Simon and Schuster, 1998).

[7] Koh, Harold H., 'Preserving American Values: The Challenge at Home and Abroad', in Strobe Talbott and Nayan Chanda (eds.), *The Age of Terror: America and the World after September 11* (2001); Klausen, K., *The Islamic Challenge: Politics and Religion in Western Europe* (Oxford: Oxford University Press, 2005); Zakara, F., *The Future of Freedom: Illiberal Democracy at Home and Abroad* (New York, Norton, 2003); Nye, J. S., *The Paradox of American Power: Why The World's Only Superpower Can't Go It Alone* (New York: Oxford University Press, 2002).

[8] Saggar, S., 'Boomerangs and Slingshots: Radical Islamism and Counter-Terrorism Strategy', *The Journal of Ethnic and Migration Studies*, March 2009, pp. 382–402.

minority integration. Britain's experience here should not be over-generalized, but equally it cannot be ignored. For one thing, there has been a steady though often imperfect trend to ethnically sensitize public policy and, in some areas at least, this has led to tangible differences in the way in which schools, workplaces, courts, and other places operate.[9] Sensitization to the needs of ethnic diversity has become de rigueur although, naturally, much still needs to be done. It is, therefore, not the greatest leap of imagination to ask whether, how far, and in what manner sensitization of public policy to a context of religious pluralism might take form. In part, the answer is already there to be seen where various accommodations in dress code, dietary requirements, and religious observance take place routinely. Britain's capacity to foster such accommodations is arguably rather greater than those seen in France, and possibly the USA, where state secular traditions tend to impinge. Nevertheless, the larger point is to think innovatively and practically about religious sensitization, and to link this to the counter-argument to Huntington.[10]

As one senior UK government official remarked to me in 2004: 'We cannot tamely preside over a situation whereby British Muslims replace the position held by Catholics in the seventeenth century.' This remark is undoubtedly correct but it is also concerning that such an outcome could be the inadvertent consequence of complacent or ill-sighted political leadership today. Or this fear may just be the kind of unforeseeable that one might expect from the forty-year history of Britons, and other Europeans, muddling through the issues of ethnic and faith identity. Though it may seem immodest to state, this book's origins and purpose, in part, lie in challenging such leadership to think and act with greater credibility.

Joined-Up Understanding

This is without doubt the most interdisciplinary book I have written and it is characterized by a series of interwoven and nuanced debates about the role of public policy and religious and ethnic pluralism in Western societies. It draws on a longish career in scholarship analysing these issues with some rigour alongside a shorter, intense period working on matching a better understanding with the needs of policy design and response.

The scholastic driver has been a most familiar one, albeit one where the fruits of specialists have only modest gains to show relative to the amount of time that has been inputted. This is a point of some regret since I have seen

[9] Messina., A., *The Logic and Politics of Post-WWII Migration to Western Europe* (New York: Cambridge University Press, 2007).

[10] Esposito, John. L., *Unholy War: Terror in the Name of Islam* (New York: Oxford University Press, 2002).

the activities of a time-rich environment at first hand. Notwithstanding this grumble, understanding of ethnic and religious pluralism in post-war immigration societies has centred around a widespread interest among scholars in identity politics of one kind of another. Such a centrifugal point has yielded a considerable volume of work examining a range of worthy topics but without much effort given to evaluating these in their institutional context. Political scientists, additionally, have been somewhat flat-footed in pursuing the role of ideas and interests in shaping causes and outcomes.[11] These together have been significant missed opportunities which are not unrelated to largish gaps in understanding within and beyond the academic community.

Exceptions to the rule exist, fortunately. For example, the insights of political economists, political geographers, and social demographers in particular have allowed key insights into distributional questions in labour and housing markets. This kind of evidence has added real value in understanding the framing of, and choices embedded in, the politics of difference. In respect of religious difference particularly, this is no small achievement. Without it, the bulk of scholarship devoted to the Western Muslim communities has skirted around central questions to do with social distance and stigmatization. Given that Western Muslims have in recent years become the subjects of a cottage industry of descriptive research activity, the need to develop solid analytical foundations could not be more pressing. Such analytical foundations can be pointed to in a variety of areas. For instance, the residential settlement and early migratory patterns of Pakistani- and Bangladeshi-descended British Muslims have played a big part in the poor labour market experiences of these groups. The importance of geography can be distilled in a quantifiable manner so that this can be evaluated alongside evidence about the role played by human and social capital. Once aggregated together, this analysis amounts to an analytical foundation of some robustness. This, arguably, is sorely needed in the face of an avalanche of research that focuses on socio-psychological, cultural, or indeed ideological discrepancies between Muslim and Western identities. Identity politics and its related engine of research has shown determination in the restatement of a problem. It has been rather less efficient in its contribution to causal explanation and understanding, never mind the task of robustly informed policy remedy. The major task, therefore, is in further extending proper analytical foundations in this skewed environment.

Religious pluralism and conflict in Western societies presents academic researchers with two related challenges.[12] To begin with, there is the perennial difficulty of exploring the limits of secularism in public life and in public

[11] Saggar, S., 'Race and Political Behaviour', in Dalton, R., and Klingerman, H. (eds.), *The Oxford Handbook of Political Behaviour* (Oxford: Oxford University Press, 2007).

[12] Lewis, Bernard, *What Went Wrong?* (London: Phoenix, 2002); Lewis, Bernard, *The Crisis of Islam: Holy War and Unholy Terror* (London: Weidenfeld and Nicolson, 2003).

policy.[13] This book begins by noting that such exploration requires a fair bit of recognition of the different secularist traditions in different Western societies. There can be a tendency among researchers to offer a grand sweep, characterizing the steady march of secular public society and life across a range of Western countries.[14] This is almost as fraught as attempting to simplify or summarize Western models of social exclusion. The variance is often substantial and needs to be handled appropriately. In any case, longer established ways of thinking about religion and faith in Western societies mean that the case of Western Muslims appears initially to be a special case. It is worth holding up the proposition that, while it may not be truly unique, there are several parallels with other and earlier patterns of religious conflict. The question of Muslims' sense of belonging to a community and underlying allegiance to the state has obvious parallel with the earlier troubled position of Roman Catholics in Protestant-led nation states. The capacity of the state to engage with groups via the latter's religious identity is another illustration.

Second, academic research, potentially, offers a more rigorous understanding of the interplay between religious identity on one hand and those factors pertaining to the objective socio-economic position of specific religious communities on the other. That is, such research certainly needs to be more rigorous than the characterizations offered by political and press commentators who commonly mix up causal factors behind political conflict. The mushrooming of robust evidence about contested identity has contributed to a pattern of viewing and understanding Western Muslims purely through such a prism. However, academic researchers must at the very least seek to go beyond this and examine the relationship with wider patterns of social inclusion and exclusion. A more rounded view, in other words, is the basic challenge facing scholars, and it is important to face up to this hurdle at the outset of this book.

The Theory–Practice Interface

In recent years, I have become acutely aware of the general failure of those directly involved in the policy community to draw on and utilize the analyses and insights of wise minds in the academic community. In some senses, much of my work over two decades has sought to address and fill that shortcoming in any case. But this book specifically sets out to operate at the interface between academic research and practical lessons for policymaking. This is no small segment either. For one thing, it is apparent that Muslim

[13] Nielsen, Jorgen, *Muslims in Western Europe* (Edinburgh: Edinburgh University Press, 2004).

[14] Perkins, Mary Anne, *Christendom and European Identity, The Legacy of a Grand Narrative Since 1789* (Walter De Gruyter, 2004).

political and religious extremism in Western societies has pretty much leapt to the top of the list of major and pressing concerns for the majority of Western democratic governments and political systems.[15] In other words, this book is dealing with terribly salient and critical issues where the risks of failure are high both in political and in personal terms. The turnaround has been swift and largely unpredicted. When I began my own academic career in the mid-1980s, it was clear that the politics of ethnic and religious pluralism was a fairly esoteric and limited volume among social science researchers and commentators. A few notable heavy guns have made intermittent contributions, chiefly in response to overt breakdowns of inter-ethnic harmony. However, in the main, the subject matter was populated by rather narrow ethnic studies specialists, many of whom worked exclusively and extensively on aspects of mass migration in European and North American societies but with little regard to the choices and dilemmas facing policymakers dealing with the knock-on tensions and controversies thrown up in areas such as education, employment, and general social cohesion. This distance between specialist research and writing on one hand, and the occasional policy turbulence felt in everyday politics on the other, has concerned me for some time, but the opportunity or need to bring minds closer together has generally not been pressing. After the attacks in Washington, DC and New York City in September 2001, all of that has changed of course. The broad issues of ethnic and religious diversity have moved centre-stage in the half-decade since, and with this development there has been a sharp increase in the policy relevance of specialist academic work in this field.[16]

I have sought to take advantage of a further opportunity in this book. This has been to tell and interpret a story that, despite extensive research and publication by others, has been poorly understood in terms of the perspective of government. That is to say, part of my purpose has been to tell that story from the viewpoint of government. By this I mean two things. First of all, there is a need to rebalance the shelves of libraries that are already crowded with weighty academic publications that concentrate on analysing, assessing, dissecting, and pondering the problem at hand. This is vital, for sure, but it is striking that the comparable shelves concerned with discussing solutions have been, frankly, rather bare. While working as a government official on a labour market inclusion policy review between 2001 and 2003, one of the staff remarked that we had seen very few serious academic submissions that highlighted promising remedies to the problems that we had digested and understood from every conceivable angle. He asked why and we quickly embarked on commissioning papers from eminent academics to help tackle

[15] Schmid, Alex P., 'The Response Problem as a Definition Problem', in Schmid, Alex P., and Crelinsten, Ronald D. (eds.), *Western Responses to Terrorism* (London: Frank Cass, 1993).

[16] Harb, M., and Leenders, R., 'Know thy Enemy: Hizbullah, "Terrorism" and the Politics of Perception', *Third World Quarterly*, vol. 26, No. 1, 2005: 173–97.

the difficulty. But even the resulting submissions were flawed in seeking, yet again, to go over agreed territory about the nature and causes of problems, while hedging bets galore about credible policy responses.

In the end, this is a comment about the hesitancy of academic researchers to draw out the policy implications and conclusions of their analyses. (One senior academic colleague recently lamented that his work could never meet the 'single sheet of paper' test to hold the attention of ministers, pleading that between one and ten of his books might be more realistic. I, of course, do not share this perspective and have sometimes concluded that it is all but impossible to challenge or reform.) That said, it is a hesitancy I can see and partly identify with. But it is overdone more than not, and it is certainly possible, in a book such as this, to set out some broad policy conclusions that will be picked up and exploited by informed and entrepreneurial policymakers. It is frustrating when such hesitancy becomes predictable and second nature. For that reason, this book should, I hope, go some way towards describing the picture that government officials and ministers typically see. This inevitably includes the complication of the unavailability or unsightedness of robust and succinct academic views about policy responses.

This book, bluntly speaking, cannot directly answer the question as to what needs to be done at 9 a.m. on a Monday morning. But it can, thankfully, recognize that such a test is all too real for those working in and for government.

The second reason why it is important to tell the story from this viewpoint is that governments frequently misjudge their capacity to pull levers to tackle problems. The corollary of the 'Monday 9 a.m.' test is the sense that 'something needs to be done'. This sense is often a major reality in government. For instance, the dangers of 'initiative-itis' are present, with no shortage of political masters seeking a response of some kind, sometimes, it seems, for its own sake. Furthermore, the pressure to act because others are calling for action, or in some way have stoked expectations for action, is a force to be reckoned with. However, the really big difficulty stems from an overestimation of the number and reliability of particular policy levers. For example, in tackling and curbing the underlying sources of radicalization among Western Muslim communities, the levers that exist are not only multiple and complex but many, in reality, are very indirectly linked to substantive outcomes. Even noting the existence of such levers can itself set off a chain reaction that equates almost all levers as equally reliable. This is rarely the case, of course. There is a notable absence of Newtonian logic between causes and effects in understanding such radicalization but, as this book nevertheless does, it is still important to pin down important factual knowledge.[17] This helps to generate a more settled picture between government and stakeholders, and

[17] Choudhary, T., 'The Role of Muslim Identity Politics in Radicalisation (a study in progress)' (London: DCLG, 2007).

even if this is not attained, there can be greater precision about the areas least subject to consensus. Identifying gaps in knowledge, and their significance in the larger task of informing government strategy, is made a touch easier as a consequence.

Pulling levers that are overblown in their reliability is one concern of this book. Pulling others that are self-cancelling, at best, and contributing to further difficulties, at worst, is an even bigger concern. However, working in an environment where levers are imagined, or get pulled despite being attached to very little, is arguably the biggest concern. For this reason, it is a significant factor informing my own motives for writing this book and also shaping the debate about aligning analyses with solutions. This book's perspective is necessarily caught up in the risky business of managing the levers that are at the disposal of government. This risk is rather poorly understood within government, particularly in the terrain that this book is concerned with. It is also a risk that is virtually unacknowledged by academic and other commentators, so in that sense this book aims to register that risk to a wider audience.

The Narrative of Political Pariahs

Western Muslim communities are today's largest political pariahs and are in turmoil. Often their presence in many Western countries is deeply resented and feared by local populations. Aspects of their various religious beliefs and social customs are contrasted with the progressive age of reason in Europe, America, and elsewhere. Leaderships within these communities are frequently caught straddling militant voices against liberal progressive influences. And probing torches are cast on Muslims' ability and willingness to show loyalty to Western nation states while observing diligently their obligation to *Ummah* or religious community. The events of March 2004 and July 2005, in Madrid and London respectively, were a wake-up call to Muslims and non-Muslims in Western societies who held that the above challenges might be managed without escalation, much of it unilateral, into religious violence and the cult of suicide bombing.

More than three years after 7/7, it is scarcely believable that British security officials and their colleagues abroad report almost no progress in penetrating the conspiracy surrounding this outrage. The identity and whereabouts of a presumed fifth bomber remain as elusive as ever. The circumstances of a late recruitment and substitution to the suicide mission team have not been unravelled. Equally daunting has been the lack of success in uncovering the identity of a mastermind behind the attacks. And perhaps even more disconcerting is the sad realization that the immediate culprits would not obviously have been recognized in any plausible intelligence reconnaissance.

Privately, and occasionally publicly, this last admission has been dwelt upon by senior members of the security services as well as by their political masters. In blunt terms, it confirms a widely held assumption that there is no realistic security solution to such a security challenge. The basic arithmetic surrounding informed estimates of the scale of potentially violent religious extremism simply falls outside the limits of realistic and reliable intelligence gathering and analysis. For example, Lord Stevens, the former Metropolitan Police Commissioner, remarked in the aftermath of 7/7 that the scale of genuine religious and political extremism within British Muslim communities was around 1 per cent of this population subgroup. With a total population size of 1.6 million, the inference was that the public policy and intelligence communities should focus upon around 16,000 individuals—in short, the outer limits of the security problem.

The thinking behind such an assessment seems attractive enough and follows broadly the analytical approach taken by practical security and intelligence policies.[18] However, this thinking contains a major lacuna. This was that potential and actual involvement in violence easily extended to potential and actual support for such action. Support, in turn, divides into a whole host of activities, some which involve practical assistance in tasks such as assembling complex explosives, transportation, as well as feeding and housing active mission teams. Such support matters in order for attacks to take place rather than gestate or be deflected or detected. All the available evidence from such missions suggests that active members can achieve a great deal themselves but are never wholly, or often remotely, self-sufficient.[19]

The support network is typically designed to be as lean and efficient as possible. This means restricting knowledge of, and participation in, conspiracies to a limited and detection-resistant group. However, this network speaks only to translating a plan of action into practical action. It does not touch upon the conversion of a communal grievance into such a plan—or plans—to begin with.

This book is, in essence, about this prior stage. It devotes energy and space to mapping the nature, scale, and implications of Muslim grievances, both within and beyond Western democracies. This book attempts to tackle head on the reasons why such grievances have come to the fore in recent times and why they have endured from earlier periods. Particular chapters are concerned with the composition of political grievance and the responses of governments and others institutions. The unifying argument that this book pursues is that

---

[18] The Salzburg Seminar, 'Muslim Youth and Women in the West', unpublished background paper, Salzburg Seminar, May 2007, p. 38.

[19] Swain, S., 'Protective security: new challenges', presentation to a conference on 'Countering Suicide Terrorism', Royal United Services Institute, 6 March 2007.

grievance politics—located in a variety of multiculturalist and assimilationist contexts—has produced the vital life-blood of religious extremism. It contends that tacit support for violence probably extends far beyond one in a hundred. Tacit support, by its very nature, both extends far beyond tight-knit particular conspiracies and supplies the vacuum into which violently minded individuals effectively disappear. It also, disturbingly, is the fabric from which new recruits to violence emerge, often self-selectingly.

This book pushes for developing an evidenced argument that allows a better shared understanding of the circle of tacit support that surrounds men of violence. It will suggest that security solutions are unlikely to be manageable or sustainable. Realistic strategies, it argues, to address the threat of terrorism require a range of policy interventions aimed at both better engagement with communities and tackling the specifically religious aspects of social exclusion. The rub is that neither of these elements commands widespread public support.

Somewhat modestly, this book also turns to consider whether, and to what degree, such an apparently hopeless political climate might be turned around. Turnarounds are unlikely to happen soon or without better policies and behaviour by governments and communities, respectively. A more hopeful trajectory should not be dismissed, partly because of the need not to submit to Huntingtonian prophecies. Better public policy is certainly one dimension that a book such as this, and by such an author, can expect to add value. As for the behaviour of religious communities, there is much to work on. Tackling tacit support for violence must start with recognizing it. Addressing it is a big leap which hangs upon its prior detection and admission. Scanning the current political landscape, I have to confess that I see precious little appetite within communities to discuss the roots of violence in an even-handed way. The men of violence know this and have a vested interest in maintaining a binary understanding of (good) Muslims besieged by (bad) enemies of Islam. This book is designed to alter that prediction and thus offer a more optimistic path ahead.

The purpose of this book is not to re-examine political Islam, both ancient and modern. But it can hope to describe the markers and preconditions of better behavioural outcomes for Muslims in Western democracies. Addressing and combating tacit support is probably the most important behavioural change that is needed. It is a major change that is long overdue. It is something that requires patience and a steady political nerve. And it needs clear thinking unconstrained by sectional interest. Identifying the credible means by which this can be achieved is, therefore, the most significant purpose of this book.

Acknowledgements

In writing this book, I have accrued a number of debts. This is my opportunity to pay a modest tribute to those who have impacted or influenced this book over several years. Whatever errors remain are, as the old saying goes, mine alone.

This book is the product of critical thinking on a vast subject. I had previously spent several years examining aspects of the subject in academic and academic-related settings. Some of that work had brushed gently against the issue of severe alienation among minority communities and had suggested that deterioration scenarios should not be excluded. The Rushdie and similar episodes in the decade after 1989 reinforced this assessment, further underlined by the growth of militant Islamist groups in London through the 1990s.[20] The potential for a downward spiral of anger and bitterness plainly existed in my thinking—and that of some others—about the future course of migration and inclusion. The security dimension surfaced during the mid- to late 1990s when I was struck by Myron Weiner and others, writing about the demographic and transnational aspects of security policy.[21] But this nevertheless remained an unpopulated territory in which particular connections were made in my own thinking without a larger debate in which to test them. Significantly, the reception to my book, *Race and Representation*,[22] published at the start of this decade warmly acknowledged my general argument; and yet reviewers largely failed to grasp its conclusion that the politics of a Muslim underclass—indeed any ethnicized or identity-based underclass—was likely to be one of the bigger, and more unmanageable, future challenges facing Western states.

I began looking in-depth at the issues underscoring this study shortly after the shocking WTC attacks in September 2001. This was of course in common with a number of other commentators, all of whom quickly realized that the Western world had, seemingly overnight, moved into a new post-9/11

---

[20] Malik, K., 'Born in Bradford', *Prospect*, October 2005.

[21] For an overview of these arguments and insights, see Weiner, M., and Staton Russell, S., 'Introduction' in Weiner, M., and Staton Russell, S. (eds.), *Demography and National Security* (New York: Berghahn Books, 2003).

[22] Saggar, S., *Race and Representation: Ethnic Pluralism and Electoral Politics in Britain* (Manchester: Manchester University Press, 2000).

epoch. However, in my case, several important seeds had been planted just a few months earlier. The most significant of these was planted by Richard Perle, then Chairman of the US Defense Board and an influential figure in the then-new and at-times controversial US Republican administration. Speaking at a private event, he spoke powerfully (and, to my mind, compellingly) of a range of perceived potential threats to Western security. His audience, largely comprising senior European policymakers, struggled to comprehend the subtext involved—and, regrettably, substituted their own into his remarks. As a participant in this exchange, I appreciated that the calculus of traditional security policy was rapidly changing. Most importantly, the idea that some of the offspring of migrant populations in Western Europe might become embroiled in this calculus was noted, but probably not fully appreciated by most of those present.

It struck me that Perle's remarks, however hostile their projection or reception, could not be sidelined. This book has followed a line of enquiry based on this initial transatlantic exchange.

The influence of my colleagues in government from 2001 onwards is another substantial debt. This time-poor environment contrasted heavily with the time-rich one of scholarly life, and immediately impressed on me the very real difficulties faced by government on a daily basis. Fortunately, the Prime Minister's Strategy Unit largely existed to establish a better grip on those pressures and to respond with policy measures that were grounded in convincing evidence. Nevertheless, gaps in knowledge also had to be managed, in real time, and PMSU again led the field in thinking and practice on this front. This was a major contextual influence on my thinking and, in due course, on this book. The work I carried out there on labour market inclusion, strategic audit, and extremism risks allowed me to gather my thoughts into a coherent story. I am particularly indebted to Stephen Aldridge, Mark Kleinman, Alison Richardson, and Tom Steinberg. Geoff Mulgan, then the Director, also encouraged me to look more broadly at the issue and to consider the policy trade-offs involved. Tom Ellis, one of my staff in 2001, also warrants a special mention: for noting the imbalance between analytical academic studies against publications focused on remedies and solutions. This book is surely inspired in part by his simple and honest observation.

My third major debt is to my academic colleagues and students over two decades. The settings included the Universities of Essex, Liverpool, Queen Mary–London, Sussex, UCLA, and, most recently, Yale. And there are many others spread across various universities in Britain, the USA, Canada, Europe, and Australia. In particular, I would like to thank Erik Bleich (Middlebury), Andrew Geddes (Sheffield), Jytte Klausen (Brandeis), Randall Hansen (Toronto), Peter Hennessey (Queen Mary–London), Anthony Heath (Oxford), Zig Layton-Henry (Warwick), Ted Marmor (Yale), Tony Messina (Notre Dame), Barry Nalebuff (Yale), Pippa Norris (Harvard), Nimala Rao

(SOAS), Sharon Staton Russell MIT, David Sanders (Essex), Amartya Sen (Harvard), Gurharpal Singh (Birmingham), Jeff Sonenfeld (Yale), Sarah Spencer (Oxford), Ken Young (King's, London), and finally, Paul Webb, James Hampshire, and Russell King (Sussex).

The period between 2003 and 2004 spent as a Yale World Fellow at Yale University provided me an invaluable opportunity to think through and test the major arguments contained in this book. The World Fellows programme, probably better described as a crash course in current big thinking on aspects of globalization, was a rich backdrop for this task. The accumulation of big thinkers and big practitioners meant that I had a wonderful chance to try out my arguments and to hear first hand the descriptions and insights of others I respected. Colleagues on the programme, drawn from interesting and influential positions from all over the world, were all masterful in their opinions. Conversations that stand out include those with Norbert Mao (Uganda), Emilia Beblava (Slovakia), Kamala Chandrakirana (Indonesia), Hoda Elsadda (Egypt), Hiddo Houben (the Netherlands), Brian Kagoro (Zimbabwe), Raenette Taljaard (South Africa), and Michael Ward (Canada), and also with Emelia Arthur (Ghana), Christine Hogan (Canada), and Abdul Tejan-Cole (Ghana). The Yale environment not only provided a timely setting for this work but also impressed on me the importance of writing and speaking to research and policy audiences with equal credibility. The World Fellows programme, of course, exemplifies this point in its philosophy and structure. Through the programme and its affiliates, I was successfully able to reach a number of voices in the US and international policy communities that were searching for fresh, compelling arguments and evidence. The friends and acquaintances made at Yale have also had a lasting influence on my thinking, not least in terms of the unmet demand for greater analytical rigour and synthesis but also in pressing ahead with this kind of project.

I am especially indebted to the wise counsel and personal friendship of Ted Marmor at Yale. His own style of intellectual enquiry made a strong impression on me in shaping the angle of argument pursued in this study. And the occasional visits and company of 'Uncle Ted' have made quite a mark on the lives of my family.

In spring 2006, I was invited to give the University of Sussex annual lecture in London. The subject matter of that address featured the security policy challenges created by radical Islamist forces in Britain. I received valuable feedback from many at the lecture and also from a number who read my text when it later appeared in published form. I am grateful to Dominic Grieve MP, the Shadow Home Secretary, for his remarks introducing my lecture and then for his ongoing feedback thereafter. Similarly, I am grateful to Zeinab Badawi, my introducer, and Sheila Dipcock of the Hansard Society, for comment and feedback when I gave the 2001 Hansard Society annual lecture in London.

A fourth, larger debt has to be repaid to the large number of colleagues I have worked with in the policy and political worlds. Over more than a decade, I have worked with a large number of individuals, either in an advisory role or in collaborative projects or as board member colleagues of public, private, and charitable bodies. This is big cast and it is certainly possible that I may have omitted to mention a name or two. Nevertheless, all have shaped my thinking on public policy in its broadest sense and also on a wide range of policy issues. Some have had detailed exchanges with me and can trace their fingerprints in this book. Others have sometimes only uttered a few lines that they should be proud that I have taken note of, and, attentive to detail, have recycled somewhere in the thinking behind this book. The specific names include Geneive Abdo (Gallup), Manolo Abella (ILO), Imam Abduljalil (Muslim Council of Britain), Stephen Aldridge (PMSU), Mockbul Ali (FCO), Rushanara Ali, MP, HE Richard Alston (Australian High Commission, London), Sir Michael Arthur (British High Commission, New Delhi), John Dauth, Australian High Commissioner, Issac Martin Barbero (Instituto de Estudios de Policía, Madrid), Ian Barr (Astar), (Lord) Amir Bhatia, Margaret Bloodworth (National Security Advisor, Canada), Douglas Board (formerly Saxton Bampfylde), Lesya Bolych-Cooper (Bank of Montreal), Rachel Briggs (Demos), Gary Brisley (TGWU), Joel Budd (*Economist*), Inyat Bunglawala (MCB), Zamila Bunglawala (Better Regulation Executive), Mark Carroll (Department of Communities and Local Government), Philip Colligan (London Borough of Camden), Evelyn Collins (Equality Commission for Northern Ireland), Mary Coussey (ABNI), George Cox (formerly IoD), Sir Bernard Crick, John Cridland (CBI), Rosa Daniel (Prime Minister's Office, Singapore), George Dragnich (formerly US Embassy, London), Christina Dykes (Special Advisor to Dominic Grieve QC MP), Julian Evans (British High Commission, Ottawa), Bill George (formerly Medtronics), Sir John Gieve (formerly Home Office), the late Norman Glass (National Centre for Social Research), Heather Grabbe (Centre for European Reform), Frances Guy (FCO), Hugh Harris (London First), Lin Homer (Home Office), Sir Peter Housden (Government of Scotland), Neil Jamieson (Citizen Organising Foundation), Sir Roger Jowell (National Centre for Social Research), Mark Kleinman (DCLG), Sadiq Khan MP, the late Ashok Kumar MP, Sir Stephen Lander (SOCA), Sarah Ladbury, Mark Leonard (Centre for European Reform), Sir Leigh Lewis (DWP), Gillian Licari (Canadian High Commission, London), John Lloyd (FT), Malini Mehra (Centre for Social Markets), Nahid Majid (DWP), Errol Mendes (Privy Counsel Office, Canada), Amobi Modu (DCLG), Claude Moraes MEP, Joe Montgomery (DCLG), Baroness Neville-Jones, Kevin O'Brien, Mark O'Neal (BP), Sir Herman Ouseley, Cem Ozdemir MEP, Dame Janet Paraskeva (First Civil Service Commissioner), Baroness Usha Prashar, (Judicial Appointments Commission) Alison Richardson (BP), Dame Jane Roberts (formerly LB Camden), Jonathan Rozenberg (*Daily Telegraph*), Jonathan Paris (Next Century

Foundation), John Prideux (*Economist*), Peter Reichwald (Harvey Nash), Abdul Rizvi (Department of Immigration and Multicultural Affairs, Australia), Sir Iqbal Sacranie (formerly MCB), Afsana Shakur (formerly DWP), Gurchand Singh (Home Office), John Taylor (ACAS), David Watt (formerly Australian High Commission, London), Jenny Watson (Electoral Commission), Robert Winder, Patrick Wintour (Employability Forum), Mark Wood (ITN), HE Jim Wright (Canadian High Commissioner, London), and David Young (Oxford Analytica).

The regulatory world that I also inhabit includes some important debts in addition. One or two of my colleagues in my incarnation as a legal regulator with the Law Society are also worth citing. Each has caused me to rethink on particular points that are not discussed directly here but have a bearing on the effectiveness of regulatory and policy interventions. Andrea Cook, Jane Furniss, Chris Hughes, Arif Khan, Michael Tildseley, and John Halliday have all made a notable contribution. Elsewhere in regulatory affairs, I am indebted to a large group of colleagues, but a few names stand out: Sir Howard Davies (formerly Financial Services Authority), Rick Haythornthwaite (Better Regulation Commission), Steve Brooker and Philip Callum (National Consumer Council), Sir Callum McCarthy (FSA), and Walter Merricks (Financial Ombudsman Service).

On a more personal note, it is impossible to believe that this book would have been completed without some real space and backing on the home front. My wife, Rita Alfred, has been patient critic of my ideas and obsessions. My father, Krishan Dev Saggar, has provided large doses of moral support. His younger brother, and my uncle, Devinder Kumar Saggar, has given his own style of steady encouragement, as has Shushila Thapar. Invaluable support of a personal kind has been supplied by Vinod Saggar, and also by Neelam Thapar who knows, more than most, the importance of solid ideas that are well presented. And the constant challenge of informing, and being informed by, our children has been one of the biggest fillips in writing this book: Shelley (currently in Cambodia as I write) has been fascinated by the central issues and has provided helpful feedback; Shaan and Symran, meanwhile, have created lots of helpful distractions; and Aaron and Luke, our nephews, have been keen to provide laughter and more besides. Beyond these individual names, there are literally countless others among our larger family—broadly defined—who have managed to chip in in one way or another. Many have simply been part of a vibrant network in which some of these issues are casually aired, while others have provided particular contributions or examples that have been woven into this book.

And a late, sentimental mention has to be made of our son, Reuben, born in mid October 2008, the week the original edition of this book went to press. He will grow up to be surprised to see his name in print so shortly after his long-awaited arrival.

If a special mention had to go anyone, it would certainly be my uncle, Ajeet Tandon. His influence has been one of the very best kinds there is: he has combined one part gentle encouragement, one part his own intellectual curiosity, and one part lessons and observations from his own rather impressive story as a Ugandan immigrant-refugee to Britain.

My publishers, Oxford University Press, also require thanks, most notably Dominic Byatt, my commissioning editor, for getting behind the project early on, and to Elizabeth Suffling and Louise Sprake in the editorial and production teams. I am also grateful to the members of the peer review panel who gave me some fresh ideas to take on board when drafting this book.

This book has been in gestation for a long while. From inception to execution has spanned a shade over half a decade. The crucial period in which my own ideas crystallized probably occurred during 2000–3. The issues at stake were also changing and the problems presented in new and unexpected ways. The basic issue is probably far from being settled in any sense. My own study is designed to nudge thinking and practice in a particular direction, and it may be that the effects of my study are seen in the longer run. The study itself may only help to answer some of the questions, and help shape newer ones for later. Nevertheless, there have been a number of people to whom I am genuinely grateful for helping to get me this far. Any who have been overlooked can take pride that their influence is at least recorded in the pages that follow.

I trust that the bulk of my debts have been cited here. However, some parts of this book may possibly be superceded by events before publication. And the arguments contained here are likely to evolve in the future in any case. The ideas I have put forward are, of course, subject to constant review by myself and by others. I will, no doubt, be the beneficiary of suggestions and influences from many others on this subject in the future. Acknowledging their input ahead of time is, I hope, one of the best ways of ensuring that the channels are kept free and open in the future.

Contents

List of Figures

List of Boxes

List of Abbreviations

ABNI	Advisory Board on Naturalisation and Integration
ACAS	Advisory, Conciliation and Arbitration Service
AHCL	Australian High Commission, London
BBC	British Broadcasting Corporation
BCS	British Citizenship Survey
BES	British Election Study
BHC	British High Commission
BMY	British Muslim Youth
BNP	British Nationalist Party
BRC	Better Regulation Commission
BSA	British Social Attitudes survey
CBI	Confederation of British Industry
CBS	Dutch Centraal Bureau Statistiek
CER	Centre for European Reform
COF	Citizen Organising Foundation
CRE	Commission for Racial Equality
CREST	Centre for Research into Election and Social Trends
CRISE	Centre for Research on Integrity, Human Security and Ethnicity
CSM	Centre for Social Markets
CT	Counter-terrorism
DCLG	Department of Communities and Local Government
DfES	Department for Education and Science
DIMA	Department of Immigration and Multicultural Affairs
DISS	Danish Institute for International Studies
DWP	Department for Work and Pensions
ECNI	Equality Commission for Northern Ireland
EF	Employability Forum
EHRC	Equality and Human Rights Commission
EMAG	Ethnic Minority Achievement Grant

List of Abbreviations

EOC	Equal Opportunities Commission
EU	European Union
EUMAP	EU Monitoring and Advocacy Program
FCO	Foreign and Commonwealth Office
FOS	Financial Ombudsman Service
FOSIS	Federation of Student Islamic Societies
FSA	Financial Services Authority
FT	Financial Times
GCSE	General Certificate of Secondary Education
HAC	House of Commons Home Affairs Committee
HMI	Human Movements and Immigration
HSBC	Hong Kong and Shanghai Bank
IEPM	Instituto de Estudios de Policia Madrid
ILO	International Labour Organisation
IPPR	Institute for Public Policy Research
IRA	Irish Republican Army
JRRT	Joseph Rowntree Reform Trust
LB	London Borough
LEA	Local Education Authority
MAPS	Muslims in the American Public Square
MCB	Muslim Council of Britain
MEP	Member of European Parliament
MORI	Ipsos MORI (Market and Opinion Research International) Research Company
MP	Member of Parliament
MPAC	Muslim Public Affairs Committee
NCC	National Consumer Council
NCF	Next Century Foundation
NCSR	National Centre for Social Research
NDC	New Deal for Communities Faith Communities Project
NF	National Front
NOP	GfK NOP (National Opinion Polls) Media
OA	Oxford Analytica
ODPM	Office of the Deputy Prime Minister
ONS	Office for National Statistics
OSI	Open Society Institute
PCO	Privy Council Office
PMSU	Prime Minister's Strategy Unit

RUSI	Royal United Services Institute
SOCA	Serious Organised Crime Agency
TGWU	Transport and General Workers Union
UK	United Kingdom
UN	United Nations
UNDP	United Nations Development Program
UNRISD	United Nations Research Institute for Social Development
US/USA	United States/ United States of America
WTC	World Trade Center
WVS	World Values Survey

1

Introduction

Modern democracies will face difficult new challenges—fighting terrorism, adjusting to globalisation, adapting to an ageing society—and they will have to make their system work much better than it currently does. Perhaps most of all, it requires that those with immense power in our societies embrace their responsibilities, lead and set standards that are not only legal, but moral. Without this inner stuffing, democracy will become an empty shell, not simply inadequate but potentially dangerous, bringing with it the erosion of liberty, the manipulation of freedom and the decay of common life.

Fareed Zakaria[1]

When I started in the United States, my sister said to me, 'Rule number one: smile at everyone 24/7'. She said because I was wearing the hijab everyone would think I was a terrorist. I took her advice—grinning at everyone like crazy.

Rajaa Alsanea[2]

Introductory Comments

Reputations matter. At present, and for some while past, the reputation of Muslims in Western societies, regrettably, is all but in shreds. Though this statement may strike some as harsh, it is no exaggeration to suggest that all-around hardly anyone has anything remotely good to say about Western Muslim communities. Meanwhile, the reputation of Western liberal societies in the eyes of even moderate Muslim opinion is little better than in the gutter. The essential elements of a siege mentality have set in, and are founded on the widespread pariah reputation attached to Western Muslims. Pariah politics, as the title of this book suggests, is the overwhelming characterization seen by

---

[1] Zakara, F., *The Future of Freedom: Illiberal Democracy at Home and Abroad* (New York: Norton, 2003).

[2] Quoted in *The Sunday Times*, 8 July 2007, p. 7.

most observers, especially those with some distance from day-to-day frictions and controversies. Why?

This is a book that is concerned with the scale and nature of such reputations, and also with the causes behind such a picture. It contains evidence and commentary around those particular points. This book is also driven to understand the reasons that explain the behaviour and outcomes that are familiar to all. It also seeks to examine this question with the benefit of historic comparison and detailed interrogation of factual evidence. This is, therefore, a book that looks at the pariah reputation problem in terms that fundamentally require full explanation, not only as an end in itself but also to support more credible, practical remedies. The benefits of convincing explanation may seem obvious for those close to one side or the other of the pariah problem itself. But these benefits are central to better informed efforts to tackle the problem as well. There are specific, strong messages in this book about the most credible strategies to arrest and reverse the pariah status of Muslim communities in Britain and elsewhere in Western democracies.

This leads to another central feature of this book. It is a book that, simply speaking, seeks to tell a familiar story from the perspective of government. Even the most casual glance at the bookshelves reveals that the literature on Muslim religious and political extremism and violence is substantial. This literature has grown massively within a short timeframe. There is probably no compelling case to write and publish yet another addition to that material. At the start of the decade, prior to the iconic attacks on the New York World Trade Centre, the shelves contained, for the most part, specialist titles produced by migration or Islam specialists. The fact of 9/11 obviously spawned many more accounts and also broadened interest such that many other disciplines and cross-disciplines were drawn upon to explain conflict and controversy. Some have emphasized the importance of values and ideologies, while others have focused more on objective circumstances. But most of the vastly expanded studies have served to stretch analysis and explanation, without much regard to the practical dimension of delivering positive change. This is a large vacuum that this title sets out to fill.

This study casts itself in that important role as much as in the job of extending knowledge. This is a book that self-consciously asks what can and what should be done to tackle the reputational problem. In some places, answering these questions amounts to identifying, with evidence, various 'whats' that cannot and should not be done or perhaps even attempted. This is chiefly because the first lessons of government is surely understanding problems well enough to know how best to avoid further deterioration of existing difficulties (undesirable) or the emergence of further unrelated problems (worse still). Avoiding either has much to be commended, not just in relation to the problems of Western Muslims but also in regard to policy problems generally. Some older academic sages have sometimes observed that doing good can often be achieved by doing little. This book in fact draws rather different conclusions, though it is very mindful of unintentional paths to even greater discord between Western Muslims and their neighbours.

Readers of this book are invited to take a closer look at the face of the problem as seen by government. This involves taking a view of the analysis and explanation offered here and linking this overtly to the proverbial 'what is to be done?' question. The job is not so much to create a better knowledge base as an end in itself but rather to think about how this might better equip policymakers—and others—to develop more effective strategic responses. The intellectual underpinnings of the response mean that a convincing case needs to be made to support one model, or discount another, to understand the problem. Even better than that is to seek to establish a better shared understanding of the mixed causes and consequences of religious and political extremism. This book is very much located in this kind of setting.

This is partly because the elegance of the intellectual insights should not be overdone. Or at least it is important that these are not overstated or over-complicated in this book. The rationale that is shared between writer and reader is to shed enough light on tackling the problem in a practical, measured way. So writing this book makes sense to someone who is interested in shaping long-term change. And reading and thinking about it makes sense to those wishing to execute or encourage particular kinds of change. In the nature of things, there will be certain kinds of change that will not be supported by the arguments and evidence in the pages that follow. In all cases, this is a book that seeks to meet the test of having something useful, and credible, to say about what to do at 9 a.m. on a Monday morning.

Reputational Politics

Returning to reputations briefly, it is important at the outset to acknowledge that pariah reputations are not specific to Muslim communities. A century ago, Jewish communities across the Western world were commonly demonized in ways that appear faintly familiar. At the start of the twentieth century, British and American society was filled with influential assertions that the absorptive capacity of either country towards immigrants had been reached. This was not based solely on calculations about homes, jobs, or hospitals, but rather it was couched in terms of foreign, alien threats to the perceived Anglo-Saxon inner character of these societies. Perceptions about Jewish values and identities meant that downbeat conclusions were drawn about long-term Jewish integration. Even a generation ago in Britain, the arrival of quite modest numbers of South Asian refugees from Uganda and elsewhere in East Africa prompted equally pessimistic assessments to be drawn. Theirs was an alien lifestyle, laced with an impenetrable value code, that meant that almost no one had anything remotely good to say, or imagine, about their presence. The city council of Leicester, a Midlands industrial city, went so far as to place an advertisement in the Kampala evening paper imploring the refugees to stay away; a generation later, the city's leaders effortlessly dine out on Leicester's new-found reputation for peaceful ethnic diversity and economic success. Like Jews before them, they were a de facto pariah group, whose ways and manners, it was predicted, would always grate against British society.

These received wisdoms were wrong in large part. Both groups have gone on to enjoy very different reputations. Their experiences are echoed by many Asian-American communities in the USA and a whole series of model minorities right across Western countries of immigration. Japanese-Americans, to be sure, went from being an interned community during the Second World War, with all the suspicions and hatreds that that entailed, to a position of substantial entry into America's educated, affluent upper middle classes.

Turnaround stories such as these are not the whole picture. Many accounts of the abandonment or shedding of pariah reputations have come at a price. For instance, trends to westernization and/or anglicization of lifestyles are closely associated with these patterns. By one account, some 50,000 individuals legally change their names by deed poll each year in Britain. No detailed accounts of the backgrounds of the name-changers is kept, but it is highly probable that the factors surrounding this behaviour are nested in socio-economic advancement and a hunger for social acceptance. In other cases, high level of marriage and child-bearing outside the group has served to shrink the pariah label. However, the broad picture also comprises various groups that are stuck with a persistent pariah reputation of some kind or another. For sure, young black men enjoyed (if that is what it was) a collective reputation as public pariahs in Britain in the 1970s and 1980s. Sadly, their sons are in much the same boat on the streets of urban Britain today. Meanwhile, there has been no detectable movement in the pariah reputation—and in the effects of such a reputation—of Romanies and travellers for several decades. Strictly speaking, their outsider status has remained scarcely unaltered for centuries across many European countries.

And even the true position of nominally successful minority groups can give cause for concern. This is because the factors lying behind economic or other strengths have come at a price, often one that reinforces the negative aspects of the group's original reputation. In the case of East African Asian communities, it is clear that the legitimacy of their right to belong to the society is sometimes brought into question. Moreover, while the capacity of the group to achieve positive outcomes economically and educationally is not doubted, it is commonly described in terms that undermine the group's right and entitlement to general respect. Indeed, success and progress are widely thought to be the products of naked self-interest and cronyism, so that they are said to be at the expense of opportunities for others. Likewise, many ethnic

Chinese communities in South-east Asian countries regularly experience a political backlash for their efforts. In terms of dominance in business and commercial sectors, these Chinese communities are routinely portrayed as pariahs.[3] They, almost alone, are said to drain resources and more from the society that neither they nor others will call their home.

Pariah-dom, in other words, contains a number of nuances and complexities. In overall terms, however, pariah groups are described not only in heavily biased and critical terms, but are also accused of having it both ways, or at least trying to have it both ways. In the case of Muslim communities living in Britain today, this is a terribly powerful and wounding criticism. At its heart is the concern that British Muslims wish to negotiate, possibly demand, a self-centred carve-out from the laws and norms of society at large. This is typically fuelled and illustrated by quarrels and tensions in relation to education, healthcare, religious observance, blasphemy, the role of women, and so on. This line of collective identity and demand is routinely ascribed to all Muslims in Britain, even though it is not shared by sizeable minorities. Moreover, the tendency among de facto leaders within Muslim ranks to project a form of political muscle based around raw group numbers only serves to entrench the group's already poor reputation. On violence alone, British public opinion broadly takes a pessimistic view of Muslim extremism. Some two-thirds of the public, when polled in summer 2006, agreed that 'Muslim extremists hate democracy and the Western way of life and, if Britain's foreign policy were different, they would find another excuse for their terrorist activities'.[4] This is a harsh characterization for sure, but it generally confirms the idea that the appetite for violence and confrontation goes beyond specific policy differences either at home or abroad.

In fact, the problem is rather worse than previously described. This is because political negotiation is often a dialogue of the deaf. In such a context, demands for greater respect for Muslims have grown considerably, at the same time as public support has receded equally considerably. The gap between outrageous demand and derisory offer is now very large and noticeable. It is not echoed in the case of any other minority ethnic or religious community, and this further underlines the apparent unpopular case of British Muslims.

The single greatest factor driving the pariah reputation today is the sense that political negotiation might slip into political demand, and that even demand might one day give way to declaration of a unilateral kind. This is a sensitive and sometimes misunderstood point. Obviously, at one end of the spectrum, there is a regular supply of loose talk about the resurrection of a European Caliphate of one kind or another. This is an unfounded fantasy as

---

[3] Chua, A., *World on Fire: How Exporting Free Market Democracy Breeds Ethnic Hatred and Global Instability* (London: Arrow Books, 2004).

[4] Populus poll, *The Times*, fieldwork carried out 1–2 September 2006.

well as a highly selective reading of Islamic and European histories. In one sense, this vision involves many cutting of corners. But this ideal, shared, it seems, by a handful of hardened enthusiasts, cannot be dismissed in terms of the reputational problem. This is because it demonstrates the enormity of the goal that partially underpins day-to-day debates and arguments about Western Muslim communities. It also, therefore, describes the mammoth challenge that secular-minded, liberal states face. It is for this reason, quite naturally, that some commentators express alarm at the mounting tensions between relatively poorly integrated Muslim populations and their indigenous counterparts across Europe. Evidence for these tensions can be seen in Spain, France, Germany, Britain, and the Low Countries on a significant scale. Similar tensions are also present and simmering in much of the rest of the continent. These tensions together frequently have identifiable links to conflicts and violence in adjacent regions such as North Africa, the Caucasus, and the Middle East.

Reputationally, many moderate Western Muslim communities who share nothing of the Caliphate fantasy can be tarred by the suggestion that the Muslim *Ummah*, or community, acts as a greater source of loyalty than citizenship of the liberal state. In some instances, this sharing of allegiance is borne out and critics understandably retort that this dynamic can only store up frustration and anger. It is notable that a number of North American—and a smaller number of European—observers have picked up on this potential for religious conflict in Europe's future. Some have even linked this with the reality of religious conflict in Europe's past. The point that is contained in this observation is one part that integration efforts have failed more than they have succeeded and one part that European governments have tended to underestimate their own problems.

This point is not to be passed over lightly. For starters, as this study notes, much of this concern is grounded in substantial evidence. In Britain's case, the very long tail of Muslim underachievement in schools and employment is magnified in entrenched patterns of residential segregation, inward-looking community norms, grievance narratives, and leadership styles that have proven to be remarkably unpersuasive about anything very much. The patterns are not notably different in the other Muslim concentrations elsewhere in Europe, and, if anything, are accompanied by a generally poorer track record, overall, in bringing post-war immigrants into the mainstream. The thinking of different European governments over several decades on these issues can appear especially alarming. This is because of the notable lack of appetite among the majority of political leaders to seek the accommodation of immigrants and their offspring. Certainly, some governments, such as Britain's, have been active in adopting integrationist measures. But this has taken place in a generally anti-immigrant and anti-minority political climate. The upshot has been that the especially difficult aspects of integration and accommodation have been relegated to the fringes of political life. Back burners have simmered away, in time becoming overloaded with the politics of exclusion and, latterly, the politics of religious extremism. This is not to try to paint an unnecessarily gloomy picture but rather to note that governments have, until recently, been caught on the back foot. The nature and scale of political grievance among Muslim minorities that has surfaced in recent years has taken place against a wider landscape of global conflict involving Islam. Back-footedness has been compounded by an element of wrong-footedness. The instincts of politicians and their officials have been to attend to the symptoms rather than the causes of extremism. In Britain, this misjudgement has sometimes taken place on a massive scale. As this book goes on to argue, acquiring the right balance of policies to address the reputational problem is terribly hard but certainly possible. Resolving the politics of Muslim extremism—and sympathy for extremism—makes the policy task that much harder.

It does not take a Caliphate dream to establish that many millions of Western Muslims are caught between opposing influences. It would be hasty to conclude that all of this stems from the Huntingtonian claim that Muslims and non-Muslims experience differences of an essentialist and unmanageable kind and are therefore set on collision. Such an argument is commonplace in many circles today. Nevertheless, sweeping generalizations need to be interrogated fully in order to assess their contribution.

What is rather more certain is that the patterns towards identity-based difference are now fairly well established in most Western Muslim communities. In some cases, these patterns are not as deeply rooted as in others. In France, for instance, there is substantial public and political pressure to erode the possibility of widespread attachment to one-dimensional social identities centred on ethnic or faith categories. In the Netherlands, there is a more recent public effort to offset religious or ethnic identities by talking up the importance of singular national identity.

Nevertheless, the die-of-sorts has been cast. Religious identity, according to this now-familiar picture, is closely bound up with religious difference. In the case of Western Muslims, this is almost endemic to the situation and self-awareness of these groups right across Europe, and to an increasing degree across Western countries in general.[5] And religion, for Muslims of all kinds, so the narrative goes, is a determinant of both positive outcomes and negative ones. In more colloquial terms, good things and bad things happen to, and are true of, Muslims—and these are explained because they are Muslims. This is a very tight circle of identity, essence, causation, and outcome. It may not necessarily be backed up by evidence since it is basically about identity-based

---

[5] Bleich, E., 'Religion, Violence and the State in 21st Century Europe', unpublished paper, 2006.

difference as cause and consequence simultaneously. It is true, in other words, because enough people believe it to be true about themselves. It is about belief, something that is certainly familiar but nevertheless also rather unfamiliar in the modern secular world.

The reputational hit that many ordinary Western Muslims face is that public attitudes are both uninformed and uncertain about the importance of faith for Muslims. This book is chiefly about Britain's experience and in this case there are numerous uncertainties about the limits of faith in public life and in society. So Muslims' variable appetites for greater recognition and respect for their faith is something that is articulated and received in an atmosphere that is undecided in any case. The particularity of Muslim grievance perhaps matters less in this context, given that this doubt is also experienced by many other faith groups. Nevertheless, the perception of the reputation of Western Muslims is almost bound to be affected negatively. It is often a specific example that questions and resists the dominance of secular values. And yet, reputation distorts matters and manages to portray Islam as uniquely occupying the mantle of resistance. This is especially damaging since the links to wider concerns and anxieties, such as the carve-out thesis, are both close by and notoriously easy to exploit.

Western Democracy and its Security

The security of Western publics facing Islamist threats is a major theme of this book. It certainly overshadows political life on a regular basis and is likely to do so for a long time. And it also represents one of the most prominent footings of newer, more complex features of political exchange. Security politics has become, and will most likely remain, part of mainstream politics in Britain and throughout Western countries. The added dimension of global anti-American sentiment is one further layer in this security question.[6] This step-change has enormous implications for the nature of political responses to terrorism. It also has vast repercussions for the nature of politics itself. With that in mind, it is important to recognize that this is not a book that is solely driven by the current security challenges created by Islamist terrorism. There are, as previously mentioned, a large number of titles that have appeared to meet that particular demand. That is, the security dimension of Western Muslim communities plainly does stand head and shoulders above all other

[6] Rubin, B., and Rubin, J., *Hating America: A History* (New York: Oxford University Press, 2006).

aspects of the issue, something no one would have failed to have noticed.[7] The writer cares enough about this single element to write a book aimed at providing better solutions to this problem. And, it follows, the reader, likewise, cares enough to read and enquire more about the credibility of one strategic response versus another.

The security peg is much larger than getting to grips with immediate plots and conspiracies. There is considerable attention paid in the main relevant chapters of this book to the specific issue of Islamist-inspired terrorism. And the main focus of that discussion is to find better ways to distinguish between participation in political violence on one hand and providing tacit support for such violence on the other. The bigger aspect of security is one that was touched on in the Preface, namely, to map out the full extent of emerging threats to the future security of Western nations. At first blush, this is, inevitably, a very large canvass indeed. It ranges from getting to grips with the template of security in the post-Cold War world, and thinking beyond the stability of bipolar ideological sources of conflict, to penetrating the motives and abilities of causes that are rooted in oppositional thinking. Modern global Islam, as many have noted, largely defines itself in terms of what it is against.[8] This can provide a very substantial rallying call for a wide range of Islamist-inspired groups and various other loose affiliates as well. The former are, in principle, easy to study and have been the subject of considerable scholarly interest. The latter are much harder to map and understand and have proven much more elusive to scholarship.

Zero Failure

Modern security thinking has to be concerned with all of these forces and more besides. It must grapple with a combination of identity and motive that is forever elliptical. The reasons that propel one category of Muslims towards extremism and worse are rarely repeated enough among others to warrant hard and fast generalizations. For sure, some generalizations can be drawn out that broadly model the underlying causes of security threats, and these are offered in the chapters that follow. But this is far from a watertight calculus. This is because there are very few fully grounded predictions on offer. At one point, numerous role models of immigrant integration have regularly been implicated at the heart of violent conspiracies. A grammar school boy from Gloucester, far from the call of the besieged Muslim ghetto, it seems, is as likely to follow in the footsteps of the 9/11 suicide team as any other Muslim.

[7] One exception appears to be Silvestri, S., 'Europe and Political Islam: Encounters of the Twentieth and Twenty-First Centuries', in Abbas, T. (ed.), *Islamic Political Radicalism: A European Perspective* (Edinburgh: Edinburgh University Press, 2007).

[8] Donohue, J., and Espisto, J., (eds.), *Islam in Transition: Muslim Perspectives* (New York: Oxford University Press, 2006).

An otherwise gentle primary school assistant from Leeds can portray himself, and his cause, at the fighting edge of Muslim anger and organized resistance to the war in Iraq. And a small handful of foreign doctors are, it appears, able to go undetected and come close to inflicting substantial carnage. In other words, the individual stories even within just one country, Britain, are forever evolving and managing to evade very considerable efforts at detection and prevention. This is not due to any particular failing in counter-terrorism policies as such but rather the result of a threat whose underlying source is too slippery to track let alone manage. This realization has enormous implications for the way in which security policy is thought about and handled in a world of loosely connected and opportunistically motivated Islamist grievance. It also has implications for the way in which security policy thinking and practice is better grounded in community and integration policy.[9]

The perspective of government in relation to security is a key feature of this particular book. Again, many of the insights and generalizations that can be established here are of importance to writer and reader alike if there is a practical spin-off. A better shared understanding of the changing nature of security is a priority but only in so far as this creates a foothold for better calibrated policy remedies. And a big element of this aim is to develop an understanding that both matches the scale and nature of threats to security and succeeds in touching Western societies' anxieties about their assured future security. The latter of these objectives is much harder to attain, not least because of inter-cultural differences and nuances about the definition of security, uncertainties about what constitutes success, and the steps that are reasonable to achieve either. And it is further complicated by a legitimate and lively debate about the nature of dissent among a religious minority that, in part, senses the pressures that have resulted from their pariah status.[10]

In terms of differences between American security thinking and that of other Western countries, there is considerable implicit disagreement about definitions, success, and means. There is little point in probing these further here other than to note that most are best accounted for by historic and cultural differences. In the USA, for example, there is a palpable sense of violation following 9/11 in a way that is muted, if that, in most of Europe. Equally, Americans have chosen, at least for now, to rally around a foreign policy security-based response to the perceived threat.[11] Britain, and others, have tinkered with this approach but have been much readier to take a longer-term,

---

[9] Saggar, S., 'Boomerangs and Slingshots: Radical Islamism and Counter-Terrorism Strategy', *Journal of Ethnic and Migration Studies*, forthcoming.

[10] Briggs, R., 'Why are We so Scared of the Respect Party? Why Dissent is our Best Hope for a Cohesive Britain', *Renewal*, 2007.

[11] Hart, G., *The Fourth Power: A Grand Strategy for the United States in the Twenty-First Century* (New York: Oxford University Press, 2005).

community-centred approach. This contrasting model of, and means for, security seems slightly strange, and possibly appeasist, to many American observers. In part, this is because of the absence outside Europe of such large-scale unintegrated Muslim communities. It is also partly the result of worries that European governments have not faced up to the problem beneath their noses and, worse still, are afraid to do so now.

Differences of these kinds over security are worth acknowledging openly in order to develop a better-informed consensus about the political choices that are involved. For example, it is all too easy to slip into a working assumption that a zero-failure regime is the only test of success. This may seem misguided when observing the problem from the pages of a detached study, but it is only too likely in the real world of policy decisions and operational detail. Zero-failure is also an attractive standard to set or at least be seen to set. It implies that the commonly quoted first duty of the modern state—namely, securing the lives of its citizens—is to be treated as an absolute principle. In reality, it is not. In fact, in many walks of life, it is a guiding principle that is routinely subject to trade-offs, some more uncomfortable than others. Typically, for example, healthcare policies, even in state-dominated systems, are not designed to avoid terminal failure at all costs. A certain level of residual failure is known and tolerated in so far as the costs and interventions of delivering zero-failure are widely known and accepted to be excessive. Similarly in tackling and preventing road traffic accidents, environmental hazards, food hygiene, domestic violence, and so on. The interventions required to prevent all cases of domestic abuse are plainly enormous, even though it is widely accepted that the moral case for doing so may be overwhelming. But it is equally accepted that a sliding-scale exists at some level whereby a small, hard-to-reach, and hard-to-protect group will not be affected. This is failure by any other name but it is common to describe it in other ways.

In tackling Islamist-inspired terrorism in Britain, for instance, there are clearly observed limits to the extent of surveillance that this society is willing to accept. This is the trade-off. It may be subject to change over time, and it can be moved as a result of political will that is deployed in the short to medium term. The trade-off calculus may even be flexible in the face of prolonged attack and suffering, but even this is at the margins of the overall settings.[12] Indeed, there is some reason to think that adjustments may be attainable in the calculus as successful attacks increase; however, even this is subject to its own tipping point that reacts to greater intrusion and cost in sceptical terms if only because the benefits of higher costs are so slow in being realized.

---

[12] Richman, D., 'The Right Fight. Enlisted by the Feds, Can Police Find Sleeper Cells and Protect Civil Rights, too?', *Boston Review*, December 2004/January 2005.

Risk Appetites and Settings

The factors within and surrounding something other than zero-failure are in fact familiar to governments. There may be tendencies to ignore these factors in a rush to embrace zero-failure benchmarks. Efforts to boost the capabilities of existing security infrastructures are one example.[13] However, underlying all of this is a harder edge that has to probe, and then set, an overall risk appetite for public policy. Such a risk-based approach to policy has gained some traction within government.[14] It involves getting to grips with the levels and kinds of failures that society is prepared to accept—or at least willing to tolerate in an involuntary sense—in relation to the degree of mitigation and prevention it is willing to adopt.

This is a bald way of putting it, but it is the gist nevertheless. In some cases, the links between the former and the latter are not widely known or appreciated. So the job of government to begin with is to create fresh transparency so as to allow a trade-off to take place, and be seen to take place. The difficulties lie in, first, establishing how far declared, transparent risk appetites are in fact to be relied upon (they may not be once the hypothetical gives way to the actual) and, second, establishing the distribution of costs to be carried for any given set of benefits. For example, if all the tangible costs of surveillance and intangible distasteful feelings of informing are thought to fall on Muslim communities exclusively, it is likely that this imbalance will not necessarily be sustainable over the long run. Or at least it will not be unless there are proactive efforts made by communities and leaders to accept responsibility for such costs.[15] This, at present, is scarcely the case, and there is rather more reason to think that many believe that these costs can be externalized forever. Meanwhile, in whatever scenario is painted, the vast bulk of benefits of a given trade-off are enjoyed by non-Muslims, that is, the rest of any given Western society. It is of course an open point to debate whether indeed all of these benefits are consumed by non-Muslims. The very heart of the reputational thesis that is pursued in this book is that the benefits will (and possibly already do) accrue to Western Muslims just as much as they accrue to non-Muslims. This is quite simply because the willingness to pay costs for generalized gains is itself a very real benefit to Muslims. This willingness is itself voluntary, it is perceived from within to be against the grain, and it has faced countless short-term disincentives. It is these factors that make such willingness acknowledged and valued in society generally.

[13] 'Boosting Security and Defence Capabilities', remarks by Whalley, R., CB, former Home Office Director of Counter-Terrorism and Intelligence, conference on 'Transnational Terrorism: Defeating the Threat', Royal United Services Institute, 9–10 November 2006.

[14] Arthur, M. (UK High Commissioner to India), 'The Global Challenge of Terrorism', speech to the Indian Supreme Court Bar Association, 9 November 2005.

[15] Kepel, G., *The War for Muslim Minds: Islam and the West* (Cambridge, MA: Harvard University Press, 2004).

The reputational risk of shunning this basic reality is great for Muslims. So the reputational gain of accepting it is potentially equally great, so long as it is sincere and sustained. Either of these features can be debated endlessly. It is therefore perhaps better to note that it is the principle of sharing reputational costs that matters most. Taking on the heaviest burden of these costs no doubt improves credibility. Staying on this path when the counter-costs are mounting, and when peer pressure is exerted to halt cooperation, is far from easy. But its value is greatly enhanced precisely because it is hard to sustain. Therefore, presumptuous attempts to test sincerity are best avoided: doing hard, uncomfortable things that are unpopular among one's own ranks is a simple and well-understood test of sincerity. Remaining committed to the difficult path is an even better test of good faith.

Holding Several Thoughts Together

In recent years, there have been two clarion calls trumpeted by observers of Muslim communities in Western democracies. One of these, already mentioned, has come from Samuel Huntington and sympathizers, critical of the delusionary mindset of governments and leaders who have sought integration and accommodation of one kind or another. The other, highlighted perhaps by Tariq Ramadan and his supporters, has focused on the practical and philosophical expansion of Western understanding of citizenship to allow Islam to flourish in its midst. These are both grand generalized viewpoints and very often contain elements that are not directly comparable. Nevertheless, these intellectual camps seek overall to shift the centre of political debate in roughly opposing directions. One set veers towards political arguments that only allow an accommodation with political Islam on tougher terms, some of which certainly questions the basis of Muslim identity for many Muslims. The other tends towards the idea that Islam at large remains more demonized than most faiths and that long-term accommodation first requires a genuinely level playing field.[16]

This study seeks above all to avoid restating these positions as a means to present argument and evidence that fits one school or the other. In fact, the central purpose here is to encourage the readership to hold more than one thought at any one time. That is to say, there are elements that must be taken seriously from Huntingtonians and their critics alike in this book. For instance, as this study makes clear, there has been a considerable understating of the extent of extremism and radicalization in Britain and elsewhere. The ideological basis of this well of extremism certainly includes violent jihadist

[16] Wiktoronwicz, Q., *Radical Islam Rising: Muslim Extremism in the West* (Lanham, MD: Rowman and Littlefield, 2005).

13

ideas that have long been in circulation but which have been underplayed by governments on a selective, instrumental basis. This factor alone ensures that there are significant numbers of individuals and groups that are today intent on promoting religious conflict as an end in itself. Huntingtonian ideas have thus had a certain self-fulfilling prophetical quality. The thorny issue of how immigrant integration policy fits with efforts to address security threats from Muslim radicals is one example of developing a shared understanding. Few today seriously doubt that both of these tasks matter and that they are closely interwoven. According to one veteran observer, the emphasis should therefore shift in a more practical direction:

Integration policy and national security are over-lapping objectives but at times in conflict with each other. Nonetheless, the question is no longer *if* it is possible to pursue security objectives in partnership with Muslim community organization. Effective counter-terrorism requires collaboration. The question is *how* to do it.[17]

In terms of a study such as this, the key lessons are that while whole models can bend and distort matters beyond recognition, it does not follow that base, essentialist views of Islam in the West can be ignored. There are just too many minds that are influenced by these kinds of views, and there is little point in merely repeating blithely that cultural identity of this kind is an oversimplification. It is, but there is more to it than that. In particular, it is this precise oversimplification that has gained popular currency on the back of day-to-day narratives of Muslim exceptionalism.[18] The task of integration and peacefulness is regularly sidelined in relation to Muslims, a pariah group that is widely thought to defy the reach of Western governments and liberal political philosophy. This one-dimensional, deterministic sense of identity permeates the landscape of political debate concerning Western Muslim communities. This is a study therefore that cannot ignore this reality, even though the evidential causes beneath this may be highly contentious.

In the end, Western Muslims are, unusually, in a much worse position in terms of their reputation in Western liberal society. To the extent that this is a book that looks at this story through the prism of reputations, it is somewhat unsurprising that the basic reputational position features as the starting point for this discussion and the analysis that follows.

This book also serves to deliver a panoramic sweep of the issue while also offering sufficient granular detail to afford a judgement about the strength of the argument. The reappraisal of accepted wisdoms about Western Muslims, and about integration into Western society, is an important task for anyone writing in this field. Almost all observers have been compelled to

[17] Klausen, J., 'Counter-Terrorism After 7/7: Adapting Community-Policing to the Fight Against Domestic Terrorism', *Journal of Ethnic and Migration Studies*, forthcoming.

[18] *Dignity and Dialogue: Civil Pathways to Peace*, Final Report of the Commonwealth Commission on Respect and Understanding (London: Commonwealth Secretariat, 2007).

re-examine their positions in recent years. Certainly, the long-term effects of the New York, Madrid, and London attacks have been substantial in terms of reappraisal. But it is the question mark over the thing that is the subject of reappraisal that stands out. The early view was that this related to either political Islam or Western integration efforts. This has steadily given way to arguments that have placed identity politics, citizenship, and belonging more at the centre of the reappraisal.[19] These are larger, more complex matters and also involve a great deal of fresh thinking about the unintended impact of poor, unshared understandings of the problem or problems. In fact, much of this has resulted in a general sense that there are several interrelated problems to be examined, rather than a single problem. The danger of confusion between one problem and another is all too present.

Imagining Political Success

This book, therefore, promotes fusion in thinking about a major multi-faceted contemporary challenge. One of the most difficult aspects of doing so relates to developing an understanding that better solutions reside not just in *what* is done, or not done, but also in *how* it is done. The 'what' questions, to a very large degree, are dependent on the 'how' questions in order to command long-term credibility.

For example, as this and other studies have noted, the issue of humiliation lives just below the surface of global Islam identity and politics. There is nothing especially new about this issue, but it has certainly grown in its prominence and ability to shape immediate political realities and choices. But the pressures that global Islam faces and nourishes are themselves not unique. Many are located in a wider narrative of a deep sense of injustice in the world today.[20] That narrative resonates against the backdrop of certain identity-based political movements more effectively in some instances than in others.[21] But all cases imply that offering dignity in the place of confrontation is a key part of the overall strategic answer.

It is worth stressing that it is not the economic hegemony of (largely) Western industrialized nations, per se, that lies behind the sense of powerlessness, but, rather, the fact that some of these nations have created 'an environment of impunity' where there are no reliable rules, only self-interest.

---

[19] Gohir, S., 'Understanding the Other Perspective: Muslim and Non-Muslim Relations', *Muslim Voice UK*, 2006.

[20] Alderdice, J., 'The Individual, the Group and the Psychology of Terrorism', unpublished paper, 2007.

[21] Sageman, M., 'Global Salafi Jihad: Empirical Assessment & Social Network Analysis', Conference Presentation to the World Federation of Scientists' Permanent Monitoring Panel on Terrorism, Erice, Sicily, 2005.

Grand narratives of Muslim humiliation in particular have dwelt on this idea.[22] This, then, plays into the hands of extremist groups and followings with a grievance agenda.

The 'how' dimension should be thought about as carefully as anything raised in this book. It is essentially about reinforcing a message that can easily be pushed into the tramlines of public policy analysis and design. This dimension is sensitive to the multiple layers of grievance and hatred that have built up among individuals and communities. These layers need not have taken generations to crystallize even though many have been in formation for long periods of time. They can be nourished quite rapidly in that the essential elements are already present in one form or another. The pattern can be further accelerated by the capacity of modern ideological movements to link together specific grievances into a grand sweep of oppositional identity. This is especially pronounced among Al-Qaeda-inspired political groups and factions, but it is also found more generally across modern political Islam.

Genuine delicacy attaches to the 'how' question precisely because it is so frequently overlooked or minimized. It is the most awkward aspect of any deeply ingrained conflict based around identity. In the Middle East, where credible technical and practical solutions are not in short supply, it is striking that there have been many fewer realistic attempts to bridge the emotional gulf between Israelis and Palestinians. Hurt, guilt, misunderstanding, and similar sentiments have been pushed to one side, partly because it is less easy to address and partly because even addressing this would serve to disrupt well-settled patterns of grievance politics.[23] Similarly, many Western Muslim communities are today caught in political arrangements that fail to address their sense of underlying vulnerability or humiliation. And addressing these is also improbable since to do so would be too much to expect and create categories with too much to lose.

The job is equally about helping to create new ways to think about the humiliation and misunderstanding that underpins conflict. This fresh way of thinking, if successful, might serve to establish fresh ways of behaving and acting. Both might then feed off each other, creating additional incentives to change and cause others to change. The short- to medium-term chances are typically very slight. So, looking to the medium to long term, it is helpful to think of ways that first create a basic level of mutual confidence and second help to allow reciprocal changes to take place. Thinking about identity-based conflict in this way can be positive because it removes the essentialist logic that often underpins the counter case. It also recasts change as comprising

---

[22] Salzburg Seminar, 'Muslim Youth and Women in the West', unpublished background paper, Salzburg Seminar, May 2007, p. 38.

[23] Sageman, M., *Understanding Terror Networks* (Philadelphia: University of Pennsylvania Press, 2004).

smaller pigeon steps that can be taken in isolation. And new ways of thinking are best advanced if offered within a larger account which accepts that:

- The challenges of global violence and hatred are by no means new to governments and the international community.
- It is worthwhile examining the nature and underlying causes of such behaviour in order to arrive at a more credible response.
- A key insight is that one-sided, imposed solutions (including those that are perceived as such) have tended to fail in carrying hearts and minds in the longer run.
- The task is to arrive at an approach or style of engagement that has credibility precisely because the measures required can and must be sustained over a long period.
- Credibility accrues from having to build and nurture coalitions of interests, from having to take into account the opinions of others, and from affording respect to those different views and values.

These are the hallmarks of an approach to thinking about politics and policy towards Western Muslim communities that is not at all apparent currently. The issue at hand is to help governments and others to address grievance and humiliation in order to curb violence and hatred. This, necessarily, implies a particular way of looking at, and thinking about, the problems identified in this study and arriving at better, shared, and sustainable solutions based on evidence about causes and also about what works.[24]

Returning to reputational issues briefly, it was hinted previously that imagining a better future is a prerequisite for attaining one. This is nowhere more apposite than in the field under discussion here. The entrenched positions are fairly easy to see. They are also rather easy to anticipate and serve to create virtually no incentives to think about change, never mind delivering change itself. Placing emphasis on how better solutions should be arrived at, and how they should be implemented, is integral to longer-term success on any conceivable scale. Therefore, the author is keen not to lose sight of these 'how' questions as a way of directly nurturing a more imaginative way to pursue better thinking and better solutions.

Reappraising Western Muslim Communities

This is a book that surveys modern religious identity and political reputation. Crudely speaking, in excess of 1.6 million Britons today enjoy a public

---

[24] Atran, S., 'Global Network Terrorism', Briefing to National Security Council, White House, 28 April 2006; available at http://www.sitemaker.umich.edu/satran/files/atran_nsc_042806.pdf and http://www.au.af.mil/au/awc/awcgate/whitehouse/atrannsc-042806.pdf.

reputation paralleled by Catholics in the seventeenth century, or perhaps a bit worse. Echoes can also be heard in the story of Anglo-Jewry about a century ago. The major driving factors behind this outcome are essentially fourfold and are set out more fully in the bulk of the chapters that follow. These are centred around (in no particular order):

- economics—that is, long tails of underachievement in schools and employment set within a general story of settled disadvantage;
- social isolation—that is, noticeable trends towards inward-looking communities that are relatively lightly influenced by mainstream society and its implicit codes about faith and about tackling exclusion;
- politics—that is, patterns of oppositional political leadership, increasingly gripped by a grievance narrative that jars with political consensus about the public interest; and
- global Islam—that is, the dynamics of which are both highly charged and unpredictable, to say nothing of being rather unconnected to policy levers enjoyed by British or other Western governments.

This is essentially a book about the view from government. That is, these points are not just examined in order to build a convincing explanatory picture. They are also examined in terms of their policy relevance and to understand better the adequacy of the policy response of government. A part of that understanding also includes commenting on the overall adequacy of existing policy levers and wider policy strategies, the starting point of which is to check whether, or how far, helpful, targeted levers exist to begin with. In some cases, it is apparent that causal factors are associated with long-established levers to deliver change or to remedy outcomes. In other cases, the match is rather more mixed. And in yet others, there is almost no credible read-across at all.

The above list of causal factors is, however, organized in an order that roughly approximates to the existence and proximity of known, tried policy levers. That is why it is important to acknowledge that the dynamics of global Islam, however pertinent to the reputational concerns identified in this book, are nevertheless very hard to influence directly from Westminster or Whitehall.

Much the same is also true from both ends of Pennsylvania Avenue, although this realization is far from universally shared across the British or American ideological spectrum. For instance, democratic change in the Arab and Muslim-majority world is widely thought to be important in terms of shaping a better understanding and dialogue with Western states. Nevertheless, the means to affect such change in any direct manner by Western governments is hardly within reach. In the case of the intervention in Iraq, it is probably just about within reach, but any minimal positive outcomes are massively outweighed by the disbenefits. Equally, the past and the future of the Arab–Israeli conflict lie close to the epicentre of global Islam's sense of collective grievance. Having accepted this constraint, Western governments have proven remarkably unable to affect change that is likely to produce an equitable, and therefore lasting, peace between the warring sides. In fact, more than half a century of conflict and hatred has eluded solutions from almost any quarter, Western or otherwise. The particular policy reputation of the USA in the conflict—crudely, as the unbreakable ally of one side—has arguably made matters worse in the sense that any capacity for even-handedness in negotiating peace has been gradually forfeited. In other words, even where fairly direct levers of foreign and security policy are in existence, they are not necessarily well calibrated to the policy challenge itself.

The view from government, therefore, is both mixed and uncertain as well as clouded by the lack of alignment between problems and levers. This book is interested in that imbalance and in helping to bring about a better strategic sense of what can be changed or influenced quickly, what can be attempted but without real promise, and, ultimately, what should be tried, if only to offset the worst features of Western society's anti-Islamic reputation.[25] The latter of these is no small job and requires careful policy design in itself, most particularly in relation to reducing the chances and impacts of counter-terrorism measures fuelling further disillusionment or worse.[26]

The overall policy challenge is essentially twofold. The first part centres on better alignment, along the lines discussed above. This requires a clearer understanding of the limitations of certain policy levers, the absence of others, and the capacity to utilize yet others in new and innovative ways. In relation to the latter, it is clear that there are already many existing levers in the overlapping fields of tackling social exclusion and isolation. Many of these levers are predicated on the principle of improving opportunity structures for disadvantaged groups within a general effort to allow all boats to rise together on a tide of growth and prosperity. These are discussed more fully in later chapters but here it is important to note that this task may require existing levers to be utilized in different ways. In schooling and employment, there is a mountain of evidence to suggest that especially disadvantaged groups are also socially isolated and therefore unable to take up new opportunities where and when they arise. This then means that intermediary policy measures are sometimes needed to build connectivity. These are basically innovative adaptations to the existing toolkit of social inclusion policy.

The second part goes beyond alignment of problem with solution and looks at the sum of all these realignment tasks. When aggregating together, there

---

[25] 'Gallup World Poll: Muslims' (Princeton, NJ: Gallup Organisation, 2007).
[26] Saggar, S., 'Boomerangs and Slingshots: Radical Islamism and Counter-Terrorism Strategy', *Journal of Ethnic and Migration Studies*, forthcoming.

is obviously a risk that small adjustments and adaptations can build into a much larger philosophical change in public policy. In the case of Britain, this is about the overall sensitization to religion and faith identity that can be achieved—and even desired—in a largely secular public policy setting.[27] Similar faith sensitization questions also hang over other Western societies and their political and policy traditions. The unspoken danger in any and all these Western cases is that such greater faith sensitization may amount to, and be perceived as, an effective carve-out for Muslim minorities. The probable political appetite for this kind of outcome is almost non-existent. Its pursuit, meanwhile, is likely only to further worsen the serious reputational problem that overshadows day-to-day political debate and controversy.[28]

There is, beyond this, one further challenge that is principally political rather than policy in nature. This is to manage a strategic response in a way that reduces, not increases, the political heat on and from Western Muslim communities. This is obviously much easier said than done, and there are numerous incentives to ensure that the issue, broadly defined, remains on the front burner of political life. A single act of terrorism or a further alpha-rated controversy is all that is needed to keep matters on the front burner. But, paradoxically, it is something of back-burner political attention that is most needed. This is not to suggest that the issues involved should be relegated to the margins. Rather that they should and need to be protected from the flames of immediate controversy and outspokenness. The midpoint between front- and back-burner politics would seem optimum in order to combine sufficient attention and risk of failure on one hand with enough space and licence to try and modify public policy levers on the other hand.[29] The latter in particular requires room to think, react, learn, and revise, in a setting that is not derailed by even the slightest hint of stakeholder controversy. This may be too much to expect, given the incendiary nature of political debate in this field. But it is not too much to aim for. One of the essential elements of long-term success is to be able to tackle problems affecting Muslims in ways that broadly resemble the approach to problems that affect all other religious and ethnic groups.[30] This would implicitly mean that policy solutions were sought and applied on a back, rather than front, burner. In relation to Muslim communities, it may be that current and ongoing sensitivities are already far in excess of what they should be. Like an open wound, inflammation cannot be easily reversed once present. But it is possible, and desirable, to identify proactively ways to reduce

[27] Johnson, N., 'We're all in this Together: The Challenge of Diversity, Equality and Solidarity', *Renewal*, Vol. 14, No. 4, 2006.

[28] Atran, S., 'Global Network Terrorism', Briefing to National Security Council, White House, 28 April 2006; available at http://www.sitemaker.umich.edu/satran/files/atran_nsc_042806.pdf and http://www.au.af.mil/au/awc/awcgate/whitehouse/atrannsc-042806.pdf.

[29] Saggar, S., 'Shifting Identities', in *The Next Decade: Understanding Change*, Final Report of the Pontingnano Tenth Anniversary Conference, The British Council, 20–2 September 2002.

[30] Amiraux, V., et al., *Faith and Secularism* (London: British Council, 2004).

the pain of nerve endings, at least in part by limiting the area for further aggravation.

Back-burner politics also brings with it an understanding that some good can be achieved. If good things can happen in difficult places, it is certainly possible to present positive gains in terms of fresh, learnt behaviour. This then allows Muslim communities the benefit of a wider and more innovative toolkit of policy responses, as opposed to the constraints of being viewed solely as a one-dimensional identity lobby. And, needless to say, the wider reputational positive spin-offs cannot be overlooked. There is, in other words, a real need to nurture a political environment in which Muslims' sentiments and perspectives are just that. Such an environment is currently terribly elusive—for all. But it is sorely needed in order to take the wind out of the sails of the reputational problem.

This outcome is largely a symptom of a post-pariah status, and so it cannot simply be willed. But it is also, at least in part, a political language and temperament. This can be proactively embraced by government and others to accelerate a post-pariah outcome.

About This Book: Who Should Read it and Why?

This study does not attempt to retell an already familiar story. It is a story that more or less surrounds contemporary politics in most Western countries today. It is without doubt a major political and policy problem that commands huge amounts of attention among academics, policymakers, think tanks, and journalism.[31]

The task pursued here is twofold: first, to build a better and more refined understanding of the position and reputation of British Muslim communities; and second, to tell a less well-known story that concerns governments and others who are committed to reversing the reputational problem. Therefore, the job in this book is to organize ideas, arguments, and evidence to pursue these two central goals. This then has implications for how this book is navigated by the reader and for bringing together its findings into generalizable lessons and priorities. To do so involves setting out three things at the front end: first, the rationale for the basic issue and problem; second, the context in which immigration, integration, and faith identity are hotly disputed topics; and third, the question of how governments should best mitigate the risks that they are faced with.

To start with, a book such as this should explain briefly why the central issue matters and to whom. At one level, ongoing controversies may serve to

---

[31] Saward, M., 'The State and Civil Liberties in the Post-9/11 World', in Dunleavy, P., et al. (eds.), *Developments in British Politics 8* (Basingstoke: Palgrave Macmillan, 2006).

answer these questions superficially for most readers. At another level, there are some deeper-seated, important rationales for carving out attention to look at the politics of Western Muslims' pariah reputation. Muslims are the second-largest religious group in the UK: 1.6 million Muslims live in the UK today. In considering the integration of British Muslim communities, there are two traditional objectives driving the interest of government and the focus of strategic public policy:

- to improve economic and social outcomes for those communities alongside other traditionally disadvantaged groups; and
- to increase the odds of social cohesion and reduce risks of conflict.

Achieving these objectives requires a better understanding of several inter-linked issues for British Muslim communities. This study aims to provide such an understanding based on testing several propositions and evidence. These are mainly around integration patterns, policy efforts to combat exclusion, and an often-charged domestic setting that is open to many international and transnational influences. Three stand out:

- The extent to which Muslims suffer disadvantage because of their religion (which can be difficult to disentangle from disadvantages due to ethnicity).
- The potential domestic ramifications from international tensions with Muslim-majority countries and countries containing large numbers of Muslims.
- The degree to which current policies for promoting long-term integration of immigrant and immigrant-descended groups across a range of areas, such as education, healthcare, housing, and employment opportunities, need to be rethought or revised to take greater account of religious sensitivities.

At present, a significant series of gaps in the underlying evidence base need to be addressed to improve understanding of this issue. In particular, demographic patterns among British Muslims and complex (including some transnational) patterns of family and community formation are not well understood. These are addressed in later chapters, mindful of a number of other equally tricky gaps in knowledge that need to be addressed as well.

Addressing religious diversity presents a number of challenges for public policy. These challenges can often be complex in character and highly nuanced in potential impact. The particular case of British Muslim communities matters in that, in common with other religious groups, the precise role of religion in shaping identity is not especially well understood. Such identity matters to government because it affects the basis on which government interacts with citizens, promotes inclusion and belonging, and builds social cohesion. There is a growing body of evidence to suggest that religion is a powerful aspect of some people's identity and interaction with others in an ethnically and religious plural society. Such identity affects the ways in which government engages with people, sometimes differentially. And the issue also matters because it is about the possibilities for building better citizen engagement.

Second, the issues discussed in this book are among the most hotly disputed in modern Western democracies. These issues also dominate the international and transnational landscape. It is not realistic to think that these disputes are mainly the spin-offs from immigration politics alone. Many mature liberal democracies have faced major debates and uncertainties in organizing their approach to mass immigration. These forces have sometimes led to turbulent political and social changes with which governments have struggled to cope. This turbulence has resulted in arguments over state reach, autonomous response, citizenship, and inclusion principles.[32] The effects have been felt across these migration countries but have been especially acute in Britain, Germany, France, and parts of the Low Countries. The resonation of these effects has also been heard, usually on a modest scale, in several New World migration countries such as the USA, Canada, and Australia.

Mass immigration has therefore not always been straightforward in political or policy terms. Whatever its political or economic consequences in each of these migration countries, much of the real controversy has been cultural in orientation in modern liberal states.[33] Many of these states are of course committed to a position of openness and tolerance of difference—or at least are committed to their self-identification in these terms. The cultural pressures stemming from mass immigration have led typically to disputes over the scope of the interventionist state, the role of women, the acceptance of counter-intuitive cultural norms, and the fostering of common cultural values and norms.

The bulk of Muslim communities in Western countries are a subset of post-war mass migration to Europe and the New World from South Asia, Turkey, North Africa, and the Middle East. The issues that these communities have brought, and the disputes that their presence has ignited, are not unique or different from other migratory settlements. These extend earlier debates and controversies, especially in relation to cultural norms and practices. But these issues are sometimes such a great extension on earlier themes that they have become recognizable and are managed in their own right. The point was made earlier in this chapter that a century or so ago it was not so strange to witness Jewish communities as subjects of a pariah status that mirrors the

---

[32] Messina, A., *The Logic and Politics of Post-war Immigration* (Cambridge: Cambridge University Press, 2007).

[33] Eade, J., et al., *Identities on the Move* (London: British Council, 2004).

reputation of many Western Muslims today. The factors identified at that time to be responsible for an unbridgeable divide were equally gargantuan in appearance. But they were also mainly straddled over a fifty- to seventy-year period. Jews in Britain today, for example, may not have fully escaped the pariah label of the past, but it is quite mistaken to think that this reputation dominates their present lives. It is a background murmur, audible to some perhaps and of significance to even fewer.

For the reader, this book is about setting the problem in some proper context that allows a better understanding as well as better informed response. This means placing the reputational lens at the forefront of the discussion. Western Muslim communities are not normally examined through this lens, but this book seeks to do so in a way that helpfully reminds us of the enormity of the problem. This is helpful because of the importance attached to the underlying narrative at play. It is not a narrative that easily allows Muslims to be seen in a positive light, but, then again, it is balanced by the equally negative reputation of Western societies in many Muslim minds.

The narrative of humiliation that is articulated and received in many Muslim communities and societies (and minds) is an important theme among commentators analysing the root causes of Islamist fervour. Some have gone further and sought to explain today's tensions in terms of a sense of collective humiliation felt by declining Islamic empires from the sixteenth century onwards. Even the most casual observer acknowledges the contemporary dynamics of global Islam in which the sense of the honour or dignity of Muslims is felt to be under attack. A perception of humiliation at the hands of Western, secularly minded governments and publics is a core element of the narrative. It has created a moral oxygen by which hatred and violence become permissible and even excusable.[34] This last element lies at the heart of this study's analysis of Islamist-inspired terrorism in Britain and elsewhere. And it has been noted by the recent Commonwealth Commission on Respect and Understanding, when describing the rise of violence in response to identity-based conflict:

Such narratives bind a community together and unite them around a common cause and this can be positive. But it can also result in portraying the 'other' in a wholly negative light, divesting them of any moral authority or legitimacy, make feelings of hate and distrust 'normal' and, in extreme cases, be used to justify violence.[35]

The reader's job is aided by the concentration placed on not just hatred and violence but also its moral acceptability in otherwise peaceful minds and communities. Indeed, this is one of the biggest challenges when examining and tackling Islamist political agendas and terror. Readers are reminded

[34] Volkan, V., *Killing in the Name of Identity* (Virginia: Pitchstone, 2006).
[35] *Dignity and Dialogue: Civil Pathways to Peace*, Final Report of the Commonwealth Commission on Respect and Understanding (London: Commonwealth Secretariat, 2007).

that moral frameworks that turn a blind eye to hatred and violence are by no means new or unique. Helpful lessons can be discerned by reference to conflicts in Northern Ireland, the Basque country, and Quebec, to name just three prominent examples. The politics of religious and political extremism among Western Muslim communities shares much in common with earlier cases, and these insights can be deployed to explain, for instance, some of the limitations of counter-terrorism strategies. But, overall, the reader is invited to ponder the depth and intractability of disputes that currently obscure all else there may be to say or think about in respect to Western Muslims. This book is about such an exploration, although shaped by a bias towards the long-term solubility of current problems. This is, therefore, an optimistic account, if anything, chiefly because it challenges the assertion that the politics of one-dimensional identity can tackle the reputational problem Western Muslims face. It almost certainly cannot, and that is itself a positive way to guide the search for credible solutions of a more complex, nuanced nature.

Finally, since this book is written with the needs of practitioners (alongside analysts) in mind, the reader is guided to the implications that arise. The most important of these is to examine problems and issues in terms of the inferences that are drawn about the applicability and effectiveness of public policy. Closely related to this is the need to track likely policy responses to see how far they chime with existing policy frameworks and traditions. In Britain, the main focus of this study, this means looking for the gaps in integration policies, the hidden opportunities in social inclusion policies, and, regrettably, some of the unintended consequences of counter-terrorism measures.

All of these can, to a large extent, be seen as commentaries on the overall effectiveness of public policy thinking and practice. The problems identified here are largely ones that serve to test the limits of strategic policymaking. The case involves, *inter alia*, evidence of settled disadvantage, extreme bitterness and anger, inward-facing postures, radical oppositional politics, unbalanced pursuit of grievance agendas, and susceptibility to globalized, grand humiliation narratives. This is a powerful combination, for sure, but one that pointedly tests the capabilities of social, economic, security, and foreign policies of government at one and the same time.

To that extent, it is helpful to think of these as ongoing and overlapping risks faced by government. Each high-level risk can be mapped to each other and to a host of lower-order ones, ranging from attainment in schools to indoctrination patterns and transnational communications. Not each can be handled in the same way nor with the same degree of importance. Evidence-based public policy is not just about linking cause to remedy. It is rather more ambitious in that there is a case for looking at the interdependencies of causes and therefore remedies. This implies a need to understand the risks better and in a way that is flexible in the face of various Rumsfeldian unknown and known unknowns.

This book seeks to explore what those unknown issues are, and how they might be thought of as risks to be managed in a holistic way. However, this book is also operating in largely uncharted terrain. The problems and issues are both new and familiar. Whether they are the ones that are claimed, and whether behaviours are influenced in predictable ways, is still uncertain. So this book ultimately is one that wishes to assist the growth of neurological nerve endings between disciplines to promote understanding. Once fused, at least in part, this book has a chance to effect important gains in the biggest gulf of all: between theory and better explanation on one hand and practice and better solutions on the other.

The Structure of the Book

In Chapter 2, we turn to look at the factual evidence surrounding the position of British Muslim communities. This chapter includes a review of demographic patterns alongside the evidence on socio-economic opportunity, residential patterns, and interaction between Muslim and non-Muslim communities. Chapter 3 is concerned with looking at the interplay between religion, faith, and identity politics. It includes a lengthy discussion of Muslim identity and the factors responsible for the recent assertion of a confrontational, hardline posture in and towards Western countries. This chapter also unpacks the case for pariah-dom as the core argument pursued in this book. The purpose of Chapter 4 is to examine in detail the situation of Muslim communities in Britain, alongside a more brief examination of Muslims in some other Western countries. This is an empirical examination that tries to go to the heart of claims and counter-claims about the unique position of Western Muslim communities, and in effect to test claims regarding the emergence of a Muslim underclass. Thereafter, Chapters 5 and 6 switch gear to look at the nature of extremism and radicalization, and to discuss the emergence of an alpha-rated reputational problem in Britain and elsewhere. In Chapter 7, we review the major strategic implications of the material raised in earlier chapters and link these to normative questions about better strategic responses. Finally, Chapter 8 serves to provide a summary and a broad-based review of the main conclusions of this book. In addition, it provides a general discussion of the lessons for the policy community on the frontlines of integration, inclusion, and security challenges.

2

Demographic and Factual Overview

Amid all the hyperbole [about a future Eurabia] a hard reality stands out. It is the importance of jobs. In America, it is easy for the newcomer to get work and hard to claim welfare; in Europe the opposite is true. Deregulating labour markets is a less emotive subject than head-scarves or cartoons, but it matters far more.

Economist, 24 June 2006, p. 11

One finds in Europe today a great deal of transnationalism activity (nominally involving 'Muslims') which has little or nothing to do with Islamic agendas and much more to do with the nature of labour migrant networks in a globalized world. [The] variegated experience means that Muslims in Europe who seek to make common cause across state boundaries often bring the baggage of their unique national (or even local) experiences with them, making it difficult to unite around a shared sense of European Muslim-ness.

Peter Mandaville[1]

Introduction

Western Europe, informed estimates conclude, includes between 12 and 15 million Muslims.[2] In the UK alone, the official census-based total is 1.6 million. This figure derives from a self-description methodology originating in 2001. Internal growth through childbirth and a young population age profile will have lifted the total substantially before the next scheduled headcount in 2011. Inward migration will also have contributed to rising numbers. At the time of publication, most reliable quasi-official estimates cluster around the 1.8–2 million mark.

[1] Mandaville, P., 'Muslim Transnational Identity and State Responses in the UK After 9/11: Political Community, Ideology and Authority', *Journal of Ethnic and Migration Studies*, forthcoming.

[2] Open Society Institute, *Monitoring Minority Protection in the EU: The Situation of Muslims in the UK*, EU Monitoring and Advocacy Program (EUMAP) (Budapest: OSI, 2002).

The bulk of recent Muslim migration and settlement to Europe has originated from South Asian as well as Turkish and North African sources. Around 40 per cent stems from Pakistan, with another 20 per cent from Bangladesh. Of course the Muslim world population is nowhere near so heavily skewed towards South Asia, heavily populated though that region is. The South Asian dimension is closely linked to post-colonial migration to the UK, although in recent years this has fanned out to include several other European countries (e.g. Mauritian communities in France, Pakistani communities in Denmark).

However, the profile of Muslims elsewhere in Europe is markedly different. To begin with, several European countries have rather larger Muslim resident populations in absolute terms. France's current population, for example, officially comprises 5 million Muslims. Many unofficial readings suggest that this number could be between 7 and 8 million in reality. The composition of this group is slanted towards North African immigrant communities, principally originating from Algeria, Morocco, and Tunisia. The Maghgreb communities make up a very distinctive French Muslim identity, both internally within French society and externally in terms of wider European perceptions of French Muslims.[3] This is further overlaid by the experience of decolonization.[4] Older generations of French Algerians in particular have strong memories of the independence movements and struggles of the 1950s, accompanied by the early experience of political violence and colonial suppression. The spectre of secular Arab nationalism, prominent in the 1950s and 1960s, further distinguishes this generation. Their younger counterparts have been partly influenced by secular forms of political conflict but have also remained connected to a high degree with political instability in North Africa. Algeria's de facto civil war during the 1990s, resulting in a formal attempt to restrict radical Islamist parties and movements, is the most prominent example that has had a marked spillover effect in France itself. Finally, the experience of patchy integration into mainstream French society and of discrimination in particular has created a further twist.[5]

In Germany, almost a tenth of the population at large fall into one immigrant category or another, equalling 7 million residents across two or three generations. Around a half of these 7 million migrants are Muslims, with the bulk drawn from Turkish origin (2.2 million).[6] The dominant aspect of

[3] Cesari, J., *When Islam and Democracy Meet: Muslims in Europe and the United States* (New York: Palgrave, 2004).

[4] Bowen, J., 'Beyond Migration: Islam as a Transnational Public Space', *Journal of Ethnic and Migration Studies*, Vol. 30, No. 5, September 2004, pp. 879–94.

[5] Kepel, G., *The War for Muslim Minds: Islam and the West* (Cambridge, MA: Belknap Press, 2004).

[6] Report of the Wilton Park Conference, 'Muslim Youth in Europe: Addressing Alienation and Extremism', 7–10 February 2005.

the German Muslim population has been the awkwardness of a large settled immigrant population with historically little more than the political or legal status of a classic guest worker community. The Turkish community in particular has been directly recruited to fill gaps in the German labour market over several decades. Its Muslim origins are different again, influenced in particular by Turkish secular traditions.

The Low Countries contain Western Europe's other significant Muslim communities.[7] In this case, these are mainly made up of Moroccan immigrants, with sizeable concentrations in the Netherlands; similar Moroccan concentrations are also found in Belgium.

Overall, however, Western Europe's largest Muslim communities are located in the UK, France, and Germany. The characteristics of these communities vary considerably both across and within these three countries. In this chapter, some detail is offered to unpack this point and to focus on the specific characteristics of particular countries and specific Muslim communities. Despite these variations, it is also important to look for common patterns and trajectories. The most striking of these relate to the demography of West European Muslims in terms of age and generation and also in terms of socio-economic status and geographic clustering. The high-level aim of this chapter is to investigate how far and in what sense accurate generalizations can be drawn about the position of Muslims in Western countries. This chapter also includes some evidence regarding the development and sustenance of collective consciousness and identity among Western Muslims (something that is discussed more fully in later chapters), thereby adding another dimension to the case for or against generalizations.

Overview of European Muslim Communities

Europe's Muslims are a highly diverse group demographically, socially, and theologically. The evidence shows that they contain various strands of religious beliefs and practices, and are primarily drawn from a series of large migratory movements to Europe one or more generations ago. These earlier movements, chiefly from South Asia, North Africa, and Turkey, have been supplemented in more recent times by smaller, yet significant, influxes of temporary and permanent migrants from *inter alia* the Horn of Africa, western and central Africa, South-east Asia, and various parts of the greater Middle East.

---

[7] Geddes, A., *The Politics of Migration and Immigration in Europe* (Sage, 2003); Geddes, A., 'Ethnic Minorities in the Labour Market: Comparative Policy Approaches (Western Europe)', Report commissioned by the Performance and Innovation Unit, Cabinet Office, 2002; available on-line at www.strategy.gov.uk.

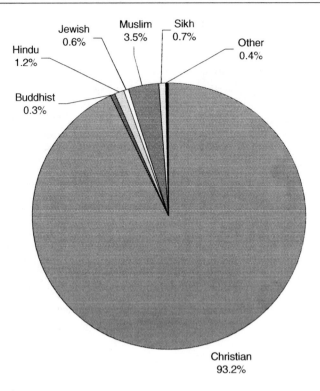

Jewish
0.6%

Muslim
3.5%

Sikh
0.7%

Hindu
1.2%

Other
0.4%

Buddhist
0.3%

Christian
93.2%

Figure 2.1. Religious background in the UK, 2001
Source: 2001 Census.

Britain

British Muslims encompass a wide range of ethnic, cultural, linguistic, and national backgrounds. The 2001 census estimated that there were 1.6 million Muslims living in the UK, making Muslims the second-largest religious group after Christians. The 2001 census was the first to include a direct self-description question on religion and, as the data has been fully mined by academic and other researchers, this has provided a rich source of information on this issue.

Figure 2.1 shows the scale of the Muslim minority in Britain alongside other religious groups. Clearly, even among the South Asian religious cohorts, it is apparent that Muslims constitute the largest single group, dwarfing the Hindu and Sikh populations.

In the past, the size of the Muslim population in the UK has been debated widely among researchers. Prior to the direct religious background question of the 2001 census, much of this debate was underscored by uncertainty and imprecision on matters of methodology. Moreover, the emergence of a vocal, mass Muslim political interest may have served to exaggerate estimated numbers in some circles. The work of Ceri Peach has helpfully summarized various estimates of population size over a twenty-five-year period in tabular form.[8] In 1980, he notes, most researchers published population size estimates that ranged between 750,000 and 800,000. By the mid-1990s, Peach's[9] own work indicated a total population size of well below a million, in sharp contrast to those publicized by the Muslim Parliament in 1992 (3 million).[10] The effects of political inflation could clearly be seen.

Significant patterns of religious diversity exist within and across ethnic lines in Britain: for example, despite some popular views of Britain as a white, Christian country, just around seven in ten are both white and Christian according to the 2001 census. Figure 2.2 tells the story.

The 2001 census collected information about ethnicity and religious identity backgrounds. Combining these results shows that, while the population is more culturally diverse than ever before, white Christians remain the largest single group by far. In England and Wales, 36 million people (nearly seven out of ten) described their ethnicity as white and their religion as Christian. Majorities of black people and those from mixed ethnic backgrounds also identified as Christian (71% and 52%, respectively). In total, there were 810,000 black Christians and 347,000 Christians from mixed ethnic backgrounds. Among other faiths, the largest groups were Pakistani Muslims (658,000) and Indian Hindus (467,000) followed by Indian Sikhs (301,000), Bangladeshi Muslims (260,000), and white Jews (252,000).

The Indian group, according to the 2001 census, is relatively religiously diverse in its composition. Thus, 45 per cent of Indians were Hindu, 29 per cent Sikh, and a further 13 per cent Muslim. By contrast, the Pakistani and Bangladeshi groups were substantially more religiously homogenous, with Muslims accounting for 92 per cent of each ethnic group.

The picture can also be examined from the perspective of the ethnic composition of religious groups. Some faith communities were concentrated in particular ethnic groups. For example, 91 per cent of Sikhs were Indian and 97 per cent of Jews described their ethnicity as white. Other faiths were more widely dispersed; significant proportions of Buddhists were found in the white, Chinese, other Asian, and other ethnic groups. But the Muslim population remains heavily drawn from Pakistani and Bangladeshi backgrounds (43% and 17%, respectively). Indians are an important subset in

[8] Peach, C., 'Britain's Muslim Population: An Overview', in Abbas, T. (ed.), *Muslims in Britain: Communities Under Pressure* (London: Zed Books, 2005).

[9] Peach, C., 'Estimates of the 1991 Muslim Population of Great Britain', Oxford Plural Societies and Multicultural Cities Research Group, Working Paper 1 (Oxford: School of Geography, 1997).

[10] Siddiqui, K., 'The Muslim Parliament of Great Britain', inaugural address, unpublished (London: Muslim Parliament of Great Britain, 1992).

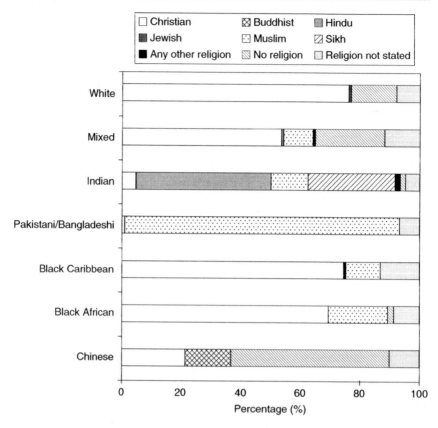

Figure 2.2. Ethnic group by religious composition, 2001, England and Wales only
Source: extracted from http://www.statistics.gov.uk/cci/nugget.asp?id=395.

addition, making up almost a tenth of the Muslim population. South Asians, therefore, amount to a little over two-thirds of British Muslims. Other sizeable ethnic subgroups among British Muslims include black Africans (6%) and those of mixed ethnic backgrounds (4%).[11] The remaining one-third, non-South Asians among the Muslim population, are therefore typically drawn from African countries, Near Eastern countries, and also from South-east Asia.

It is also useful to set these figures in the context of those with no expressed religious faith. Overall, 15 per cent of the English and Welsh population reported having no religion, although variation by ethnicity was marked. Just over half of all Chinese people, and a quarter of people from mixed ethnic backgrounds, stated they had no religion. Asian, black African, and

[11] http://www.statistics.gov.uk/statbase/Expodata/Spreadsheets/D6892.xls.

Irish people were least likely to have no religious affiliation. Fewer than 1 in 200 Pakistanis and Bangladeshis reported having no religion, although this should not be taken as firm evidence of having no religious background whatsoever. Interestingly, 14 per cent of people in the other black group chose not to answer the religious background question, almost twice the average for England and Wales as a whole. Similar proportions of people in the black Caribbean and mixed ethnic groups also gave no answer.

Britain's Muslim communities represent a diverse range of different theological and immigrant descendant groups. The UK Muslim population's doctrinal traditions can also be measured, albeit in approximate terms. The Oxford Leverhulme survey of UK Mosques suggests that 87 per cent of mosques are within the Sunni tradition, as against just 7 per cent that are Shi'a mosques. The remainder, including groups that are not fully recognized by the majority of Muslims and cross-denominational mosques, comprised 6 per cent.[12]

The Pakistani and Bangladeshi populations are also synonymous with Muslim communities. Furthermore, and significantly, these national ethnic groups are also synonymous with relative poverty and disadvantage in the UK context—and at least in comparison with other South Asian ethnic groups. It is less widely known or appreciated that both are also largely drawn from an agrarian peasant background: mainly from Punjab and Azad Kashmir among Pakistanis and from the Sylhet region among Bangladeshis.

There are few detailed, reliable sources giving a breakdown of British Muslim communities by country of origin. However, available estimates show that Muslims of Pakistani and Bangladeshi origin are the two largest groups but may still only constitute just under two-thirds of the total Muslim population. Significantly, South Asian Muslims originate from a small number of areas such as Gujarat among Indians, Mirpur in southern Kashmir among Pakistanis, and Sylhet and Chittagong among Bangladeshis.

Other significant ethnic and national groups that comprise the total Muslim population include the Turkish (including Turkish-Cypriot), Somali, Malaysian, and Nigerian communities. The Arab Muslim communities in particular include a range of national origins, and there are numerous examples of relative economic success particularly in central London-based self-employment. According to Whine:[13]

Britain's Arab communities are small and often transient, composed of students and businessmen who temporarily locate to Britain during the summer to escape the intense heat of the Middle East. However, the Lebanese civil war and political turmoil in some

---

[12] Cited in Peach, C., 'Britain's Muslim Population: An Overview', in Abbas, T. (ed.), *Muslims in Britain: Communities Under Pressure* (London: Zed Books, 2005).

[13] Whine, M., 'The Penetration of Islamist Ideology in Britain', *Current Trends in Islamist Ideology*, 1, 2005, 50–8.

Arab states has led to the relocation of many Arab media outlets to London, which now serves as a major Arab language news publishing centre.

Estimates of converts to Islam stretch between 5,000 and 10,000 (around half of whom are from the black Caribbean community). However, the rate of Muslim conversions is the subject of some dispute.[14] A number of contributions to the British Muslim media have suggested that not only is Islam the fastest growing religious group in Britain, but the sources of conversion are disproportionately from white non-religious backgrounds as well. This in turn has fuelled a lively debate about the attitudes of non-white Muslims towards white converts.[15]

Finally, the multi-ethnic, diverse Ismaili Muslim community—itself part of a significant and influential transnational network—represents a powerful counter-intuitive example among Western Muslims. Its principal significance lies in its success in defying familiar stereotypes of Muslim underachievement in schools and employment (to say nothing of the face of oppositional, grievance politics) that has become familiar in Britain at least.

The Muslim presence and contribution to British society dates from the Middle Ages, mainly resulting from the expansion of Islamic empires and European Crusades.[16] For example, sailors from the Indian subcontinent, some of whom were Muslims, settled in port cities 300 years ago, and significant populations were established in London, Cardiff, Liverpool, and South Shields (containing Britain's oldest Yemeni community). The first purpose-built mosque was established in Woking in the 1880s, and a Trust to build the well-known Central London Mosque (at Regent's Park) was created in the 1920s.[17]

Fresh migration from India, Pakistan, and East Africa in the 1960s and 1970s, followed by an intense wave of migration from the young state of Bangladesh in the late 1970s and 1980s, increased the Muslim population considerably. This also contributed to a far greater degree of internal differentiation among British Muslims in terms of national, cultural, and linguistic backgrounds. Contrasting profiles also emerged in the socio-economic profiles of particular subgroups. For example, some 20,000 of the 150,000 South Asians of East African origin were Muslims and typically possessed key advantages over other Muslim groups drawn directly from the Indian subcontinent. Such advantages made a critical difference in terms of

---

[14] Nielsen, J. S., *Muslims in Western Europe* (Edinburgh: Edinburgh University Press, 1991). One estimate in the *Financial Times* (23 January 2002) suggested that 'white' converts to Islam alone might exceed 10,000.

[15] Rosser-Owen, I., 'British Muslim? A Venting of Steam', *Q-News*, May–June 2003.

[16] Breton, J.- M., 'Muslims in France and Britain', unpublished report of conference, Paris, November 1998.

[17] The present mosque was only completed in 1977, although a pioneering Islamic Cultural Centre was opened by King George VI on the site in 1944.

long-term patterns in education, jobs, housing, and social mobility. Three elements creating an advantageous foundation stand out.[18] First, this smaller group has experience of living in urban centres with similarities to British cities. Urbanization in the country of origin on this scale has been relatively scarce among other immigrant groups to Britain. Second, they boasted wide exposure to English as the public lingua franca of East African societies. Again, this attribute contrasted sharply with the very limited exposure to English found among other South Asian immigrants. Third, they brought with them various white-collar business and professional backgrounds that were relatively easily transferred to the UK context. Such white-collar educational and employment experiences, with similar educational aspirations following settlement, have been widely commented on. All of these factors, when combined together, have presented a strong match to the changing labour market, urbanization, and entrepreneurial needs of the modern UK economy.

Precise estimates of the composition by national background of Britain's Muslims are limited. One study indicated that South Asian Muslims comprised around three-quarters of the total Muslim background population of Britain, although this figure takes no account of the depth of religious faith found in each of these communities.[19] Significantly, around 400,000 Muslims live in Britain who are not drawn from South Asian origin. A significant minority of these Muslims are Arabs and are also highly concentrated geographically in central parts of London. Figure 2.3 describes the internal variety of UK Muslims by national background.

The demographic profile of Britain's Muslims points to a young, tightly clustered, and often deprived community. Age profiles differ greatly between people of different religions. For example, Muslim and Sikh populations have a very high proportion of young people: 33.8 per cent of Muslims are aged 0–15 years and 18.2 per cent aged 16–24 years; for Sikhs, some 24.5 per cent are aged 0–15 years and 16.7 per cent are aged 16–24 years. The average across the whole population is 20.2 per cent aged 0–15 years and 10.9 per cent aged 16–24 years. The age profile of Buddhists, meanwhile, is older than the Muslim and Sikh groups, and children (aged 0–15 years) make up only 12.0 per cent while 52.0 per cent are aged 25–49 years.

Overall, Muslims continue to be significantly younger in their age profile than most other religious groups. The modest concentration within the Muslim population who are in or near retirement is also a characteristic of other South Asian religious groups, as Figure 2.4 demonstrates.

To a fair degree, the age distribution of different ethnic groups follows the same pattern, largely because of the South Asian dominance within UK

[18] The Report of the Runnymede Trust Commission on British Muslims and Islamophobia, *Islamophobia—A Challenge for us All* (London: Runnymede Trust, 1997).

[19] *Muslims in Britain* (Minority Rights Group International, 2002).

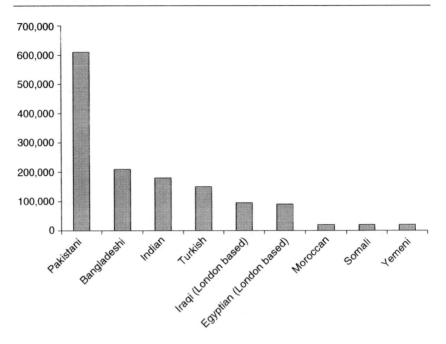

Figure 2.3. Estimates of British Muslim population by country of origin, late 1990s
Source: Muslims in Britain (Minority Rights Group International, 2002).

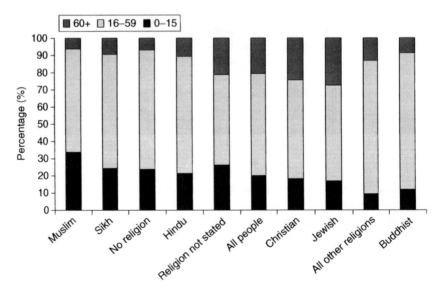

Figure 2.4. Religion by age group, England and Wales, 2001
Source: 2001 Census.

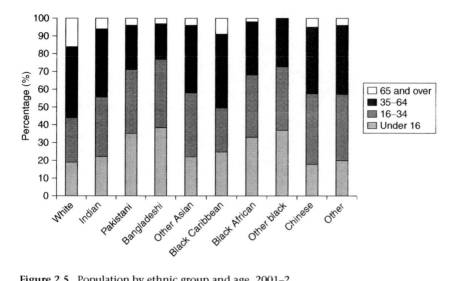

Figure 2.5. Population by ethnic group and age, 2001–2
Source: Annual Local Area Labour Force Survey (ONS, 2001).

Muslim communities. This is seen in Figure 2.5, which draws not on census data but rather on pooled Labour Force Survey data gathered around the time of the 2001 census.

Most people in England and Wales describe themselves as Christian (71.7%), but Christians tend to be towards the older end of the age spectrum—19 per cent are sixty-five years of age and over compared with 16.0 per cent of the overall population. Only Jewish people have a higher proportion of older people—22.3 per cent are aged sixty-five years and over and 12.5 per cent are aged seventy-five years and over. Part of this distinctively older age structure is shaped by growing affluence which, in general terms, is associated with smaller and later household formation and childbirth patterns. Some is also shaped by a broader tendency of immigrant descended groups to exhibit, over relatively long periods of time, a pattern of merging with larger (and usually lower) societal fertility rates. Only about 2 per cent of the Buddhist, Hindu, Muslim, and Sikh populations are aged seventy-five years and over.[20]

Certain areas in urban England have emerged as places with a strong local Muslim presence. For example, in inner East London, 36 per cent of the population of Tower Hamlets and 24 per cent in Newham is Muslim. These comprise a large number of Bangladeshis who tended to settle in London's East End during the 1970s and 1980s. Pakistani communities, many of whom originally settled in the 1950s and 1960s, tend to be located in the Midlands, the North West, and large cities in Scotland. These traditional manufacturing

[20] http://www.statistics.gov.uk/cci/nugget.asp?id = 349.

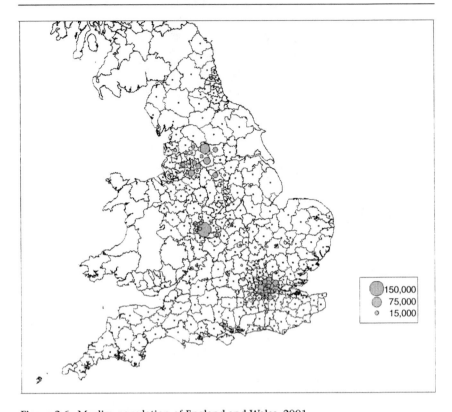

Figure 2.6. Muslim population of England and Wales, 2001

Source: from Peach, C., 'A Demographic Profile of the British Muslim community', presentation to the Centre for the Study of Democracy conference, 'Muslims in Britain: The Making of a New Underclass?', University of Westminster, November 2004.

areas of the UK have seen a significant decline over the last thirty or forty years owing to the changing structure of the UK economy, which has tended to favour service-based industries often, but not exclusively, located in southern regions of the UK.

Bangladeshis, by contrast, have a much shorter settlement history, with the bulk of this group arriving in Britain during the 1970s and 1980s; they are also disproportionately located in east and central London. Their proximity to buoyant demand for labour in central London and the City of London's professional services sector has thus far made rather little impact on employment and progression rates. Figure 2.6 highlights the main areas of Muslim population concentration in England and Wales using 2001 census figures.

It is worth overlaying this picture of the geographic spread of religious groups with some understanding of the geographic distribution of poverty. For the population as a whole, the greatest concentration of people living

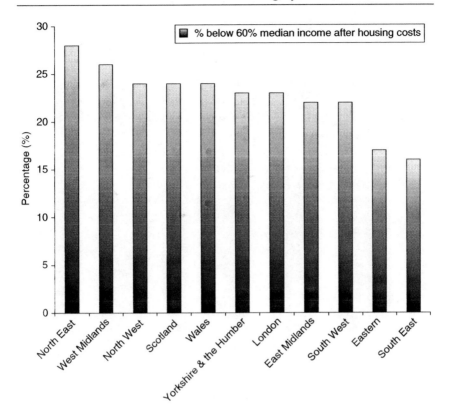

Figure 2.7. Percentage of all UK households below 60% median household income, 2001

Source: Households Below Average Income Series (DWP 2001).

below 60 per cent median income is located in the North East, West Midlands, North West, and Scotland—see Figure 2.7. Two of these regions are especially associated with Pakistani ethnic settlement patterns that typically occurred two or even three generations ago. The degree to which these communities have experienced internal mobility away from these regions and into generally more economically prosperous regions can be added to the picture. Broadly speaking, such mobility has been modest, to say the least.

Pakistani and Bangladeshi communities have lower levels of disposable income than other ethnic groups. After accounting for housing costs, a colossal 60 per cent of Pakistani and Bangladeshi people are in the bottom quintile of the income distribution compared to 27 per cent of black Caribbean and 26 per cent for Indian communities. This contrast is shown in Figure 2.8. A number of commentators have linked this concentration in poverty to the levels of employment and economic activity among Pakistani

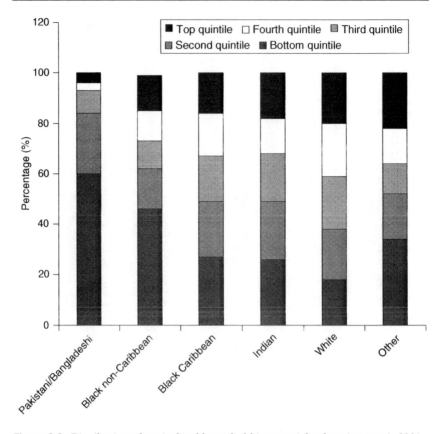

Figure 2.8. Distribution of equivalized household income (after housing costs), 2001
Source: Households Below Average Income Series (DWP, 2001).

and Bangladeshi women. Women's participation in employment is discussed later in this chapter but it is worth noting that the presence of twin-earning households is a common predictor of the avoidance of poverty generally and the incidence of economic shocks at household level specifically. Resilience to economic turmoil of this kind is an important factor when assessing the overall economic integration and progress of minority faith and ethnic communities.

These specifically Muslim (or rather, what are better described Pakistani and Bangladeshi) demographic characteristics and patterns need to be placed in the context of assessing the progress, especially in economic terms, made by post-war immigrants to the UK. For instance, the educational and linguistic advantages of second-generation groups clearly distinguish their labour market experience from that of first-generation migrants. Evidence suggests that the second generation is faring somewhat better than the first, both in terms

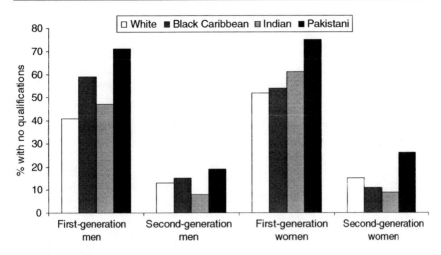

Figure 2.9. Percentage of people with no British qualifications, by ethnic group, gender, and generation, late 1990s

Note: first generation refers to those born in 1940–59 and surveyed in the 1970s; second generation refers to those born in 1960–79 and surveyed in the 1990s.

Source: Panel one—cumulated GHS 1973–9; Panel two—cumulated LFS 1991–7 in Britain.

of access to mid-skilled white-collar jobs and professional and managerial jobs and in terms of earnings. The flip side of this positive assessment is that it focuses on comparison over time within an ethnic or religious group and thus obscures the rather more pertinent comparator, namely, the position of other ethnic groups of the same generation. In this respect, the evidence points to poorer records of achievement between most Muslim groups and other religious communities.

Overall, the gap between immigrant-descended minorities and whites appears not to have closed with respect to employment levels, suggesting that native birth brings occupational improvement but does little to mitigate unemployment. According to Heath, the evidence in Figure 2.9 shows that:[21]

- In the 1970s, all first-generation minorities suffered higher rates of unemployment than British-born whites of the same age. While Indians came close to the British-born white figures, the most disadvantaged group in the first-generation were black Caribbeans, with an unemployment rate around twice that of whites.

- In the second generation in the 1990s, there is no sign that matters had improved. Indeed, white British versus ethnic minority differentials have

[21] Heath, A., 'Explaining Ethnic Minority Disadvantage', unpublished paper commissioned by the Prime Minister's Strategy Unit, October 2001. See www.strategy.gov.uk.

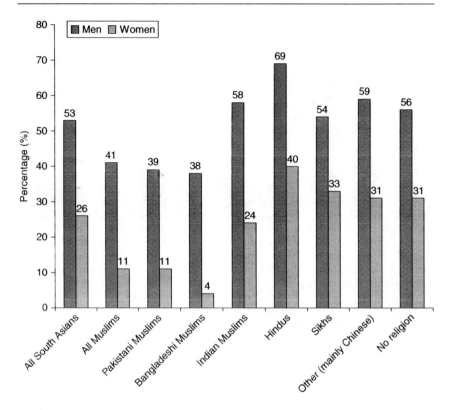

Figure 2.10. British South Asians in full-time employment (%), 1997

Source: based on Brown, M. S., "Religion and economic activity in the South Asian Population" *Ethnic and Racial Studies* 23 (Nov 2000).

increased in all three cases. Unemployment rates of second-generation black Caribbean and Pakistani men were over twice those of white British men of the same age.

These data show that labour market achievement varies between the first- and second-generation groups. Pakistanis men experienced a considerable surge in unemployment from the first to the second generation, but this was in common with patterns found among other non-Muslim ethnic minority groups.

Broadly speaking, religious background is not a clear driver of outcomes in employment. Evidence on the outcomes of the different ethnic groups who make up Britain's Muslim community describes a complex picture in which being Muslim is not so obviously a clear predictor of achievement in labour market terms. However, from what data are available (see Figure 2.10), it appears that Pakistani and Bangladeshi Muslims have worse labour market outcomes than other Muslim groups.[22] Pakistani and Bangladeshi men have 39 and 38 per cent full-time employment rates respectively compared to 58 per cent for Indian Muslims and 53 per cent for South Asians as a whole.[23] The evidence is therefore mixed in drawing clear assessments about the link between religious background and economic participation. It does, however, point to an important and far from fully understood country of origin effect that appears to enable Muslims of Indian origin to escape the worst aspects of Pakistanis' and Bangladeshis' weak performance. This has led, regrettably, to some odd and illogical leaps among researchers, commentators, and special interests seeking to identify a rationale for intervention in public policy to remedy a perceived 'religious penalty' that it is not borne out in evidence.[24] In addition, there are significant data deficiencies since these tentative conclusions are themselves drawn from large-scale surveys that were in the field in the mid-1990s.

There is some evidence to show a wider pattern within Muslim groups, whereby Muslims of Pakistani and Bangladeshi origin have worse social outcomes than other Muslim groups. This is at least associated with geographical location, age structures, and aspects of social capital among these groups, alongside persisting discrimination. The main point to note is that perceptions of UK Muslims are undoubtedly heavily conditioned by the Pakistani and Bangladeshi experience, although there is evidence to show that there is considerable variance once Muslims from other national and ethnic groups are factored in.

There may be many non-religious aspects driving differential outcomes among Pakistani and Bangladeshi communities. But, practically speaking, the extremely high proportions of Muslims within these groups (96% and 95%, respectively) mean that religion cannot be ignored when analysing

[22] A firmer assessment of relative advantage or disadvantage in the labour market requires a multivariate methodological approach to the data that can separate out, where possible, the effects of religious background beyond the impact of ethnicity. Such work has already been pioneered in respect to ethnic and gender effects in assessing labour market outcomes. See Prime Minister's Strategy Unit, *Ethnic Minorities and the Labour Market: Final Report* (London: Cabinet Office, 2003). See also *Fairness and Freedom: The Final Report of the Equalities Review* (London: Cabinet Office, 2007). In the UK, work by the Office for National Statistics has been carried out to identify the scope to carry out such a study of religious effects. See 'Ethnicity and Religion in the British Labour Market' (unpublished) draft analysis plan, ONS Social Analysis and Reporting Division: Ethnicity and Identity branch, January 2005.

[23] Modood, T., et al., *Ethnic Minorities in Britain: Diversity and Disadvantage* (London: Policy Studies Institute, 1997)—also known as the 'Fourth National Survey of Ethnic Relations'.

[24] An example of the confusion and muddle among think tanks and others can be seen in the report published in summer 2004 by the Open Society Institute which makes great play of the lack of detailed evidence or understanding about religious 'penalties' in labour markets while simultaneously recommending that policymakers adjust policy programmes to take account of faith differences. See 'Aspirations and Reality: British Muslims and the Labour Market' (Budapest and New York: OSI, 2004), esp. pp.30–3. See also 'Muslims in the UK and the Labour Market', chapter 3 in *Muslims in the UK: Policies for Engaged Citizens* (Budapest: OSI, 2005).

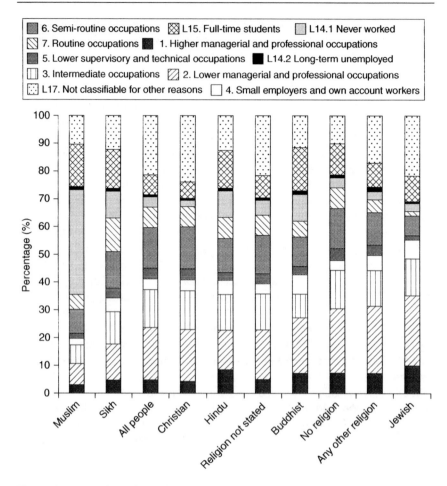

6. Semi-routine occupations   L15. Full-time students   L14.1 Never worked
7. Routine occupations   1. Higher managerial and professional occupations
5. Lower supervisory and technical occupations   L14.2 Long-term unemployed
3. Intermediate occupations   2. Lower managerial and professional occupations
L17. Not classifiable for other reasons   4. Small employers and own account workers

Figure 2.11. Females: religion by occupation, England and Wales, 2001

Muslim communities and when formulating policy responses to tackle disadvantage and discrimination within these communities. Tackling education and labour market disadvantage issues typically involves a response based on ethnic differences, making for an uneasy understanding of the overlapping or distinctive influence of religion. By contrast, reconciling negative reactions to international tensions and crises will probably involve a more religiously sensitized approach to dealing with religious issues.

Labour market achievements also vary by gender, as set out in Figure 2.11. There is a greater difference in employment across ethnic groups for women than for men. Bangladeshi women, for example, are approximately three times less likely to be economically active than their black Caribbean counterparts. Intra-group variances in economic activity rates by gender are again particularly marked in the case of Bangladeshis, with the economic activity rates of men from this group over 40 percentage points higher than those of women.

Trends in occupational attainment and income for women are similar to those for men, although smaller proportions of women from all groups hold professional or managerial positions. Similarly, though women's unemployment rates generally tend to be slightly lower than those of men, the same basic pattern holds, with black Caribbean, Pakistani, and Bangladeshi joblessness significantly higher than that of whites. But the most telling aspect of Figure 2.11 is the very large proportion of Muslim women who are either long-term unemployed or have never worked. This subgroup is vastly greater than anything found among other religious groups. This describes a position of great distance from the world of work and the dynamics of the mainstream labour market. According to Peach:[25]

[It] reflects tradition Islamic values of *purdah* (protecting Muslim women from contact with men outside their immediate family) and *izzet* (family honour). Unlike the Hindus and Sikhs, where both husbands and wives often work and there are dual incomes in the household, Pakistani and Bangladeshi households often have only one breadwinner.

There are, additionally, striking human capital disparities between groups of different ethnicity, age, and gender, as measured by the proportion with no qualifications.[26] Figure 2.11 also highlights the fact that Pakistani men and women (who are overwhelmingly Muslim groups) fare especially poorly.

The picture in relation to housing patterns continues a familiar story. This is shown in Figures 2.12 and 2.13. The former examines patterns of household formation in the context of family circumstances and size. By focusing on Muslim households, we can quickly pick up the fact that the tendency to comprise households of two or more dependent children is especially pronounced. Indeed, well over half of all Muslim households were in this position according to the 2001 census figures. By contrast, this description matched considerably fewer households of other faith backgrounds including other South Asian faith backgrounds.

Turning to Figure 2.13 for a moment, the picture is completed with evidence of all South Asian faith background households tending to comprise married couples at about the same rate. There is little by way of a distinctive Muslim story in these data.

A brief final word is needed on the question of the extent of social and cultural similarity between different ethnic groups. Specifically, an older

---

[25] Peach, C., 'Britain's Muslim Population: An Overview', in Abbas, T. (ed.), *Muslims in Britain: Communities Under Pressure* (London: Zed Books, 2005), p. 30.

[26] Some of this difference is accounted for by the fact that first-generation migrants may have foreign qualifications.

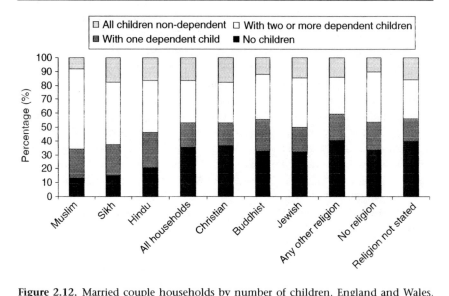

Figure 2.12. Married couple households by number of children, England and Wales, 2001

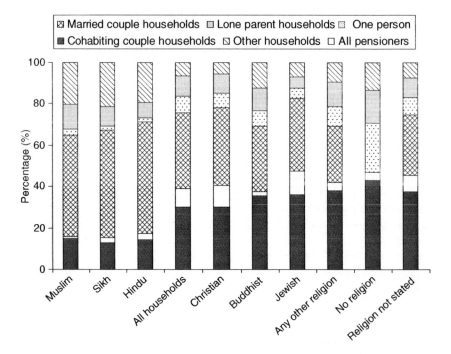

Figure 2.13. Household types by religion, England and Wales, 2001

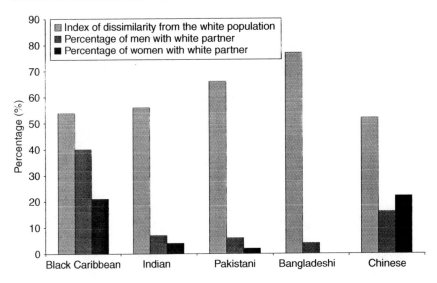

Figure 2.14. Aspects of similarity/dissimilarity: residential patterns and choice of spouse

Source: Heath, A.; *Explaining Minority Disadvantage* (2001).

sociological school of thought has held that objective differences in outcomes in education and employment are likely to be associated with the degree of separate identities among and between groups. Some groups may be much more likely to live apart and marry within than are others. This pattern of relative separation or integration in other aspects of society can be used to inform the expected patterns that might be seen in educational and labour markets. One is not a driver of the other but a degree of association might nevertheless be unsurprising. In the case of Britain, for instance, the reaction of commentators to the early waves of post-colonial immigration was to note that black Caribbean communities were in some obvious senses 'most like' the indigenous population. Distinctions of language and religious faith were not notably large obstacles to integration at the point of entry and settlement in Britain, somewhat unlike the position of migrant settlers from South Asian countries. The 1949 Royal Commission of Population itself reflected this concern, and commented on the perceived barriers facing one set of migrants as against another.[27]

Figure 2.14 throws some light on the evidence behind this proposition. Its conclusions should be interpreted cautiously, but it does certainly provide some evidence of the degree of difference in personal relationships and in housing and settlement concentrations. By using a composite index of

[27] Saggar, S., *Race and Politics in Britain* (Hemel Hempstead: Harvester Wheatsheaf, 1992).

similarity or dissimilarity based on ethnicity of partnerships and residential mixing, it is apparent that some big contrasts exist between South Asian patterns on one hand and black Caribbean patterns on the other. However, it is equally the case that Pakistani and Bangladeshi communities are taking a path of distinctiveness and even separateness that is not so obviously pronounced among their Indian counterparts. Residential mixing among the latter, for instance, essentially mirrors the picture among the larger white ethnic group. Later in this study, we will return to discuss the social capital inferences that can be drawn from these data.

France

The most striking feature of France's Muslim experience has been its overriding attachment to the principle of *läicité*—or official secularism. There are long historic roots that have been responsible for the secularism of French politics and society, and these are commonly referred to in everyday public debates over French Muslim communities.[28] The most immediate outcome is that France does not officially enumerate its population on the basis of religious belief or faith. Thus, official data sources describing Muslims in France are largely beyond the scope of French public policy.

Despite this secular orientation, there are various estimates of Muslims in France. All broadly accept that Muslims account for the largest religious minority in France: 3 per cent (of a population of 61.2 million) is the most frequently cited estimate. (This estimated figure, incidentally, is a shade larger than Britain's official tally of Muslims who constitute just under 3 per cent of a population of England and Wales of 52 million in 2001.) The actual size of the Muslim population is most likely to be rather higher than the widely quoted, 3 per cent mid-point estimate. For example, a recent House of Commons Home Affairs Committee report on terrorism and community relations reported that estimates of Muslims in France were as high as between 4 and 6 million (i.e. 6.5–10% of the population).[29] Non-official sources indicate that French Jews make up 1 per cent of the population.

The dearth of factual demographic information about religious and ethnic minority groups in France has itself been the subject of heated dispute. The modern advocates of this model emphasize that it is a constitutional principle that has taken more than a century to evolve into its current form. Moreover, the purpose it fulfils continues to have relevance in French society,

[28] The 1946 and 1958 constitutions both specify and underpin the constitutional principle of *läicité*. Article 2 of the 1905 Law 'does not recognise, pay or subsidise and form worship'. See Caeiro, A., 'Religious Authorities or Political Actors? The Muslim Leaders of the French Body of Islam', in Cesari, J., and McLoughlin, S. (eds.), *European Muslims and the Secular State* (Aldershot: Ashgate, 2005).
[29] House of Commons Home Affairs Committee (HAC), *Terrorism and Community Relations*, Sixth Report of Session 2005–05, Vol. 1, HAC 165-I, 2005, p. 31.

even though the nature of the religious diversity and identity has changed massively over that period. Set against this argument is the claim that the absence of objective evidence about population subgroups and their material circumstances can create a barrier to formulating properly informed public policies. Tackling discrimination using legal rights adopted by French lawmakers starts to become hollow in practice if enforcement regimes lack knowledge of the size and circumstances of population subgroups. These are examples of arguments that are pitted against each other in accounting for the general French approach to integration policy and managing ethnic and religious diversity. Certainly, it is widely accepted that the vast bulk of Muslims in France are North African in origin, live in strong concentrations in and especially surrounding the country's major northern industrial and Mediterranean cities, and generally experience high levels of social and economic exclusion. However, this broad picture is not based on reliable data that can be further interrogated by the research and policy communities in a bid to gain better understanding of French Muslim communities.

In recent years, there have been a number of high-profile campaigns to challenge either the spirit and/or the impact of French national attachment to the principles of *läicité* and *communautarisme*. The challenges have come from a combination of younger anti-racism activists as well as from leaders of French mosques who have been concerned about the negative impacts of these principles in practice. Muslim leaders, in particular, have found themselves caught between a number of competing and vocal expectations of Islam in France. The 2004 law passed by French lawmakers to ban the overt display of religious symbols in schools led to the most controversial oppositional campaign of all. The ban was aimed at all such religious symbols and technically covered a range of possible kinds of religiously linked clothing and related accessories. Sikh turbans, Jews' kippas, and Christian crucifixes were all rolled into the same category of unacceptable and, following the law's passage, inadmissible symbols. The reality, inevitably, was that the law's most pronounced enthusiasts were known to be motivated by worries about Muslim dress codes generally and the adoption of Muslim headscarves by girls specifically. It was aimed, and understood, therefore, as a policy aimed towards French Muslims communities, and it is not surprising that it resulted in a sharp clash of values.

The argument in reality hinged on the degree to which the law served to create a dichotomy between French and Muslim identity. Critics abroad largely interpreted the reform as clumsy at best and over-zealous at worst. But in France too, criticisms were voiced by traditional supporters of the approach that such a move would, inadvertently, only increase the everyday appeal of stricter, less-liberal Islamic identity. The risk, in other words, was that the move would play into the hands of radical Islamists who regularly preached that Muslims were not at peace with Western liberal societies such as France.

49

The series of public demonstrations against the proposed law culminated in December 2003 when tens of thousands of Muslims (and some others) marched on the streets of Paris and other major cities. Gilles Kepel, a veteran observer of French Muslim communities, described the scene and its meaning for the politics of social and national cohesion:[30]

The women draped themselves symbolically in a great display of red, white and blue, to invoke their rights as French citizens. Liberty, equality and fraternity were the rallying cries raised to defend the right to wear veils at school. Fundamental questions about the contract of citizenship were being raised, with integration and separatism for Muslims in Europe hanging in the balance.

Europe's largest Muslim communities live in France and are surrounded by a secularist and colour-blind political culture that has no real parallel elsewhere. The French model is regularly cited in explanations offered for the rise of radical political Islam, both in France and in Europe generally. The theory and practice of this model contains a number of subtleties that are not readily apparent to even close observers. The lack of reliable data on the lives, homes, education, employment, and networks of French Muslims means, if little else, that sweeping, uncorroborated generalizations can be made about Muslim identity and its relationship with French identity. It also means that broad-brush claims are commonplace in the face of manifest failures such as the riots that swept urban France in 2004 and 2005.

France also represents an unusual case within Europe because of the spectre of Islamist-linked terrorism prior to the post-2001, Al-Qaeda-inspired wave of radical extremism and violence. In the 1980s and 1990s, France was the subject of two separate waves of political violence closely linked to Islamist groups. The first episode stemmed from Iranian-inspired Lebanese Shia militants, while the latter was the result of Algerian Islamists operating on French soil a war of proxy against the increasingly repressive Algerian state. Despite both waves originating from explicitly foreign sources, the short-term impact on France's own radicalized Muslims was not clear. The response of the French government at the time was characteristically uncompromising, and chiefly motivated by a wish to keep foreign Islamist leaders at arm's length from France's domestic population of largely excluded and alienated North African communities.

It is important, therefore, that discussion of French thinking and experience in relation to Islamic extremism and violence is placed in a context that is conditioned by the general influence of the so-called French model and the specific exposure to Islamic terrorism. The aim is to promote understanding that best appreciates contrasting ideas and practices across Europe as well as

[30] Kepel, G., *The War for Muslim Minds* (Cambridge, MA: Harvard University Press, 2004), p. 246.

probes the larger impact that France's reputation has had—and is having—on the development of internationalized, radicalized Islamic identity. The substance of these points is reserved for the discussion in Chapter 4 of this book that considers larger comparative integration and belonging questions.

Germany

Unlike the UK, there are no direct statistical sources for assessing the size and composition of the Muslim population of modern Germany. German public officials do not routinely record information on the religious background of immigrants, thus making any high-level analysis of Muslims in Germany very difficult to pursue. That said, Germany does periodically gather information on the religious orientation of the population at large. The most recent effort in this regard took place in May 1987, so the findings are necessarily two decades out of date and very possibly limited in their use as a result. At that point, however, the census revealed that 1.651 million people within the then West German state were Muslims. This headline number comprised some 1.325 million Muslims who were in fact Turkish citizens at that time. In addition, 40,000 German citizens also declared their Islamic background for census purposes. Among the Turkish nationals, the overlap with Islam was very pronounced (93% were recorded within the Muslim religious community).

The generation since these data were collected has seen no further comprehensive attempts to gather data on religion in modern Germany. Estimates, therefore, have prevailed and been profound in their generation. Gesemann for example notes that a response to a parliamentary question tabled in January 2000 indicated that it was 'officially' thought that the Muslim population of the former West Germany alone was between 2.8 and 3.2 million. Again, foreign nationals generally and Turks specifically, it was estimated, made up the bulk of the total (between 2.5 and 2.7 million were believed to be non-German resident aliens). The number of Muslims within this count who were estimated to be German citizens had grown substantially since the 1987 census: by 2000, it was thought that around 370,000–440,000 Muslim German nationals lived in the former West Germany. This figure probably reflected some degree of naturalization by Turkish immigrants despite the comparative difficulties of doing so in modern Germany.

The German Central Institute Islam Archive provides a rich source of data on Muslims in Germany. This yields a familiar headline Muslim population in unified Germany of 3.2 million, with one-third of the total shown to be born in Germany. The proportion who are German nationals within this total is also quite high compared with earlier studies. The Archive indicates around a million as citizens of Germany, mainly driven by comparatively large numbers of foreigners who have become full citizens of Germany. Figures from the federal government point to 640,000 former Turkish nationals who acquired German citizenship in the period 1988–2004. However, among Turks, the vast majority continued to be foreign nationals despite often long-term residency in Germany (1.8 million). Notwithstanding the Turkish dimension, Germany is also home or host to significant numbers of Muslims from other immigrant backgrounds. Arab countries make up 0.5 million of the 3.2 million total; those from Bosnia-Hercegovina 186,000; from Iran 129,000; from Afghanistan 95,000; and from Pakistan 49,000. The total number of resident alien Muslims in Germany according to this source had by end 2004 risen to 2.4 million, and the naturalized total was estimated to be around a million. Put together, these more recent estimates indicated an overall Muslim population of close to 3.5 million individuals.

The demographic profile of Muslims in Germany is a familiar one given the immigrant background of much of this population. The Archive suggests that 850,000 were below eighteen years of age. Federal data shows that in the case of 1.76 million Turkish nationals living in Germany, some 450,000 were under eighteen years of age. Significantly, 88 per cent were German born, reflecting the lengthy duration of these communities' presence in Germany. The current picture of younger Muslims is not quite the same thing as assessing the pipeline effect of Muslim births on German soil. A federal government press notice issued in summer 2005 revealed that 9.1 per cent of all live births were to Muslim parents (64,000 newborns) in 2004 alone.[31]

Debates about the extent of immigrant and/or Muslim spatial concentrations and links to disadvantage are often quite muted in comparison to similar debates in the UK. However, there is a growing appetite in public life to discuss the circumstances of these population groups and also to set findings in a wider context about long-term strategic attempts to integrate newcomers into German society. One of the central elements of traditional German assessments of citizenship has been an undifferentiated understanding of ethnic and religious attainment records. This has then blocked efforts to examine social conditions and educational outcomes among Muslim communities. Participation rates can be measured fairly directly, however. These show that a tenth of the German school roll in aggregate comprised foreign national school children. Again Turks make up the largest single group (43%). Significantly, the proportion varies across both distinctive strands of the German sub-federal compulsory education system—18.7 per cent of children in the vocationally oriented Hauptschule schools were foreigners as against a much smaller 4.1 per cent in the academically geared Gymnasium institutions.

Attainment by religious background is virtually impossible to track reliably in German education, so the rough proxy of national background is useful.

---

[31] Quoted in Gesemann, F., 'The Integration of Young Male Muslims in Germany: Education and Training as Key Areas for Social Integration' (London: Friedrich Ebert Stiftung, 2005).

This reveals a complex picture in which attendance and success in schools, which allow an academic pathway to higher education, is as high as half of Iranian male students; meanwhile just a quarter of Turkish male students are enrolled in such schools and less than a fifth of Moroccans. One half of the former are found in schools, with minimal prospects of acquiring a school leaving certificate. Attainment figures bear out this pattern of heavy concentration on non-academic pathways. Overall, 70 per cent of German national children were awarded a Realschule or Gymnasium leaving qualification in the 2004–5 school year; by contrast, a similar level of qualification was earned by just 40 per cent of non-German school children.[32] An interesting gender disaggregation of these results can also be identified. For example, while 22 per cent of foreign males held no qualifications at all in 2004, among foreign females this proportion was 14 per cent (among German men and women the figures were 9 and 5%, respectively). At the other end of the scale, 12 per cent of foreign females—compared with 9 per cent of foreign males—held a qualification that permitted entry into higher education. (The gender gap among German nationals was even wider, with a fifth of men compared with almost a third of women holding this optimum qualification according to 2004 figures.) At first glance, these data cause us to question some of the stereotypes regarding the limited appetite and scope of immigrant communities for female education.

The main insight is obtained from data concerning participation in vocational education. Strong vocational qualifications and experience have traditionally played a central part in shaping long-run success in the German labour market. Gesemann reports the particularly weak position of foreign nationals in this picture. For example, the proportion of foreigners holding apprenticeships in the former western states stood at 6.1 of all apprenticeships in 2003, although the proportion of foreign nationals in the 18–21 age cohort was roughly twice as large. Turkish apprentices made up 38 per cent of all foreign apprenticeships, but 50 per cent, according to one large survey, did not complete their training (compared with 29% of Germans on similar training programmes). The position among individual foreign groups is generally no more impressive. However, the really big factor at work has been the considerable reduction in the total number of apprenticeships that are open to young people in Germany. The German Federal Commissioner for Migration, Refugees, and Integration has noted this obstacle and how it leads to tougher competition in an already vulnerable sector. The downward cycle of foreigner 'deficiency' that then supports stereotypes about groups' ability to 'fit in' has also been commented on by the Commissioner:[33]

[32] German Federal Bureau of Statistics, *Topical Matters* 11, Series 1 (2005).

[33] Federal Commissioner for Migration, Refugees and Integration, *Bericht der Beauftragten der Bundesregierung für Migration, Flüchtlinge und Integration über die Lage der Ausländerinnen und Ausländer in Deutschland*, Berlin, 2005.

Foreign youths, and Turkish youths in particular, are often assumed to have disruptive behaviour patterns or insufficient familiarity with the language or with the German business culture. Specific cultural practices are felt to be a disturbance to operational routines. This is aggravated—particularly among small and medium-sized companies— by an assumed lack of customer acceptance.

The Netherlands

The Dutch Government's official estimate of the country's Muslim population is 900,000 (or 5.5% within a population of 16.2 million). Following a familiar pattern, the vast majority is concentrated in the country's larger urban areas, and in Amsterdam specifically. The city's residents comprise an estimated 13 per cent from a Muslim background. It is also home to most of the country's minority ethnic groups descended from post-war immigration. The bulk of that demographic change began and took root during the 1960s and 1970s. Between 1970 and 1997, the overall numbers of Muslims in the Netherlands, from a variety of national backgrounds, increased tenfold. The bulk has migrated from Turkey and Morocco, although it is striking that neither had prior colonial or other close links with the Netherlands.[34] Instead, Dutch policies towards asylum have tended to drive the scale and nature of the country's immigration in the past. Various countries including the former Yugoslavia, Somalia, Iran, Afghanistan, and Iraq have featured strongly in the asylum cohorts. Surinam has also contributed large numbers, although in this case a complex colonial legacy has independently shaped migration to the Netherlands. Asylum has combined with a large amount of chain economic migration to produce today's significant Turkish and North African communities. Census results show that the Turkish population comprises 328,000 while the Moroccan population stands a little lower at 296,000. In terms of citizenship, census data indicates that overall around half of Muslims living in the Netherlands are citizens of the state.[35]

The remaining demographic profile of Dutch Muslim communities contains elements that are shared with British Muslims, although again the disaggregated picture shows considerable variation within and between these communities. For example, the age profile of Dutch Muslims shows that two-fifths are below twenty years of age. Such youth places them in the same boat as their British counterparts, and reflects the general age structures of migrant population movements to Western Europe as well as the high birth rates of most of the national subgroups involved. Both the Turks and Moroccans comprise a slightly larger male–female ratio than is found in the Netherlands in general (52:48 and 53:47 among these two groups, respectively), and again this is

[34] House of Commons Home Affairs Committee (HAC), *Terrorism and Community Relations*, Sixth Report of Session 2005–05, Vol. 1, HAC 165-I, 2005, p. 31.
[35] Centraal Bureau Statistiek [CBS], 2006.

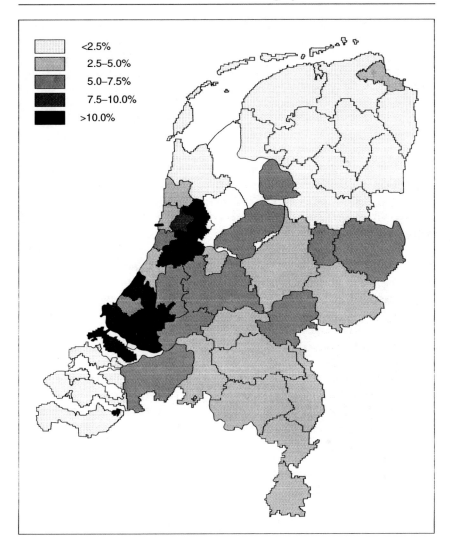

	<2.5%
	2.5–5.0%
	5.0–7.5%
	7.5–10.0%
	>10.0%

Figure 2.15. Muslims in the Netherlands
Source: www.scp.nl; www.nigz.nl.

the legacy of asylum and economic migration flows.[36] The geographic spread means that four cities dominate (Amsterdam, The Hague, Rotterdam, and Utrecht) and the average Muslim presence is just over one in ten. Figure 2.15 shows this settlement pattern.

[36] E-Quality, *Emancipatie van Vrouwen met een Islamitische Achtergrond* (Den Haag: E-quality, 2004).

As in Britain, there is a convention that most data concerning economic participation is enumerated in terms of ethno-national rather than religious groups. However, in the case of the largest communities, this is less awkward in practice than it may first seem given that ethnic and religious labels are largely co-terminous. Ninety-four per cent of Dutch Turks and 97 per cent of Dutch Moroccans are in fact Muslims, an overlap between ethnic and religious categories that mirrors that found among British Pakistanis and Bangladeshis. Nevertheless, the larger point is that Dutch researchers and policymakers operate in a long-held tradition of observing ethnic-based variance in economic and social inclusion, and, like Britain, have adapted this orientation to the needs of religious identity and diversity.[37]

The employment market in the Netherlands exhibits a number of significant variations in achievement across ethnic lines. Unemployment rates of each of the largest minority groups (Turks, Moroccans, Surinamese, and Antilleans) stand higher than the Dutch average. The latter in 2005 was recorded at 5 per cent, and at 14 per cent among Turkish-Dutch and 22 per cent among Moroccan-Dutch, respectively. There is some evidence to indicate a higher unemployment rate among men relative to women in these communities. This type of finding is interesting because it reverses a pattern commonly found among the largest Muslim communities in Britain where, typically, female participation in the labour market has been scarce. Earnings data follow a similar path in the Netherlands, but it is the heavy concentration of Muslim-majority ethnic groups in low- and poor-skilled occupations that stands out most. Fifty and 60 per cent of Turks and Moroccans, respectively, are occupied in low-skilled employment and with it the lower earnings of such work. Meanwhile, official figures show that around a third of native-born Dutch workers are employed in low-skilled occupations. This kind of work is especially pronounced among refugee groups, with 80 per cent of Somalians and 70 per cent of Afghans, respectively, working in low-skilled jobs. Self-employment is found among 12 per cent of native Dutch, whereas this occupies rather less Turks and Moroccan (8% and 3%, respectively).[38] The under-concentration in self-employment is itself significant since it reverses a pattern that is well established among many migrants to European economies. The propensity of various Dutch Muslim communities to be, or become, economically active is an area that is not adequately underpinned by factual data. Understanding is therefore limited.

The work of Phalet, Van Lotringen, and Entzinger has sought to shed fresh light on this area, and has suggested that the cultural norms and expectations that women from these groups should occupy domestic roles serve to

[37] Sunier, T., 'Interests, Identities, and the Public Sphere: Representing Islam in the Netherlands since the 1980s', in Cesari, J., and McLoughlin, S. (eds.), *European Muslims and the Secular State* (Aldershot: Ashgate, 2005).
[38] Centraal Bureau Statistiek [CBS], 2006.

constrain their ability to be economically active in the formal labour market.[39] A similar observation and interpretation has been picked up in Britain in relation to the socio-demographic analyses provided by Peach. This cultural orientation towards male workers and bread-winners is an important aspect of the picture, but rather less is known about the degree to which Dutch Muslim groups tend to follow this approach in comparison with non-Muslim minority communities. The pattern of single-income households among British Pakistani and Bangladeshi households has been especially marked in contrast to other minorities and has been widely cited in explanations for economic insecurity and exclusion faced among working families.

The educational participation and attainment picture points to a weak position among these groups. Nimwegen and Beets report that lower levels of attainment are commonplace among virtually all visible minority immigrant groups in comparison with native Dutch students.[40] However, the largest variance is accounted for by generational differences, and second-generation groups mostly record much higher rates of attainment than first-generation students. The Dutch Surinamese community now boasts attainment rates that outstrip native Dutch scores and thus represents a powerful example of variation within and across minority communities. Detailed studies of Muslims' educational participation are scarce in the literature, although there is some evidence pointing to Muslim girls gaining stronger scores and qualifications later in their education as a result of early family restrictions on their independence.[41]

Religious identity among Muslims in the Netherlands has become a growing source of research interest in recent years. The findings and insights provided by this literature are, arguably, highly contextual in nature as a consequence of Dutch traditions towards group-based politics and the impact of Dutch pillarization. These historic and ideological factors are discussed more extensively in a later chapter dealing with integration and identity matters. However, for the moment, it is important to remember that the task of integrating and incorporating Muslims into Dutch society has often involved an appetite for a pillarized approach. Most significantly, such a model, by its inherent nature, permitted considerable scope for Muslims—and indeed other distinctive religious groups—to enjoy rights to establish institutions that would specifically cater to Muslims. This followed such an approach for Catholics and Protestants over several centuries. The upshot has been that Dutch Muslim leaders have, in general, grown accustomed to

---

[39] Phalet, K., Van Lotringen, C., and Entzinger, H., *Islam in de multiculturele samenleving* (Utrecht: Ercomer Report, 2000).

[40] Nimwegen, N, and van and Beets, G., *Nederland Immigratieland* (Den Haag: Netherlands Interdisciplinary Demographic Institute, 2000).

[41] Dagevos, J., Gijsberts, M., and van Praag, C., *Rapportage Minderheden 2003* (The Hague: Sociaal en Cultureel Planbureau, 2003).

such a right as a hallmark of belonging to Dutch society. Muslim identity has evolved, therefore, in this comparatively unusual context and has meant that some have characterized this outcome as resembling a form of state-sponsored religious identity. Certainly, Muslim identities in the Netherlands contain many influences and variations, but the role played by the state pillarization model has usually been in evidence in some manner.

Sentiment on belonging and identity also contains some interest patterns. For instance, Phalet, Van Lotringen, and Entzinger report that around four-fifths of Turks and Moroccans in the Netherlands continue to feel mainly Turkish or Moroccan in their identities. Surprisingly, perhaps, only 2 per cent reported feeling mainly Dutch in this survey, although hybrid identities were most popular among a fifth of these two communities. The question of Islamic identity is more sensitive, not least because affinity to such an identity appears to be as high (or higher) among second- and third-generation groups than among first-generation ones. The classic study of Dutch pillarized society and identity was published by Arendt Lijphart almost forty years ago. In this book, he described an environment in which largely separate and free-standing identities were not so much accepted as actively promoted and even celebrated. In a memorable passage, he wrote:[42]

Rival subcultures may coexist peacefully if there is little contact between them and consequently few occasions for conflict [in which] distinct lines of cleavages promote the internal political cohesion within each subculture and consequently the latitude that the leaders have to strike bargains with the leaders of rival subcultures.

Only later did he add that 'there needs to be some degree of national solidarity'. This intellectual footnote has meant that recent and current debates over the Dutch approach to Muslim integration have been among the most heated in Europe. It has been driven by manifest shortcomings in terms of the behaviour of radicals and extremists within the country's Muslim communities. It has also been fuelled greatly by a vocal counter-reaction to the perceived excesses of Dutch multiculturalism in facing the separate and conflict-ridden identities.

The Dutch case has undoubtedly received disproportionately large attention internationally in recent years. The principal reason for this was the Theo van Gogh affair in late 2004, and, before that, the political rise of the populist anti-immigration campaigner Pim Fortuyn. The murder of van Gogh, a controversial film-maker, at the hands of an Islamic fanatic stimulated a major national debate concerning the country's approach to immigrant integration and to the thorny question of Islam in Dutch society. The murder also directly led to an upsurge in racially and religiously motivated violence against a range of

[42] Lijphart, A., *The Politics of Accommodation: Pluralism and Democracy in the Netherlands* (Berkeley: University of California Press, 1968).

visible minorities, Muslim and non-Muslim, in the Netherlands.[43] This debate confirmed that the Netherlands, in common with several other European countries, contained a complex interplay between societal fears about terrorism and underlying anxieties about the long-term integration of Muslims in particular. The wider context revealed that much of this deterioration in public attitudes had already taken root in the post-9/11 environment. A survey reported by Frerichs in 2006 showed that just over half of Dutch respondents felt that the Dutch at large perceived their Muslim counterparts and co-nationals with 'too much hostility'.[44] Another survey reported in 2005 that Dutch feeling towards Muslims at large worsened among 95 per cent of the population and substantially among 50 per cent of respondents.[45] These findings were consistent with other Western nations, all of whom have faced specific domestic ramifications from the events of September 2001.

The critique of Dutch pillarization-inspired integration policy has been that it has spawned incentives that have actively kept Muslim communities away from the mainstream. This was reflected, according to this critique, not just in schools, employment, and housing but also in terms of awareness of and engagement with Dutch society, culture, and legal norms. Paul Scheffer has characterized the disjuncture and, in his judgement, political over-reaction as follows:[46]

It wasn't so much that they didn't adapt to Dutch culture and Dutch law; they kept to themselves, they spoke in their own language, and, apart from their jobs, they hardly knew there was such a thing as Dutch culture or Dutch law.

Kramer, writing for a transatlantic audience, has argued that the shortfall in the Dutch experience, relative to other caricatures of European attempts at integration policy, has been especially sour:[47]

It could be said that each European country misreads its immigrants in its own way and that way becomes a kind of self-portrait. France assumed that it could turn millions of poor North African workers into French republicans by conferring citizenship on their children at birth. Germany practiced *jus sanguinis*, and never even opened the

---

[43] Nyman, A. S., *Intolerance and Discrimination against Muslims in the EU: Developments since September 11* (Vienna: International Helsinki Federation for Human Rights, 2005).

[44] Frerichs, R., *Nederlanders niet eens met standpunten WRR-rapport: Wel draagvlak voor politiek van verzoening* (Amsterdam: TNS NIPO, 2006).

[45] Nieuwenhuizen, E., and Visser, J., *Racisme in Nederland: Stand van Zaken* (Rotterdam: Landelijk Bureau Racisme, 2005).

[46] This citation relates to an anonymous paper refereed by the present author; see in Anon, 'Framing Anti-terror Policies' MSS, p. 27. The author of the paper, Paul Scheffer, previously published an inconoclastic paper about the failure of multiculturalist policies in the Netherlands; see Scheffer, P., 'Het multiculturele drama' [The multicultural disaster], *NRC Handelsblad*, 19 January 2000.

[47] Kramer, J., 'The Dutch Model: Multiculturalism and Muslim Immigrants', *New Yorker*, 82, 3 April 2006.

possibility of citizenship to its two million Turks until the late nineties. But it's safe to say that no country was as smug as Holland in its particular misreadings...

Changing Muslim identity in the Netherlands is shaped, therefore, in a context that has seen widespread attacks made on past models of immigrant integration. The politics of recognition for Dutch Muslims and other minorities initially emerged as a contentious issue in the 1980s and 1990s when pillarization thinking dominated Dutch society and when Dutch society first became sensitized to Muslim identity controversies such as the Rushdie affair, the Iranian Islamic revolution, and the stirrings of modern political Islam in international affairs.[48] The contemporary debate, however, has been fuelled by a number of additional factors. The influence of Muslim imams upon second- and third-generation Turks and Moroccans has been hotly debated in the Netherlands, with widespread calls for the ending of the supply of foreign-trained Muslim clerics. Disputes over Islam's attitude towards homosexuality have been another prominent source of reappraisal by left and centrist political elites in the Netherlands. The latter, to be sure, has especially driven the wider Dutch concerns about the long-run compatibility between Islam and putative Dutch values of sexual liberalism.

Fortuyn's earlier murder in 2002, at the hands of an environmental extremist, had followed extensive revisiting of Dutch policies. One key argument in this process was that, while Dutch society had successfully edged away from binding religious identity, the case of Dutch Muslims represented a new group that would make political demands that had been largely consigned to history. The particular character of the religion that sought to go against this grain has been hotly contested in the Netherlands. A Dutch Islamic 'fifth column' was a product of this counter-reaction from 2001 onwards. According to Sunier:[49]

And this was not just any religion. [Islam] was known for its anti-modern character. In such a dominant discourse, Muslims are seen as passive, fatalistic people who are inward-looking and who rely so heavily on their faith. The current discourse is highly polarising and suggests that Muslims will never become 'Dutch citizens' unless they abjure their religion completely.

The significance of the Dutch experience has clearly extended well beyond the Netherlands. It has demonstrated the limits of an arguably liberal and non-prescriptive approach to integration. Much of that experience, it seems, has been inverted in recent years in one of the most startling and speedy turnarounds in integration politics and policy seen anywhere in the Western

[48] Anon, 'Framing Anti-terror Policies: Debates in the United Kingdom and the Netherlands', refereed by the author for *Comparative Political Studies*, 2006.

[49] Sunier, T., 'Interests, Identities, and the Public Sphere: Representing Islam in the Netherlands since the 1980s', in Cesari, J., and McLoughlin, S. (eds.), *European Muslims and the Secular State* (Aldershot: Ashgate, 2005), pp. 90–1.

world. The experience of Dutch Muslim communities has not been merely incidental to that story. It has, if anything, been a driving force in the dramatic and radical Dutch reappraisal of national policies. Ironically, the prominence and proximity of domestic issues and controversies involving Islam has meant that the Dutch case has been only partially affected by the rise of international security concerns. These concerns are not absent in the Netherlands; they are, however, just another set of factors behind substantial disquiet about the interface between modern Dutchness and Dutch Muslim identity.

Conclusion: Collective Identity and Consciousness

This chapter has provided a factual overview of the Muslim populations of several European countries. In total, this is a large religious minority population. However, as this chapter has shown, there are a number of important distinctions between Muslims in and across each of these countries. The most significant of these is the national origins of Muslims, which, in large part, are a reflection of the migratory stories associated with different European countries. For instance, the North African origin Muslim communities of France are largely not reflected in Britain where Muslims are overwhelmingly from South Asian origins.

This chapter has also examined aspects of the socio-economic position of these various Muslim communities. The purpose of this part of this chapter has been to pin down highlights of the evidence base that has been collected and analysed, and also to identify the most significant gaps in knowledge. For instance, by comparative standards, a great deal is known about Britain's Muslims in terms of economic and economic-related opportunity structures. By contrast, similar data is not readily gathered or easily accessed in relation to Muslims in France. This difference has not prevented Muslim politics and controversies from being discussed and debated among French intellectual commentators, and in many ways these issues are just as sensitive in France despite the patchy evidence base. But the comparisons are not just between national settings. They can also be thematic and sectoral. For instance, available data on Muslims in higher education and involvement in the professions in any of these countries is thin. More significantly, the available data tend to be socio-economic in nature. As a result, rather less is known about the internal dynamics of the communities themselves.

In a later chapter, this book explores the question of collective consciousness and identity among Muslim communities in Western countries. This is an area that is central to the concerns of this book but it is not, generally speaking, terrain that has been fully navigated by empirical research findings. Indeed, as the later chapter notes, most accessible findings in relation to

Muslim identity appear to stem from a relatively small, recent handful of surveys that have probed attitudes towards radicalization, extremism, and political violence. These surveys are useful and provide some important findings, but they also reveal an ongoing gap in knowledge and understanding that is of concern.

Committed researchers and casual observers both have an appetite for greater knowledge and understanding of the fabric of Western Muslim communities. This is, in truth, not a random interest but rather one that is fuelled by deep-seated concerns about alienation and radicalization among segments of these communities. For instance, the potential contributory causes of alienation and radicalization amounts to a long, largely disconnected list of factors. These range from Islam-centred claims to moral superiority and an explicit willingness to embrace violence, based upon religion, among Muslim youth through to personally experienced injustices and society's failure to recognize any collective religious identity. These are then compounded by factors such as discrimination, modernity, patterns of inward-looking, self-segregating communities, rejection of 'modern' educational values, and intergenerational conflict within Muslim communities and families. These factors are routinely cited in a wide-ranging literature but are hampered by an absence of a well-integrated analysis. The causal drivers certainly do not inevitably culminate in violent action, but it is important to develop a much better shared understanding of these factors in public debate.

The comparative social researcher will start by asking what is reliably known about the sources of group cohesion and identity among various otherwise distinctive Muslim communities across different Western societies. It is clear that political campaigns exist to develop such cohesion, largely in order to create and champion a sense of corporately owned and managed Muslim identity. But beneath such politics, it is important to gain an understanding of group dynamics that will feed, or possibly repel, political attempts to collectivize Western Muslims. This understanding is partial at best. It is returned to in extended discussion in the next chapter which looks at identity politics in the round and the difficulties of exaggerated single identities in particular.

3

Thinking about Religious Identity, Politics, and Public Policy

The blurring of the distinction between being a Muslim and having a singular Islamic identity is driven by a number of confusing concerns, of which exclusive reliance on crude civilisation categories is certainly one. However, the emergence of reactive self-conceptions in anti-Western thought and rhetoric also contributes to this conceptual clouding. Culture, literature, science and mathematics are much more easily shared than religion.

Amartya Sen[1]

Nowadays we all have to incorporate into our lives countless ingredients that come to us from the most powerful of the world's cultures. But it is vital that we should all be able to see that elements of our own culture—individuals who have distinguished themselves, fashions, works of art, everyday objects, music, food, words—are also adopted all over the world, including North America, and form part of the universal heritage of all mankind.

Amin Maalouf[2]

Introduction

A compelling debate has emerged in recent years about the role of religious faith and identity in political affairs. This debate is not about the extent or indeed the nature of religious faith that is or is not made to feel welcome in shaping political matters. That is a rather separate question and one that is touched upon, briefly, later in this chapter and the next. Instead, what is at issue is how far religious faith is underscored by one-dimensional collective

[1] Sen, A., *Identity and Violence: The Illusion of Destiny* (London: Allen Lane, 2006), p. 102.
[2] Maalouf, A., *In the Name of Identity: Violence and the Need to Belong* (New York: Penguin Books/Arcade, 2000), English edn., p. 120.

identity. In the case of some faiths in the modern world, this tendency towards a single faith-based identity has been significant and almost overwhelming. Muslim groups in Western societies are a noticeable case in point. Among others, faith identities have played a smaller—and sometimes a negligible—role but this has been part of a larger interplay between a variety of identity-based political movements on one hand and the workings of political and social change on the other.

In this chapter, our attention is given to the above debate. This chapter aims to provide a theoretically grounded basis for this book's broader enquiry. As such, it is about exploring the intellectual curiosity of readers' interest in a highly visible and topical matter.

This chapter contains three main elements. To start with, this chapter looks at the emergence of large-scale identity politics in the case of Western Muslim communities. For instance, the issue at hand most immediately is the degree to which this recent development now helps or hinders progress in meeting social inclusion objectives faced by governments in general. Second, this chapter looks at Muslim-based faith and related identities to assess the mechanisms through which the religious and the political are related. It does not seek to take a particular position in this sometimes rocky debate. Rather, this section purports to introduce some rigour into arguments about identity politics and impacts on the political process. Finally, this chapter ends with a discussion about how far religious identity and sensitivity can be incorporated into general governmental concerns, including those over social disadvantage and social integration and also in relation to broader social cohesion objectives. Aspects of this capacity and appetite can be transnational and international in character so some important issues need to be faced in this regard.

Facing the Challenge of (Muslim) Identity Politics

The starting rationale for this chapter, previously mentioned, is in fact about the rationale for this book more broadly. That is to say, there is a clear need to give coherence to a general investigation into religious faith identity that allows us to understand better why identity matters at all. However, in order to address this rationale more satisfactorily, it is necessary first to look at the reasons why identity categorization takes place, particularly in the Western liberal world, and to examine whether this is proportionate to the issue or issues at stake.

Everywhere in modern societies we can see countless manifestations that dividing people into tighter or looser categories is at least quietly assumed to be helpful. But it can be both helpful and a hindrance at the same time. For example, in autumn 2006, Britain dwelt heavily on the findings and conclusions of the Turner report into long-term pensions policy. The Turner report's position was and will be much debated in the country's relevant policy communities, and doubtless parts of its body of knowledge will and are having influence in shaping pensions policy in other similar countries. A central unit of analysis for such a report has, almost by definition, to be age or generational cohort. That is, the need for a credible pension arrangement for a twenty-five-year-old starts to take on different meaning once such an individual becomes forty-five or fifty-five years of age. It is also shaped, sometimes fundamentally, by the view taken by twenty-five-year-olds of those who are currently a generation or two older. The putative head start that the twenty-something-year-old has is essentially time, roughly a generation's worth of it, if the pension arrangements are established then rather than in early middle age. This is age at play, or rather the basic effects of time, for someone or a whole collective group of people who are born at one point, hoping to hang up their proverbial boots fifty or sixty or even seventy years later. So the young are a category, but not immutably. They will age and become the formerly young in due course.

By contrast, another building block of Turner's work involves looking at generational groups. This category is obviously linked to age but also carries other, unrelated meanings as well. In this case, for example, a notional pensions policy might be required to answer the question: how far, if at all, should younger members of a scheme or club be required to pay for the deferred income of older members? There are many answers to this that can be rehearsed but the detail does not matter greatly here. What does matter is that whole groups of individuals have been parcelled up according to their closeness or proximity to receiving benefits as opposed to making contributions. Thus, one potential answer to the question would be to ask another by seeking to clarify whether intergenerational claims of any kind either existed or needed to be recognized. In everyday terms, pensions depend to a large extent on a semi-codified way of sorting out reciprocity between a society's older, retired workers and its younger, economically active members.

The purpose of the discussion based on the pension policy example is merely to draw out two very obvious group categories, namely age and generation. These are partly related categorizations, but they are certainly not the same. Many others could also be discussed, such as workers and non-workers, the better versus the less well paid, and so on. These are all generally analytical categories that are needed to break down a large issue such as pensions. But, in truth, they also allude to identities—or rather, aspects of multiple identities— that have some degree of resonance in society. Certainly, retired groups of pensions can and have established fairly well-known identity categories and even organizations to solidify and represent their interests, to say nothing about reminding others that their interests need to be protected. Younger, non-retired individuals arguably do not exhibit much sense of identity in terms other than being the opposite of current pensioners. An identity based on becoming a future pensioner, to all intents and purposes, cannot be said to resonate to the same degree. More specifically, individual pension providers have had to manage an increasingly tense relationship between some members who have certainty about future benefits (generally earlier membership recruits) and those who do not (current and future cohorts). This is not quite in resonance with everyday feelings of identity, certainly. But the caveat is that similar groups of people, who find that they are being treated in profoundly dissimilar and arguably unfair ways, may all too easily find reason to rally around an identity centred on hidden unfairness. In more colloquial terms, there is plenty of scope for people to fall out over money, and this can become a tangible grievance to focus on and promote. Identity is often not far behind as a way of expressing and taking forward all of this. It may even pre-exist the fault line of division or anticipated conflict.

The Turner report is a relatively uncontroversial illustration of analytical and everyday identities coming into play with one another. When journalists write that a particular event or initiative will give rise to support or condemnation by one group—perhaps with the opposite outcome with another group—then a lot of lines of real and assumed identity have been summarized into one claim. For example, if women stand to lose out from a pension policy of getting out roughly what you put in (chiefly because, in Britain, of rather different lengths of working lives between men and women), it is not hard to make sense of this argument. Most women, who are more likely to be absent than men from the ranks of those with forty-year-long paid working lives, will have fewer benefits than most men. Being a woman, in itself, is not the direct cause of this differential treatment. However, the current lives of most women (not the lives that might or could exist) mean that losing out in this way is rather hard to avoid in the circumstances of rules of entitlement that negate, for instance, the value of time away from paid employment to bear and raise children. It is basically a forced, indirect disadvantage that would be mitigated or even removed under somewhat different rules. So the rules of this particular game, many have observed, are far from fair across one group of workers against another. For most women, there are very few ways to escape the downside. Rules such as these are commonplace, although the appetite to change them has clearly grown considerably in recent years. But for the time being we are describing rules that are not gender-neutral. If they are not neutral, they are biased against the interests of a category that has limited scope to escape the consequences. The identity that is involved appears to be one that already resonates in everyday life and society. It is usual for people to think of themselves and others in gender terms.

The centrality of this kind of identity varies considerably, however, with some so closely attached to this outlook that it is virtually a prism through which most other things are viewed. Others are less attached, suggesting that gender identity competes much more fluidly with a whole host of other kinds of multiple identities. That said, the sting that applies in the case of pension rules is that such an example of distributional unfairness is, despite its complexity, something that can resonate quite easily with gendered forms of identity. Thus, any examples of evidence of existing disadvantage faced by women in the workplace become the context within which the apparently additional pension disadvantage is understood. It is almost a double disadvantage, despite the clichéd packaging. Women workers, some of whom are concerned about the return in pay and progression to their efforts, are now also anxious that longer-term pension benefit arrangements will bring more unfairness. The identity is not just about resonance with everyday lives; it is also about chiming with existing feelings of fairness and unfairness.

The greater insight from this type of example is the extent to which one line of identity can be responsible for building strong lines of solidarity among its ranks. Can it in fact create a common bond that can be deployed as a political force? And, related to this, can it operate in this one-dimensional way to cancel out the influence of multiple identities?

The answers to both questions are all too often 'yes'. Details, however, matter in shaping the answers. For example, the juxtaposition of members of one identity against members of other groups within the same identity frame of reference is crucial. Two different member identity categories may be described as being on a collision course with one other, but this basic, blunt account will depend heavily on drawing out the caveats and also the other sources of potential identity and senses of affiliation. In our example involving men's and women's pension rights, the collision course scenario is probably rather more apparent than real. It is real in the sense that it involves tangible monetary benefits although these only collide, and thus conflict, after the passage of long periods of time. Collision is not so much averted as kicked into the long grass of what will happen decades hence. As such, it is potentially hard to present gender interests as fundamentally, never mind immediately, at odds with each other. The interests of members of one category or another do not align and the rationale for this are hard to justify in modern society accustomed to gender equality alongside other kinds of symbolic and substantive fairness.

However, the fundamental clash between one side and another cannot be dismissed altogether. For instance, it is not hard to see the likely consequences of serious attempts to reform rulemaking that examine every conceivable long-term misalignment of beneficial rights except those around gender. In addition, presenting distributional issues in strictly zero-sum terms is likely to accentuate the sense of zero-sum identity. Thus, 'men must give up something' for women to have more of that thing is the most crude way of expressing such a one-dimensional identity and the (self-) interest that goes with it. And this argument can extend one stage further with claims that men's rights will not be reduced in order to increase the rights of women—because of the lower value the former accords to the latter in economic terms. This line of argument comes closer to viewing identity in essentialist terms; that is, the choices available are limited by membership of one camp or another.

The limiting effects of an excess of one-dimensional identity politics have been noted by a number of commentators. In particular, the extent to which identity serves to make things appear to be inevitable and predictable has been a source of controversy.[3] This is seen nowhere more vividly than in the role of identity in framing and even explaining conflict and violence. In many cases, the explanations afforded imply that the assertion of one group's identity is in order to combat the rise of another's. This puts both sides on a collision course of some kind even before closer examination can be made of the nature and merits of group-based rights and claims specifically. By employing a universalist and determinist frame of reference, it quickly becomes possible to view inter-group relations as about the avoidance of dominance or much worse. The groups, it is widely thought and said, are locked in conflict that has always been present to some degree—thus, its avoidance or mitigation is seen as a form of rescuing victory from the inevitable jaws of defeat. Individuals caught up in the scenario are absolved of either individual understanding of the other or the need to exercise choice and responsibility. Both of these elements are surrendered to the identity group and all too often to group leaders with particular agendas and motives. The rank and file in this setting have almost no role to play other than in terms of reinforcing the exclusionary nature of a single form of identity.

Depressingly, it is not that hard to see how battle lines can be drawn in this type of setting. One of the most typical means of creating in-group solidarity comes not just by framing the out-group as threatening or parasitic or worse. An effective hold over the group also comes from denying the commonality of experience and interest that lies across and between groups. In the case of systematic, organized sectarian violence, this element must be central to the ability to rally supporters and target a single common foe. Thus, 'they' are and will always remain 'them', who will not and cannot share anything with 'us', let alone ever become part of 'we'. Put differently, the sense of the other side having an identity and experience that equates with one's own is something that must necessarily be denied. Only through this can the other side's identity be reduced to the one thing that severe conflict requires, namely, that any other group's identity is simply to rob or to threaten or to challenge whatever is valued to begin with. Their identity, in short, is to be or been seen universally, as pariahs par excellence.

---

[3] Ali, T., *The Clash of Fundamentalisms: Crusades, Jihads and Modernity* (London: Verso, 2003).

The theme of pariah-dom runs throughout this book, and it is useful to note the characteristics of this problem in its severest form. For the time being, two interim observations stand out. The first is that such extreme circumstances are hallmarked by the politics of non-negotiation. That is to say, one side's willingness to discuss and negotiate the shape of grievance or concern to the other side is completely undermined by the inability to see the other side in terms that are recognizable or having inherent value. The most extreme version of course is to see the other side in non-human terms, thus obviating the need to justify hatred or violence. No or few excuses are needed if the incitement to action is directed against those who do not share one's human characteristics.

The second observation is that one-dimensional identity is fundamentally flattening in its purpose and outcomes. It is designed to deliver an all-powerful lens through which the world is seen, though not always required to be understood. Wearers of the lens are provided with a world view that is sufficiently all-encompassing that individual choice is relegated to the margins at best. In extreme conditions, it supplies a plentiful source of nourishment to build and sustain hatred.[4] The lens cares little for the nuance or complexity of lives that often involve multiple identities and even greater ways of understanding and deepening understanding. In fact, understanding and meaning are required to have limits, rather shallow ones at that, which prevent the possibility of association and sentiment across boundaries. The effects, if not the purpose, can be easily seen and sometimes mitigated separately. The most notable effect is to reduce heavily the possibility of social linkages being imagined, let alone created, that blur one-dimensional identity. The odds against mutuality, or interlocking lines of empathy and solidarity, are terribly heavily stacked as a consequence. They are made even smaller if ethnic identity is seen as the sole basis for understanding and explaining conflict.[5]

The rise of identity politics of this kind is far from novel. Even in modern times, there are no shortages of vivid illustrations of powerful, exclusionary, hate-driven identity politics and movements that have denied even the most minimal value or dignity to others.[6] National Socialism in Germany in the mid-twentieth century is arguably the most well-documented example that remains a lesson in the subject. The partition of India in the 1940s was characterized by the same elements, most notably the sudden evaporation— denial in many cases—of cross-community links and bonds. And, the chapter on African slavery in the New World (to say nothing of the related chapter

[4] King, R., and Ladbury, S., 'The Cultural Reconstruction of Political Reality: Greek and Turkish Cyprus Since 1974', *Anthropological Quarterly*, 1984, pp. 1–17.

[5] Gilley, B., 'Against the Concept of Ethnic Conflict', *Third World Quarterly*, Vol. 25, No. 6, 2004, pp. 1155–66.

[6] Cramer, C., 'Inequality and Conflict: A Review of an Age-Old Concern', Identities, Conflict and Cohesion Programme, Paper 11, UNRISD, October 2005.

on indentured labour throughout the European imperial world) from the sixteenth to nineteenth centuries is a compelling example of the assignment of one racial identity as a means of creating political and cultural dominance.

But, even putting these large examples to one side, it is equally important to note a general trend towards the growth of one-dimensional identity politics. This has been observed in both the developed and developing worlds. As a partial result of globalization, it has meant that particular kinds of identity-based conflict are now much more rapidly projected in a range of otherwise quite dissimilar societies. For instance, contentious and campaigning forms of collective identity have emerged in recent years that centre around opposition to the homogenizing effects of globalization. These identities have found it relatively easy to fuse or find common cause with related concerns about the economic domination of global corporates, threats of environmental degradation, and failure to tackle perceived regional injustices. Such pressures and rapidly changing environments have in turn created new demands on existing systems and understandings of global governance.[7] It is quite possible, and even expected, to form campaigns of opposition to all of these things at one and the same time. Moreover, the strength of feeling against large, powerful, corporate interests is not unrelated to other strands of oppositional sentiment. Indeed the opposition can be interlocking and self-reinforcing. This is much more likely if an overarching value system can be pinpointed to describe the basis for being against each and all of these forces. The narrative of anti-globalization movements is a simple, ready-made way of supplying such a narrative, and this has had remarkably powerful effects in shaping a sense of common understanding. This is all the more remarkable given that the dynamics of a globalized economy are far from being well, let alone properly, understood. Nevertheless, a form of single dimension of identity has emerged that has been impressive in appealing to the multiple identities that underpin concern and opposition to various aspects of globalization.

One-dimensional identity trends are also apparent at a more subtle level. This is in relation to the ability to keep alive older, familiar inter-group conflicts. In many cases, these conflicts have transgressed beyond responsiveness to particular sensitivities or grievances. These particular concerns can and have been addressed, at least in part, and yet there has been an unusual and unexpected tendency towards reimagining single, mutually exclusive identities.

The case of Northern Ireland is a pointed one in this regard. At one level, significant progress has been made in a short period of time towards the economic integration of two communities, confidence-building measures to avert violence, and the removal of symbolic causes of hatred. And yet,

---

[7] Kahler, M., and Lake, D., *Governance in a Global Economy* (Princeton, NJ: Princeton University Press, 2003).

the gaps in inter-group recognition and respect remain all too large. One convincing explanation for this is that issues of humiliation and profound disrespect have remained unaddressed. The reasons for doing so are powerful and compelling in each case. However, by trying to take the more sensitive, uncontroversial route, there is a risk in post-conflict societies of unwittingly denying the original causes of severe disrespect and hatred. Those causes may no longer be present in a direct sense but they can live on in the collective imagination. Thus, in the real world, there has been real achievement in building mixed, multiple-identity based communities either in workplaces or in schoolrooms or in neighbourhoods. And yet, in the imagined, yet equally important world, there has been much less movement. Minds remain fixed on past, clearly understood, and easily recounted examples of injustice and humiliation.[8] Those humiliations cannot be the focus of change and to build new bridges where older ones have collapsed or never existed. However, denial of humiliation and injustice, wherever deeply felt, is much harder to achieve.[9] It may not be achievable in the end, and it may simply magnify and distort over time. Imagined identity of this kind can thus serve to divide in that it prevents the growth of resilience against other powerful influences that dilute common, bridging identities. The task, in other words, is not just limited to addressing evidenced barriers to multiple, nuanced identities. It also involves an appreciation of the psychological, historical, and cultural impediments to developing relationships through a process that is capable of not just tolerating but also respecting.

Lord Alderdice, a former Speaker of the Northern Ireland Assembly, has commented on this most difficult of barriers. It involves individuals who can respect others, as well as desist from causing harm to others. It is inherently complex since such barriers can often lie deep in the collective, hidden consciences of oppressed groups. It can even stain the implicit moral purpose of oppressing groups. Two possibilities exist nevertheless that can help to break down imagined grievance. One is to isolate intelligently the opportunity or space to speak about perceived injustice or humiliation. Victims of atrocities or equivalent, therefore, require the room to express the human consequences of inhuman behaviour. Senator George Mitchell's message to the warring parties in the Northern Irish peace process began with a clear invitation to them to hear things they did not want to hear. This, he argued, was an effective way to give and be seen to give respect to those who had previously

---

[8] McGuire, P., and Eyben, K., 'What Now? Reflections Report on a Political Education Project with Young Adults in the Rural Loyalist Community', Supported by International Voluntary Service—Northern Ireland, 2004.

[9] Alderdice, J., 'Understanding Terrorism—the Inner World and the Wider World', unpublished submission to the Commonwealth Commission on Respect and Understanding—summarized in various working papers and available at the Commonwealth Secretariat website, www.thecommonwealth.org.

been severely disrespected. The other, related possibility lies in the expectation that particular institutions can be given respect and even detached reverence, even if different groups are unable to show respect to one another. Thus, behaviour in the public sphere is respectful to the institutions and processes of society. The political process is an obvious place to start, particularly if key institutions and offices can be reformed to deliver a neutral outcome.[10]

The key gain is that, through negotiation, the outcome of otherwise differing and conflicting groups agreeing to observe a common platform. This platform has less to do with agreeing with one another on aspects of difference or identity, but rather on the need to have some, or more, common institutions that bind society together. It is these institutions, and their attendant processes, that require the formal display of respect by different groups. One notable result from this kind of approach is that patterns of respectful behaviour are driven by practice in a more neutral sphere than would be the case if groups had to display overt respect for one another's values or belief systems. Indeed, the former can be an effective means to the latter, first by creating practice and habit in a less-charged terrain and second by creating space within which the perspectives of opposing identities can be expressed. Expression of this kind, as Senator Mitchell observed, was likely to lead to otherwise closed identity groups hearing what had previously been unheard. In its own modest way, the two can engender respect across traditionally fixed boundaries. Human stories, especially involving the robbing of human dignity, are both expressed and heard as a way of nurturing a dialogue about aspects of common, overlapping identity. Thus, respect for identity and respect across identities can be achieved, although this, by its nature, requires an appreciation that imagined identity is often reinforced by feelings of humiliation and worse.[11] It is a large assumption to make, and often can only be made after the experience of extreme sectarian identities associated with political violence.

Flattening Identity

The concern with identity politics as a flattener of meaning has been discussed by a number of commentators and in a vast array of settings. For example, the publication in late 2006 of the official Stevens enquiry into the death of Princess Diana strayed into the possibility that the late princess had considered converting to Islam. The evidence was by no means solid or compelling but the question had been raised in the context of personal opposition that friends, family, and others may have expressed about a former senior

[10] Lord Alderdice, unpublished written submission to the Commonwealth Commission on Respect and Understanding, December 2006.

[11] Sen, A., 'Global Causes of Violence', unpublished lecture given at the Chinese University of Hong Kong, February 2005.

member of the royal family taking on such a new faith identity. Of course, this was not just any faith but rather one that, even in the mid-1990s, had enjoyed a somewhat troubled relationship with any variety of Christian faith identities. Significantly, it was suggested that the princess's relations with her stepmother had been breached on this specific question shortly before the former's demise.

This example matters not for its details—or indeed lack of reliable factual details—but instead for the manner in which a single dimension of identity is placed centre-stage to the exclusion of all other aspects. The causes said to be linked to the possible conversion relate to a possible engagement to marry—not the high-profile Dodi al-Fayed but rather the lower-profile Hasnat Khan, a London-based surgeon. The late princess, who undoubtedly encapsulated a variety of complex, interwoven identities into a single public personality that sometimes bordered on a cult, if not a brand, moved from the multiple into the singular in an instant. The effects of the unevidenced story (for that is largely what it is) are that the spectre of a 'Muslim Diana' (dubbed the 'hidden face') dominates almost all other considerations.[12] The nature of the possible conversion, the reasons for its ascent and decline as a scenario, the experiential issues that gave rise to it, and the issues of hybrid identity in such a public figure are all largely put to one side. All these remain fascinating and substantive issues, of course, and many have commented at length on one or another of these associated points. However, their complexities rapidly give way to a singular, untextured view of a monolithic faith identity. So, even in this unusual context, the identity of Islam is projected and received in one dimension alone, and with flattening consequences for meaning.

The flattening of meaning in this way has also been the focus of the recent writings of Amartya Sen. In *Identity and Violence*, Sen advances the argument in respect to what he sees as the false illusion that fixed identity without choice or meaning cannot be thwarted through reason and engagement. The area where this is most corrosive, he argues, is the appearance of the world as comprising a fixed set of identities, or federations of identities, in conflict with one another. He writes:[13]

Underlying this line of thinking is the odd presumption that people of the world can be uniquely categorised according to some *singular and overarching* system of partitioning. Civilisational or religious partitioning of the world population yields a 'solitarist' approach to human identity, which sees human beings as members of exactly one group. (Emphasis in original)

This is certainly a depressing outlook since it makes more likely the emergence of one-dimensional identity politics. Whether this is the cause or the

[12] Daisy, W., 'Diana's Hidden Face', *The Sunday Times*, News Review, 17 December 2006, p. 4.
[13] Sen, A., *Identity and Violence: The Illusion of Destiny* (London: Allen Lane, 2006), p. xii.

consequence of tendencies towards conflict is not so clear, however. On one hand, it could be argued that an excess of this kind of identity politics presents a highly favourable backdrop to narratives of unavoidable friction and conflict.[14] The argument is as follows: all members of one identity group have their myriad complexities reduced to one dimension only. This dimension juxtaposes with much the same thing among other groups. Such groups, despite national, territorial, and cultural distinctions, can and do command an overarching loyalty. This loyalty serves to transcend all other relationships, bonds, and responsibilities. Indeed, as already noted in this chapter, loyalty of this kind is founded on a form of identity that relieves the individual from the responsibility of having to consider responsibilities to and with others who lie outside the domain of the loyalty. They are absolved, and take their cue from all that follows from group membership alone. This has a bearing on the question of how respect and mutual understanding can be sustained across various kinds of identity or doctrinal divides. It echoed for example in the arguments put forward by the recent Commonwealth report, *Civil Paths to Peace*:[15]

Respect is about acknowledging a common human-ness, and a preparedness to treat everyone, no matter how different their world views, with the dignity they deserve because of their humanity. There is an important distinction to make between respecting persons (and their right to hold their own views) and indiscriminately respecting what they believe in or how they behave. We can show respect to others without agreeing with their particular doctrines or their actions.

However, the causality can also run the other way. That is, corralling people into pens that preclude all others is often a symptom of relations that have already encountered friction. It is not unnatural or unusual for group-based identity to take on a single overarching dimension in the face of threat, real or perceived. In such times of crisis, individuals understandably seek assurance and protection if needed under the broad wings of a single identity. Why such an identity is selected or emerges over all others is no mystery. It is all too often an identity that carries with it an existing, albeit limited, discourse of opposition, suffering, and protection. This limited narrative can be rapidly expanded to offer a generalized view of the world, its most prominent threats, and how these can be met.[16] In this sense, therefore, one-dimensional identity politics is as much a reaction as a driver of trends towards conflict.

A small anecdote can be introduced here to highlight this problem in relation to the sensitive question of Western Muslim communities. This

---

[14] The opposite line of reasoning is pursued for instance in Gilley, B., 'Against the Concept of Ethnic Conflict', *Third World Quarterly*, Vol. 25, No. 6, 2004, pp. 1155–66.

[15] *Civil Paths to Peace*, Final Report of the Commonwealth Commission on Respect and Understanding (London: Commonwealth Secretariat, 2007).

[16] Sen, A., 'Poverty, War and Peace', unpublished Nadine Gordimer Lecture, Wits University and the University of Cape Town, April 2007.

relates to the framing of security policy alongside community-based counter-terrorism intervention, a policy subject area that has emerged as a salient and complex area in the past few years. For instance, over three years between summer 2004 and summer 2007, the author attended more than a hundred invited academic and policy meetings on the broad topic of the integration of Western Muslims. The hosts and sponsors ranged from prominent domestic think-tankers (IPPR, Demos, Fabians, and so on) to research and analytical specialist meetings (Oxford Analytica, the US National Intelligence Council, parliamentary Select Committees, and so on), research institute and foundation audiences (Carnegie, the Salzburg Seminar, Barrow Cadbury, Rowntree, and so on), and various groups of senior officials in government departments and agencies (FCO, DCLG, DWP, Home Office, and so on). The salience of these discussions was obvious enough in the context of the New York, Madrid, and London attacks. Of course, the vast bulk of these discussions also involved highly interested and committed participants, many from governments, and also a large proportion of think-tankers and journalists. Debate ranged in each setting, highlighting deep-seated disagreements about the shape of the policy problem or problems, to say nothing of the strategic responses that carried weight by way of solutions. Typically, some at these meetings (from a variety of backgrounds) argued passionately that the genuine risks related to only a tiny fringe element bent on violence and confrontation. Others, just as typically it must be said, pressed exactly the opposite analysis (much as this book does in later chapters), arguing that the picture resembled other episodes of terrorism. Some voices (including a few very senior ones) framed the strategic response in terms of globalized, universalist value systems to be met, and overcome, by different value systems.[17] The test of enlightened modernity, it was argued, was at the heart of how militant Islamists must be tackled. Other voices (sometimes no less influential) made the case for a somewhat contrasting response. These could be based around the incorporation of moderate Muslim identity into inclusive civic ideas of citizenship or possibly the more imaginative use of policy levers to deliver greater economic and social inclusion.[18] The lines of debate and disagreement continued (and continue) on many other aspects of the topic. Together, this cottage industry of experts, advocates, and others could not conceivably have contrasted more in their analyses and prescriptions. The debate over Muslim integration challenges lived up to the true meaning of the word 'debate'.

At one level, this is obviously an encouraging development. It implies that few stones were left unturned. And that is largely borne out in terms of the scope of the debate internationally. A common understanding (albeit a

---

[17] Speech by George J. Tenet, Director of Central Intelligence, Nixon Center Distinguished Service Award Banquet, 11 December 2002.

[18] Saggar, S., 'A Makeover is not Enough', *Guardian—Comment is Free*, 24 November 2006.

very notorious one) largely exists. In that sense, it can be said to be a better and shared understanding given that almost all legitimate, non-violent participants now have heard and have an appreciation of perspectives that differ rather a lot from their own. For example, heated dispute has raged over the centrality of foreign policy—the Iraq war specifically—as accounting for the London and Madrid bombings. No one, in all seriousness, can claim to have misread or been shielded from this viewpoint, no matter how strongly they might take issue with such a claim. Equally, the claim that fervent Western secularism has served to deny Muslims a faith identity is an argument that has received a considerable and full airing. This does not normally attract a large amount of sympathy, for sure, but it has been widely understood for its authenticity and even its sincerity, if little else.

However, there appears to have been a downside to the otherwise positive character of this debate. This is described as a downside in the sense that virtually all participants sought to isolate the relative importance of being Muslim as a conditioner of exclusion and, with it, grievance. Even those generally sceptical about ethno-religious categories as ways of trying to account for difference accepted the point that Islamic identity or identities lay at the heart of the question. Such identity, particularly in Western settings, either contributed to, or was the outcome of, contested identity of one kind or another. For example, in tracking the extent of socio-economic disadvantage faced by Western Muslim communities (remembering that some of these communities, according to the evidence, in fact encountered rather few barriers to opportunity and achievement), the question was continually posed: are these patterns and experiences distinctive to Muslims rather than others? To be sure, this question was repeated and pondered in a single month at the dining table of a prominent High Commissioner to London, an influential London-based, left-leaning think tank, a major Brussels-based foreign relations institute, a UK prime ministerial sounding board, and an EU intelligence network summit. It was, needless to say, returned to time after time, often politely, occasionally directly. The Muslim identity card, crudely, became the focus of attention.

Partly this was led by the intuitive logic of members of the senior policy communities involved (i.e. did one particular faith group have experiences, chiefly negative, that were attributable to anti-Islamic prejudice?). But this was also partly fuelled by an acknowledgement that many forms of Western Muslim identity had begun to embody an element of an excluded mindset, or victimhood as many have dubbed it. Thus, there was, almost unavoidably, a self-fulfilling Muslim card to consider precisely because this is a newer, collective form of consciousness that is characterized by opposition, grievance, and complaints of stigmatization. Muslims in the West as oppressed minorities, is how this position is articulated. If nothing else, it is associated with something of a self-fulfilling prophecy.

In one discussion, for example, hosted by the British Fabians in late 2006, this already familiar exchange developed into a larger difficulty. This related to applying the issue to the wider debate over how far faith identity was, or should be, central to government's efforts to engage with its citizens. It was not helpful, it was pointed out by supporters of extended engagement with Muslims, if various other aspects of people's identities were to be used as tools of engagement while excluding faith-based identities. The counter-pressure to exclude, or at least give less importance to, faith carried with it a risk that members of particular faiths would be impacted more adversely than others. So the conclusion drawn was that faith identities ought not to be unfairly treated for fear of making worse the concerns of many Muslims. However, the rival viewpoint was just as compelling. This argued that a particular kind of flattening Muslim identity had begun to dominate all debates over integration, belonging, and citizenship. Thus, single-dimensional identity politics was serving to prevent Western Muslims from holding, or being acknowledged to have, a vast variety of additional identities and frames of reference, to say nothing of dissenting political outlooks. The picture painted was that of brown, middle class, bourgeois-minded British neighbours who had become Muslims to the exclusion of all else, sometimes almost overnight. French, Algerian-descended men without job opportunities on suburban housing estates had come to be, and be seen as, Muslims alone. And highly entrepreneurial, successful, and fully-settled immigrants to Canada had also taken a similar trajectory. In the end, simplified political Muslims now shone through where before complexity, hybridity, and ambiguity had existed.

The difficulty lay in developing a coherent response to this picture. To say rather blithely, with however much evidential backing, that factors beyond faith and Islam lay behind poor opportunity structures and achievements risked the charge of ignoring the proverbial 800 lb gorilla that sat in the corner of the debating room. To engage this gorilla at the start ran the opposite risk of subsuming identity based on multiplicity and granularity into ready-made singularity void of deeper meaning. Both approaches contain strong elements of intellectual coherence and practical relevance. And yet both do not get us very far in terms of a currently particularly estranged and volatile mixture of Muslim identity politics and grievance politics.

Root Causes and Embedded Inequality

One approach to this dilemma has been to try to link ethno-religious conflict to explanations that sit outside of identity politics. For example, the question of conflict between members of different groups can be understood in terms of competition for scarce resources and advantages. Similarly, cooperation across ethnic boundaries might be explained in terms of factors that are mutually rational across groups or unite members of different groups that go beyond one-dimensional essentialist identity.[19] The terms of the advantage or benefits enjoyed by a particular group may have been established at a much earlier point. Defence of that advantage has tended to reinforce the importance of projecting the identity of the group. For groups at the losing end of the relationship, there are powerful motivators to see their loss as a result of the exclusion of their group's identity, and also to view strategies to cope with or overcome the deficit through the prism of one-dimensional identity.[20]

Nevertheless, the politics of access, opportunity, and privilege is chiefly about resources of one kind or another. Many of these will be essentially economic in nature, but some may be more directly related to the freedom and scope to dominate subordinate groups. In other words, the power of the more and most powerful is something that requires maintenance and retrenching, and this involves keeping challenges to existing power relations in check and limited to fringe issues. The political science literature has sought to explain this in terms of the mobilization of bias against the right or legitimacy of weaker groups or interests to have a say or a place at the proverbial table.[21] Much of these can be experienced as inter-group relations in which identities are central. However, identity is as much a conduit as an engine of the relationship.

This observation takes us to the question of what are the underlying causes of extreme, entrenched, and bitter identity politics. In thinking about root causes, it is useful to look closely at conflict that results in violence. A number of commentators have noted that ethnic and religious identities are rarely the root causes of violent conflict.[22] However, these identities are often presented as though they exclusively drive conflict. Factually speaking, this is rarely true and directly challenges conventional wisdom about the ethnic or religious basis of such severe conflict. In analysis presented to discussions of

[19] Fearon, J., and Laitin, D., 'Explaining Interethnic Cooperation', *American Political Science Review*, 1996, pp. 715–35.

[20] Stewart, F., 'Horizontal Inequalities: A Neglected Dimension of Development', Centre for Research in Inequality, Human Security and Ethnicity (CRISE), Working Paper 1, University of Oxford, 2004.

[21] Bachrach, P., and Baratz, P., *Power and Poverty: Theory and Practice* (New York: Oxford University Press, 1970).

[22] See for example Cohen, A., *Two-Dimensional Man* (London: Routledge and Kegan Paul, 1974); Gilley, B., 'Against the Concept of Ethnic Conflict', *Third World Quarterly*, Vol. 25, No. 6, 2004, pp. 1155–66; Rao, S. K., *Poverty, Democracy and Development: Issues for Consideration by the Commonwealth Expert Group on Democracy and Development* (London: Commonwealth Secretariat, 2004); Stewart, F., 'Policies towards Horizontal Inequalities in Post-Conflict Reconstruction', Centre for Research on Inequality, Human Security and Ethnicity (CRISE), Working Paper 7, University of Oxford, 2005.

the Commonwealth Commission on Respect and Understanding in 2006, it was noted that:[23]

People do not fight because their customs are different or because they adhere to different faiths. If they did then one would expect a fairly high incidence of conflicts between overtly different ethnic groups living close to one other. Yet evidence suggests the opposite—most multi-ethnic societies are peaceful. Between 1960 and 1979, of all the potential conflicts that could have arisen between ethnic groups in Africa because they lived side-by-side, it was estimated that only 0.01% of relationships became violent.[24] This is not to suggest that groups of people defining themselves in terms of one racial or ethnic group are not in conflict with those defining themselves otherwise. Some are. But this doesn't mean that their ethnic identity is at the heart of the conflict and can explain it. Group A may pit itself against Group B because it has grievances for which it holds Group B responsible or because it has aspirations that Group B is thwarting. These and other factors are more likely to underlie the violence than the ethnic or religious characteristics associated with Group B.

Floating Identities and Statistical Generalization

The argument thus far has been to note the limitations of one-dimensional identity and to observe that few cases of inter-group conflict are directly driven by such identity. Instead, the factors behind conflict and violence are often laced with issues of embedded inequality and grievance coupled with perceptions of humiliation. These are important conditioners for mistrust and suspicion across ethnic or religious lines, and it is important to make this distinction relatively early on in this book.

At this stage, it is worth developing the argument in another, related direction. This has to do with the extent to which distinctive claims can reliably be made about particular social, ethnic, or religious groups. At a basic level, for instance, all manner of everyday claims are made in politics and in public life about the characteristics and likely behavioural norms of specific groups.[25] For example, in Britain and elsewhere, it has long been taken for granted that working-class voters are more closely aligned to the Labour Party, a party traditionally of the centre-left and also born out of the collective struggle for economic and political rights by the British working class in the

[23] Ladbury, S., and Saggar, S., 'Towards Respect and Understanding: An Essay on the Causes of Violence', unpublished paper written for the initial meeting of the Commonwealth Commission on Respect and Understanding, December 2006; available at www.commonwealth.org.

[24] Fearon, J., and Laitin, D., 'Explaining Interethnic Cooperation', *American Political Science Review*, 1996, pp. 715–35.

[25] A current, topical illustration that such generalized claims are, in fact, underpinned by some rather mixed evidence can be seen in Malik, M., 'Discrimination, Equality and Community Cohesion', *Muslims in the UK: Policies for Engaged Citizens* (Budapest: Open Society Institute, 2005).

nineteenth century. In broad terms, this type of alignment only makes sense and is worth citing if, all things being equal, it actually delivers a markedly greater chance of working-class voters favouring Labour over its main rivals. In fact, a similar (though less well observed) link between class background and voting behaviour operates in reverse, binding together middle-class voters with the Conservative Party. This is the core model of the group–party nexus in other words.

Two important qualifications, however, demonstrate both the utility of this kind of model and its inherent limitations. First, there is a need to bottom out just how far the statistical pattern between the group and a particular behavioural pattern endures over time. In psephological analyses, therefore, a familiar question over more than half a century of investigation has been to map levels of class–party support and the underlying relationships that drive the class–party nexus. Some have postulated a very tight alignment, implying that other conditioning forces have been pushed to the margin. For example, one electoral commentator wrote in 1967 that 'class is the basis of British politics, all else is embellishment and detail'.[26] According to this account, social class stood head and shoulders above all rival explanations. Indeed, in the 1950s and 1960s, the relationship between class and party was recorded to be a strong one, which means that class-deviant voting was generally uncommon. Sophisticated methods were developed and deployed to uncover this point.[27] The job of political parties, and of the wider political process, was thus limited to trying to mobilize voters to behave in a class-consistent manner. Labour's task, crudely, was to get its troops to back it in the polling booths. With working-class voters broadly outnumbering middle-class ones, Labour notionally began with an advantage. Of course this did not prevent it being defeated if it was ineffective in mobilizing its troops or if it was indifferent to its rivals' ability to appeal to aspects of working-class aspirations. However, this same logic meant that the Conservatives were forced to operate in a context that necessitated appealing to voters beyond their own traditional class base. Electoral victory, by definition, involved trawling in unfamiliar waters to catch a haul that opponents would have normally taken for granted. Cross-class thinking and behaviour of this kind was not unusual for one of the major political parties and also underpinned its considerable post-war electoral success. Moreover, gradual shrinkage in the size of the traditional working class, accompanied by an expansion of the middle class, meant that, over time, the counter-intuitive behaviour of the Conservatives became increasingly the norm for parties seeking victory. In other words, the conditioners of political difference and of political behaviour have become

---

[26] Pulzer, P., *Political Representation and Elections in Britain* (London: Allen and Unwin, 1967).

[27] Butler, D., and Stokes, D., *Political Change in Britain*, 2nd edn. (Basingstoke: Macmillan, 1974).

less fixed and rather more fluid over this period. Or at least academic interest and understanding of such conditioners has taken such a turn, since much of what is known in this area of human behaviour, like others, is heavily dependent on trends and norms in intellectual categorization.

For class, one can also look to rival explanatory accounts that appear to be linked to large-scale political difference. Take for instance the electoral engagement of Britain's post-war Commonwealth immigrants and their offspring. Broadly drawn from South Asia, the Caribbean, and Africa, these immigrant cohorts have developed into today's widely recognized British black and Asian communities. In shorthand terms, they are known as (New Commonwealth) ethnic minorities, although there are many newer distinctions arising from non-Commonwealth immigration that are challenging this term. Nevertheless, one of the most striking features of black and Asian political behaviour has been their collective electoral support for Labour.[28] Successive studies have driven home this basic observation. The author has previously written of the 'iron law' of ethnic minority voting behaviour: in all elections going back to 1974 (when reliable data was first gathered), of those who registered and turned out to vote, an astonishing four in five supported the Labour Party.[29] This iron law is all the more impressive once account is made for the fact that a significant slice of this period was associated with Labour's long-term electoral decline and wilderness during the 1980s and early 1990s. The upshot of the observation is that blacks and Asians hung on to and stuck with Labour in its hour of need (in contrast to other groups of voters). The usual factors shaping the party's appeal and rejection were largely absent in the case of this group of voters. So, in terms of the link between group and behaviour, the overarching message is that ethnicity (or membership of a distinctive set of ethnic groups) undoubtedly shaped (and continues to shape, it must be said) outcomes to the virtual exclusion of other forces. Specifically, social class has been heavily muted in its influence, although the author's own investigations have revealed an important class effect at play alongside the better-known ethnic effect.[30]

The class–party or ethnic–party nexus seems to hold water in other words. It cannot be easily dismissed since there is a wealth of empirical evidence to back up claims that political difference and political behaviour are indeed driven by these group categories. The inference is that a fair amount of one-dimensional

[28] This is widely documented in early authoritative studies such as McAllister, I., and Studlar, D., 'The Electoral Geography of Immigrant Groups in Britain', *Electoral Studies*, Vol. 3, 1984, pp. 139–50; Layton-Henry, Z., and Studlar, D., 'The Electoral Participation of Black and Asian Britons', *Parliamentary Affairs*, Vol. 38, 1985, pp. 307–18.

[29] Saggar, S., *Race and Representation: Electoral Politics and Ethnic Pluralism* (Manchester: Manchester University Press, 2000).

[30] Saggar S., and Heath A., 'Race: Towards a Multicultural Electorate?', in Evans, G., and Norris, P. (eds.), *Critical Elections: The 1997 British Election in Long-term Perspective* (London: Sage, 1999), pp. 102–23.

identity politics is at work bonding and reinforcing groups to more or less predictable outcomes.

This is not always borne out in practice, however. The most obvious departure comes from other sources of identity and affiliation that interrupt the smooth linkage between ethnic or class identity and behaviour. Interestingly, both the ethnic- and class-based models of voting behaviour that have been so influential in voting studies in many Western countries have also been adapted or watered down to allow for alternative conditioners of behaviour. Ethnic-based accounts, particularly in relation to immigrant-descended groups, have been especially muddied by the effects of mainstream class influences and also by the trend among second and third generations towards political integration.[31] One notable mark of such political integration has been the rise of a multiplicity of conditioning forces as opposed to a singularity found among second- and third-generation ethnic minority cohorts. Thus, not only are class effects likely to take hold but so too are the influences of gender, occupation, geography, and also access to opportunity structures. With class-based accounts, a similar process of alternative influence has been important such that, in Britain for instance, distinctions in voter outlook can be linked to public versus private sector employment, education levels, housing tenure, and social mobility, to say nothing of the impact of ethnic, gender, and youth culture, and so on. When placed together, it is important to check to see how far a basic class-related way of thinking about identity and politics serves to explain political difference. Most notably, in the 1983 general election in Britain, class background became a rather poor predictor of party choice generally. In the case of the class composition of Labour's support (in an election where the party was routed on a scale not seen since the 1920s), working-class membership became as likely a predictor of non-Labour support as of Labour voting. In other words, the class–party nexus for one of the major party forces contained hardly any real explanatory value at all. To think of potential supporters as one-dimensional members of a social class was, in this case, fundamentally to misunderstand the picture.

Reading politics through the prism of class in this one-dimensional manner was, and remains, of course largely a hangover of the past. It is a lens that worked, sometimes rather well, in previous times when party politics was largely organized around the social cleavage of class membership. Politics was largely about classes in competition and conflict with one another, so it was hardly surprising that new generations of voters were brought up on a diet of social class nourishment. This view of the world—not just the political world—resonated in everyday lives and activities. Social and

---

[31] Malik, M., 'Inequalities of Integration: The British Experience in Comparative European Perspective', unpublished paper to a Policy Network seminar on Inequalities of Integration, London, November 2007.

geographical mobility was on a very small scale in comparison with con-temporary patterns. This meant, typically, that whole communities lived in worlds that were largely socio-economically distinct and unconnected with others.

Psephological commentators have been interested in describing and under-standing the effects of social distance created by class-based communities that knew of, but not about, each other. The effects were easy enough to map and assess, not least because of the reinforcing tendencies of thinking and outlook that were sustained. Typically speaking, working-class pit-valley communities had little tangible experience of privilege, wealth, or access to power. That is not to say that they had no feeling or judgement about massively more advantaged communities. Indeed, the former adopted a wide range of equally one-dimensional perceptions of other individuals and groups who were, if anything, unlike themselves. The unlikeness stemmed from seeing the values and behaviours of others from a distance and thus taking these to be charac-teristics of a group that could not possibly have anything in common with one's own community.

Likewise, upper, gentried, and middle classes had no need, and even less appetite, to see the poor material conditions of the working class. Theirs were worlds that strived to be apart from the sight and smell of poverty. To be a member of these more advantaged communities was at least partly defined by the collective stigmatization of not just poverty but also of the poor themselves. The latter in the minds of the former were different in just about every conceivable way from themselves. They represented values, behaviours, and pathologies that could easily be labelled as morally threatening and worse. The poor's perceived lack of moral fibre was just one obvious way in which to create distance and to reinforce a relentless one-dimensional way of looking at the other. In this context, it was relatively easy to demonize another world and its inhabitants. Having to share space with such another world was to be minimized if at all possible. Significantly, where and when it was not possible, it was commonplace to view members of other class groups and communities as pariahs, both capable and keen to threaten society at large.

In the case of social class identities, the post-war era in Britain has witnessed considerable mobility and softening of much older stereotypes. Cloth caps and bowler hats have diminished considerably, leading one commentator to quip that Britain has become metaphorically and literally all but hatless. The two or three principal classes have gained first-hand knowledge and experience of one another. Sometimes where this has been slow, it has been greatly accelerated by the influence of the mass media. Widespread ownership of a television from the 1950s onwards ensured that the working and middle classes were able at least to see and hear, via cathode ray tubes, artistic and light-hearted representations of communities that they had previously only vaguely heard about. Geographic mobility and transportation were further accelerants, as were the effects of limited mixed housing and educational policies. Segregated, isolated communities came under pressure to open up, mix, and thus change.

Similarly, the theme of this book is about the factors lying behind severe isolation and separation, parts of which are as much psychological and cultural as they are literal. This is not the only driver behind the emergence of conflictual, oppositional politics between and among Western Muslims and other communities. But is it a central way in which political grievance, disrespect, and overt intolerance are organized and re-created in the consciousness of Muslims and non-Muslims alike. One-dimensional identities are the recurring part of the story that allows pariah groups and those that feed their pariah status to be so effective in fuelling division.[32]

Collectivized Muslim Identity

The preceding observation conveniently leads to the second qualification to the argument about uni-dimensional group identity. This qualification is less about the quantum or degree of group-driven behaviour and more concerned with the nature of the underlying relationship or relationships.[33] Thus, although we can easily observe that there are many more things that make up the character and reputation of Western Muslims than faith identity, it is equally important to note that this single kind of identity undoubtedly has the capacity to overshadow and marginalize other competing identities. This is often unmistakable and overwhelming in its impact. Thus it cannot be ignored as aberrant to the general picture of mixed, complex, and interwoven identities, especially when thought of in terms of discourses of violence and hatred.[34] It is arguably more than that since any instance of a single identity trumping all other identities carries genuine risks of essentializing both the identity and the consciousness it is built upon.

For this reason, space needs to be given to addressing such essentialist ideas about identity generally and about religious identity in particular. Examples abound of attempts to essentialize religious identity in this way.[35] Many are usually based on a familiar single dimension of what it means to be a member of or belong to a religious community currently. One handy illustration of the problem can be seen in the advocacy in early 2007 by Safraz Manzoor, a

---

[32] Slim, H., 'Violent Beliefs', Centre for Humanitarian Dialogue, Geneva, 2005.

[33] Ramadan, T., *Western Muslims and the Future of Islam* (Oxford: Oxford University Press, 2004).

[34] Volkan, V., *Killing in the Name of Identity* (Virginia: Pitchstone, 2006).

[35] Williams, R., interview on the *Today Programme*, Radio 4, 31 October 2006.

journalist, that an opportunity lay for mainstream Britain to move towards embracing so-called Muslim values. He wrote:[36]

It is easy to dismiss Muslim parents as old-fashioned and traditional, but when the rest of the country is busy wondering how to respond to a culture of rampant disrespect, it is worth considering whether they could learn from Muslim values. Whether the danger is religious extremism, drugs or crime, those involved are largely third-generation Muslims who are so integrated into white society that they are emulating its worst characteristics. Integration did not save them, it created them.

This otherwise poorly informed op-ed spoke directly to the belief that in modern Britain all individuals and communities could be divided along Muslim and non-Muslim lines. In the former camp lay all members of a religious group whose core ethical values and sentiment was at odds with the rest of society. The same could be said in reverse of the latter in that they were characterized by a notably hedonistic, undeferential, and disrespectful value system that contrasts with that of their Muslim neighbours. The Manzoor argument goes on to make a number of wild yet all-too-common generalizations such as that: 'Muslim children are more likely to be brought up in two-parent families rather than the single-parent households that are increasingly common in Britain' and that 'Muslim parents also tend to be less interested in child-centred parenting and more into parent-centred parenting'. The weakness of this claim is that, as many corresponding readers have noted, it confuses elements of the migration and settlement of Muslims from South Asia with patterns generally found among all migrants, the bulk of whom are not Muslims.[37] It seeks a faith-related explanation for a phenomenon that is, in truth, anything but related to faith. Also, much the same could be claimed for, say, the Jewish community or communities in Britain, or by Hindus, leaving similar gaping questions about causality and also about the legitimacy to speak on behalf of Anglo-Judaism or Anglo-Hinduism.[38]

Furthermore, the argument contains the familiar trait of drawing on the statistical odds behind one behavioural pattern or another. Thus, according to this viewpoint, if proportionately more Muslim mothers stay at home to care for young children than non-Muslim mothers, a reasonable inference can be made that this pattern reflects a different value system regarding the rearing of

[36] Manzoor, S., 'Britain Should Integrate into Muslim Values', *Guardian*, 4 January 2007.

[37] One Internet blog, by 'Disraelian', responded dismissively to the claim by pointing out that: 'The reason Muslim families are closer must have something to do with the fact that they are recently immigrated families from largely rural countries. Look at the Italians in North America and you see all the same phenomena—this has I'm afraid nothing to do with Islam. It's sociological. The point is that in rural communities such community sanctions work but they break down in cities—in cities they break down because you can easily move away and there are more opportunities to move away.' See http://gracchii.blogspot.com.

[38] Alderman, G., 'Who Really Speaks for Jews in Britain?', *Guardian—Comment is Free*, 6 February 2007; Gledhill, R., 'Hindus say it's Time to Ditch the Asian Tag', *The Times*, 11 July 2006.

children. However, it may just as equally reflect a contrasting set of attitudes about the role of women, especially in terms of discouraging roles outside of the family and home. Alternatively, this statistical pattern of family behaviour may be intimately shaped by other patterns of full-time working involving long working hours and shift work among men (husbands, sons, fathers) to whom these Muslim mothers are related. The pattern therefore is the result of the weak socio-economic position of men, whose working patterns negate the possibility of involvement in child-rearing. This may be reinforced by cultural norms about male and female roles within the family.

The inference, in other words, is just as likely to be false as not. Moreover, it takes existing behavioural patterns to be illustrations of more or less essential traits. These are accorded the status of being inherent and characteristic of a group as a result of their membership of a single faith identity.[39] Of course many members of the group will share this behavioural pattern and outlook but the argument rather misses the key point that many others, who belong to other faith or ethnic or national groups, may also share this in common with Muslims. The reasons in the case of these other faith groups cannot be circumstantial (i.e. migratory patterns, generation, rural influences, and so on),[40] while being attributed purely to faith identity in the case of Muslims.

But the base observation that Muslims are mostly one thing or another is the point most at issue here. It is an observation that is fleeting, possibly flawed, in its empirical accuracy and also extraordinarily myopic in mistaking statistical generalizations (albeit weak ones) with deeper meaning through identity. It is this point that needs to be challenged and made an issue of, if it is not one already.

Theorizing Identity, Consciousness, and Behaviour

Plainly, all sorts of claims can be made on a variety of grounds about the pertinence of one kind of identity or another in shaping outlook and behaviour. In the case of the earlier discussion of voting behaviour, what is striking is that political scientists and others have devoted extensive effort and resources to mapping patterns of political engagement among distinctive ethnic and religious groups.[41] Ethnic voting, so to speak, has emerged as a

---

[39] Falk, R., 'False Universalism and the Geopolitics of Exclusion: The Case of Islam', *Third World Quarterly*, Vol. 18, March 1997, pp. 7–24.

[40] Bhachu, P., *Twice Migrants: East African Sikh Settlers in Britain* (London: Tavistock, 1985).

[41] This is now a substantial literature in Britain alone spanning over forty years. See for instance Deakin, N., *Colour and the British Electorate* (London: Pall Mall, 1965); Crewe, I., 'Representation and the Ethnic Minorities in Britain', in Glazer, N., and Young, K. (eds.), *Ethnic Pluralism and Public Policy: Achieving Equality in the United States and Britain* (London: Heinemann, 1983); Studlar, D., 'The Ethnic Vote 1983: Problems of Analysis and Interpretation', *New Community*, 11, 1983, pp. 92–100; FitzGerald, M., *Political Parties and Black People*, 2nd edn. (London: Runnymede Trust, 1987); Layton-Henry, Z., and Studlar D., 'The Electoral

robust, specialist cottage industry. However, despite documenting patterns of distinctive voting behaviour, rather less attention has been devoted to better understanding the reasons for behaviour based around a single dimension of identity. In other words, the theoretical underpinnings of political behaviour among demographic subgroups have remained weak and unconvincing. In order to address this gap, it is important to advance a brief discussion of an ethnically or religiously related theory of political consciousness and behaviour. Such a theory, or theories, will enable a more fruitful understanding of the ways in which ethnic or religious identities influence the dynamics of group consciousness at large.

Identity-related theories of political behaviour involve two related spheres: first, questions of political thought and outlook (socio- or cultural-political orientation being an obvious focus) and second, questions of political involvement and participation (political action as well as inaction). When combined, these perspectives seek to model some central questions. First, precisely what, if anything, can be said about ethnic and religious relationships as a force that shapes political behaviour? Second, to what degree do different ethnic and religious groups deviate, both from one another and from dominant 'norms', for their political behaviour to be thought of as sufficiently distinctive and thus worthy of comment? Finally, how well do identity-related theories of political behaviour cope with examples of non-identity-related political behaviour, or, more pertinently, evidence of mixed and interwoven influence that touch upon ethnicity or religion only spasmodically? The last of the questions is the most disputed area of all because it requires otherwise simplistic theories to tackle complex terrain and also because it deals with the notion of partial, indirect, or mixed causal relationships. Identity politics and complex consciousness and behaviour require nuanced explanation.

The above questions, while important, nevertheless present ethnic and religious identities as having an impact on the outlook and behaviour of discrete demographic subgroups. This is only one way to look at impacts. Another way to think about the potential of ethnicity and religion to shape political behaviour is to look at how new identities are managed by existing political institutions and processes.[42] After all, a great deal has been made

Participation of Black and Asian Britons: Integration or Alienation?', *Parliamentary Affairs*, 38, 1985, pp. 307–18; Gouldbourne, H., 'The Participation of New Minority Ethnic Groups in British Politics', in Blackstone, T., Parekh, B., and Sanders, P. (eds.), *The Politics of Race Relations* (London: Routledge, 1998); Le Lohé, M., 'Ethnic Minority Participation and Representation in the British Electoral System', in Saggar, S. (ed.), *Race and British Electoral Politics* (London: UCL Press, 1998); Saggar, S., 'Ethnic Minority Political Mobilisation in Britain: Competing Claims and Agendas', in Martiniello, M. (ed.), *Reflections on Two European Multicultural Societies: Belgium and the United Kingdom* (Utrecht: ERCOMER, 1998).

[42] Dench., G., Garron, K., and Young, M., *The New East End: Kinship, Race and Conflict* (London: Young Foundation, 2006).

about the capacity and track record of Western political parties, political elites, and political organizations to respond to the ethno-religious pluralism brought about through post-war mass immigration. For example, in 1965, Nicholas Deakin published a landmark study of immigration and electoral behaviour, *Colour and British Electorate*[43]; it was fairly obvious that the main focus of academic and practitioner thought was on the ways in which the indigenous 'white' electorate had responded to the immigration issue. The response was divisive and largely negative in that strong feelings against black and Asian immigration could easily be exploited by parties and leaders. Thus, the influence of ethnicity was thought of entirely in terms of the effects of ethno-religious diversity and change upon a homogenous 'white' electorate. Such an approach makes sense in the context of such pioneering studies. However, carrying out similar analytical exercises more than four decades on would appear less credible in most Western democracies. For one thing, the ethnic and religious composition of many of these societies (and to some extent in their electorates) has changed considerably. Furthermore, the reactive stimuli of immigration (involving many non-European settlers, and the form of social change it embodied) has gone beyond the old-fashioned anti-immigration politics of the 1960s and 1970s. The effects are arguably more salient two generations on, with widespread impacts in terms of culturally and religiously informed controversies. However, the effects of ethnic and religious difference are still being measured in the sense that these are primarily independent variables.[44] Identity-related theories of political behaviour, therefore, must take care to ensure that their applicability is extended to all groups and subgroups, not merely those descended from post-war mass immigration.

Another related question, then, might be to ask how far ethnic and religious identity serves as a contextual feature of mainstream participatory politics. This is needed to account for voters' and others' responses to issues, events, and other stimuli that are generally thought to be affecting the ethno-religious character of society at large. Whether empirical measurement is focused around one identity group or another hardly matters as the analysis is about unlocking the simultaneous dependent and independent aspects of changing and contested identity at one and the same time. Something rather similar applies in relation to changing influences on, and effects of, gender identity and also disability and sexuality. In the case of gender, many Western societies have adapted, sometimes imperfectly, to the significant change in the consciousness of women over the past forty years in respect of non-domestic

[43] Deakin, N., *Colour and the British Electorate* (London: Pall Mall, 1965).
[44] Cramer, C., 'Inequality and Conflict: A Review of an Age-Old Concern', Identities, Conflict and Cohesion Programme, Paper 11, UNRISD, October 2005.

roles. This has taken place roughly at the same time as, and has been the main cause of, the considerable expansion of female employment in many of these countries. However, what is as important has been the consequences of this development on the identity awareness of men in these societies. Many traditional labour market roles have been reformulated as have a number of roles related to domestic life and child-rearing. Although few would claim that these have been revolutionized, what is important is that identity frames of reference have been influenced that go beyond the boundaries of one-dimensional identity politics.

Theoretical enquiry can conceptualize the role of ethnic and religious identity in a number of ways. The most prominent aspect of this has been to look at the question of an ethnic or religious political agenda, sometimes referred to as a race agenda or perspective, or perhaps as a Christian, Islamic, or other group-based agenda.[45] The evidence surrounding this idea has been hotly contested over the years and it is still unclear in its main conclusions. At an empirical level, the debate has revolved around the degree to which members of a single identity group have been stimulated and motivated exclusively by identity considerations in their political outlook and behaviour. At one end of the debate, there has been something of an essentialist viewpoint that has stressed the importance of a powerful and discrete set of common values and priorities among members of an identity group. At the other end, so-called sceptics have poured scorn on this claim, suggesting that any major inter-group variations are fully explicable either through circumstantial factors or else as the ever-diminishing product of transitional change. In addition, the debate has featured lively and pointed dispute over the role of identity derived from community-based organizations.[46] Participation organized around specific cultural, religious, or similar ties has plainly played an important part among some minority communities, most notably at the local level. The task has been to map the political potential of these forms of quasi- or alternative community-based organizations. For instance, are they merely significant in ad hoc, single issue terms? Or, more robustly, can it be said that they are genuinely autonomous and possibly rivals to orthodox political institutions such as political parties? The traditional view held that they amounted to

---

[45] Messina, A., 'Ethnic Minorities and the British Party System in the 1990s and Beyond', in Saggar, S. (ed.), *Race and British Electoral Politics* (London: UCL Press, 1998); Marable, M., *Beyond Black and White: Transforming African American Politics* (London: Verso, 1995).

[46] Shukra, K., 'New Labour Debates and Dilemmas', in Saggar, S. (ed.), *Race and British Electoral Politics* (London: UCL Press, 1998); Shukra, K., *The Changing Pattern of Black Politics in Britain* (London: Pluto Press, 1998); Ali, Y., 'Muslim Women and the Politics of Ethnicity', in Saghal, G., and Yuval Davis, N. (eds.), *Refusing Holy Orders* (London: Virago, 1992); Hall, S., 'Politics of Identity', in Ranger, T., Samad, Y., and Stewart, O. (eds.), *Culture, Identity and Politics: Ethnic Minorities in Britain* (Aldershot: Avebury, 1996); Kalka, I., 'The Politics of "Community" Among Gujarat Hindus in London', *New Community*, 17 (3), 1991.

potentially important learning zones in which newcomer groups could absorb the customs and mores of the mainstream political system.[47] Though dated, this view still holds sway in some quarters.

In assessing political examples of ethnic and religious identity and group loyalty, it is important to observe two basic tests. The first is to ensure that the evidence is not excessively or unnecessarily contaminated by signs of non-political, leisure, or cultural-led activity among the particular identity group that might distort assessments of political difference. While community-based activity to secure better distributional outcomes for restaurateurs or sports teams is a worthwhile area to study, it is not always obvious how these directly serve to shape the link between ethnic or religious identity on one hand and political outlook and behaviour on the other. The link is often an indirect one and it is helpful to be reminded of this. Such a trap can be slipped into quite casually and unknowingly, leading to some quite preposterous and immeasurable claims about the politics of ethnicity and faith. This leads to a second check: how far is ethnic and religious identity, both overtly in the political realm and elsewhere, the source of a permanent, stand-alone cleavage in the politics of particular Western societies? In the USA, for instance, it has been widely trumpeted that racial identity (among black African-Americans) consistently trumps class-based identities in influencing partisanship and voting choice. The inference is that this kind of racial identity has sufficiently deep and immovable roots that it amounts to such a stand-alone political cleavage. To many observers of the legacy of the racial scar on US society, this assessment is credible and far from exaggerated. It chimes, in other words, with a trove of other sources of understanding about the depth of one-dimensional identity in American society over several centuries.

This stand-alone question in fact forms the basis of the empirical aspects of this book. Subsequent chapters present a range of empirical evidence to help isolate the distinctiveness of Muslim identity and behaviour in a variety of settings. These chapters ask, in other words, how far it is fair to view Muslim experience and political outlook as symptoms of a religious cleavage in Western societies.[48] In essence, it is a question that has enormous implications for thinking and practice towards the long-term integration of Muslim communities into these societies.[49]

---

[47] Hill, M., and Issacharoff, R., *Community Action and Race Relations* (London: Oxford University Press for the Institute of Race Relations, 1971); Katznelson, I., *Black Men, White Cities: Race Relations and Migration in the United States 1900–30 and Britain 1948–68* (London: Oxford University Press for the Institute of Race Relations, 1973).

[48] Cesari, J., *When Islam and Democracy Meet: Muslims in Europe* (New York: Palgrave, 2004).

[49] Gul, A., Deputy Prime Minister and Minister of Foreign Affairs, Republic of Turkey, comments to an international symposium on 'Civilisation and Harmony: Values and Mechanisms of the Global Order', Istanbul, 3 October 2004.

Identity Straitjackets and Political Representation

The recurring theme of this chapter has been that of collective interests based on a platform of common, shared identity. The evidence to back this assessment undoubtedly varies but, as important as this is, the fact is that the meaning attached to the collective and common also stretches across a wide spectrum. An obvious question that arises is to explain how and why individuals can think and act beyond the constraints of one particular dimension or another. For instance, what is the potential for cross-group identification and is this merely another form of identity constraint, or is it something different and possibly better?

The conventional view on this question in many Western societies has been that any cross-group identification was likely to be fairly limited and of minimal, passing consequence. This was primarily because of the dominance of essentially non-ethnic and religious-based political parties in attracting and retaining the identification of political participants. Although aspects of religious difference continued to shape, partially, political norms in countries such Belgium, Germany, and the Netherlands, the larger distinction has been between faith-based identity as against secular kinds of identity. In addition, it was thought that social group identification only came into the limelight in the private realm or at least far removed from the domain of public affairs. In any case, conditional identification with the social group was felt to be a long way from social representation in its full-blown form. The latter required considerable organizational and mobilization input, much of which could be supplied and therefore displaced by formal political organizations. It has not been a role routinely assigned to private social or community organizations, although the evidence in fact points to extensive mobilization results by these organizations. An alternative viewpoint, however, has suggested that the social and demographic characteristics of political participants do in fact matter, at least to the extent that this creates potentially powerful forms of allegiance and representative muscle. These allegiances have either been capitalized on by or within political parties or been steadfastly ignored.[50] This counter-view is important because it not only acknowledges the difficulties associated with the interface between social and other notions of representation but also through its appreciation of the internal management of these social identities by mainstream political institutions and by government. It is, arguably, the politics of this interface, and the management questions that it raises, that is potentially so interesting in studying representative theories in action in modern liberal democracies.[51]

[50] Norris, P., and Lovenduski, J., *Political Recruitment: Gender, Race and Class in the British Parliament* (Cambridge: Cambridge University Press, 1995).

[51] Ramadan, T., *Western Muslims and the Future of Islam* (Oxford: Oxford University Press, 2004).

The social identity that gives rise to a coherent form of collective identity and interest lies at the heart of the matter. These social identities may be quite numerous and vary from one country to the next, or even from one place to another within the same society. In modern Britain, for example, it is fairly clear that the social composition—which includes a range of descriptive identities ranging from gender, sexual orientation, generational, and so on—of the general population tends to generate considerable exposure and attention.

Not all of this is benign. For instance, most social representation arguments are centred on the social class, gender, generational, or regional composition of a society. But it is hard to draw any grand generalizations about the relative importance of specific notions of social representation in the British political system. What is clear is that social representation claims and counter-claims have become pretty vocal today in a way that would have been impossible to imagine, let alone predict, a couple of generations ago. The idea that prominent, organized faith groups would routinely dominate national political debate would have been a highly dubious prediction even thirty years ago.[52] This emphasis has led to a strong counter-reaction among those who argue that social or descriptive representation can be taken to absurd lengths. For instance, several years ago a correspondent in *The Times* colourfully lambasted political leaders for overdoing the spirit of representation-by-social-microcosm:[53]

The idea that women are better represented by women, blacks by blacks and gays by gays is a modern fallacy. Last week...a candidate announced that as the only openly gay candidate he had a special responsibility to homosexual voters. How is this different from a racist candidate declaring a special responsibility to 'whites'?

The point of contention is that grand generalizations can be and have been made about a group developing as a collective political constituency. This may be dubious from the point of view of outside observers. Crucially, it may also be unconvincing from the perspective of notional insider members. Thus, in Britain, the interests and influence of ethnic and religious minorities (historically linked to mass Commonwealth immigration) as a collective political constituency are to an unprecedented degree now structurally embedded in the Labour Party and its policies.[54] There has been little serious qualification of this assertion in empirical research for over three decades, although the impact, since late 2005, of the Cameron-led Conservatives in this regard cannot be fairly or fully judged at the time of writing. But this raises substantial

---

[52] Cohen, A., *Two-Dimensional Man* (London: Routledge and Kegan Paul, 1974).

[53] Rankin, A., 'If Parliament is to be a Mere Statistical Mirror, 19 per cent should be Unable to Read and We should Recruit More Manchester United Supporters', *The Times*, 30 November 1999, p. 24.

[54] Messina, A., *The Logic and Politics of Post-war Immigration in Europe* (Cambridge: Cambridge University Press, 2007).

doubts about the efficacy of such an arrangement and also about the limits of identity politics.

Take the case of voting behaviour among ethnic minorities. The 'ethnicity counts' argument has been centred on the idea of an ethnically based way of explaining political thought and action. Its logic can be equally applied to faith identities and communities. Accordingly, ethnic minority voting behaviour is approached in terms of a model of ethnic bloc voting which implies a vast subtext of uniform ethnic group swing, the influence of so-called ethnic issues, and the en bloc mobilization of voters.

The evidence to back up this subtext is patchy to say the least. However, the model is also couched in the language of the potential behaviour of minority voters and therefore attaches great weight to minority group socialization and capacity-building efforts. For instance, the growth of South Asian minority community-based organizations is seen as a sign of an underlying trajectory for ethnic-based voting to take off.[55] These discrete groups of voters, it is con-tended, perceive political mobilization through the lens of ethnic solidarity and, therefore, voting campaigns built around this base are thought to be a natural and fairly inevitable outcome. At the local level, there have been some solid signs to support this line of argument. For example, a decade ago in the 1997 general election, such ethnic voting campaigns in constituencies such as Bethnal Green and Bow in London's East End had a clear impact. By the general election of 2005, ethnic identity had combined with explicit religious and ideological ideates to deliver even larger impacts. However, these cases tend to be pretty rare. The question that matters is whether they symbolize an unfolding pattern that is ascendant or merely uncharacteristic blips that can easily be ignored. One school of argument stresses the former, chiefly because these examples provide clear grounds for theories of ethnic- and religious-based electoral mobilization. A similar conclusion can be inferred about the political mobilization of electors in general.

The 'ethnicity counts' perspective, therefore, rests on the processes of group membership being linked, perhaps equated, with group identification and interest. This is a central point of dispute between commentators, not least because it goes somewhat farther than trying to flesh out any distinctive theory of ethnically or religiously linked political participation. In fact, this point leads to the setting for an even larger debate, namely, over the long-term political integration of ethnic and religious minorities.

The racial or religious exclusion paradigm has been influential mainly because it effectively links an important strand of sociological analysis of institutional policies and process with behavioural political science interest in

---

[55] Samad, Y., 'The Politics of Islamic Identity among Bangladeshi and Pakistanis in Britain', in Ranger, T., Samad, Y., and Stewart, O. (eds.), *Culture, Identity and Politics: Ethnic Minorities in Britain* (Aldershot: Avebury, 1996); Lyon, M., 'Ethnicity in Britain: The Gujarat Tradition', *New Community*, 2 (1), 1972; Eade, J., *The Politics of Community* (Aldershot: Avebury, 1989).

patterns and levels of representation. Indeed, from this interface has emerged one of the key points of concern and dispute, namely, over theories of under-representation in political life. There are various prime arenas in which to evaluate under-representation claims and counter-claims, including school-ing, employment, housing, health, and descriptive political representation. However, all of these arenas are important because they lend themselves to three closely aligned arguments about procedural and substantive democracy. The first is that disaggregated levels of political participation are important as they provide a passing, though useful, comment on the legitimacy and relevance of political institutions.[56] Political communication, for instance, normally relies on this type of argument to generate support for the principle of social inclusion. Second, the quality and reputation of the democratic processes, beyond that of specific institutions, may be at stake when examin-ing democratic system performance questions among different groups within society.[57] The sentiment of ethnic and religious minorities in considering how far the society and its institutions are to be valued, distrusted, conditionally accepted, or fully embraced is a recurring feature of this academic and political debate.[58] Third, certain patterns of under-representation might mask consid-erably deeper forms of political and social alienation.[59] If large pockets of society—in this case, specific minority faith groups or communities—remain substantially aloof from mainstream participation norms, then it is likely that liberal interpretations of under-representation will be challenged.[60]

The larger point is that the understanding of representation by social group is based entirely on parity indicators. The implication of this is that, even where large-scale breakthroughs can be secured, these remain distinct from any discussion of the representation of the distinctive collective interests of a political or social group.[61] The idea that British Muslims have such distinctive

[56] Pattie, C., and Johnston, R., 'Voter Turnout at the British General Election of 1992: Rational Choice, Social Standing or Political Efficacy?', *European Journal of Political Research*, 33, 1998, pp. 263–83.

[57] Saggar, S., *Race and Political Representation Reconsidered* (London: Hansard Society, Kings-land Papers Series No. 2, 2001).

[58] An early illustration of this concern can be seen in Layton-Henry, Z., and Studlar, D., 'The Electoral Participation of Black and Asian Britons: Integration or Alienation?', *Parliamentary Affairs*, 38, 1985, pp. 307–18.

[59] In their unrelated work on ethnic and religious minority local councillor attitudes, Jessica Adolino (1998) and Kingsley Purdham (1998) both make the wise point that forms of political involvement can and should be measured across a range of indicators relating to political interest, political knowledge, and ad hoc participation in public affairs or events. See Adolino, J., 'Integration within the British Political Parties: Perceptions of Ethnic Minority Councillors', in Saggar, S. (ed.), *Race and British Electoral Politics* (London: UCL Press, 1998); Purdham, K., 'The Political Identities of Muslim Local Councillors in Britain', *Manchester Papers in Politics*, No. 3/98, 1998.

[60] Klausen, J., *The Islamic Challenge: Politics and Religion in Western Europe* (Oxford: Oxford University Press, 2005).

[61] Portillo, M., 'Our One-cudgel Approach to Islam is Costing us Dear', *The Sunday Times*, 1 August 2004.

and collective interests in politics has been regularly debated in Britain and is further considered, along with some detailed evidence on this question, in subsequent chapters.

It is clear, however, that such a claim hangs on a view of the group as a sufficiently distinctive and self-identifying category to justify the cause of a political interest or set of interests. Two views have emerged on the nature and causes of such supposed distinctiveness. One of these holds that common ethno-religious origins and cultural ties are the long-term basis for the political interest, while another view contends that it has been the common experience of migration and conflict with the indigenous society that has, somewhat circumstantially, built the basis of a particular political interest. The former is essentially a positive bond while the latter is largely a negative shaped influence. And there is obviously something much more temporary and conditional about the latter perspective than the former. Nevertheless both accounts see the prize as mobilization through politics—formal and informal—to realize common and distinctive interests.[62] In other words, it is substantive representation of these interests that is valued and not, significantly, representative positions held by minorities alone.[63]

This is a potentially powerful divide within social theories of representation, and one with important implications for the argument pursued in this book. It is arguably the relationship between these potentially rival views that really matters perhaps because of the implicit suggestion of a tension, even a trade-off, in terms of mobilization. If so, a number of questions arise about the symbolic character of representative institutions as well as the ability of identity groups to call to account both institutions and individuals.

The Relationship between Religious Faith and Society

There is, at first glance, little need to qualify our interest in the relationship between religion and society. This book is, after all, interested in examining this relationship in order to gauge how far the political outlook and sentiment of one prominent religious minority, Muslims, is affected by underlying ideas about the inclusion of religious faith in setting norms for society as a whole. This appears a straightforward task. However, an important caveat is necessary even at the outset, given a growing literature on cross-national variations in religiosity.[64] This is to draw attention to the basis of the relationship

[62] Somerwille, W., *Immigration Under New Labour* (Oxford: Policy Press, 2007).

[63] Pitkin, H., *The Concept of Representation* (Berkeley: University of California Press, 1967).

[64] See for example Norris, P., and Inglehart, R., 'God, Guns, and Gays: Religion and Politics in the US and Western Europe', Paper for APSA 3rd annual Political Communication Section Conference: 'Fun, Faith, and Futuramas', held prior to the Annual Meeting of the American Political Science Association, September 2004, University of Illinois, Chicago; Greeley, A.,

and to probe whether or not it is in fact a relationship to begin with. A largely secular viewpoint would hold that religious and faith communities were distinguished by their greater or lesser attachment to the values and outlook of their co-religion members. Moreover, in looking at a religiously plural society, it would be necessary to isolate the nature and extent of the influence of faith-based identity on the working of the society at large. In order words, the former would amount to an independent variable used to account for change in the latter.

The difficulty with this perspective is that it may serve to overstate, or even misstate, the relationship. In the case of certain faiths, attachment and adherence to the values and teaching of a religious doctrine may make it hard to separate out membership of the faith group from membership of society as a whole. This is frequently observed in contemporary Islam and has been a notable feature of Western Muslim communities.[65] This critique has even been framed in terms of Western Muslims facing *the* structural and ideological disadvantage of widespread societal secularism. But it is not the degree of society's generally secular character that is the source of disquiet, but rather that secular values negate the possibility that faith groups will be seen as anything other than an external influence, a pressure group of sorts, on government policy.

The charge of 'secular fundamentalism' has been used—somewhat effectively it must be said—to convey the sense of frustration and impotence felt by Muslim self-help groups. This is an important charge. It infers that the historical and ideological framework for examining the relationship between religious faith and society is of less worth than many had imagined. In particular, it suggests that a fuller exploration of identity-based politics is needed that helps to explain whether, and how far, religious faith drives political sentiment and behaviour. In doing so, the most important caveat to appreciate is that we are also aware of faith in, and as, society, as alongside any other understanding.

A Muslim Faith Agenda?

The aim is to take forward the above qualification and to set out a variety of ways in which Muslim identity can be viewed as a shaper of political outlook and action. The central issue at stake is to develop a better informed understanding of collective identity in wider political terms.

Religion in Europe at the End of the Second Millennium. (New Brunswick, NJ: Transaction, 2003); Robert, C. Fuller, *Spiritual, but Not Religious: Understanding Unchurched America* (New York: Oxford University Press, 2002).

[65] Gray, J., 'How Marx Turned Muslim. Not Ancient, But Modern: John Gray Argues that Islamist Militants have Western Roots', *Guardian*, 27 July 2002.

This issue is by no means unique to the currently sensitive and high-profile case of Western Muslim communities. Similar issues have underscored the politics of ethnic and racial pluralism in many Western societies for at least the past half-century. And echoes can also be detected previously in a whole host of modern developing societies characterized by ethnic or faith divisions.[66] The issue is one that in fact regularly punctuates debates concerning the creation of cross-ethnic and religious identity solidarity in the development of democratic institutions and accountability on environmental objectives in developing societies.[67] As such, the discussion has sources and relevance beyond the example of Western Muslims that this book is primarily concerned with.

There is an important tension in the literature on identity and political engagement. This centres on the extent to which it is possible to make claims for ethnic or religious groups as a discrete and coherent political interest.[68] A wealth of attitudinal survey research has pointed to differentiation among Western Muslims.[69] A report by the Minority Rights Group in 2002, for example, vividly showed sharp distinctions within even the younger British Muslim population: between a vocal, radical minority hallmarked by a narrow interpretation of Islam, a second cohort who retained Islamic identity while integrating on most usual indicators, and a third, sometimes overlooked, group of nominal Muslims who no longer identified overtly with their Muslim origins.

The same point has been observed in respect of immigrant and immigrant-descended populations. For example, writing in relation to immigrant-descended ethnic minority groups in Britain, Messina, a veteran observer of these issues, notes that the difficulty has arisen from a failure to answer two questions.[70] First, since 'non-whites and whites share similar policy priorities', it is not at all easy to see how their collective political interests can be said to be sufficiently distinctive from their more numerous white counterparts. In other words, while some minorities—ethnic or

---

[66] See *Alliance of Civilisations: Final Report of the High Level Group* (New York: United Nations, 2006); see: http://www.unaoc.org.

[67] Wangari Maathai, comments on Radio 4, 'Start the Week', 5 February 2007—see http://www.bbc.co.uk/radio4/factual/starttheweek.shtml.

[68] Davultoglu, A., *Civilisational Transformation and the Muslim World* (Kuala Lumpur, Malaysia: Mahir, 1994).

[69] This can also be seen in surveys that focus especially on attitudes towards radical, violent interpretations of political Islam. In one study on the Dutch case, considerable variation in attitudes was reported suggesting that many Western Muslims share preferences with non-Muslims on issues of radicalism. See Pressman, D. E., 'Measuring Integration and Radicalization: A Role for Education', presentation to EU Transatlantic Security Roundtable 4: Educating for Migrant Integration—Integrating Migration into Education: European and North American Comparisons, University of Toronto, September 2006.

[70] Messina, A., 'Ethnic Minorities and the British Party System in the 1990s and Beyond', in Saggar, S. (ed.), *Race and British Electoral Politics* (London: UCL Press, 1998).

religious—adhere to a strongly distinctive platform of interests and concerns, the same is not true of the bulk of ethnic or religious minorities. This creates a significant problem in terms of mapping the route and style of minority political representation. Second, and perhaps even more awkwardly, there is growing evidence to show that ethnic and religious minorities are far from an ideologically homogeneous social group within society. Thinking of these minorities as democratic participants reveals that attitudes tend to vary on a range of public policy questions, and elements of these intra-minority divisions tend to follow ethnic or faith lines. Thus, opinion among Muslims alone can and does vary so that younger Muslims report markedly different views to those of their parents.[71] Indeed, the absence of a single body of opinion among Muslims also extends in part to some of the traditional concerns of minority faith groups such as faith schools, the link between church and state, dietary restrictions in schools and prisons, faith observance in the workplace, and so on. The upshot is that, once again, the job of articulating a strategy for the representation of these collective interests becomes yet more elusive.

Messina concludes that 'it is far from clear what these shared interests are'[72] when writing about ethnic minority groups. If this is indeed the case, then it is also important to accept that quite a lot has been claimed in the name of Muslim representation that is founded on lines that are distinctive, if not occasionally separate, from the political representation of non-Muslims.

All this leads to an even bigger question, namely, the extent to which Muslim communities and their interests are satisfactorily integrated into the mainstream political process. This question also includes the possibility that political integration is stymied by charges of grievance and humiliation, however reasonable or unreasonable these may be.[73] In order to address this question, it is necessary to do two things. First, we must unpack and clarify the confusion over the political concerns and interests of Muslims; and second, we need to explore the factors that have led to the belief, however poorly founded in evidence, that these interests are not adequately served by political institutions that cater for the representation of all political interests.

At one end of the spectrum, the claim has been made that Muslims are characterized by a separate and discrete set of opinions and attitudes on issues, and that these are not shared by non-Muslims and probably rejected by non-Muslim opinion as being religiously divisive. The most obvious ground for this view has not been any casual sense of collective group consciousness but rather the perception that religious discrimination generally, and anti-Muslim

---

[71] Mirza, M., Senthilkumaran, A., and Zein, J., *Living Apart Together: British Muslims and the Paradox of Multiculturalism* (London: Policy Exchange, 2007).

[72] Messina, A., 'Ethnic Minorities and the British Party System in the 1990s and Beyond', in Saggar, S. (ed.), *Race and British Electoral Politics* (London: UCL Press, 1998), p. 49.

[73] Manji, I., 'Why don't we Muslims Grow Up?', *The Times*, 20 May 2005.

discrimination specifically, is widespread in many Western societies.[74] Specifically, it is the suggestion that anti-Muslim feeling is commonplace and that ongoing religious exclusion persists on a large scale in British society. In sloganeering terms, it amounts to the cry that 'Britain is an Islamophobic country', and that specific institutions, notably those of public authority, are guilty of treating Muslims in an inferior or slanted way in comparison with non-Muslims—including, it should added, other non-Muslims from a South Asian background.[75]

In Britain in recent years, there has been little doubt that such a viewpoint continues to hold sway in several quarters. Radical Muslim leaders have repeated the charge during and beyond a number of controversies including the Rushdie affair, the events of 9/11 and 7/7, and the Danish cartoons episode in early 2006. In the case of the latter, the claim was advanced that if institutions such as the British Foreign and Home Offices saw no reason to intervene to ban the allegedly offensive images, then there remained little reason to believe that the fate of Muslims would be any better in society at large. Of course those taking this position from the Danish cartoons episode were joined by a sympathetic chorus among influential members of the press and other public commentators.[76] It is hard to know in this case whether the label of 'Islamophobia' meant anything more than strong or endemic criticism of Muslim-led campaigns to try to ban the controversial images from UK publications.

It has become rather more common to come across strong claims of this sort. For one thing, it has become somewhat easier to sustain a rounded, coherent view of the world that is founded beyond the viewpoints of religious extremists, both Muslim and non-Muslim.[77] One prominent illustration of an attempt to build an institutional fabric based on such universalistic thinking about religious difference can be seen in the experience of the various umbrella representative organizations among British Muslim community groups. The emergence of the Muslim Council of Britain, a putatively moderate-led body, into a national role of dialogue and partnership with government after September 2001 illustrates this. Although MCB's leadership broadly held to a moderate, participatory view of social change through government policy, it was nevertheless at the receiving end of much harder-line protests from its various affiliates. Some of these organizations undoubtedly pursued an agenda from 2001 onwards to highlight the indelible split between

---

[74] Remarks by the (then) Director of Central Intelligence, George J. Tenet, at the Nixon Center Distinguished Service Award Banquet, 11 December 2002.

[75] Ansari, H., *Muslims in Britain* (London: Minority Rights Group International, 2002).

[76] Eatwell, R., 'Community Cohesion and Cumulative Extremism in Contemporary Britain', *Political Quarterly*, Vol. 77, No. 2, 2006, pp. 204–16.

[77] Davultoglu, A., 'The Clash of Interests: An Explanation of the World (Dis)order', *Journal of International Affairs*, Vol. 2, No. 4, December 1997–February 1998.

Muslims and their co-nationals in Britain, not least at a time when external and internal pressures were fuelling a polarization of mass attitudes. The argument that ran through the spine of MCB's grassroots movement was that a Muslim faith dimension to British politics had effectively been frozen out of high-level, serious debate over a number of years. The principal reason for this exclusion, so the criticism ran, was that a form of blind, unwitting anti-Muslim prejudice—echoed in various timely contributions—had been present throughout. Ultimately, it was argued that the British government's own limitations in addressing its internal religious exclusion was rather more than a residual irritation faced by ordinary Muslims who had disproportionately supported the Labour Party in (and out of) office. Rather, this tension constituted a major flaw in Labour's long-term ability to aggregate and represent the supposedly discrete interests of its Muslim minority members and supporters.

The question of how far the Labour Party has succeeded in tackling this task is a matter that is taken up more extensively later in this book. However, the important point to stress here is that this critique of Labour and Britain had, by the early years of the new millennium, resulted in strong pressure to establish a tough counter-narrative of exclusion. Many of these pressures were equally resisted by others taking a more moderate line and also taking issue with the core criticism that held that Britain was riddled with anti-Muslim policies, procedures, practices, and values.

The point to draw out of the rise of MCB's internal hard-line is not so much that radical and moderate voices differed in their assessments of anti-Muslim prejudice but, rather, that the eventual lines of disagreement were also mapped on the basis of group membership. In other words, MCB (like many other umbrella organizations) was also involved in a basic debate over the relevance of the common experience of anti-Muslim prejudice. This experience, said to bind together other minorities, some religious, others not, was in essence conceptualized in religiously exclusive terms. That is, it was the personal and collective experience of Muslims, whether actual or in principle, that counted in determining the calculus of authenticity and conviction. The role of non-Muslim opinion was viewed, at best, with caution and suspicion. Indeed, the prevailing value system that had placed weight on cross-group campaigns to tackle anti-Muslim prejudice within and beyond politics was taken by many radicals as a target to be assaulted. The position of Tony Blair specifically, once one of the most vocal opponents of anti-Muslim sentiment, particularly encapsulates the division. His argument, championing the liberal cause, centred on the indictment that Muslim tendencies towards separatism stood to legitimize religious barriers and exclusion—or 'reverse faith Apartheid' in the slogan of the times. This, liberals argued, would undermine more general efforts to remove religious discrimination from society.

However, the counter-criticism launched against Blair and similar figures, more-or-less personally, was that his argument represented an outdated form of paternalism that would render ethnic and religious minorities ever more dependent on existing political leadership.

Sources of Political Difference

At its heart, the dispute revolved around this basic question of how far, if at all, progressive non-Muslim opinion could empathize with and internalize the experience of Muslim minorities. The question has been put in a number of more complex ways against the backdrop of controversial episodes from 2001 onwards. It highlights very effectively the intellectual and tactical position taken by radicals in their philosophy of autonomy based on authenticity of experience and perspective.[78] Additionally, the new movements not only reflected but also contributed substantially to the growth in such thinking in British religious and ethnic politics.

The leadership of all the major political parties has been clear in its rejection of discrete institutional bodies for the purposes of Muslim representation, yet has also been willing to accept that a limited degree of autonomy cannot—and probably ought not to—be resisted. Pragmatic politics, in other words, has meant that, contrary to common belief, key aspects of the discrete faith agenda advocated by MCB and others have been recognized in mainstream British politics. These movements may have yielded little by way of genuine sectional autonomy, but their passion and commitment has undoubtedly meant that a 'faith dimension' is taken more seriously in mainstream political circles. As the discussion later in this book goes on to observe, the evidence on Muslim minority political attitudes shows that the argument might be taken a little too seriously.

The difficulty faced by researchers and commentators in this area is to find a way of gauging the extent to which the political attitudes and outlook of Muslims is founded *overwhelmingly* or *exclusively* on religious difference. It may be quite easy to show that minorities have some degree of sympathy with the notion that minority group membership sets minorities apart from their non-minority counterparts in terms of their experiences and ability to empathize with minority experience. However, this may be a long way short of deep and widespread sympathy (though there is disagreement over how this sentiment might be reliably measured).[79] Additionally, there remains a powerful distinction between underlying support for this position on one hand and willingness to accept religious divisions as informing and influencing political

---

[78] Fukyama, F., 'Identity and Migration', *Prospect*, 131, February 2007.

[79] Chaitin, J., 'Stories, Narratives and Storytelling', in Burgess, G., and Burgess, H. (eds.), *Beyond Intractability* (Boulder, CO: Conflict Research Consortium, July 2003).

attitudes on the other. Voting or any other kind of political mobilization on these kinds of grounds is yet another matter, the evidence for which remains patchy and not easy to interpret. Research that is to be meaningful must, therefore, seek empirical evidence that shows a *sustained pattern* of political attitudes exclusively, or even overwhelmingly, based on religious difference and division.

It is on this basis that it may be possible to speak meaningfully of a Muslim faith agenda in British politics. Such an agenda, to be sure, is a powerful interpretative tool for those seeking to explain Muslim participation in British politics. Sustained supportive evidence of this kind amounts to reliable grounds for a religiously related theory of political behaviour noted previously. The challenge in theoretical terms is to identify and describe the religious faith and faith-related prism through which the world is perceived and understood politically.

It is no secret that empirical evidence to support this position has been extremely limited and often reliant on interpretative stretching of one kind or another. Take for instance the notion that a core Muslim faith agenda might be based on a collective view held by Muslims which sees Britain in religiously hostile terms. A survey published in 2007 by Policy Exchange, a London-based, centre-right think tank, reported, somewhat surprisingly, that well over four-fifths of Muslim respondents accepted that Britain was a society in which opportunities for advancement among Muslims were generally widespread. It was not, in other words, an example of a society especially characterized by religious exclusion against its Muslim members.[80] However, two caveats are attached to this powerful finding. First, the attitudes of younger Muslim respondents, who might have been expected to follow a similar path, were less emphatic: a large minority of younger Muslims dissented from the favourable characterization offered by their parents. Some have suggested that such a proposition merely reflects attitudes that commonly follow socio-economic progress among different ethnic groups, but it is important to remember that the Muslim faith agenda thesis is essentially a faith cognitive prism rather than a faith monitor of experience. In any case, the socio-economic profile of younger Muslims tends in almost all cases to be stronger than for older Muslims. The two dimensions are undoubtedly interlinked as experience ordinarily informs frameworks of perception. However, we should be concerned that a large number of younger respondents dissented from this view in comparison with older respondents. The second caveat is that these data do not extend to non-Muslims so the element of direct, informed comparison is lost. It is not known how many non-Muslim respondents also adopted the same view. If the evidence showed that this positive viewpoint was commonplace

---

[80] Mirza, M., Senthilkumaran, A., and Zein, J., *Living Apart Together: British Muslims and the Paradox of Multiculturalism* (London: Policy Exchange, 2007).

among non-Muslims (and it is likely that this is indeed the case), then the grounds for a Muslim faith agenda tend to weaken further.[81] Such a finding would in fact render obsolete the idea that quasi-universal views based on religious difference are the product of actual minority group membership. In fact they are not, and the closeness of the cross-faith group findings are significant barriers to the development of any world view of a Muslim faith agenda.

That said, earlier work from writers such as Miles[82] and Troyna[83] reminds us that attitudes about racial and ethnic distance might be less reflective of a white-dominated society and more intertwined with feelings of strong reactive ethnic pride. So-called cultures of resistance, as some have put it, draw equally on counter-hostility toward 'white society' and white-dominated institutions on one hand and on group assertiveness and self-promotion on the other. The point that matters, then, is that talk of a discrete faith agenda ought probably to allow for minority attitudes that are not just focused on British society but also sensitive to group consciousness and solidarity. The latter can be a potentially powerful resource for the creation and sustenance of collective political identity and action.

An even more ambitious attempt to identify the basis for a Muslim faith agenda has been the suggestion that Muslims may be distanced from broad visions of British history and traditions. Some of these visions, it is argued, are at best indirectly hostile to the historic background of minorities generally and Muslims specifically and, at worst, might be cynically designed to incite greater inter-faith chauvinism than already exists. A pamphlet published almost a decade ago by the Institute of Public Policy Research, a left-leaning think tank, made the complaint that a progressively minded Labour administration was guilty of using old, out-of-date visions of British history that could only alienate ethnic minority Britons. Quoting Tony Blair's 1996 remarks acclaiming 'a thousand years of British history' and boasting of 'the largest empire the world has ever known', the report's author responded dismissively with the claim that:[84]

Black and Asian Britons are unlikely to feel much enthusiasm for this particular British achievement. [Blair's speech is] a case of political leadership attempting to address the aspirations of one section of the population at the expense of the rest.

The logic of this indictment was that ethnic and religious minorities stood on one side of this vision of national history while their white and Protestant

---

[81] Alam, M. Y., and Husband, C., *British-Pakistani Men from Bradford* (York: Joseph Rowntree Foundation, 2006).

[82] Miles, R., 'Racism, Marxism and British Politics', *Economy and Society*, 17 (3), 1978, pp. 428–60.

[83] Troyna, B., 'Differential Commitment of Ethnic Identity by Black Youths in Britain', *New Community*, 7(3), 1979.

[84] Alibhai-Brown, Y., *True Colours: Public Attitudes to Multiculturalism and the Role of Government* (London: Institute for Public Policy Research, 1999).

counterparts remained on the other. Indeed, at one level, the proposition could hold sufficient weight if tested against the likelihood of different ethnic and faith groups attaching themselves to such a vision. However, looking beyond likelihood measures, there is also a need to consider whether the levels of tacit approval of, even endorsement for, such a speech in fact vary between different ethnic and faith groups. Furthermore, there remains the obvious Achilles heel in the IPPR author's charge: how far does the evidence directly point to opinion dividing according to ethnic or faith background? The claim, in other words, takes as read that some people—whites and Christians from an indigenous background—cannot possibly support an anti-imperialistic or critical line in relation to British history. This cannot be defended in the sense that a range of opinion can be found on this vision among the society at large and, it might be added, even among some ethnic and faith minorities. If quasi-imperialist visions of national history are said to be the kinds of building blocks underpinning a Muslim faith agenda, the primary difficulty lies in demonstrating in evidence that this fissure both exists and goes beyond differential likelihood.[85] Certainly, the US case often reminds us that Southern Confederate models of national—or just even regional—history can certainly act as a powerful ideological and cultural cleavage between racial and ethnic groups. In that sense, the IPPR claim must necessarily be taken seriously. However, such a claim requires extensive empirical probing in order to allow useful conclusions to be drawn. Such a rigorous exploration remains patchy in the literature, though some further light is thrown on this question later in this book.

The polling examples cited above illustrate another continuing problem. That is, although some survey data can reveal evidence of common feeling and sentiment about ethnic- and faith-related matters, they are less successful in mapping the *depth* of such attitudes. Opinion comparing ethnic and faith groups, and even subgroups, on a particularly sensitive and reliable indicator might be skewed in one particular direction according to certain data. However, little can be deduced about how strongly such attitudes are held. Indeed, one of the biggest bugbears in the academic literature is the recurring tendency of researchers and commentators to assume that minority ethnic and faith group voters are equally motivated by a set of core concerns. To compound this basically ill-informed assumption, the analytical distortion is made substantially worse by the accompanying belief that these supposed ethnic or faith concerns are either the biggest influences on minorities (at best) or an exclusive causal influence pushing out all other factors (at worst). The latter is a restatement of the analytical approach taken by supporters

[85] Appiah, K. A., *Cosmopolitanism: Ethics in a World of Strangers* (New York: W. W. Norton & Co., 2006).

of the Muslim 'faith agenda' school of thought (discussed earlier), and it is certainly a large and questionable assumption to make casually.

The evidence over the years has pointed to a striking high level of similarity between the political agenda of different ethnic and faith groups in Britain.[86] Variance has been uncovered in some polling evidence but it has often been at the margins. That is to say, where ethnic or religious minorities (or minority subgroups) highlighted attachment to specific issues that did not fully square with the pattern shown by their non-minority counterparts, this difference was normally easy to explain and thought to be linked to apparently known factors. For instance, a 1991 survey of Asian voters by Harris Polling revealed that a noticeable 37 per cent of respondents felt that racial attacks were the most pressing issue they faced.[87] The findings of this evidence have been replicated through more recent surveys and these also show similar patterns. However, the main point about the long-dated 1991 results was that the racial or ethnic dimension of political issues was conspicuously not interpreted in any generalized, non-specific terms. Quite the contrary was true, namely, that race and racism were explicitly linked to hostility and/or violence.

This did not imply that these respondents were unconcerned about the effects of racism in other spheres, and indeed one interpretation might be that sentiment about racial attacks was the tip of a much larger iceberg that related to wider feelings of victimhood, both individual and collective, held by Asians. The impact of race appeared to leave more than a third of Asians feeling especially vulnerable to a particular kind of violence and intimidation. This interaction is much in the same way as Muslims in general may feel exposed and liable to casual assumptions and charges about their faith group's association with modern acts of terrorism. The psychological effects of this exposure at group level, priming the individual to stand up defensively, are critical.[88] The priority of the issue could possibly be limited to a set of law-and-order concerns but might equally be a mask for much deeper-seated worries over security. The former spin would allow us to conclude that the 'race agenda' amounted to a racialized aspect of otherwise mainstream issues of law and order. The latter, however, is less easy to force into this type of analytical straitjacket. This account suggests that a form of personal and group vulnerability, leading to the potential for defensive group consciousness, was hidden beneath the superficially narrowly defined issue of racial attacks. Likewise, recent years have witnessed plenty of examples of Muslim groups and

---

[86] Saggar, S., *Race and Representation* (Manchester: Manchester University Press, 2000).

[87] Harris Research Centre (1991), 'Asian Poll 1991', survey conducted for BBC Pebble Mill, unpublished data set JN99245.

[88] Alderdice (Lord), J., 'The Individual, the Group and the Psychology of Terrorism', *International Review of Psychiatry*, Vol. 19, No. 3, June 2007.

leaders describing feelings of isolation, victimhood, and frustration through a single lens defined not just by faith but rather by endemic religious conflict.[89]

There is great scope for generalization about the impact of ethnic or religious identity seeping into numerous indirectly connected issues and, possibly, shaping the agenda for new political issues altogether, a point made earlier. We can see, then, that advocates of the Muslim faith agenda school of thought also rely on a somewhat broader reading of the evidence. Placing groups' attitudinal responses against each other does not end by merely reporting overt lines of departure between them. Rather there is an assumed need to account for these differences in a way that is not just circumstantial but also geared to uncovering the cross-cutting and indirect influence of ethnic or religious identity among political issues as a whole.

Conclusions

This chapter has been concerned with how to think about identity conceptually. It has looked at a range of ways to organize identity and identities, only some of which relate directly to religious faith. The overriding issue has been to assess how far particularistic identities can be used to inform and organize political choice.

But has anything useful been added to our understanding of the shape of political choice by focusing on identity and identity politics in this way? This is important if scholars and practitioners are to obtain a handle on faith-based identity as a way for governments to relate to citizens. Moreover, the nature of the task is such that policymakers will be interested in particular ways of constructing corporate identities if this is at all possible.[90] Looking at the outlook and behaviour of Western Muslims, for instance, does not tell us a great deal to start with. Therefore it is necessary to think, however artificially in terms of hard evidence, about these communities as if they subscribed to and operated with a sense of unified, collective identity.

For social researchers and theorists, the challenge is to examine the case for (and against) a faith identity-based theory of political thought and behaviour. There are several possibilities. First, it can be argued that Muslims can, in principle, be moved politically according to completely different and discrete criteria not shared by non Muslims—something that supporters of this standpoint would claim amounted to a Muslim political agenda. The evidence to

---

[89] Blick, A., Choudhary, T., and Weir, S., *The Rules of the Game: Terrorism, Community and Human Rights* (Democratic Audit/Joseph Rowntree Reform Trust/University of Essex Human Rights Centre, 2007).

[90] Friedman, T. L., *Longitudes and Attitudes: Exploring the World After September 11th* (New York: Farrar, Straus & Giroux, 2002).

back this is undoubtedly patchy, but there is no mistaking the political head of steam that has been established by particular lobbies and pressure groups in support of such a position.

Second, it may be suggested that the political outlook and actions of Muslims are based on the same range of issues and concerns as non-Muslims but on slightly (perhaps greatly) reordered sets of priorities. For example, we already know that the age profile and demographic structure of many Muslim communities in Western societies is sufficiently different from others in those societies. It is little wonder then that the political importance of schools stands out in terms of its saliency given the large family sizes and high birth rates that are involved. The main point is that Muslim identity of any kind is only very indirectly driving the agenda of salient concerns for these communities. For the most part, these are the result of skews in population structures and characteristics.

A third possibility is that while Muslims may have precisely the same agenda of issues and concerns as non-Muslims, beneath this, virtually all issues are perceived through a faith-related lens—a 'Muslim twist' so to speak. This stems from two sources. The first is the claim made by numerous Islamic theorists about the all-encompassing remit and reach of Islam into society and family. The idea of a public (secular) domain is one that is frequently dismissed, suggesting that Islam's influence is not indirect or via segmented personal choices. The other source, particularly in recent years, has been the tendency to accentuate the religious faith identity of Muslims-in-conflict in particular and to see this in uni-dimensional terms.

Finally, a fourth way of thinking about faith and corporate political identity has been to reject the suggestion that Islam (or indeed faith) has a particular or even relevant role to play. Thus, the political agenda of this religious minority group is but a microcosm of the outlook and behaviour of society at large. It has to be said that the political outlook and behaviour of Muslims in countries such as Britain is, in fact, somewhat unlike that of society at large. The real debate instead falls on the sources of political difference and specifically the extent to which this is caused by Muslim group identity of one kind or another.[91] There is, in fact, growing evidence to point to circumstantial reasons for such political difference. The likelihood of effective understanding of Muslim communities through a conceptual lens that negates the importance of Muslim identity is, however, rather slim.

The policy implications of these conceptual distinctions can be considerable. For instance, a number of political campaigns have been waged in Western societies aimed at the articulation and registering of distinctive ethno-religious claims. Some have been fuelled by a 'fair shares' logic that

---

[91] Zunes, S., 'Political Islam: Revealing the Roots of Extremism', Centre for Policy Analysis on Palestine, 2005.

has concentrated on distributional outcomes in politics and in economics, sometimes at the expense of ignoring participatory norms about democratic inputs.[92] This tendency, of course, has been most pronounced in the USA in relation to the racial scar of slavery and its aftermath. But it is an approach that is heavily dependent on strong lines of collective, corporate identity held by particular ethnic groups to begin with. By contrast, equal opportunity strategies pursued more vigorously elsewhere have taken a more relaxed view of group identity. The job is mainly to concentrate on identifying barriers to participation, and to remove these in proportionate and timely ways, so as to maximize opportunity structures working to benefit those who have previously experienced exclusion. Strong identity groups among the disadvantaged are helpful lubricants in this process, but a commitment to uni-dimensional identity politics probably is not.

This book is about a number of national country cases that straddle this distinction. It is, therefore, not desirable to make larger or more generalizations than are strictly necessary about the longer-term impacts of recent tendencies towards heightened faith-based identity among Western Muslims.[93] What is more useful is to make the point that national traditions towards social inclusion, especially when underpinned by ethnic and religious diversity, are important conditioners of outcomes that require some consideration.

[92] UNDP, *Human Development Report 2005*, 'International Cooperation at a Crossroads: Aid, Trade and Security in an Unequal World' (New York: UNDP, 2005).

[93] UNAoC, *Alliance of Civilisations Report*, Final Report of the High-Level Group, 13 November 2006.

4

Integration and Identity Politics

When you have a pathway to a man or a woman living in big mansion high on a hill, you tend to focus on the path and on achieving your dreams. When you have no pathway, you tend to focus on your wrath and on nursing your memories.

Thomas L. Friedman[1]

The idea that Americans—residents of the most powerful land in history—are now truly living in fear of Bin Laden has failed to impress the majority of people around the globe, whose concerns about terrorism are dwarfed by the challenge they face in simply staying alive despite the ever-present perils of poverty, hunger and disease.

Madeleine K. Albright[2]

Introduction

Western Europe, and increasingly North America, has in the later part of the twentieth century become associated with significant Muslim-minority populations as a result of large-scale immigration. Descriptions of those migratory flows and the Muslim populations that have settled in Western Europe were provided in Chapter 2. That chapter noted the large element of internal differentiation and heterogeneity in the various Muslim communities of Western Europe. Although a number of those communities are associated with post-war labour migration into growing industrial economies, it is also clear that the sources and circumstances of their migration has varied a great deal. The Turkish guest worker-derived community of Germany differs in important ways from the North African communities of France, for example. The heavy influx of refugee communities into the Netherlands, many

---

[1] Friedman, T., *The World is Flat: The Globalised World in the Twenty-first Century* (London: Penguin, 2005).
[2] Albright, M., 'Bridges, Bombs or Bluster?', *Foreign Affairs*, Vol. 82, No. 5, September/October 2003, p. 19.

from Muslim regions such as the Horn of Africa and the Maghrib, has resulted in a different dynamic. Meanwhile, Britain's more recent Bangladeshi influx has tended to originate from a poor, rural, agrarian background to a much greater extent than its other longer-standing South Asian communities. In this chapter, the focus of the discussion changes to examine in some detail the dominant ideas and approaches towards the inclusion of migrants and foreigners across Western Europe. The localized context of migrants and the descendents, in other words, is sufficiently important as a set of explanatory variables. Therefore, some space needs to be devoted to exploring not just the varied experiences of European Muslims but also the specific historical and ideological environments in which they live, if not always easily, with their non-Muslim neighbours.[3]

The aim of this chapter is to introduce some appropriate context for understanding on one hand the trajectory of settlement and progression patterns and on the other the soil in which the roots of alienation and extremism have taken hold.[4] It is not reasonable to claim, casually, that Western Muslim communities are locked in conflict with European societies, let alone much larger claims about feelings towards Muslims operating as fifth column aliens in Europe. Grains of truth in these sweeping claims do not obviate the need to investigate the nature and reasoning of different national traditions and approaches to the rapid appearance of ethnic and religious diversity. This chapter is interested in how and why the inclusion of migrants and minorities varies across Europe and elsewhere. This chapter is also interested in examining the peculiarities of religious identity in different Western countries and linking this to thinking about and approaches to social inclusion.

The case of Western Muslim communities, as we shall see, sits in a range of complex national traditions, and it is therefore unattractive to view Muslim grievance or agitation in entirely stand-alone terms. Of course this is precisely the temptation that a number of other analyses have succumbed to, all too often resulting in a picture of Western Muslims standing indelibly outside the mainstream of Western economies and societies.[5] In many cases, there is evidence to reinforce this picture but it is often something that runs counter to extant thinking and practice about the integration of Muslim communities.

The bulk of this chapter deals with Britain and its substantial grounding in responding to ethnic pluralism. The challenge of religious pluralism is not altogether easily grafted on to institutions and practices geared to sensitizing

---

[3] 'Culture Clash: Islam in Europe', *Economist*, 15 July 2006, p. 46.

[4] Coussey, M., 'Framework of Integration Policies', Council of Europe, Strasbourg, 2000.

[5] Saikal, A., *Islam and the West: Conflict or Cooperation?* (Basingstoke: Palgrave Macmillan, 2003).

public policy to the needs of ethnic differentiation.[6] Thereafter, attention is given to a series of other Western cases, most but not all sitting along a rough spectrum in which, in general terms, Britain has been keenest—and France the least keen—to accept ethnic and religious identity in the public sphere. Europe's 12–15 million Muslims are spread widely across these cases. This chapter also looks briefly at some non-European Western examples including Australia and Canada, both of which have been heavily conditioned by multiculturalist ideas and doctrines of group identities and rights. This chapter ends with a discussion of how and the degree to which localized context has contributed to the politics of alienation and support for strident interpretations of radical political Islam. Contests for the backing and loyalties of Western Muslim communities, it would appear, take place within a variety of contexts, some of which have been pilloried more than others for their negative consequences.[7] This chapter looks at the rationale and evidence for these critiques and feeds this into a better understanding of the causes of radicalization and extremism.

Europe's Muslims or European Muslims?

Notwithstanding the range of diversity found in the experiences and settings of European Muslim communities, it is probably worth starting with some broad visions that have been articulated about the future of Europe and its Muslim citizen members. That is to say, Europe's broad-brush experiences and ideas towards religious diversity generally, and Muslims specifically, needs to be considered before particular national-level differentiation is examined. This task is one that leads many commentators to probe the issue of how far, if at all, Muslims in Europe might be expected to vary in their experiences and outlook from the bulk of immigrants and newcomers who have established new lives across the continent.[8] Muslims, therefore, have either followed broadly within a range of comparable groups of migrants and their offspring or, alternatively, they have veered towards an exceptional path of their own. This assessment is largely independent of the growing appearance of conflict Islam and European societies, but eventually there is—or there must be, unavoidably so—some cross-fertilization of evidence and evaluation.

---

[6] Saggar, S., 'Boomerangs and Slingshots: Radical Islamism and Counter-Terrorism Strategy', *Journal of Ethnic and Migration Studies*, forthcoming.

[7] See, for example, Sayyid, B., *A Fundamental Fear: Eurocentrism and the Emergence of Islamism* (London: Zed Books, 1997).

[8] Portes, A., 'Globalisation from Below: The Rise of Transnational Communities', *Global Networks: A Journal of Transnational Affairs*, Vol. 1, No. 3, 2001, pp. 181–94.

This question in turn is linked to some longer-run debates about the role of secular influences and secularism in Islam and among Muslim communities.[9]

One of the most striking has been advanced by Gilles Kepel, a French commentator, who has tracked the rise of political Islam within Europe. He posits an 'optimistic vision' in relation to the second and third generation of these migrant communities as the 'ideal bearers of a modernity' drawn from their European environment. The significance of this characterization lies in the vision it establishes for the future direction of Islam and the Muslim world, to say nothing of the development and democratization prospects for those parts of the world. Against current received wisdom, he writes convincingly of the possibilities for borrowing and learning across the Muslim and non-Muslim divide:[10]

[Western Europe's Muslims] . . . are potential purveyors of these values [of modernity] to the countries from which their families emigrated. They offer an alternative to increased religiosity, which has served as both an ideological shield for corrupt authoritarian regimes and as outlet for the social rage of a dispossessed population. Europe's young Muslims will become the international vectors of a democratic project whose success they themselves embody—by blending innate Arab or Muslim traits with acquired European ones.

This is an imaginative and even inspiring account of the future development of European Muslim identity. It contains strong elements of transnational links and identity that may be harnessed for objectives that have hitherto not been especially associated with European Muslim populations. But, most important of all, the Kepelian vision propels us to consider more rigorously the question of Muslim and European identity. There is an implicit presumption that European traditions for the development of social inclusion public policies are sufficiently flexible and oriented to the needs of Muslim communities. There is certainly a lively debate on this point alone, and it must be remembered that social inclusiveness of this kind remains a fairly large challenge already.[11]

However, Kepel is pushing in a more ambitious direction altogether in describing such European Muslim integration as a natural bulwark against the attraction of extremism. Moreover, the positive vision is also a powerful fresh means for Western societies to bridge with the traditional Muslim world. It is this world that remains the biggest source of destabilization and extremism,

---

[9] Boroujerdi, M., 'Can Islam be Secularised?', in Ghanoonparvar, M. R., and Farookh, F. (eds.), *In Transition: Essays on Culture and Identity in Middle Eastern Societies* (Centre for Middle Eastern Studies/University of Texas, 1994).

[10] Kepel, G., *The War for Muslim Minds: Islam and the West* (Cambridge, MA: Harvard University Press, 2004), p. 249.

[11] Sardar, Z., 'The Excluded Minority: British Muslim Identity after 11 September', in Griffith, P., and Leonard, M. (eds.), *Reclaiming Britishness* (London: Foreign Policy Centre, 2002).

according to this view, because of the corrupt and distortive use of Islam that is commonplace. Kepel's account is therefore not just about trying to foster successful, integrated Muslims in Europe itself. It is also, rather controversially, about 'assisting North Africa, the Middle East and Pakistan emerge from the quagmire'. Hitherto, it should be recalled, the capacity of European and Muslim countries to engage has been at a more pedestrian level. Any hint of engagement with the future trajectory of Muslim countries has been fiercely resisted by post-imperial generations who have been keen to assert national self-determination. The involvement of European Muslims in such an ambit is therefore a new ingredient but nevertheless one that represents sorely needed fresh thinking. It is further reinforced when looking at America's Muslim communities in terms of basic understandings of participation and democratic process.[12] At a more basic level, this account also implies that the Western governments will have the capacity and willingness to tackle the real difficulties facing their Muslim communities in terms of accessing better opportunity structures in the future.[13] This is obviously a debatable point. It is something that will be returned to later in this chapter as well as in Chapter 7, which is concerned with the strategic responses of governments to the simultaneous risks of exclusion and extremism.

Set against this vision is a much more pessimistic one that has inevitably received greater attention in recent years. This account is largely predicated on seeing Muslim communities remaining in weak and precarious positions in education and the labour market. Moreover socio-economic weakness is coupled with a social and cultural disengagement with Western society. Elements of this pattern are already evident on the outskirts of many French cities[14] and in the inner city areas of most medium-to-large British cities. The living of separate or parallel lives by young Muslims in these places is especially concerning and surprising given the wealth of attention given by policymakers to ideas of second-generation improved circumstances coupled with steady dispersal. Younger Muslims, in other words, will increasingly choose a form of cultural separatism in communities that are more and more inward-looking.[15] The external Western environment may be rejected and also kept at arm's length by institutions such as mosques and schools, however unintentionally. Routine contact with workplace colleagues or neighbours drawn from outside Muslim communities will be as rare as it is

---

[12] Poston, L. A., 'Da 'wa in the West', in Yazback (ed.), *The Muslims of America* (Oxford: Oxford University Press, 1991).

[13] This familiar suggestion is advanced in general terms, for example, by Radcliffe, L., 'A Muslim Lobby at Whitehall? Examining the Role of the Muslim Minority in British Foreign Policy-Making', unpublished M.Phil. Thesis, University of Oxford, 2003.

[14] Kapil, A., 'Les Parties Islamistes en Algerie: Elements de Presentation', *Maghreb-Machrek*, Vol. 133, 1991, pp. 103–11.

[15] Samad, Y., 'Book Burning and Race Relations: Political Mobilisation of Asians in Bradford', *New Community*, Vol. 18, No. 4, 1992.

welcome. Issues of foreign policy and Western governments' posture towards the 'Muslim World' may exacerbate tensions further.[16]

This picture is obviously unattractive to many European governments who already have signalled their determination to avoid such an outcome. Nevertheless, such a reality is already to be found on a significant scale in a number of European countries.[17] The more sinister part of this vision stems from the political opportunities it creates for a variety of extremists. Some may use the social and cultural isolation of these Muslim communities to promote the appeal of living at a distance from 'corrupt' and 'immoral' practices of Western society.[18] The withdrawal into a separate Muslim world, within a non-Muslim one, appears attractive to many who have become embittered by the criticisms of Islam heard routinely in the society at large. The semi-involuntary nature of the community's collective withdrawal from wider society can certainly be presented as a natural, defensive response to the fractious relations between Muslims and non-Muslims. Being 'forced' to withdraw because of the lack of legitimacy afforded to a pariah community can, itself, generate significant ideological fodder for radical organizations.[19] Some of these organizations will be content with cultural distance as an end in itself to minimize, if not eliminate, the harmful influence of an 'unbelieving' secular society. Others, however, will wish to capitalize on the hostility shown to Muslims to encourage an aggressive, potentially violent, response in kind. Muslims, in these circumstances, would be regularly reminded of their obligation to defend Islam, and fighting against Western society, institutions, or symbols can be easily defined as an appropriate and proportionate outlet for such grievance. Weakening or damaging non-Muslim society thus becomes one readily available means of supporting and strengthening Muslim communities. Violence, in such a scenario, is presented as an unavoidable lubricant in a mechanistic battle to defend Muslims' faith and creed.[20]

Significantly, both kinds of withdrawal are in reality closely interwoven. That is, there is no easy means of describing withdrawal without the aggressive grievance from withdrawal that goes with it. Kepel and others have noted that both forms are closely linked to Salafist thinking and movements, some of which see themselves in equal combat with Western and Arab governments. The latter have become known as 'jihadists' and have labelled

[16] Sahgal, G., 'Blair's Jihad, Blunkett's Crusade: The Battle for the Hearts and Minds of Britain's Muslims', *Radical Philosophy*, Vol. 112, 2002.

[17] Esposito, J. L., and Mogahed, D., 'What Makes a Muslim Radical?', *Foreign Policy*, November 2006.

[18] Miles, H., 'Think Again: Al Jazeera', *Foreign Policy*, July/August 2006.

[19] Mandaville, P., *Transnational Muslim Politics: Reimagining the Umma* (London: Routledge, 2001).

[20] Lawrence, B. B., *Shattering the Myth: Islam Beyond Violence* (Princeton, NJ: Princeton University Press, 1998).

Western countries as a land of war (*Dar al-Harb*) in which religious-inspired violence against apostates is condoned.[21] The idea of the integration of Muslims into the mainstream of Europe is deeply threatening to organizations and groups that operate within this framework of belief.[22] Therefore, the success of policy measures to integrate Muslims is viewed with suspicion. The foundations for doing so are essentially a rejection of the moral fabric of Western society coupled with a formal statement of belief that sees Muslims in the West as required to take to battle to combat the enemies of Islam.[23]

This is so deeply pessimistic a vision that it fuses the alienation and grievance of young Muslims with a political message of aggression and violent conflict.[24] The isolated, ghetto identity of European Muslims is a prerequisite for this vision, and much of the remainder of this chapter is devoted to examining national approaches to mitigate the risk of such an outcomes in different parts of Europe.

Britain's Race Relations Model

The integration of Commonwealth immigrants into British society has become a long-term objective of governments of all shades of opinion for half a century. The task has thus appeared both familiar and instinctive for British policymakers. It has become, and remains, a common piece of the political landscape, although there are contrasting ideas and political approaches to the practice of integration. So while liberal thinking has dominated the framework of public policy over most of this period, there has been no shortage of conservative critiques of integration policy as being too one-sided and insufficiently grounded in British history and values.[25] Radical critics, meanwhile, regularly decry the culture of inexplicitness over race, and racial discrimination, they argue, hallmarks the British approach to integration.[26]

[21] Ansari, H., 'Attitudes to Jihad, Martyrdom and Terrorism among British Muslims', in Abbas, T. (ed.), *Muslim Britain: Communities Under Pressure* (London: Zed Books, 2005).

[22] Muoz, G., *Islam, Modernism and the West* (London: I. B. Tauris, 1999).

[23] Malise, R., *A Satanic Affair: Salman Rushdie and the Rage of Islam* (London: Chatto and Windus, 1990).

[24] Kepel, G., *Allah and the West: Islamic Movements in America and Europe* (Cambridge: Polity Press, 2000).

[25] Saggar, S., 'Integration and Adjustment: Britain's Liberal Settlement Revisited', in Lowe, D. (ed.), *Immigration and Integration: Australia and Britain* (London: Bureau of Immigration, Multi-cultural and Population Research, Australia/Sir Robert Menzies Centre for Australian Studies, 1995); Saggar, S., 'A Late, Though not Lost, Opportunity: British Ethnic Minority Electors and the Conservative Party', *Political Quarterly*, 69, 1998, pp. 148–59.

[26] Saggar, S., and Geddes, A., 'Negative and Positive Racialisation: Ethnic Minority Political Representation in the UK', *Journal of Ethnic and Migration Studies*, 26, 2000, pp. 1–29.

Britain has rapidly established an official multicultural doctrine that openly recognizes and celebrates ethnic and religious distinctiveness. The cultural traditions and practices of immigrant groups are valued both for the strengthened identity that they provide for newcomers and for the variety that they contribute to society at large. The doctrine has not been without its tensions or controversies. For example, a standard point of concern has been the capacity of multicultural ideas to promote equally the principles of commonness and shared national values. The criticism has been that, in the rush to support and respect diverse identities and cultures, there has been a distinct weakness in building a cohesive, national sense of Britishness. Another, related controversy has been the question of where and how far limits to cultural distinctiveness can be set by the state. Certainly in the case of religious and cultural dress codes, the British government and courts have struggled to find a suitable balance between the projected claims of discrete minorities against the putative interests of all others.

However, despite these occasional difficulties, it is clear that Britain has gained a reputation for tolerating and often backing a far greater degree of cultural separateness than any example found elsewhere in modern Europe. Thus, Britain's self-image includes a strong reference to its own culturally diverse communities—something that, for example, underscored its claim to host the 2012 Olympics. Equally, the image of Britain received among its European neighbours contains a strong element of both official and societal diversity. Its reputation, in other words, is that of a modern industrial society that has supported the growth of multiple ethnic and religious cultures and identities which, despite setbacks, are not seen to be at odds with membership of the nation at large. This is obviously a delicate balance in practical terms since Britain, in common with other European democracies, has been scarred by racial violence and urban unrest on several occasions.

The distinctiveness of Britain's model also stands out because of its close association with US race relations. Indeed, large aspects of Britain's domestic anti-discrimination legal regime and policy framework have an intellectual pedigree that is derived from American thinking and practice towards racial desegregation and civil rights. There are major debates about the relevance of US race relations in the context of post-war immigrant integration to a medium-sized British economy geared to industrial recovery. Nevertheless, the link with the USA has meant that group identities and rights have been more rapidly feathered into the political lexicon of Britain than elsewhere in Europe.

The Muslim communities in Britain's multiculturalist model have encountered a twin-edged sword in pursuing their claims. On one hand, Britain has provided an environment that is relatively sensitive to the desires of cultural minorities to retain and promote their own identity. This has been a far more open setting to pursue such objectives than, say, France, which is officially wedded to assimilationist values requiring minorities to shed distinctive identities. Consequently, elaborate social and cultural ties uniting various minority groups are commonplace throughout Britain, and are especially deeply embedded among the country's Pakistani and Bangladeshi communities. These communities have by and large flourished in their capacity to recreate distinctive identities among their members. It could be said that elements of their strength are derived from the British tradition of allowing space and attention for groups to pursue such distinctive goals and identities. On the other hand, a number of Muslim political leaders have felt hindered by British multiculturalism's comparative neglect of rights based on religious identity and equality. Thus, the absence until recently of specific legal provision to prosecute against religious hatred has angered Muslim communities and their leaders. Equally, the lacuna in existing anti-discrimination law that has protected some religious minorities (e.g. Jews) but not others (e.g. Muslims) has been an especially sore issue among British Muslims. In other words, Britain's approach has readily sought to sensitize public policy to the needs of ethnic pluralism but has been not so overtly geared to the task of religious sensitization. This mismatch has fuelled a sense of grievance among Muslim communities who fear that the public reputation of Islam means that Muslims will be afforded the status of second-class citizens.

The approach taken by British governments to Muslim communities has evolved over many years. However, the approach tends to follow the logic of trying to facilitate the long-term integration of immigrant groups into British society. There are tensions within this immigrant integration policy in respect of both the unique aspects of different religions and its relevance for the circumstances of second- and third-generation immigrant-descended groups, many of whom identify with a faith thought to be under siege.

Immigrant integration objectives focus on the barriers to long-run access and achievement faced by the full range of immigrant and immigrant-descended groups. The religious backgrounds of each of these groups are treated as largely irrelevant from the point of view of integration policies. British Pakistanis and Bangladeshis are two important groups that have been subjects of this type of approach. The fact that both groups are predominantly made up of Muslims—who are internally differentiated on theological, linguistic, caste, class, and other grounds—is largely treated as being coincidental. The barriers that they face to integration can be identified on a range of fronts including educational choice and attainment, healthcare access and outcomes, employment opportunity, and achievement. However, many of these barriers are common to other, predominantly non-Muslim, immigrant

117

and immigrant-descended groups—for example, black Caribbeans and South Asian- and East African-origin Indians.[27]

The promotion of integration is a broad objective for government but has links to a range of other objectives. In Britain, it most closely related to the task of building a stable, cohesive society that is not overtly littered with mistrust and hatred across ethnic and religious lines. A more detailed consideration of the religious aspects of barriers to integration among different immigrant groups may enhance the economic and social outcomes for these groups. The evidence base supporting such barriers is mixed and difficult to interpret. This will be examined in more detail later in this chapter.

There are several strands of thought concerning integration policy. One of the major difficulties in application of the concept of integration is that it can often have different meanings. This may depend on precise usage but more commonly is the result of some genuine conceptual disputes over how far this embodies a two-way process of adaptation and mutual adjustment. If the underlying emphasis is on a one-way process in which immigrants and newcomers are the prime focus, it is possible to see that culturally distinct groups may react adversely. This may in fact be interpreted as a form of assimilation in which distinctiveness in cultural or other terms is seen as the source of the problem for policy to begin with. It goes without saying that assimilationist thinking and rhetoric has been scarce in the public domain in Britain precisely because of the negative backlash it might be expected to trigger from immigrant and minority leaders as well as from liberal opinion. At the heart of multiculturalist thought lies the belief that integration hangs upon the profile and progression of groups as a whole. Upward social mobility is judged, for instance, by the average record of the group relative to others although some attention may be paid to the spread of progress. The systematic lack of progress among some groups is understood at group level, the point at which various rights and opportunities are ascribed. Individual achievement, or lack of achievement, or opportunities structures facing individuals, or their absence, are all framed within the experience of the group at large.

In practice, multiculturalist and assimilationist ideas have been interwoven and played a part in shaping national debates about the absorption of immigrants as well as cultural and religious difference. British governments' policies have rarely addressed this ambiguity and tension explicitly. There are advantages and disadvantages to this approach. On the plus side, policies can be and have been tried that promote convergence between immigrant and immigrant-descended groups and their white counterparts which focus mainly on British-born groups. The position of first-generation groups matters less, in that time will shrink their relative size and impact on

---

[27] 'Keeping the Borders Open', *Economist* (Leader), 5 January 2008, pp. 8–9.

overall integration. On the down side, many policies can get bogged down because of a failure to win support from communities who fear dilution of their cultures and traditions. Even policies that have no purchase over cultural values and practices can be tarnished by the rejection of assimilation (Box 4.1).

Box 4.1 Aspects of Integration

Socio-economic integration[28]

Socio-economic integration refers to the utilization of acquired rights in the education system and labour market. In this area, the emphasis has tended to be on:

- Language training;
- Education;
- Employment and the development of social networks linked to the labour market; and
- Anti-discrimination.

Civil/Political integration

Civil/political integration refers to citizenship both as a formal status denoted by nationality laws and as a process of inclusion in the key institutions of modern society such as the welfare state and the political system.

Cultural integration

Cultural integration refers to processes of cognitive, cultural, behavioural, and attitudinal change in people. This raises the obvious questions of 'from what?', 'to what?' and 'by whom?' At the very least, this involves a shift from one form of heterogeneity to another with cultural requalification affecting both newcomers and members of the host society.

The question of Muslim communities' integration into British society has become the subject of considerable debate and dispute in recent years. The argument goes further than the well-rehearsed indicators of integration based on socio-economic progress, political participation, and even shared values, although these areas reveal some significant discrepancies of their own. Rather, the debate has shifted towards the degree to which religious identity and group rights are recognized as a means through which government policies can reach citizens. Thus, it is something of a means from integration policy efforts to having credibility and meaning among particular groups, of whom British Muslims are the best known for their position. The criticism voiced against government and public policy, in other words, has been that a blindness to faith identity has contributed to a lack of engagement between

---

[28] Adapted from Geddes, A., 'Ethnic Minorities in the Labour Market: Comparative Policy Approaches (Western Europe)', Report commissioned by the Performance and Innovation Unit, Cabinet Office, 2001; full report available at www.strategy.gov.uk.

citizens and the state. One notably colourful description has complained of a 'secular fundamentalism' rooted in government policy. Although this is a distortion in many ways, it does nevertheless capture the tone of the disillusionment, even resentment, felt by some Muslims, to say nothing of other faith leaders.

A fairer assessment would be to acknowledge that faith identities have not featured at the heart of integration policies chiefly because of the existing importance of ethnic identities, most of which are thought to subsume religious identities. In addition, public policy towards ethnic pluralism has regularly included aspects of religious observance and sensitivity as a matter of course. This can be seen in areas such as dietary requirements for hospital patients and prisoners, swearing of oaths in criminal and civil courts, and also in aspects of dress codes in state schools. Faith, in other words, is recognized and catered for in some areas of public policy, but the matter of degree and universal application is clearly much more variable. So far as Muslim communities are concerned, the response is largely coincidental and implicit in nature. The degree of explicitness and universality is the main area of contention.

Religion—and therefore the challenge of reasonable religious sensitization—is implicit in many existing public policies. Public policies that are appropriately and proportionately designed to take into account the legitimate sensitivities of different faith groups are, therefore, a powerful counterbalance to such complaints.

But, that said, it is equally important to ensure that policymakers avoid over-reach in their sensitization agendas and efforts. These religious sensitization policy adjustments may be successfully identified in principle, but they can prove hard to deliver in practical terms. For example, rebalancing the dietary policies of schools and hospitals can often be done with minimal controversy but the content of the religious education curriculum or dress codes in state schools often results in heated local disputes. By extension, policies to expand faith schools that are funded through public resources have, in Britain, attracted enormous dispute. With these practical reservations in mind, it is only fair to say that some such policies, or an excess of zeal in implementing or defending their indirect consequences, can serve to create new political problems. For instance, religious sensitization policy agendas might seek to deliver outcomes that protect certain faith groups from offence of one kind or another. This is terribly difficult to do in a mature liberal democracy and is likely to be wrong-headed in the sense that liberal democracies can seek to curb offence that is designed to incite hatred or violence, where this link is reasonably direct, but these political systems cannot automatically offer shields from criticism of one group by another. The goal of religious sensitization is therefore one that should be seen in its context, namely, to rebalance and adjust policies and programmes that unintentionally exclude religious minorities, particularly unpopular ones. This goal can be chimerical if it is used to shield faith communities entirely from critical comment, and can contribute to the underlying problem.[29]

The evidence that is currently available does not unambiguously point to British Muslim groups standing wholly separately from other immigrant and immigrant-descended groups. This suggests that either the British Muslim experience is not sufficiently distinctive (from other comparable groups with different religious backgrounds) or that the evidence base remains patchy and in need of refinement.

There is a further explanation that should be considered. This is that research and policy communities are poorly equipped to understand the religious dimension when formulating and implementing policy. The lack of understanding can be linked to the paucity of evidence. It should be possible to tackle this constraint. However, it may also be linked to the absence of a clear and transparent framework for understanding the religious aspects of social exclusion.[30] Among policymakers and interest groups, the example of Muslims in the labour market has been a good example to illustrate the lack of a clear consensus about such a framework. This is explained below in relation to the labour market disadvantage experienced by Pakistanis and Bangladeshis (most of whom are Muslims).

Religious Exclusion: Absence of Evidence or Evidence of Absence?

There is a growing body of research and interpretative literature (in Britain and elsewhere) examining the nature and causes of Muslim economic exclusion and the potential relationship to sources of radicalism. Despite this literature, there is very little reason to conclude that there is a common, shared understanding of these issues. The capacity of policymakers to craft suitable policies to address labour market achievements of British Muslims is, therefore, highly constrained as a result.

There are five co-related reasons why a lack of shared understanding remains a barrier to policy formulation.

- *Data sources*. The claim repeated frequently at the margins of the policy debate has been particularly poorly informed about the nature of evidence supporting a relationship between faith and outcomes in employment or education. This has suggested that 'we have the data', when in fact there is a confusion about different types of data and data analysis. A direct religious background item in the 2001 General Census allows some basic bi-variate analysis against a range of human capital outcomes and

[29] Joppke, C., 'Repressive Liberalism: State-Sponsored Integration of Muslims after 9/11', *Journal of Ethnic and Migration Studies*, forthcoming.
[30] 'The New Wars of Religion', *Economist* (Leader), 3 November 2007, p. 13.

labour market achievements. Moving to multivariate analysis of these data should not be quite the effort or risk that sceptics have portrayed. This would be a very helpful start since the historic use of country of origin as a rough proxy for Muslim is woefully inadequate. Indeed, to carry on while omitting a staggering 40 per cent of cases (using country of origin indicators) is worrying, especially if a much better alternative exists. Furthermore, as we have seen so often in studies of minority groups, placing faith in averages is often misleading, if not worse. The variance around the average position for Pakistanis and Bangladeshis (often collapsed together in any case) is simply too weak methodologically.

• *Religion and ethnicity*. Specifically, those who are doubtful about the analytical robustness of studies examining the relationship between faith and outcomes have argued that religion and ethnicity are highly co-linear. It is difficult to understand this claim for several reasons. First, it applies when looking at two of the recognized five ethnic minority groups (Pakistanis and Bangladeshis are around 96% and 98% of those of Muslim background) but does not apply when examining the story from the perspective of religious groups (40% of Muslims are neither Pakistanis nor Bangladeshis). Second, roughly 10 per cent of British Muslims are drawn from an Indian country of origin. This matters because of the startling evidence about their much better educational and labour market experiences, relative to Pakistani and Bangladeshi Muslims. This is at least prima facie evidence of an equally important country of origin effect alongside any inference regarding a religious effect. (Unpacking the Indian case, incidentally, could throw fresh light on the relationships and interactions at play since the absolute numbers are rather larger than their one in ten proportion suggests. Moreover, ethnographic and sociological research on chain migration, transnational links, settlement patterns, domestic circumstances, and so on points to key similarities and differences with Indian non-Muslims [a first comparator] and with Pakistani and Bangladeshi Muslims [helpfully, a second comparator]. To say that none of this story can be unpacked through statistical analysis is to draw an odd and rather arbitrary line in terms of research methodology.) Finally, supplementary sources of data about other important Muslim subgroups, for example Arabs (themselves subdivided on a variety of ethnic, country, and linguistic lines) and Ismailis (rather more homogeneous by comparison), suggest that religion and ethnicity are far from overlapping and co-linear.

• *Penalties and explanation*. There has been an unfortunate and rather predictable confusion about the term 'penalty', whether ethnic, religious, or both.[31] This is understandable since the term is deployed in a number

[31] Open Society Institute, *Aspirations and Reality: British Muslims and the Labour Market* (Budapest: OSI EU Monitoring and Advocacy Program, 2004), esp. section 4, pp. 30–2.

of sometimes inconsistent ways. Arriving at a balanced and sensible regression model requires an effort to go beyond bi-variate analysis. Selecting relevant factors to control for is important. However, the result is just what such a model claims to be: a quantitative estimate about unexplained variance. It is not a claim about penalties as such since this implies that the controls in the model are complete (exhaustive is the usual benchmark to aim for). Equally, there are inferences that can be read into multivariate analysis of this kind but much depends on the selection of controls, overall quality of data, and secondary issues such as missing data, weighting, use of proxies, and so on. However, the much bigger point is that if inferences can be drawn about 'penalties' that amount to a commentary about the extent of discrimination, it is only fair that other explanations are taken with equal seriousness. A front-runner here is the role of social capital broadly and of employment-related social networks more specifically. A number of commentators have been quick to make the former inference while overlooking schools of thought such as the latter (which is one of several alternative, or rather, additional, accounts). This is a common enough aspect of the literature and debate and it is helpful to spell out that there is unexplained variance. But being wedded to simplistic explanations of such variance is probably counter-productive.

- *Causal relationships.* This is ultimately the point that matters in this otherwise narrow and, it sometimes seems, obsessive debate. Developing a balanced regression model would be a helpful development. It goes without saying that further judgements about what is and is not significant in this model will depend on the results and also showing some sensitivity to the limits of such a model. It does not seem credible to say that developing such a model will add nothing whatsoever to causal explanation. If this were true, scholarship would not have arrived at the multivariate literature that already exists on ethnicity and labour market outcomes and no one seriously suggests that this has no value in terms of assisting causal explanation. So taking such a defensive position cannot be sensible in the longer run.

- *Policy relevance.* For the reasons already mentioned, it is hard to conclude that a suitable multivariate analysis to draw out specific effects would not be policy relevant. Quite the opposite conclusion appears valid, although a lot depends on being open to a range of explanations for any variance that is not accounted for. In any case, all insights, however off-beam or counter-intuitive, hang upon a willingness to develop a robust regression model—or models—to take the discussion forward. It is striking to note the healthy proliferation of such analyses in the USA based on ethno-racial difference, and the comparative richness of the related policy debate that has resulted. This is far from thinking, as many activists often clamour for, that blind mystery shopping investigations, however illustrative, are a sufficient answer to the challenge. The whole point of the development of such investigations has been to complement multivariate analyses and to throw light on particular circumstantial factors. For example, a high-profile BBC investigation in 2004 concluded that a cross-section of British employers could distinguish accurately between 'Muslim' and 'non-Muslim' surnames. This is misleading, to say the least. If this were true, Britain would have a remarkable set of employers, suitably religiously sensitized to some fairly subtle distinctions. For one thing, such a spurious claim implies that employers routinely see no religious distinction in surnames as common as 'Patel' or 'Shah', both of which comprise Hindus *and* Muslims.

The above example is by no means unique. Several similar intellectual and practitioner disputes about the framework of understanding implies the need for a much clearer rationale for examining the position of British Muslim communities. The absence of such a framework is something of a priority for social research and policy formulation work on religion, British Muslims, and engagement with potentially alienated groups. Beyond this, there are three main rationales for governments wishing to foster a larger and better informed presence for Muslim communities on the public policy agenda. First, the limits of existing strategy and policies to address social exclusion can be tested for the case of British Muslim communities. The task underpinning this effort is to adapt the existing framework to meet the test of relevance among a range of religious groups generally and among Muslim communities specifically. It is not obvious how a broadly secular framework can be applied to groups whose identity and outlook are so clearly defined by religious values and principles, and British Muslims are only a case in point in understanding and meeting such a challenge. Of course, as Chapter 5 notes, a clear sense of religious identity varies considerably within the British Muslim community, and significant differences can be seen in the attitudes and perspectives of second-generation Muslim South Asians alone. To that extent, the test of relevance will have different meanings within the Muslim population. Government strategy towards social exclusion may not be fully understood or utilized to begin with, thus opening up a risk that Muslims come to perceive particular policy measures to be indirectly discriminatory towards their needs and aspirations. For many years, the slow pace of recognition and expansion of Islam schools within the state compulsory education system resulted in considerable resentment among Muslim communities, including those who expressed no known preference for such school provision.

Second, there is a threat of alienation among those who feel that religious background and orientation fails to count in mainstream public policy. The outlook of British Muslim groups may harden in that their experiences and preferences are perceived as 'not counting' in the eyes of government. This has been a particular challenge faced over many years by the Commission for Racial Equality, the lead anti-discrimination watchdog, and is likely to persist for its successor, the Commission for Equality and Human Rights. The specific test that has been regularly raised by Muslim organizations, sometimes in alliance with other faith organizations, has been the relative degree of legal protection against discrimination on religious grounds afforded by a range of UK and European legislation. Combining religious and non-religious strands of equality in large public anti-discrimination watchdog bodies has always been a difficult task, not least because of the practical need to disentangle religious aspects of discrimination from other factors such as language or ethnicity. Addressing religion as a strand that 'counts' therefore involves a balance being struck in a large number of cases between overtly religious factors and a number of non-religious contributory factors.

Third, there is the ever-present danger of government inconsistency and the appearance of double standards. There are to begin with general public concerns about the degree to which any group should be thought of and targeted explicitly in terms of group membership. There may be an inconsistency here in that British Muslim groups can legitimately complain that many among them are singled out by the media as Muslims wholly and exclusively and whose Britishness is often forgotten in sensationalist press coverage. Yet, in policy terms, there is relatively little appetite to adopt group-targeting in place of existing approaches that target on the basis of circumstances (income, qualifications, etc.) or geographic clustering (funding streams to alleviate general social disadvantage, urban regeneration, etc.). This reflects a long tradition in British social policy in which group membership and attendant rights have remained marginal to consideration. By contrast, there is a well-rooted tradition of targeting via circumstantial and geographic proxies, both of which have the capacity to capture very substantial proportions of an impoverished, thickly clustered group.

Tackling Discrimination

Anti-discrimination laws are only a partial answer. The pattern of inexplicitness about religion as a source of disadvantage and exclusion is not just a characteristic of government thinking in shaping the agenda of public policies to combat disadvantage. It is also reflected in the position taken by the courts in interpreting Britain's anti-discrimination laws. The results of judicial involvement are a patchwork picture by which certain religious groups have found themselves protected by the provisions of anti-discrimination legislation while others are not. Nevertheless, particular ethnic groups that share particular religious backgrounds enjoy some coverage in law. This has depended in practice both on the nature of the ethnic group and on the nature of the discrimination complaint and response. Over time the legal lacuna for Muslims in particular has come at a high costs in terms of protests and campaigns to remedy this. This has resulted in moves to address religious discrimination more explicitly. Thus, the UK government committed in 2003 to changes brought about by Article 13 of the Employment and Race Directives of the European Union that will focus more explicitly on tackling religious grounds for discrimination.

The Directive however contained no definition of 'religion or belief'. The UK government's approach has been to avoid giving further definition to the term, except to say that belief should refer to a religious or similar belief and not political belief. Legislation makes it unlawful for employers to discriminate directly or indirectly when dealing with issues such as requests for leave or religious observance, or in laying down rules on dress, uniform, etc. The legislation will not require employers to automatically grant all requests for leave for religious observance, but they must avoid both direct and indirect discrimination. In addition, the CRE has updated its Code of Practice in Employment. A strong case can be made for employers wishing to see and make use of a single updated Code that has purchase on religious equality in the workplace.[32]

Differences in the treatment of a person, based on differences of religion or belief, are permissible only in two special circumstances: first, for posts that have a 'genuine determining occupational requirement' for a particular religion (e.g. Church of England Chaplain in the armed forces) and second, for churches and other public or private organizations whose ethos is based on religion or belief. In the case of religious schools, the government's policy has been to continue to allow governing bodies of schools with a religious character to employ teachers who have a commitment to the particular faith or denomination concerned.

In conclusion, the ability of government to operate with clear goals in relation to British Muslim communities is hampered first by the effects of an existing framework that links to religion only in passing and second by political uncertainties about the supposed uniqueness of the position and outlook of Muslim groups. The former obstacle represents a medium-level risk to government and a potentially large source of frustration among particular Muslim community leaders and their followers. The latter, arguably, is an unknown, though clearly volatile, risk to government and to British society at large.

---

[32] Updating the 1984 Code of Practice was one of the twenty-eight recommendations of the 2003 Strategy Unit report on employment and integration—see *Ethnic Minorities and Labour Market—Final Report* (London: Cabinet Office, 2003).

Economic, Social, and Political Integration Across Europe

West European societies contain a range of models and experiences of social inclusion and this study is naturally sensitive to such variance.[33] At the most immediate level, we need to examine the general credibility of assertions that multi-ethnic Britain, and its distinctive policies towards race relations, is the exception within Europe. Britain's experience is often presented in such a light, suggesting that read-across insights and lessons from other countries' experiences of ethnic and religious pluralism are of limited, if any, value. However, at another level, it is worth reminding ourselves that no European country follows the tradition of the USA or Canada by actually describing, if not defining, itself as a country of immigration and immigrants. The challenges of ethnic and other forms of diversity that have been associated with large-scale post-war immigration are thus more usually thought to be factors that conditionalize the applicability and receptiveness of mainstream social inclusion policies and their underlying frameworks. Explicit, front-footed integration policy, therefore, is often absent in many European countries (although not in Britain) in a way that is hard to imagine in a country such as Canada that has devoted considerable effort and resource to this kind of task. All European countries tend to contrast with this approach and have struggled to accommodate immigration-related diversity.

The accommodations in terms of policy responses have varied considerably but have contained several recurring elements. These have frequently involved interventions in language training provision, in the workplace to deliver information, in schools to bolster low attainment records as well as poor linkages with immigrant families, and in employer awareness of particular worker needs and concerns. Less-common responses across Europe have been anti-discrimination interventions and policies to widen the social networks of immigrant groups.

However, any significant trends or patterns in the conceptualization of policy problems and in policy responses are rather more difficult to tease out. This is because of the huge diversity in the national and historic contexts across European countries.[34] Immigration and its related questions are never quite understood in the same way from one place to another in Europe and this is perhaps not so surprising after all. For one thing, the kinds of immigration flows have varied from country to country, or sometimes between groups of

---

[33] Apospori, E., and Millar, J. (eds.), *The Dynamics of Social Exclusion in Europe: Comparing Austria, Germany, Greece, Portugal and the UK* (Cheltenham: Edward Elgar, 2003).

[34] See, for example 'Centre for Dialogues', *Muslim Youth and Women in the West: Source of Concern of Source of Hope?* (New York: Centre for Dialogues: Islamic World–US–The West, 2007), esp. 'Background Paper' (pp. 98–152).

countries or regions. Certainly, it is possible to identify older versus newer immigration countries in the sense that several southern European countries (Spain, Italy, Portugal) have been barely touched until comparatively recently by the large-scale labour migrations that affected industrial northern Europe from the 1950s onwards. Britain, France, and Germany are all large economies with major urban industrial centres that absorbed a significant volume of labour migrants and their families almost two generations ago. Similar patterns have really not been seen since and certainly not in Mediterranean societies that have themselves been involved in developing modern industries from the 1970s onwards. The relevance of labour organizations and welfare state arrangements in these contexts has been qualitatively different in these newer immigration countries, and with fewer direct lessons for older immigration societies. If similarities are to be found, it is by examining some of the older cases together.

Two further distinctions to aid understanding are provided by the work of Andrew Geddes on this subject.[35] First, he points to the multi-level nature of integration policies and infrastructure arrangements. By this is meant that it is mistaken to think that national governments monopolize policy discussion and development since important roles are increasingly played by city-regions and by supranational government such as the EU. This pattern is very much in evidence when examining immigrant integration programmes and initiatives in large cities associated with immigrant and refugee settlement in Europe. Cases such as Rotterdam in the Netherlands,[36] Birmingham in Britain, Berlin in Germany, and Marseilles in France all drive home the point that integration policies are frequently organized and delivered at sub-national level. This typically involves city-wide or regional layers of government and their involvement in housing and educational programmes, as well as time-limited, ad hoc, public sector-led bodies involved in fields such as urban regeneration or employment training initiatives.[37] The result is that it is hard, and possibly meaningless, to draw significant inferences from national, stand-alone integration policies since these can easily create a distorted picture of integration measures as a whole. Much the qualification needs to be made when examining the increasingly active and ambitious role of the European Union in both shaping and implementing integration policy measures of its

---

[35] Geddes, A., 'Ethnic Minorities in the Labour Market: Comparative Policy Approaches (Western Europe)', paper commissioned by the Performance and Innovation Unit, November 2001; see www.strategy.gov.uk.

[36] de Graff, T., Gorter, C., and Nijkamp, P., 'The Effects of Ethnic Geographical Clustering on Education Attainment in the Netherlands', Tinbergen Institute Discussion Paper (Amsterdam: Tinbergen Institute, 2000).

[37] Garbaye, R., 'Ethnic Minority Participation in British and French Cities: A Historical–Institutionalist Perspective', *International Journal of Urban and Regional Research*, 26 (3), pp. 555–70.

own. This latter trend has led some observers to describe the emergence of a 'Europeanization' of immigration and integration policy.[38]

Second, any attempt to assess the nature and effectiveness of integration policy across different European countries has to pay attention to the importance of the so-called non-policy. What is meant by this term is that plenty of countries fall into, or nearby, the category of having few if any public policies explicitly geared towards immigrant integration. This absence of identifiable policy does not in itself mean that researchers should necessarily place practice and experience in these countries into a null or void category. This is because of the potentially important integrative effects of many other policies such as general labour market and workforce development policies. There is no direct correlation between countries with comparatively unbounded quantities of integration policies such as the Netherlands and substantial evidence of successful integration in practice. Indeed, the current Dutch experience demonstrates the risks of drawing any such positive correlation inference. Moreover, at the heart of the present Dutch debate over immigration and integration lies a very clear perception that whatever progress may have been gained, this has generally been in spite, rather than because, of public policy towards integration. Such a critique is obviously highly damaging, not least for public intellectuals and policy practitioners who have pursued a traditional Dutch approach to integration based on relatively high backing for cultural and other forms of autonomy for immigrant minority groups. Nevertheless, the high-level observation has less to do with settling debates about Dutch misgivings towards past integration thinking and practices. The point instead has to do with being sensitive to cases such as Germany where explicit integration policies have been scarce by comparison. There is some evidence to show that integration in employment and educational terms in Germany has fared at least as well as in countries associated with substantial integration infrastructures. In Germany's case, the role of particular institutions such as the apprenticeship system and the works' councils is important because of the ways in which these have been associated with delivering positive labour market outcomes for immigrants and their offspring. This also means that any reduced role for such institutions associated with Germany's traditional corporatist welfare state may also be linked to a reduction in the integrative effects for immigrants.

Employment, Housing, and Educational Non-policies

If non-policies matter for integration, the same can also be said for the need to observe and measure the role played by mainstream employment,

---

[38] Geddes, A., 'International Migration and State Sovereignty in an Integrating Europe', *International Migration*, 39 (6), 2001, pp. 21–42.

housing, and educational policies. The resulting effects upon integration may be difficult to pinpoint with great accuracy, but the causal relationships are sufficiently strong to matter in terms of securing better and deeper integration. There are, of course, a range of ways of identifying and promoting particular definitions of integration, although this is not the purpose of the discussion at this point. Rather, it is worth trying to make a preliminary assessment of the broad effects on integration of particular kinds of policy interventions in jobs, neighbourhoods, and schools. To take one example, British educational policies in the compulsory schooling system have traditionally been reluctant explicitly to identify and cater for ethnic pluralism. Exceptions have been significant, and include, for example, the Ethnic Minority Achievement Grant (EMAG), preceded by the so-called Section 11 funding arrangement, for schools with large immigrant and immigrant-descended pupils.[39] In the last two decades, however, the really large and influential policies in school education have been those that have created sharper incentives for schools to deliver enhanced attainment levels (e.g. the floor target regime) and vastly improved transparency for parent user groups (e.g. the publication and dissemination of attainment records at school level).

There have been many other policy interventions besides these two, but they nevertheless reflect the importance of mainstream policy levers in shaping educational opportunity structures and outcomes. The impact has been substantial in many cases, and as much for immigrant groups as others. Discussions of education and integration policies, therefore, can easily miss their target unless a broad-sweep assessment is made of the role and effects of tools such as the accountability and funding arrangements for state schools. Furthermore, with a growing body of evidence to show that different immigrant and ethnic minority groups follow different, or at least differing, paths in educational terms, it is doubly important to examine the differential impacts of mainstream policy measures.

In other words, there is much less interest in deploying, panoramic policy measures to address immigrant integration across the board. The factors that can be identified to do with poor or failing progression in education and employment, for instance, will not only vary from group to group, but also from place to place as well as over time. As a result, a more granular approach to addressing these barriers is likely to have a more effective chance of success in terms of immigrant integration. The policy lens of those concerned with immigrant integration may therefore be usefully primed to look at a range of policy levers including the effects of existing mainstream measures to build

[39] The EMAG funding programme provides a financial subsidy to local government for the education of immigrant children and has its origins in legislation first adopted by British governments in the mid-1960s.

human capital, improve employability, enhance education- and employment-related networks, and promote labour mobility and flexibility. All of these goals are likely to be more or less in tune with the priorities of policy in these areas broadly, and cannot be ignored in the name of identifying the effectiveness of measures targeted at specific ethnic or immigrant groups. Both approaches are important in seeking to assess the reasons why particular immigrant or immigrant-descended cohorts are or are not associated with improved educational and labour market outcomes. This rounded picture, then, allows a better informed understanding of integration, especially in the case of particular groups or subgroups where concerns arise about long-run progression.

Welfare Policies and Hard-to-reach Groups

At a more specific level, comparative assessments of the effectiveness of policy frameworks across different countries reveals some sharp contrasts in relation to so-called hard-to-reach social groups. Particular subgroups of immigrants and their offspring will often fall into this category, and the case of first- and second-generation Muslim women has stood out in both Britain and Germany, where policy thinking and approach has been not at all similar in nature.[40] For example, evaluative studies of Sure Start, a flagship multi-agency programme in Britain to deliver interventions for young children and parents at high risk of exclusion, has operated without any direct markers for ethnic or religious background. Instead, in common with a long tradition in British social policy, geography is used as a proxy to identify areas containing large concentrations of the targeted group or groups. In the past, only very mainstream policy initiatives have succeeded in incorporating a weighting element for immigrant populations. The early phase of the Urban Programme, from 1969–77,[41] for instance was a rare exception during which time resource allocation was altered from central to local government to tackle multiple deprivation found in areas of acute urban decline. The presence of a sizeable immigrant population was not so much a factor linked to urban distress but rather a marker of the scale of social need that was likely to exist in the poorer, less dynamic inner cities where newcomers were attracted by sluggish property markets.

Nevertheless, using mainstream policy levers to identify and address specific hard-to-reach pockets remains one of most enduring challenges in domestic social and economic policy. The pedigree behind Sure Start, an arguably

[40] Wietholz, A., 'The Educational "Integration" of Ethnic Minority Children in Germany and the UK: Moving from "Ethnicity" to a "Class" Policy?', unpublished paper presented to the Transatlantic Security Roundtable/Educating for Migrant Education Conference, University of Toronto, September 2006.

[41] McKay, D., and Cox, A., *The Politics of Urban Change* (London: Croom Helm, 1979).

highly effective if rather expensive package, partly emanates from the USA where similar Head Start programmes have operated since the early-mid-1990s. These programmes have emphasized the need to identify specific risk factors associated with the actual experience of social deprivation as well as greatly increased odds of marginalization and exclusion from mainstream educational, housing, health, and labour markets. Thus, the emphasis has been placed on groups or individuals in particular locations who lack characteristics that might protect them from the risk of exclusion. For example, poor awareness of early childhood health and development needs can be addressed via measures that raise knowledge and awareness and also deliver increased take-up of health and related services. Similarly, language deficits can be met through language provision, and with this a range of services to allow recipients to be in touch with training and skills advice and intermediate employment opportunities.

The logic is clearly one of trying to remove each risk factor one at a time while encouraging the self-help removal of other factors through a virtuous circle. The nature of the exercise is that, in the case of immigrant populations perhaps from culturally distinct backgrounds, the chances of successful engagement are enhanced by some degree of cultural or other sensitization of policy delivery. Cultural neutrality may appear attractive at several stages of distance, but it is stymied by the immediate cultural and related needs of targeted groups. The ability to engage with some of these groups in mother tongue languages is obviously one simple example. In the case of groups where cultural sensitization stems from or is tangibly linked to religious background or faith, the issues can start to become clouded rather quickly. Delivering language classes or 'mother and toddler' social development programmes that fit around religious prayer timings or dietary needs can easily be described as on-the-ground flexibility and effectiveness. Unfortunately, it can also as easily be characterized as a small but significant departure from the secular provisions of the state and its public policies at large.

There is little point in debating the sharply contrasting perspectives on offer. It is more useful to observe that cultural and religious diversity, often by its nature, can place some awkward demands on policymakers who are keen to avoid creating markers for ethnic or religious background. The danger is that by weighting policy in the direction of distinctive religious requirements may be to start to establish a religious or faith policy by the back door. In countries with strong secular traditions in policy thinking, this is an alarming possibility. Moreover, the cultural or religious sensitization of policy may be opposed because of a failure to think through and articulate its interim rationale. Policy interventions that cannot easily separate out tools from outcomes can easily be attacked for naively encouraging separatism mindsets that do not value or even recognize integration as a shared outcome.

The discussion hitherto has largely dwelt on the ways in which large policy frameworks can and sometimes have adapted to meet the needs of specific population subgroups. This is a very large debate indeed and is supported by a considerable literature. In the case of hard or difficult to reach groups, it is not clear how far the characteristics of the group are viewed as transitory or indelible in shaping the outlook and priorities of policymakers. Governments operating in strong ideological frameworks for social inclusion have, either way, to manage the challenges brought about by ethnic and religious diversity. Even without such an ideological context, there are numerous practical questions that need to be settled in implementing measures to an ethnically and religiously differentiated population. In part, the solution lies in balancing ethno-religious sensitization of the policy framework as a whole (for which there is often only very limited public support) against sensitization of specific and limited aspects of policy delivery (for which public backing is both more relaxed and less critical). In France, the importance of getting this kind of balance right is critical, not least because of a prevailing general consensus that is resistant to the recognition of ethno-religious difference in public institutions and policy. But even in Britain, the need to obtain balance is important as a result of scepticism about the longer-run, non-intentional effects of past measures to promote integration via multicultural notions of recognition and celebration of difference. The German case is rather more complex, mainly as a result of the limited scale of special integration measures accompanied by the social inclusionary rationale and effects of mainstream social and economic policies. Balance here is more a matter of selective flexibility in delivery, particularly in the context of significant disjunctures faced by a large asylum population, while retaining strong connections with the effects of mainstream schooling and work councils in employment.

National Traditions of Welfare and Entitlement

The remit needs to be broadened at this stage to take account of national welfare and entitlement traditions. Clearly, no single set of values or norms dominates the approach taken by one country. Nevertheless it is worth examining the sorts of predisposition towards immigrant integration that are brought about through existing dominant ideas about entitlement to belong and identity categories (citizenship, for example) and material benefits and support (welfare programmes, for example). In Germany's case, this means that some allowance must be made for its social insurance model of welfare. This has led to a traditional pattern of relative generosity in access to, and payments from, welfare state programmes. Significantly, the vast bulk of these economic entitlements have been extended to the country's guest worker population, starting as early as the 1950s when trade unions first began campaigning on this front. Welfare state incorporation of very large numbers of foreign guest workers, chiefly from Turkey, has been the result, even while Germany has proceeded to exclude these groups from an ethno-national conception of German identity and citizenship. Alongside welfare incorporation and ethno-nationalism, a third ideological strand underpinning German thinking towards immigrant integration has been a variable importance attached to human right doctrines: the impressive national value of collective obligation towards persecuted groups and individuals. The origins of this trait lie mainly in the post-war era and are linked to the national projects of reconciliation towards the victims of Nazi aggression and the West German preoccupation with reunification with East Germany. But it is the simultaneous inclusionary and exclusionary features of these different strands that matter. According to Boswell et al.:[42]

This combination of two conflicting patterns of thought—an exclusionary ethnonational conception of membership and a more inclusive welfare system—produced an approach to immigrant membership that has been dubbed 'social citizenship'.

For our purposes, it is important to note that Germany's relative absence of distinctive policy measures to target and promote integration has only partly affected its ability and willingness to integrate newcomers. Those who fall outside its own narrow understanding of German identity and belonging have found it difficult to gain political–legal citizenship and the recognition that goes with this. However, as long-term foreign workers with de facto settlement patterns, they have been grafted on to large parts of the worker entitlements to welfare generosity and to employment security. More recent debates about reform of German welfare provision have focused on the capacity to deliver more contingent services and benefits that support, for example, labour market flexibility. A feature of this kind of move is that the across-the-board entitlements that have been afforded to long-term foreign workers are, at least in part, also potentially at risk. Social citizenship's value can be eroded this way, albeit with potential gains to offset this by way of deeper labour market integration. Any considerations of securing a more 'lean and mean' German welfare model, more closely resembling Anglo-Saxon principles of labour flexibility and restricted entitlement, are closely intertwined with the integration issues affecting guest workers.

Integration: Historically, Rhetorically, and Practically

The interaction between labour market, educational attainment, and changing welfare state factors provides the backdrop for assessing integration rhetoric and practice in the round. The bulk of this chapter thus far has

[42] Boswell, C., Chou, M. H., and Smith, J., *Reconciling Demand for Labour Migration with Public Concerns about Immigration: Germany and the UK* (London: Anglo-German Foundation for the Study of Industrial Society, 2005).

concentrated on this backdrop. However, it is not the only one that shapes national, and increasingly cross-national, debates about immigrant integration in Europe. Other dimensions stem from civic–political measures of integration (in which, for example, levels and patterns of mobilization in the mainstream political process are fairly central) and also from cultural–educational measures (where, typically, attention is paid to the character of the educational curriculum in building a shared identity or common understanding of the past). As regards the latter, research on Germany, France, and Britain has pointed to some sharply divergent understandings of the scope of public education in shaping belonging, identity, and common values. For example, Ohlinger and Traunmuller's recent study of political and history teaching in German schools reveals the importance of two challenges facing policymakers in this area.[43] The first arises from the country's negative historical narrative. This has hampered severely the capacity for educationalists to foster much sense of positive national identity. The ethno-national nature of past debates concerning nationhood in particular have made this hard task even harder. The second challenge comes from increasing ethnic diversity itself brought about through migration and long-term settlement of foreign nationals. These numbers have been significant both within Germany and by European standards. The result has been an increased pluralization of domestic debates about Germany's contemporary and more distant history.

The arrival of migrants' histories is also having a substantial impact on opening up perspectives on and of the past. One feature of this has been a lively and growing 'whose history?' debate in Germany in which children of migrants report a greater interest than other children in accessing international history and not just German history alone. This recent tendency has also had its effects on German schooling in general by fuelling a larger debate about the limits, if any, of teaching about so-called multiple pasts.[44] Interestingly, four-fifths or more of politics and history teachers reported that issues of migration and ethnic diversity were absent from their own higher education and teaching training. Meanwhile, a similar proportion of students at large felt that history was or should be mainly about German history. A similar proportion embraced the view that the history of migration ought to be required history teaching in schools.

In Britain, by contrast, the forces driving political and historical understanding of migration and diversity through compulsory education have

[43] Ohlinger, R., and Traunmuller, R., 'Towards Multiple Pasts: Teaching History and Politics in Germany's Immigration Society', unpublished paper presented to the Transatlantic Security Roundtable/Educating for Migrant Education conference, University of Toronto, September 2006.

[44] Saggar, S., 'Whose History? National Narratives in Multiracial Societies', in Brivati, B., and Seldon, A. (eds.), *Contemporary History: A Handbook* (Manchester: Manchester University Press, 1995), pp. 50–60.

been rather muted. The recent introduction of citizenship into the National Curriculum in 2004 has inevitably created fresh room for such education to take hold in schools.

Integration was once termed a 'treacherous metaphor' by Michael Banton.[45] This part of this chapter has alerted us to the fact that integrative and disintegrative effects can result from a range of contributory causes, some of which are central to national debates and understanding about social inclusion and welfare legitimacy and others of which lie within a relatively small confine of official immigrant integration policies. It is this context that stands out and, with it, the need to examine strategies for social inclusion of distinctive ethnic and faith communities in a way that takes proper account of wider causes and drivers of those causes.

Social and Economic Disadvantage

Concentrating on Britain for a moment, the evidence shows that, on some counts, many British Muslim communities are endemically part of a left-behind fringe. On other counts, the evidence is more nuanced. Perhaps the most important factor to acknowledge has been the widespread social and political rights enjoyed by the bulk of South Asian Muslims at the point of their or their parents' and grandparents' entry to Britain. Much of this occurred in the 1950s and 1960s, although the Bangladeshi community tends to have a shorter history in Britain. Nevertheless as members of the Commonwealth, South Asian migrants tended to be full citizens following entry and settlement, putting them on a par with their indigenous counterparts. Therefore, there have been few legal or citizenship impediments to South Asian Muslims' participation in the economy and political process of their country of adoption. This has meant a de facto level playing field in judging British Muslims' participation and progress over several decades. The only notable fly in the ointment has been the problematic nature of British Muslims' protection from discrimination under successive laws passed in 1965, 1968, 1976, and 2000. Given the multi-ethnic and transnational character of Islam in Britain, it has proven hard to afford such protection in the way in which Jews, Sikhs, and Hindus have enjoyed on the basis of the overlap between ethnic and religious categories.

Theories of Immigrant Succession

The economics of British Muslims is a mixed picture. On one hand, by concentrating purely on Pakistani and Bangladeshi origin Muslim communities,

[45] Banton, M., 'Progress in Ethnic and Racial Studies', *Ethnic and Racial Studies*, Vol. 24, No. 2, March 2001, pp. 173–94.

the objective position of other Muslim groups gets relegated to the periphery. Most data have been collected on these two groups, who together only account for two-thirds of British Muslims. Indian Muslims, for instance, perform significantly better in the labour market than Pakistanis or Bangladeshis. Equally, the generally impressive story of the Ismaili community, or South Asian Muslims with an East African dimension, points in the other direction. This is also the case in relation to British Muslims of Arab, Turkish, and Mauritian background. This therefore implies a country of origin effect, rather than a religious effect.

Theories of immigrant succession have assumed that long-term progression in employment would follow smoothly for the offspring of first-generation immigrants. Tomorrow, so the idea goes, would be a better day for their children, thereby offsetting some of the hardships endured by pioneers. Ideas of this kind have been important all over the advanced industrial world. The Canadians, for example, are fond of boasting that for almost all immigrant groups, measurable gaps in earnings, on a like-for-like basis, virtually disappear within a generation or less. This claim was largely borne out in evidence until comparatively recently, and even where it is not, there is ample scope in existing public policy to focus on groups that experience sustained lack of progress. Canadian policymakers are keenly aware of their own settled disadvantage stories. The Australian case is also one that displays a strong appetite to identify weak progression among specific migrant groups and pursue remedies that are aligned with the causes of poor performance. Targeted English language programmes, skills and qualification retraining, and access to business start-up knowledge and employment advisory networks are all typical elements in this toolkit. The overriding principle in such programmes is the need to intervene proactively to limit, if not prevent, the emergence of migrant or minority pockets that are cut off from the mainstream economy and society. The risks of non-intervention are significant and involve not just social and economic isolation but also a much increased chance of separatist cultural and political influences taking hold. Such an environment is deeply undesirable because of the breeding ground it often creates for the open preaching of religious hatred and a range of assorted religio-political grievances.[46]

The factors that mitigate against settled disadvantage among Western Muslim communities are not always properly isolated or widely appreciated. In Britain, the Sunday newspaper supplements' fixation with East African Asians' success stories is a case in point. This remarkable performance in education, employment, business life, and latterly in public life has been as dramatic as it was unpredicted. Scarcely a single serious commentator in Britain in the 1970s

---

[46] Klausen., J., 'Counter-Terrorism after 7/7: Adapting Community Policing to the Fight Against Domestic Terrorism', unpublished paper, May 2007.

foresaw a future thirty years later in which this multi-religious and partly multi-ethnic cohort would integrate fully in British society. Indeed most such commentators predicted that East Africans, like other South Asian-descended migrants, would cling to their historic cultures and remain only partly connected with mainstream society and institutions. The forced, involuntary nature of their departure from East African countries—Kenya in 1968, Uganda in 1972, and Malawi in 1976—also played on the minds of commentators who argued that this aspect of their settlement meant that they would be unlikely recruits to the British nation and British identity. A better informed account of the relative chances of integration for this subgroup might have given greater weight to factors such as language, employment skills and experiences, and urban background. The advantages of English language as the lingua franca of the sending country, coupled with high levels of urbanization and participation in white-collar employment, have all made for a terrific match with the labour needs of Britain's economy in the past thirty or forty years. The link between this group's background in and reputation for micro-enterprise and business innovation has also exploited a latent gap in British commerce.

The evidence for differences in pay and unemployment produces a complex and nuanced picture. It reveals relative disadvantage among some sectional pockets of Britain's immigrant-descended minorities, alongside considerable advancement among others.

To begin with, there are large headline differences in unemployment, earnings, occupational attainment, and self-employment between different ethnic groups. From this picture, the influence that relevant characteristics such as age, generation, gender, and education have on labour market achievements can be seen. For sure, focusing on disaggregations of gender, generation, and geography, it is apparent that large variations in achievement exist. For example, a first-generation Pakistani woman in Oldham cannot expect to be on the same page as a second-generation Indian male in suburban London. Only 4 per cent of the former have been economically active on a sustained basis as against 84 per cent of the latter.

Research analysing large-scale survey data from the mid-1990s suggests that religious background is rather poorly linked to labour market outcomes. Figure 2.9 in Chapter 2 showed for instance that Muslims of Indian national heritage were considerably more likely to be in full-time employment as compared with their South Asian, non-Indian counterparts. Pakistani Muslim men for instance exhibited an employment rate around 20 per cent below that of Indian Muslim men. Meanwhile the employment rate among Bangladeshi Muslim women stood at just 4 per cent—a sixth of the rate for Indian Muslim women. Hindus and Sikhs—both men and women—significantly outperformed Muslims in general but the gap was significantly smaller in relation to Indian Muslims. The latter, in other words, appear to have as much in common with some similar non-Muslim groups as with co-Muslims with whom they share their religious background. There are similar patterns with regard to earnings and progression in this research, all of which points to Indian Muslims as significant outliers in a general picture of poor outcomes for British Muslims.

Drilling into relevant labour market data further extends our knowledge of Pakistani and Bangladeshi members of the labour force. One notable weakness arises from the prevalence of unskilled, poorly qualified workers in these two ethnic groups. This story is exceptionally prevalent among Pakistani women, three-quarters of whom from the first generation had no British qualifications at all. Among the second generation, this had shrunk considerably to just a quarter (see Figure 2.11 in Chapter 2). However, the better comparator might be the levels found among other second-generation South Asian women; this was around half that of Pakistani women of the same generation suggesting that this subgroup continued to be poorly qualified. The shrinking in the ranks of unqualified, unskilled Indian women from one generation to the next stands in stark contrast.

Ethnic Penalties

These differences in labour market achievement persist after taking into account things such as qualifications, skills, and experience. It is important to compare the position and progress of different ethnic and gender groups on a like-for-like basis. This involves a methodology to statistically adjust the raw numbers to treat all groups as being equally human-capital rich or poor. Thus, if a sample group or subgroup is especially poorly represented in the ranks of those with above-average qualifications, the test is to investigate their labour market performance in the hypothetical circumstances of enjoying much better qualifications. Multivariate analysis allows such an insight so as to investigate the relative influence of a single characteristic, such as ethnic background, in shaping labour market outcomes. Pioneering work to analyse the role of religious background is being carried out at present, but, for now, detailed reliable results are only known for the impact attributed to ethnicity. To some degree, this distinction does matter a great deal when assessing the labour market stories of British Pakistanis and Bangladeshis since both ethno-national communities are almost entirely Muslims as well.

What is the adjusted gap between, say, Pakistani and Bangladeshi men and their white male counterparts when comparing weekly earnings? Figure 4.1 shows a simple worked example using Labour Force Survey data over several years and provides some answers.

Take the case of a Pakistani or Bangladeshi man in Britain. In average terms, on the streets of London as it were, the data summarizes his typical lower weekly earnings relative to an average white working man. The figure reveals that his earnings deficit is large and depressing, especially if you are such a

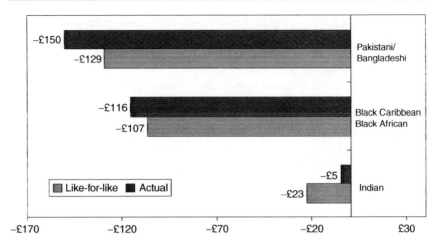

Figure 4.1. Male weekly earnings, relative to white counterpart
Source: R. Berthoud, 'Ethnic Employment Penalties in Britain', 2000.

man. However, the conventional explanation for this poor performance has been to link it to the poor qualifications and skills of this particular group. In fact, such working men are notoriously human-capital poor in Britain and largely remained so over more than one generation. For example, among younger Pakistanis and Bangladeshis, there is evidence to show considerable weakness relative to other groups at the point of entering the labour force. Less than 40 per cent of them leave school with five good GCSEs (grades A–C), compared with almost 60 per cent of whites at the same point. In relation to Indians and Chinese, the gap is even larger. Figure 4.2 tells the story across all major ethnic groups in Britain.

So, allowing for this, what happens when you treat a Pakistani or Bangladeshi man as if he were white in human capital terms, that is, with a bundle of advantages found among white men? It is clear from the figure that the darkly shaded column, although moving in the right direction, remains largely stuck. In fact, the earnings gap after the statistical adjustment has taken place stands at £129 per week, down, but not substantially, from its level prior to the adjustment. And much the same is true for black men using such an analysis of the raw data. It is important to stress that, under normal circumstances, this kind of model would predict the elimination or near elimination of any earnings gap at all. Weekly earnings across men from different ethnic backgrounds, who also enjoyed identical human-capital profiles, should ordinarily be identical to one another. Any small variations that remain can be attributed to factors that lie outside the variables that have been included in the multivariate model. In other words, the analysis leaves us with a level of earnings variance that cannot be explained by the factors, such as education

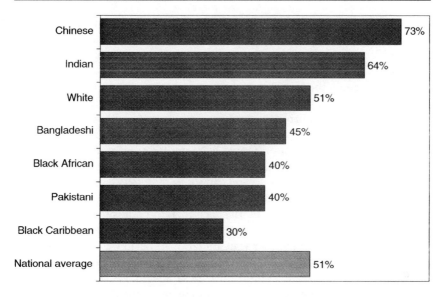

Figure 4.2. Attainment of five 'good' GCSEs (grades A–C), 2002

and qualifications, that have been assessed. The variance is thus linked in prima facie terms with the sole factor that has not been explicitly controlled in the model, namely, ethnic background. In one, direct sense, therefore, it is possible to argue that differences in ethnic origin—or skin colour, more prosaically—are linked to very substantial differences in earnings. The analysis does not conclusively demonstrate a causal relationship between ethnicity and earnings but it does highlight a very considerable, unexplained relationship of some kind. For this reason, a number of commentators, especially in the USA, have seized upon these kinds of findings and have drawn various broad conclusions. To some, the results showing large like-for-like earnings gaps are known as 'ethnic penalties' in the sense that ethnic background is all that is left to which such variance might be attributed. Such a term is obviously emotive, and may not fully reflect the nuance of the findings. Nevertheless, it captures a powerful inference of these results that has salience politically and beyond. A gender analysis, incidentally, provides a similar picture for minority women in comparison with their white counterparts.

The story in relation to black and Indian origin men is interesting. In the case of the former, substantial unexplained earning variations remain even following statistical adjustment, although of a lower-order magnitude than those found among Pakistani and Bangladeshi men, almost all of whom were also Muslims. Black men, in other words, share a similar story of large differences in earnings relative to white men, both before and after adjustment taking into account human capital and other relevant factors. Both face very considerable economic barriers to inclusion via the labour market. When it comes to Indian men, a different account is apparent. The headline weekly earnings for this group shows parity with the white reference group, so, at one level, the findings are rather encouraging. The monetary barriers are simply not there in the way observed among other minority groups. However, by adjusting for the human capital and circumstantial background of this group to make them mirror the profile of white men, a like-for-like picture emerges. This shows, surprisingly, a rather larger gap than at first seen. In fact, the darkly shaded column moves in a counter-intuitive direction and is larger after the control. This matters given that the outcome is a significant monetary amount (£23 per week) and cannot be remotely described as having converged with the comparator of white earnings. However, the explanation for this perplexing result lies in the fact that the adjustment has largely involved scaling Indian human capital levels down (rather than up) to reflect those of white men. Put another way, Indian men begin by enjoying greater advantages in terms of qualifications and skills than their white counterparts. Any adjustment necessarily diminishes these advantages and, with them, labour market outcomes. So while Indian men are in the envious position of similar weekly earnings to white men (a positive outcome), it is also the case that these earnings are rather lower than they might reasonably expect with the advantages they already possess (a worrying outcome). Typically, many are better qualified and skilled for the jobs they hold and the remuneration they receive than their white counterparts in such roles. One way to look at this dynamic is to avoid the concept of a direct ethnic penalty that serves to keep a lid on already poor labour market performance (as seen in the case of Pakistani and Bangladeshi men, for example). Instead, the penalty facing Indian men is one that is more subtle since it represents a dimension of additional performance that has not been crystallized but where the raw ingredients for such performance are already present in abundance.

This is a highly nuanced picture and one that is difficult to translate effectively from analytical to political and policy salience. After all, the group in question is not only widely perceived to be performing successfully in the labour market, the evidence shows that the perception matches the facts.[47] Indeed the degree of inter-generational gain in performance among Indians is now widely acknowledged in political and business circles. However, beneath this success lies a blemish that is unique and distinctive. It only impacts on this minority ethnic group since it colours and qualifies what remains successful performance. The success of Indians is therefore a bitter-sweet one, and is

---

[47] This awkwardness and tension is seen throughout a recent major policy report looking at the profile of Britain's Hindus, the bulk of whom have Indian ethnic identity and national origins; see *Connecting British Hindus: An Enquiry into the Identity and Public Engagement of Hindus in Britain* (London: Department of Communities and Local Government/Hindu Forum of Britain, 2006).

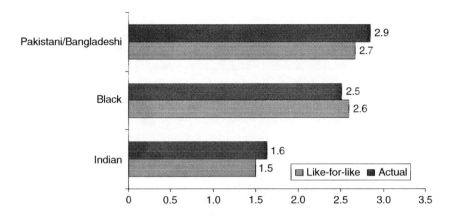

Figure 4.3. Male unemployment risk, relative to white counterpart

Source: F. Carmichael and R. Woods, 'Ethnic Penalties in Unemployment and Occupational Attainment', 2000.

conceptually both the same as and yet different from the position of their South Asian counterparts from Pakistani and Bangladeshi backgrounds. In public policy terms, it is not at all clear that the barriers to even better performance facing Indians ranks as a priority comparable to the barriers facing other much less successful South Asians. This must presumably make for a further twist in assessing the pertinence of the Indian example for understanding labour market inclusion.

Turning to unemployment as a labour market performance indicator, this kind of analysis reveals a largely similar pattern when examining unemployment risk. Figure 4.3 sets out the detail across the groups already examined: in short, the lightly shaded columns barely shift at all, whereas we would expect significant reduction in unemployment risk. The pattern revealed in the figure describing earnings gaps is largely repeated when it comes to analysing unemployment risks on a like-for-like basis across ethnic groups. In the case of the latter, Figure 4.3 shows a small decrease from 2.9 to 2.7 among Pakistani and Bangladeshi men. Nevertheless, as mentioned previously, such a model would anticipate a major reduction in, if not elimination of, any gap. This is not reported in the analysis and we are left with a further reminder of the logic of an ethnic penalty. The findings for black and Indian men tend to confirm this general picture, albeit that the latter, once again, appear to face lower-order unemployment risks. Nevertheless all three minority ethnic groups examined exhibit significant, unexplained unemployment risks implying a link with ethnic background that goes beyond the factors included in the multivariate model.

Finally, a gender disaggregation can be used to assess how far particular ethnic categories of women are performing relative to white women.

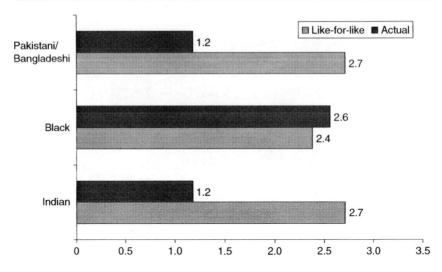

Figure 4.4. Female ethnic minority unemployment risk, relative to white counterpart
Source: F. Carmichael and R. Woods, 'Ethnic Penalties in Unemployment and Occupational Attainment', 2000.

Figure 4.4 captures the results in respect of unemployment (small sample sizes and missing data prevent such an analysis for earnings). The findings are quite surprising in their own right and also contain echoes of the like-for-like results for men. Specifically, both Pakistani/Bangladeshi and Indian women exhibit outcomes after adjustment that are substantially worse than their actual position. This implies a degree of hidden unemployment and under-employment in both groups, elements of which may touch on cultural factors that serve to either prevent female participation in employment or to restrict participation to a very narrow range of occupations and sectors.

These unexplained gaps found among men and women are increasingly referred to as ethnic penalties in Britain. Some analysts and commentators have played on this particular term to emphasize the importance of discrimination in explaining persistent, adjusted differences. The model incorporates many of the usual factors that account for labour market achievements, namely, education, qualifications, skills, experience, language, transport, family background, family circumstances, and so on. Discrimination provides an important, but only partial, explanation, however. Other factors are also at work, in all probability, and employment-related social networks are likely to be crucial as well. The ability of specific groups to achieve adequate returns on their investment in human capital in the labour market is a controversial area.

This ability also depends, without doubt, on the bearing down of discriminatory practices and reputations. But it equally hangs on the presence and development of various informal networks that colour employment decisionmaking and more besides. The interplay between causes and outcomes is therefore highly nuanced. This influence is especially important in the case of immigrants and immigrant-descended population subgroups for whom the maintenance of existing in-group networks can often be seen as a priority. Its impact, over time, will change and sometimes diminish but it will continue to affect not just the employment participation patterns of groups but also their sense of collective identity. Those who are able to bridge into newer, more promising employment fields are most likely to develop new social networks that go beyond existing ones. And the reverse is equally the case, since incrementally formed new networks will mould the kinds of employment and careers that are deemed to be most attractive. Social capital, in other words, has an impact in shaping these outcomes and an extended discussion of its role will be taken up in Chapters 6 and 7 of this book.

The Politics of 'Faith Penalties'

The awkward aspect of the evidence reviewed thus far is that it does not control directly for religious background. It is worth emphasizing, therefore, that we are *not* describing a religious penalty in jobs. The degree to which this may exist is not fully known at present.

There are some serious implications nevertheless. First, a demographic quirk arising from a comparatively young minority population means that the projected growth in the black and brown workforce will be considerable (Figure 4.5). They are over-represented in the optimum age cohorts for child-bearing and rearing. In this decade alone, around half the increase in the labour force will come from minorities, more than half of whom will be Pakistanis or Bangladeshis, almost all of whom are Muslims by background. Fifteen or twenty years from today, the bulge will have declined considerably as fertility rates and family patterns converge. Figure 4.5 describes the patterns among various groups entering the labour market.

Second, there are signs of persistent disadvantage not just in pay and unemployment but also in progression. For instance, around one in twenty men of Indian origin are employed as doctors or in professions allied to medicine. Significantly, the contrast could not be starker when looking at men of Pakistani origin: of those in jobs, one in eight works as a taxi driver. And one in three Bangladeshi men is a waiter or a chef. Meanwhile, Indian and Chinese men now are more likely than whites to hold jobs at professional or higher managerial levels. This marks dramatic progress but, again, arguably less than the rates commensurate with their qualifications and skills. Such findings serve to challenge perceptions that discrimination is exaggerated and cannot apply to those groups that are notionally 'successful' in the labour market.

Research undertaken by Ceri Peach, a social demographer, has interrogated the socio-economic data in some considerable detail. This body of research

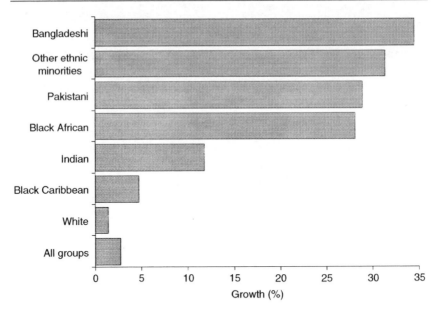

Figure 4.5. Projected growth in the working age population of ethnic groups, 1999–2009

Source: LFS data, cited in D. Owen and A. Green, *Minority Ethnic Participation and Achievements in Education, Training and the Labour Market*, CRER/IER, University of Warwick, 2000.

is rather broader and incisive than the evidence of labour market patterns cited previously. A fuller picture is better arrived at by looking at a range of indicators alongside the labour market. These include the settlement, family, and household formation patterns found among different ethnic groups generally and among Muslim communities specifically. Peach's conclusion is that, taking into account schooling, settlement, mobility, and employment, there is little to sustain the charge of systemic exclusion of British Muslims.[48] Specifically, he draws attention to the tendency among Pakistani and Bangladeshi households to have a single, male breadwinner, albeit one who is all too often, as we have seen, characterized by poor earnings and patchy avoidance of unemployment. In such circumstances, it is little wonder that the economic integration of these communities is weakened. This is largely down to exceptionally low rates of female employment, if a single causal factor could be identified that stood above all others. Less than 4 per cent of first-generation Pakistani women are economically active, for example. There are a number of cultural and generational causes behind this pattern

[48] Peach, C., 'A Demographic Profile of the British Muslim Community', presentation to Centre for the Study of Democracy Conference, 'Muslims in Britain: The Making of a New Underclass?', University of Westminster, November 2004; Peach, C., 'The Social Geography of Exclusion', presentation to the Salzburg Seminar, 15 May 2007.

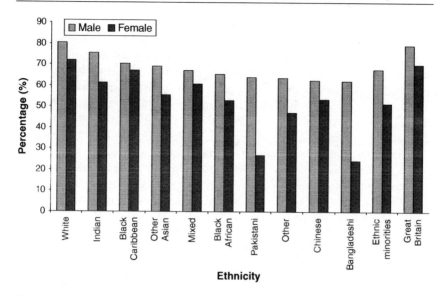

Figure 4.6. Employment rates by ethnicity and gender, 2003

Source: Peach, C., 'A demographic profile of the British Muslim community', presentation to Centre for the Study of Democracy conference, 'Muslims in Britain: The Making of a New Underclass?', University of Westminster, November 2004.

(Figure 4.6). As the *Economist* wrote, the fact remains that families made up of two earning partners are heavily protected against economic shocks and with it the risk of economic exclusion.[49]

The discussion in this section has revolved around the patterns of socio-economic inclusion among different ethnic groups in Britain. The emphasis has been on the labour market and on paid employment. Peach's work is a reminder that a broader picture needs to be drawn in which employment features centrally but alongside a number of other related factors that shape, usually indirectly, access to and prospects within various opportunity structures. For example, it is worth considering the range of causal drivers that impact on employment that go beyond education and qualifications, even though this area is cause for concern in itself.

On the demand side, account needs to be taken of the settlement and mobility patterns of different groups. Equally, industrial restructuring and regional economic development patterns have reshaped the nature of labour demand, sometimes wholeheartedly, to leave skilled, trained workers entirely cut off from employment. This has been identified previously when reviewing the historic settlement demography of Pakistani and Bangladeshi communities.

[49] Ceri Peach cited in Centre for Dialogues, *Muslim Youth and Women in the West: Source of Concern of Source of Hope?* (New York: Centre for Dialogues: Islamic World–US–The West, 2007), pp. 25–8.

In the case of the former, settlement patterns that go back to the 1950s result in a heavy concentration in the industrial belt of northern England. Typically, cotton, textiles, and manufacturing in the historic industrial towns of Yorkshire and Lancashire were favoured by early settlers from Pakistan and remained the centres of population concentration in the decades thereafter. While strong, thickly knit Pakistani communities were successfully established in these geographies, the downside lay in the steady and substantial erosion of the industrial base of northern England from the 1970s onwards. The cumulative negative impact on Pakistanis has been considerable over this period, and contrasts with the lower exposure to such industrial decline faced by immigrant groups, such as Indians, who favoured settling in the Midlands and the South East.[50] In the case of Bangladeshis, settlement and growth patterns have taken place more recently, stemming from the 1980s, and have been very heavily geared towards the capital city. At face value, this has been a beneficial pattern compared with the Pakistani community. Again, thickly knit and vibrant Bangladeshi communities have been established in the capital and these have in themselves given rise to indirect advantages such as access to resources and new ethnic niche markets. However, the disadvantages have operated at a slightly lower level in terms of the micro-geography of their settlement in East London. The capital's four most central-eastern boroughs (Newham, Tower Hamlets, Camden, and Islington) contain almost two-fifths of the country's entire Bangladeshi population. These boroughs have also tended to be the capital's most deprived boroughs characterized by higher-than-average unemployment, poor schooling, low status employment, and below-average earnings. In other words, London's Bangladeshis are heavily over-exposed to the city's historically most fragile economy, relative to other corners of the capital. This has brought with it high levels of deprivation among Bangladeshis. (The renaissance in London's East End, further under-scored by investment surrounding the 2012 Olympics, suggests that this community is relatively well placed geographically in relation to future economic trends.) On the positive side, potentially, is the fact that East London enjoys close proximity to the buoyant economy of central London. This has created an ample demand for wide range of labour, especially among service sector occupations, on the immediate doorstep of London's East End.

The supply side also contains important determinants of outcome. For instance, the poor human-capital profile of the Pakistani and Bangladeshi communities has already been the subject of extensive examination and discussion. A further variant on this theme is to look at the gains in human capital from one generation to the next. Scholars of migration have often

---

[50] Virdee, S., 'England: Racism, Anti-Racism and the Changing Position of Racialised Groups in Economic Relations', in Dale, G., and Cole, M. (eds.), *The European Union and Migrant Labour* (London: Berg, 1999).

emphasized the importance of looking at the trajectory of a group either at or on the way to a generation after initial arrival and settlement. Theories of immigrant succession have dwelt on this point and have sought to look for potential barriers to immigrant groups' progress. The idea has been that convergence with the dominant, non-immigrant population in terms of educational participation and qualifications would be the ideal end point over a single generation. However, set against this is the need to recalibrate assessments of progression in the light of the starting point of different immigrant groups. Some have entered and settled with much greater economic activity and human capital than others, so convergence will depend on the extent of any gap to begin with. The extent of extreme human-capital poverty among all groups, men and women, has diminished from one generation to the following one (see Figure 2.11 in Chapter 2). Among Pakistani men and women, there have been large improvements over this spell and certainly current generations are much less likely to have no qualifications at all. That said, the figure clearly demonstrates that almost a third of second-generation, British-born Pakistani women hold no qualifications whatsoever. This is a vaguely tolerable position to be in, once account is made for the position of their first-generation mothers. But, it is an exceptional position to occupy by the standards of an increasingly better-qualified younger labour force.

Looking at higher education for a moment adds a further layer of understanding. This not only represents an important route away from or out of deprivation and economic fragility, but it is also an opportunity structure that has undergone significant expansion in recent years.[51] Figure 2.11 in Chapter 2 describes the improved participation and attainment profile of all groups inter-generationally. In this instance, however, the evidence shows that Pakistanis— both men and women—have soared ahead relative to their first-generation parents. Moreover, their attainment profile now matches or exceeds that of whites, arguably a more appropriate comparator than their parents. A number of notable sectoral patterns have developed over many years linking particular ethnic and religious groups to employment niches. Each of these has some bearing on drawing general assessments about labour market participation and progression trends.[52]

A quick glance at the figures on attainment in compulsory schooling reveals that Pakistani and Bangladeshi children either bump along the bottom or just above. In higher education, by contrast, perhaps somewhat surprisingly, Pakistanis are faring better and this augurs well for their longer-run ability to access opportunity structures in employment, housing, and beyond.

[51] Reay, D., et al., 'Choices of Degree or Degrees of Choice? Class, "Race" and the Higher Education Choice Process', *Sociology*, 35, 2001, pp. 855–74.

[52] For instance, see Hussain, A., and Ishaq, M., 'British Sikhs' Identification with the Armed Forces', *Defense and Security Analysis*, Vol. 18, No. 2, June 2002, pp. 171–83.

The Search for Common, Core Values

Although it is important to recognize that fractious identity politics has been exacerbated by structural inequality, standing back, it is as important to pinpoint why and how barriers to common belonging have developed. For example, it is the case that core values and implicit ties matter, particularly where these might impede the development of a positive reputation for Western Muslim communities. They matter not least because of the shared assumptions they then deliver about citizens' rights and responsibilities.

David Goodhart, editor of *Prospect* magazine, has asserted that a common Britishness has been threatened, in part by a reluctance to pin down the sources of shared identity and co-responsibility. Historic and geographic development, he argues, has become a neglected source, and changes brought about through post-war immigration have been underestimated in their impacts on society's hidden glue. He states:[53]

... talk about the 'British people' refers not just to a set of individuals with specific rights and duties but to a group of people with a special commitment to one another. Membership in such a community implies acceptance of moral rules, however fuzzy, which underpin the laws and welfare systems of the state.

There are, however, some loose ends that arise from this argument. First, what compelling evidence is there to suggest that special commitments to one another have been especially difficult to generate across ethnic lines, given the short timescale within which such relationships have been possible, in Britain? Most readings of the large volume of data in this area would lead to caution about such an inference. Second, is there a particular reason to believe that the acceptance of moral rules has failed among minority groups at large or among some subgroups in particular? In response, there is very little to back the former but, yes, arguably, there are notable pockets where such a moral universalism is simply not apparent. The pariah politics of British Muslim communities stands out. Young, black, male subculture, increasingly violent, is another.

There are worrying undertones attached to Goodhart's argument. For starters, his claim, if forcefully pursued, can switch from a background promotional message into a prescriptive panacea, eye-catchingly placed in the foreground. Thus, minority groups (particularly unpopular ones) with putatively distinctive cultural backgrounds may believe that they must rapidly shed their cultural heritage in order, purely, to get ahead or to fit in.[54] At a local neighbourhood level, there may be a premium in keeping a low profile by being effectively forced to abandon any semblance of distinctiveness.

[53] Goodhart, D., 'Too Diverse?', *Prospect*, February 2004.
[54] Mondal, A., 'Liberal Islam?', *Prospect*, January 2003, No. 82.

'Behaving white' or even 'behaving non-Muslim' becomes something of a survival strategy in these circumstances. There can be incentives to those who are seen to discard prominent aspects of a 'foreign' culture. One recent estimate suggested that as many 50,000 name changes by deed poll take place in Britain each year, and it is simply unknown how many of these are cultural and ethnic minorities seeking one less barrier to achievement.

A further concern is that this argument implies that inter-ethnic ties will be unlikely in Britain today. In fact, they are increasingly common. The 2005 comedy hit *Little Britain* is quite sharp in making the same point. (Dear) Maggie and Judy, shorthand takes on bigotry in the rank-and-file of the contemporary Tory party, amount to between a quarter and fifth of Britons. But the real joke lies not in the scale of the prejudice but rather in the relative emotional gap between this fringe, isolated bunch who are casually racially offensive, and the rest of the British public, who never thought they were racist to begin with. (The best line, for those not in the know, is when Judy is formally asked to meet the village cub scouts and brownies. Realizing that these children comprise a fair number of Asian kids [and several in non-Western dress], she duly pats heads, shakes hands, drapes medal, and then, vomits over them, screaming that 'All the brownies are, err, brownies!' If it is funny, it is because these two ladies are a dying breed, figuratively and literally.)

A further observation is that overly simplistic solutions should be treated with caution. These may contain highly artificial ties and unsustainable forms of bonding. There is also a risk that small misreadings of public mood by government can in fact stifle the kinds of diversity that are valued, particularly in terms of business environments, commercial competition, and social innovation.

The message to the scholarly community is that the underlying relationships between bonding and bridging social capital have been poorly investigated and understood. In particular, the relationship between both kinds of social capital require further thought and particular caveats. Two illustrations will suffice. First, little regard has been given to short-term versus long-term impacts. There is every possibility that particular minority groups may exhibit higher than normal levels of bonding social capital in the short run, most notably in the initial period following settlement in their new society. This is partly because they will have left behind many of their wider social networks and will face clear and immediate obstacles to acquiring replacement networks in the new society. Additionally, the ties that bind them together on grounds of kith and kinship will be an important asset in navigating new challenges. In the longer run, however, the importance of these drivers will be likely to wane as second and third generations begin to operate with a more tailored mix of bridging and bonding relationships. Indeed, own-group ethnic ties may be approached with a combination of tacit obligation and an *à la carte* expediency. Second, researchers have only minimally considered the idea that bonding relationships are precursors to bridging relationships. Throughout the policy debate over diversity and solidarity, there is an implicit assumption that bonding and bridging social capital may be operating in tension with one another. Thus, there is said to be an inverse relationship between them as a way of fleshing out policy choices. Bridging relationships, with all the benefits they bring in terms of wider access to opportunities and greater social cohesion, are thought to be conditional on loosening bonding relationships. This is a strikingly modernist view and is questionable empirically. The experience of British Jewish communities illustrates the contrary: bonding and bridging relationships exist in large supply simultaneously and may even be drivers of one another. Robust empirical studies of Turkish communities in Amsterdam, Koreans in the Bay Area, and Indians in suburban London all point to similar pictures.

The focus has shifted in recent years to the position, outlook, and aspirations of younger generations of British Muslims. Three key trends are apparent among them. First, a small yet vocal minority has become radicalized and has sought to construct a relatively narrow interpretation of Islam, something that is pursued more extensively in Chapters 5 and 6. There are various sources of this radicalism, some of which are clearly drawn from transnational and international influences. Second, a larger group has largely successfully retained an Islamic identity while adapting to and integrating with mainstream British society. This group has met numerous obstacles in bridging between traditional norms and behaviours and those of a pluralistic, and often secular, society. A determination to allow an Islamic identity to flourish in a Western environment is an unmistakable feature of this group. Third, a large group does not any longer identify positively with its Muslim origins although it freely recognizes the importance of faith to other members of the Muslim community.[55]

Attention often falls on the first of these three groups for fairly obvious reasons. However, the nature of those in the second group and the relationship with the former group is probably more important in shaping the overall profile and reputation of British Muslims. The common link is the assertion of a common and binding Muslim identity, and the degree to which such an identity is seen as part of British identity and values.

[55] Open Society Institute/EU Accession Monitoring Program, *Monitoring Minority Protection in the EU: The Situation of Muslims in the UK*, pp. 77–8.

5

Grievance Politics

We do no wish to add to the stereotyping of the British Muslim community. But British Muslims are more likely than any other groups to feel that
they are suffering as a result of the response to international terrorism. A
broader anti-terrorism strategy should include measures to support British
Muslim leaders to resist extremists. We reject any suggestion that Muslims
are in some way more likely to turn to terrorism. We conclude that the
United Kingdom is well placed to deal with the issue of terrorism and
community relations.

House of Commons Home Affairs Committee[1]

The terrorist threat that Britain faces comes overwhelmingly from British
or foreign Muslims; it does not come from Welsh hill farmers or US
investment bankers. So it follows that most terror-related investigations
will focus on Muslim communities. This isn't picking on Muslims; it is
simply a fact of life.[2]

David Goodhart

Introduction

The post-9/11 environment has frequently heightened tensions about Islam
in the West that were already present in many Western countries. The degree
of such tensions is widely disputed by commentators as are the local, country-
specific variations and causes. For instance, in France, the spectacular demonstration of radical Islamist political violence, linked to Algerian political turmoil, in the mid-1990s had already created a context in which deep tensions
had been registered. The strictly non-French dimension of this conflict had
precious little effect on its internalization into domestic politics at the time.
A decade later, the French public debate over the (non-) right of Muslim girls

[1] House of Commons Home Affairs Committee, *Terrorism and Community Relations*
(London: House of Commons, HC 165-I, Sixth Report of Session 2004–05, Vol. 1, 2005).
[2] www.guardian.co.uk/comment/story/0,3604,1528953,00.html.

to wear headscarves at school took place within a political environment that had already been deeply coloured by events in the 1990s.

Likewise in Britain, the response to 'home-grown' extremism after the London bombings of 7/7 was hardly new in terms of disputes and tension between Muslims and the state. Indeed, many Muslim groups had been actively engaged in political interest mobilization and lobbying in the cause of religious identity for at least a decade prior to the World Trade Center attacks in 2001.[3] Organizations such as the MCB have long asserted that their broad cause had been pursued at one level regardless of immediate tensions and animosity on the ground. At another level, however, moderate manifestations of political Islam have certainly been coloured by the perception of great threats to Muslims since 9/11.

While it is possible to identify and track societal attitudes towards Muslims in a number of Western societies, it is more difficult to isolate these from general sentiment towards migrants. Indeed, a number of commentators have argued that responses to these are closely interwoven and all too often conflated by politicians and the media. Again the post-9/11 context has undoubtedly raised the underlying salience of concerns about Muslims and about migrants generally to the extent that political debate has shifted in many countries to the capacity and willingness of governments to limit either or both in the face of perceived threat. Irrational though this may seem, it has been a frequent pattern in many Western countries.

A related difficulty stems from the need to identify difference between general societal sentiment towards either Islam or the reputation of Islam on one hand, and the perception of various different Muslim communities in particular countries, within and beyond the Arab world, on the other.[4] This is about isolating the specifically Muslim aspects of positive or negative public perceptions towards migrant and migrant-descended communities who previously have not always been viewed through the prism of religious affiliation. British Muslims (like Muslims in many Western countries) in other words are a group about whom many views are frequently expressed, but it is important that these same communities were largely thought of as British Asians, or possibly Pakistanis or Bangladeshis, until comparatively recently. Equally, mixed German public feeling towards Turks in Germany is a long-running saga, and may only now be a phenomenon that is articulated and understood partially in terms of Muslim identity. Political Muslim-ness, thus, is comparatively new and a reaction to tension and conflict experienced by a variety of Muslim communities in Western societies.

---

[3] *The 9/11 Commission Report* (New York: Norton, 2004).

[4] Wright, L., *The Looking Tower: Al-Qaeda and the Road to 9/11* (New York: Alfred Knopf, 2006).

Growing Resentment and Alienation

Meanwhile, there is a growing body of evidence about general societal prejudice towards post-war immigrants including some data to suggest change over time. Some of the most unpopular groups in the 1960s and 1970s have become either less vilified or have been eclipsed by new targets of unpopularity.[5] On the other side, migrant groups from South Asian, North African, and Turkish backgrounds in Britain, France, and Germany have begun to be at the receiving end of anti-Muslim prejudice that had largely not existed until comparatively recently. In each case, political, social, and cultural identity based around Islam, in any otherwise familiar environment, has emerged as the new source of contention and prejudice. Anti-Muslim prejudice is a recurring issue that can single out Muslims from other minority communities, although, as already noted, disentangling the elements within the evidence is far from straightforward.

The same can also be said of the portrayal of Muslims and of Muslim values and cultures across the globe. This is typically bound up in a kind of 'Islamophobia', the contours of which are widely rehearsed in academic and public policy literature. However, at the same time, there is the problem of what has been dubbed 'Westophobia' pillorying and demonizing the often dominant—though not necessarily domineering—influence of rich, Western societies in economic, social, and cultural spheres.[6] Much the same point has been made in relation to tendencies, perhaps even habits, that have grown up that serve to undermine the reputation of the USA (and not just US foreign policy) in global affairs.[7]

Many Muslim groups and the British media often sight 'Islamophobia' among non-Muslim groups as being a key source of discrimination. 'Islamophobia' is thought to constitute a two-stranded form of racism and societal hostility rooted in the different physical appearance and cultural presence of Muslims and an intolerance of their religious and cultural beliefs.[8] The term is thought to signify the modern epidemic of a historical fear and prejudice against Islam by Western society, although there are a number of interpretations on its lineage. The first known printed usage of the word 'Islamophobia' appears to be in an article printed in the February 1991 edition of the US

[5] Centre for Research into Election and Social Trends (CREST), based on British Social Attitudes data, 2002.

[6] Iqbal Riza, Special Advisor to the UN Secretary-General on the Alliance of Civilisations, quoted in Centre for Dialogues, *Muslim Youth and Women in the West: Source of Concern of Source of Hope?* (New York: Centre for Dialogues: Islamic World–US–The West, 2007), pp. 10–11.

[7] Lieven, A., and Hulsman, J., *Ethical Realism: A Vision for America's Role in the World* (New York: Parthenon, 2006).

[8] Muslim Council of Britain, *The Quest for Sanity: Reflections on September 11 and the Aftermath* (London: Muslim Council of Britain, 2002).

periodical *Insight*. The term has been included in the *Oxford English Dictionary* since 1997.

A survey of (perceptions of) religious discrimination by the Home Office in 2001 found that 86 per cent of Muslims thought that to some degree ignorance of their religion by others was a serious problem. The survey reported that 37 per cent of Muslims thought that hostility was a 'very serious' problem and 28 per cent cited physical abuse as a problem. Muslims also saw the policies and practices of organizations in relation to Islam as being a serious concern, more than any other religion. It is a moot point as to how far this perception was based on a general hostility against religion and religious groups as opposed to being thought of in terms that single out Muslims. The main reason for adding this note of caution is that non-Muslim respondents to this survey, who were also from religious minorities reported similar things. Similar proportions of Hindus and Sikhs, the other two main South Asian religious communities in the Britain, felt that the practices of organizations resulted in 'quite serious' problems for them. British Muslim respondents certainly contained a lower threshold of those who tended to dismiss the problem. Equally, however, around a fifth of Muslims did not know whether this constituted a problem or not, a proportion very much in line with several other religious minorities (and indeed the majority Christian group). The upshot of these data is that there is a question mark as to how distinctive Muslim sentiment really is on this point.

Elsewhere, there is reason to think that interpreting these data into grass-roots sentiment is not necessarily straightforward. The main reason for this is the idea that, for Muslims, religious membership and affiliation may amount to a more significant aspect of individual and collective identity than for other religious groups. So, for instance, a proportion within this religious group who sense and then report through survey research that very serious problems exist in society in terms of their acceptance as a religious community cannot directly equate to a similar proportion holding similar views in a different religious group. This is because the underlying intensity of their views—themselves underscored by a more intense attachment to religious identity—is not picked up through survey evidence of this kind. The distribution of views is known, as is the strength of those views. But placing them in a proper context involves asking whether it is reasonable, based on what is known in research data, to take as read that Muslim identity is as central for Muslims as another religious identity is for another faith group.[9] It is not a simple assumption to make or rely on. The 2001 Citizenship Survey, sponsored by the UK Home Office, revealed that British Muslims preferred to identify themselves in religious terms to a far higher degree than other religious

[9] Bleich, E., 'Religion, Violence and the State in 21st Century Europe', unpublished paper, 2006.

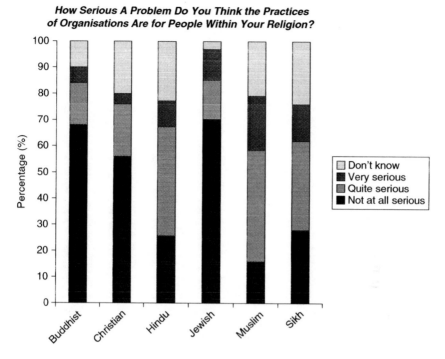

Figure 5.1. Perceptions of religious understanding and tolerance
Source: Religious Discrimination in England and Wales (Home Office, 2001).

groups.[10] This at least implies that we are not strictly comparing apples with apples in interrogating evidence such as the 2001 religious discrimination survey. Figure 5.1 tells the story.

There is evidence that Islam is often portrayed by the British media and others as being backward or chauvinistic in comparison to an 'enlightened' modern Western society.[11] The previously mentioned 2001 Home Office survey found that 48 per cent of Muslims thought media representations were a serious problem for their religion.

A 2002 survey commissioned by a UK-based Muslim organization showed that 73 per cent of non-Muslims felt that they knew little or nothing about Britain's Muslim communities; moreover, 66 per cent cited newspapers and television as their biggest single source of information about Britain's Muslim communities.[12] The events of September 11, according to these findings, were

---

[10] O'Beirne, M., *Religion in England and Wales: Findings from the Home Office Citizenship Study 2001*, Home Office Research Study 274 (London: Home Office, 2004), p. 20.

[11] *Islamophobia: A Challenge for us All* (London: Runnymede Trust, 1997).

[12] 'Attitudes Towards British Muslims: A Survey Commissioned by the Islamic Society of Britain and Conducted by YouGov', November 2002.

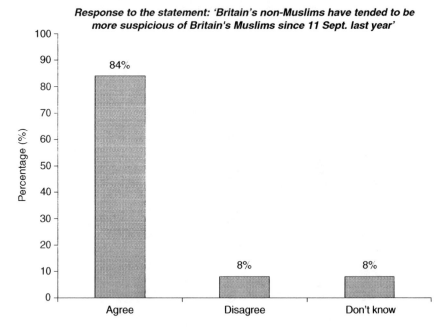

Figure 5.2. Suspiciousness towards British Muslims

Source: Attitudes towards British Muslims: a survey commissioned by the Islamic Society of Britain and conducted by YouGov, Nov. 2002.

seen to have a significant negative impact on perceptions of Britain's Muslim community by non-Muslims (Figure 5.2).

Somewhat older data from the World Values Survey paint a fairly bleak picture of attitudes towards Muslims in different Western countries—see Figure 5.3. Although dated, it is interesting that, according to this survey, as far back as 1990 for instance almost 17 per cent of British respondents confirmed that they 'would not like to have Muslims as neighbours', twice as many who felt similarly about having neighbours from a different racial group. British sentiment was fairly typical of the countries surveyed in the WVS study. Though dated, this evidence points to an additional burden of prejudice that is often endured by Muslims, that goes beyond existing sentiment against ethnic minorities.

Following the events of September 11, the Italian Prime Minister declared that Islam was inferior to the West, although he was widely condemned for doing so. Samuel Huntington's *The Clash of Civilisations* describes a single, monolithic 'militant' Islam that poses a great threat to the West. Similar sentiments have been expressed by a range of scholars, journalists, and public figures across Europe and beyond. For example, Francis Fukuyama's recent book, *America at the Crossroads*, makes great play of a lack of realism in the

On this list are various groups of people. Could you please
sort out any that you would not like to have for neighbours?

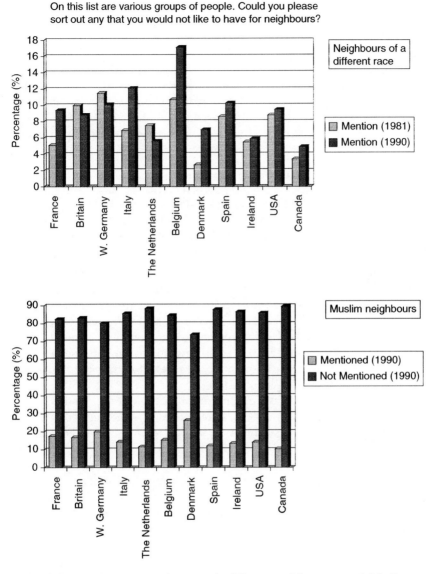

Figure 5.3. Comparative attitudes towards different racial groups and Muslims as
neighbours, 1981 and 1990

way in which European societies and political leaders view the presence of
large Muslim minorities in their midst.[13]

[13] Fukuyama, F., *America at the Crossroads: Democracy, Power, and the Neoconservative Legacy*
(New Haven, CT: Yale University Press, 2006).

The main point of contention is the degree to which active social and economic integration strategies have been pursued in Europe, where, according to Fukuyama, the contrast with immigrant integration and assimilation in the USA could not have been sharper. This disagreement in turn has tended to fuel related debates about European and American understanding of the causes of religious radicalism and political extremism linked to violence. Citing the anniversary conference following the Madrid bombings, entitled Terrorism and Democracy, Jonathan Paris, a security analyst, describes the range of additional 'route causes' placed on the table and their growing appreciation in American quarters:[14]

A(nother) difference is the European emphasis on analysing the root causes that allow fanaticism to spread. Poverty, social exclusion and humiliation, lack of education, and failed states were cited at Madrid. Palestine [is] frequently mentioned as a root cause, namely the 37-year occupation of the West Bank and Gaza, although some speakers added that even if that conflict is resolved, many other problems in the Islamic world still need to be addressed.

Some views expressed by neo-conservative and other commentators are highly critical of Islam as a whole and have provided fuel for reactionary forces within Britain, especially in relation to perceived terrorist threats. Aspects of these criticisms have focused on Muslim political and religious leaders' outlook towards sexuality and towards Jewish communities.[15] Bernard Lewis's earlier identification of external Muslim resentment towards the West has been extended by various commentators to describe the outlook of some Muslim leaders within Western societies.[16]

Oversimplification and potential misrepresentation of this kind is important. The terrorist bombers of 9/11 were extremely well-educated individuals. Their outlook towards Muslim–non-Muslim tensions within and beyond Western societies has been rarely probed. Despite that, attempts to try to place a single brand on such a diverse and sophisticated group miss key details and nuances about understanding and misunderstanding of Islam within and among Western societies.[17]

Negative portrayals of Islam in the British media have also been combined with a sense of humiliation and anger among Muslim communities at the treatment of many Muslim countries by the West.[18] It is clear that there are many transnational linkages between British Muslims and Muslims of other nations. Overwhelmingly, these transnational drivers, such as pilgrimage and

[14] Paris, J., 'European vs. American Approaches to Terrorism: Contrasts and Convergences', *Asharq Alawsat*, 21 March 2005.

[15] Browne, A., 'Anti-Jewish? Anti-gay? Welcome to Britain', *The Times*, 6 July 2004.

[16] Lewis, B., 'The Roots of Muslim Rage', *Atlantic Monthly*, September 1990.

[17] Baubőck, R., *The Integration of Immigrants* (Strasbourg: Council of Europe, 1995) PO-S_MG(94).

[18] Freeland, J., 'In the Grip of Panic ', *Guardian*, 22 January 2005.

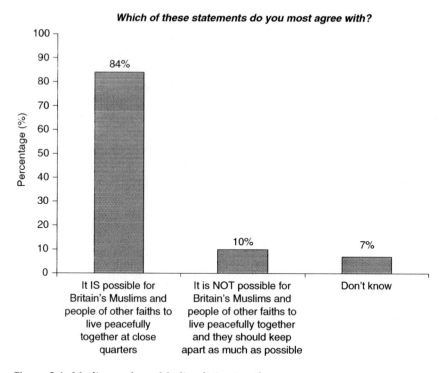

Figure 5.4. Muslims and non-Muslims living together

Source: Attitudes towards British Muslims: a survey commissioned by the Islamic Society of Britain and conducted by YouGov, Nov. 2002.

family contacts in other countries, are positive forces. However, negative sentiment as a result of the war on terrorism and the conflict in Iraq has led to a strong sense of anger and isolation among many British Muslims, particularly young men, who may be targets for extremist Islamic organizations.[19] There is also reason to think that this has produced significant short-term damage to the electoral strength of the Labour Party in this voting constituency.[20]

It will take a great deal of time, patience, effort, and political success to break the link between humiliation and modernization perceived by many Muslim groups.[21] However, the YouGov survey, shown in Figure 5.4, also showed that British people were overwhelmingly optimistic about the prospect of

[19] Saggar, S., 'The One Per Cent World', annual University of Sussex London lecture, 16 March 2006; available at http://www.sussex.ac.uk/Units/alumni/pages/prof_lectures/shamit_saggar.html.

[20] Bodi, F., 'Ties that no Longer Bind', *Guardian*, 5 May 2005.

[21] Bunting., M., 'Elephants in the Room', *Guardian*, 21 January 2005.

Muslims and non-Muslims living peacefully together. There is no inevitability in Western hatred towards Muslims in the West and Islam generally.[22]

Notwithstanding this piece of encouraging evidence, the 2001 Home Office survey also found that Muslims, along with many other religious groups, thought that non-religious factors played a significant role in driving discrimination. Some 54 per cent of Muslims thought that ethnic or racial factors were a 'large or main part of the reason' for discrimination on the basis of religion. Therefore, one reasonable inference from these data is that anti-minority sentiment and/or behaviour is not easy to disentangle from those driven by anti-Muslim feeling and behaviour.

Looking at government policies and programmes, the vast bulk of initiatives are organized around the conceptual building block of race equality and inequality.[23] It is not surprising then to see that the problem of disentangling race and religion persists. Of course, a larger anti-Asian problem, explained in terms that are separate from religious background, may colour the overall picture. Equally, the danger is that being a Muslim may act as an additional obstacle to progress, with the effects of anti-Muslim attitudes serving to reinforce the fragile position of certain at-risk groups (e.g. second- and third-generation Pakistani boys who currently exhibit very low attainment in the compulsory education system).

Muslim Identity and Collective Religious Consciousness

The basic premise lying behind debates about Western Muslim communities is that these are in essence a common social and political group. Malik puts the argument in the following way:[24]

Muslims are a group whose membership is determined according to common faith-based beliefs, sentiments, experiences and attitudes. In short, there is sufficient similarity amongst Muslims to allow us to speak about them meaningfully as a social group. [For example], religion has become a more significant marker of identity than ethnicity for Muslims in the UK.

This proposition may appear clear-cut at one level, but it opens up as many questions as it purports to answer. To begin with, it must at least be open to empirical testing to assess the degree to which such common faith-based beliefs, sentiments, and attitudes are present and whether these are independently driven or more closely attached to one another. Evidence later in

[22] Saggar, S., 'Left Out', *Guardian*, November 2004.

[23] Reed, J., 'Young Muslims in the UK: Education and Integration', briefing paper for FES/IPPR seminar, IPPR, December 2005.

[24] Malik, M., 'Discrimination, Equality and Community Cohesion', *Muslims in the UK: Policies for Engaged Citizens* (Budapest: OSI, 2005).

this chapter will explore this further. Second, the proposition pushes against the argument that suggests that Muslims are sufficiently internally differentiated to mean that we are, in practical terms, describing a plurality of social groups.[25] Britain, for example, comprises a number of Muslim communities, where important national, linguistic, migratory, theological, and other differences can be isolated in some detail. Much was made of this differentiation in Chapter 2. The differentiated picture can be further added to by examining the degree to which socio-economic variations are associated with demographic distinctions. For example, by disaggregating for gender and generation, we can immediately contrast the economic activity rates of first-generation Pakistani women with that of second-generation Pakistani men. The findings show that their economic activity rates are more than 40 percentage points apart, suggesting that this is a major line of internal differentiation. Third, the claim that the development of common identity is the result of internal factors is worth examining more closely. An alternative argument may be to assess how far Muslim categories of social identity have developed externally to the group.[26] Muslim-ness allows us to understand the features and concerns of the group, but it is not terribly helpful in helping to explain the sources of political and social difference.

A parallel debate has existed for many years in relation to the nature and extent of ethnic difference as a source shaping substantive economic, social, and political differences, in countries such as Britain and the USA. The example of the political participation and behaviour of different ethnic groups illustrates the point well.[27] On one hand, it is possible, in the British case, to point to robust evidence to show that the political orientation, attitudes, and behaviour of various ethnic minority groups follow a path that contrasts rather sharply with the white majority reference group. The higher propensity of black and Asian voters, compared with whites, to support the Labour Party has been an obvious manifestation. This pattern has been relatively insulated from trends in the popularity cycle of the major political parties, so that Labour's long wilderness years in the 1980s and early 1990s were perversely accompanied by steady and high levels of electoral support among its ethnic minority constituency. Finally, the evidence indicated that the usual sources of political difference—typically social class, education, and housing—were rather poor predictors of electoral preference among blacks and Asians. All of this caused commentators to speak of ethnic minorities as a distinctive

[25] Birt, Y., 'Between Nation and *Umma*: Muslim Loyalty in a Globalizing World—Musings on the Britannic Crest', *Islam21*, 40, January 2006, pp. 6–11; available at http://www.yahyabirt.com/?p = 64.
[26] Legenhausen, M., 'A Muslim's Non-Reductive Religious Pluralism', in Boase, R. (ed.), *Islam and Global Dialogue: Religious Pluralism and the Pursuit of Peace* (Aldershot: Ashgate, 2005).
[27] Evans, H., 'Narcissism on Stilts', *New York Sun*, 16 November 2006.

political constituency and of the notion of an 'iron law' of minority voting behaviour. The difficulty arose in testing how far the drivers of commonness were in fact fundamental as opposed to circumstantial. Multivariate analysis revealed a limited social class effect taking place within otherwise high and saturated levels of Labour voting. The implication is that, while ethnicity clearly matters in shaping political outlook and electoral behaviour, it did not matter quite as much as many commentators had previously claimed or inferred. Likewise in the case of British or indeed Western Muslims, there is a distinct possibility that commonness is the result of both fundamental and circumstantial factors. To describe Muslims in this context as a distinctive community is probably to stretch analytical understanding too far. A fairer assessment may be to acknowledge the limiting aspects of common identity as a result of circumstantial reasons, while at the same time emphasizing the political construction of Muslim identity as a deliberate act and process. The politics of recognition plays a central part in the latter and allows us to make sense of Western Muslims in a more appropriate context. This is particularly noticeable when examining the influence of ethical values and traditions that arise from within, and transcend, particular ethnic or religious identities.[28]

Although the research literature has grown significantly in recent years, there is little systematic evidence on Muslim collective identity and consciousness.[29] Anecdotal evidence from a range of sources points to generally rising levels of religious consciousness and self-identity among British Muslims.[30] O'Beirne, for example, has observed that for British Muslims there is growing reason to believe that religion has now emerged as a central part of identity, and that this largely transcends ethnic and national origins which have previously contributed heavily to distinctions of identity.[31]

The other important contextual remark to make is that this emerging force in Muslim group identity has taken place against the backdrop of generally declining societal identification with or through religion or faith. Added to this observation is a broader debate over secularization in modern industrial societies. Theories of secularization tend towards seeing tensions and incompatibilities between religiosity on one hand and modern society on the other.[32] For instance, the development of modern social welfare provision

[28] Appiah, A. K., *Cosmopolitanism: Ethics in a World of Strangers* (New York: Norton, 2006).

[29] El-Affendi, A., 'On the State, Democracy and Pluralism', in Taji-Farouki, S., and Nafi, B. M. (eds.), *Islamic Thought in the Twentieth Century* (London: I. B. Tauris, 2004), pp. 172–94.

[30] See for example Catherwood, C., *Why the Nations Rage: Killing in the Name of God*, 2nd edn (Lanham, MD Oxford: Rowman and Littlefield 2002), esp. ch. 11; see also Ansari, H., *Muslims in Britain—Report* (London: Minority Rights Group International, 2002), pp. 13–14.

[31] O'Beirne, M., *Religion in England and Wales: findings from the 2001 Home Office Citizenship Survey*, Home Office Research Study 274 (London: Home Office, 2004).

[32] Sardar, Z., *Beyond Difference: Cultural Relations in the Twenty First Century* (London: British Council, 2004).

by the state has, it is widely argued, contributed to the decline in religious observance and identity as church-based contributions to social assistance have waned. Analysis of British Social Attitudes data, for example, indicates that there is no sign that secularization has been halted in Britain or indeed in other comparable Christian societies.[33] Muslims in Britain are therefore generally surrounded by an environment of low church attendance, moderate belief in the existence of God, and declining church membership.

Surveys of Muslim identity and consciousness show that influences from internal sources are themselves conditioned by the external reputation of Islam in Britain and internationally. For example, a unique survey by the Federation of Student Islamic Societies (FOSIS) conducted in the months after the 2005 London attacks showed that a clear line of anxiety was evident within the surveyed group. On one hand, the survey revealed continuing, strong backing for pride in British identity. On the other hand, this appeared to sit uneasily with group fears that Muslims as a whole were being tarnished with the brush of extremism and violence. The same survey revealed that 43 per cent of Muslim students and recent graduates accepted that, generally speaking, society's wider perceptions about Islam had worsened following the July 2005 attacks. More specifically, nine in ten reported a deterioration in the standing of Muslim students among their peers following the attacks.[34]

The international dimension highlights the rapid pace of absorption of collective grievance that is, or can easily be, distilled into a common religious bond. Building solidarity on such religious lines that span nation states is a real possibility. Again the 2005 FOSIS student survey reflects this point. It showed several related things. First, some 93 per cent of respondents felt that the mass media was either critical or very important in shaping public opinion and sentiments towards Muslims. Nine-tenths also felt that the media's image of Muslims needed to be changed. However, once attention in the survey turned to the question of the causes behind the actions of the London bombers, a striking 32 per cent cited foreign policy and a further 30 per cent mentioned the Iraq war as the first and second most important factors, respectively. Thereafter, 83 per cent reported their dissatisfaction with British foreign policy (just 5% felt content about this). When probed about what elements caused greatest dissatisfaction, 36 per cent cited Iraq, followed by the Israel/Palestine conflict (21%), and Afghanistan (8%).

[33] De Graaf, N. D., and Need, A., 'Losing Faith: Is Britain Alone?', *British Social Attitudes: The 17th Report* (London: Sage, 2000).

[34] The Federation of Student Islamic Societies, 'The Voice of Muslim Students: A Report into the Attitudes and Perceptions of Muslim Students Following the July 7th London Attacks', FOSIS, 2005; available at http://www.fosis.org.uk/resources/general%20_literature/FullReport.pdf.

The radicalization and Islamization of conflicts in Israel/Palestine, Kashmir, the Indonesian province of Aceh, Chechnya,[35] and elsewhere are frequently transmitted as religious divisions with claims on the sympathies and loyalties of British Muslims. In exceptional cases, British Muslims can and have become a recruitment pool for extremist beliefs and violent action. The example of the pair of British suicide bombers who in 2003 targeted 'Mike's Place', a seaside bar in Tel Aviv, is well known. There are numerous other less well-documented cases that fall into the same general category, confirming in a piecemeal way the existence of a small though significant pool of British-born or -based Muslims committed to suicide missions to achieve wider political goals.[36]

Connectedness and Cohesion

Behind these particular debating points regarding Muslim integration lie one or two large questions about the nature and extent of connectivity between people across ethnic and religious boundaries in Western countries. And with this comes a set of immediate questions to do with establishing new mechanisms for contact and routine connectivity across traditional boundaries as a means of re-establishing respect and understanding, where there might otherwise be a risk of lack of contact and understanding.[37] For any society to create a common vision for itself, it is necessary for it to find effective ways to nurture a sense of belonging among its members.[38] These members are not merely required to be of that society; they are also entitled to be treated in a way that values them as integral to the society. Belonging is a mild way of expressing this requirement. A more imaginary and ambitious way is to think, perhaps, of them as being rooted in that society.[39] For this reason alone, arguably there has to be some public endorsement and acceptance of identity even if there are plural identities involved.

A traditional liberal understanding of societal membership has tended to focus on recognition of individuals as citizens. However, this can create a rub since it is not explicit about recognition of the group identity or identities through which the relationship between citizen and state is conducted. Identity, in other words, can amount to an essential lubricant for common

[35] In 1998, Islamists joined Chechen commanders and began a jihad to drive Russia from other areas of the Caucasus, including neighbouring Dagestan, aiming to create a single Islamic republic. See http://www.ceip.org/files/Publications/2002-11-03-lieven-nytimes.asp?pr=2&from=pubdate.

[36] http://www.guardian.co.uk/attackonlondon/story/0,16132,1527359,00.html.

[37] Gray, J., 'Easier Said Than Done', *Nation*, 30 January 2006; available at http://www.thenation.com/doc/20060130/gray.

[38] See for example Werbner, P., *Imagined Diasporas Among Manchester Muslims* (Oxford: James Curray, 2002).

[39] Madani, H. A., *Composite Nationalism and Islam [Muttahida Qaumiyat aur Islam]*, translated by Hussain, A. H., and Imam, H. (Delhi: Manohar, 2005 [1938]), pp. 76–7 and 79–80.

belonging and inclusion to work. Western secularism—and its reputation in largely theocratic, spiritual, and conservative societies—is an obvious potential impediment to belonging and inclusion based on faith.

The task is to build the foundations of a community that is both cohesive and diverse in its composition. According to Maleiha Malik's especially thoughtful reflection on Muslim collective identity, this involves several elements whereby:[40]

- There is a common vision and all communities have a sense of belonging.[41]

- The diversity of people's different backgrounds and circumstances is appreciated and positively valued.[42]

- Those from different backgrounds have similar opportunities. Language fluency and language barriers to entry into particular occupational categories are prime examples that can prevent this.[43]

- Those from different backgrounds develop strong, positive relationships in the workplace, in schools, and within neighbourhoods. Thus, perceptions, however, ill-informed, of freeloading can be very damaging.[44]

At the heart of the above is a conception of what it means to be a successful, cohesive society. The emergence of radical Islamist political movement and identities in Western societies represents one of the biggest challenges seen or imaginable in post-war integration politics and policy. And at the centre of strategies to understand and counter such radicalization sit 'sociological theories which suggest that it is those without any stake in society who become primary candidates to turn against it, [that is] theories that posit "discontent" of various forms as a rationale for terrorist violence'.[45] What is at issue is not whether or how far discontentedness fuels Muslim youth radicalization, but rather whether this logic provides a set of necessary and sufficient conditions for such radicalization to begin with.[46]

[40] Malik, M., 'Discrimination, Equality and Community Cohesion', *Muslims in the UK: Policies for Engaged Citizens* (Budapest: Open Society Institute, 2005), p. 55.

[41] This point is adequately reinforced by, for example, Council of Europe, 'Framework of Integration Policies', 2000.

[42] Evidence to support such an analysis can be found in Page, B., 'The Second Death of Liberal England', MORI, 2004.

[43] This argument is also reflected in the unpublished submission by the Advisory Board on Naturalisation and Integration to the Commonwealth Commission in Respect and Understanding, February 2007.

[44] Dench, G., et al., *The New East End: Kinship, Race and Conflict* (London: Young Foundation, 2006).

[45] Unpublished submission by Archbishop of York to the Commonwealth Commission on Respect and Understanding, February 2007.

[46] Cozzens, J., 'Identifying Entry Points of Action in Counter Radicalisation', DISS Working Paper 2006/6 (Copenhagen: Danish Institute for International Studies, 2006).

The challenge of Islam and Islamic identity in Western societies is perceived to represent a major task for policymakers with relatively few short-term options. The familiar objective of integration over time, with immigrant succession ensuring that the future remained, figuratively and actually, a brighter day for Western-born offspring, appears less credible in the face of (a) settled disadvantage, (b) growing opposition cultures, and (c) the rise of radicalized, confrontational strands of Islamic identity.[47] Furthermore, the dynamics of global Islam have become difficult to read, let alone anticipate. The position of Muslims in the West presents a further complication to such dynamics, especially when considering the issue of doctrinal teachings on civil disobedience and dissent.[48]

A more fine-grained understanding emerges from the insights of anthropological and socio-legal studies of Islamic identity and of the dynamics of global Islam.[49] A striking debate exists on the sources and consequences of international and transnational Muslim identity.[50] The intersection between spiritual and political objectives has been at the heart of this debate, and one manifestation of this has been differing interpretations of the role and meaning of secular power in both Middle Eastern and Western societies.

The sources and consequences of international and transnational Muslim identity stand out as a major debate with important policy implications. The intersection between spiritual and political objectives has been at the heart of this debate, and one manifestation of this has been differing interpretations of the role and meaning of secular power in both Middle Eastern and Western societies. Clifford Geertz, a commentator on contemporary Muslim societies, summarizes the question and its potential impacts:[51]

More than any other single thing, it has been the rising tendency to ideologise faith in so much of the Muslim world that has made it increasingly hard to arrive at summary accounts of what is happening there. The movement from religion to religious-mindedness, from Islam to Islamism, from a rather quietist, withdrawn and scholastic immersion in the fine details of law and worship, the ordinary piety of everyday life, to an activist, reformist, increasingly determined struggle to capture secular power and turn it to spiritual ends, has transformed what once was, or seemed to be, a historical macro-entity to be set beside Christianity, the West, science, or modernity, into a disorderly field of entangled differences about which it is difficult to say anything at all except that it seems at once various and volatile.

---

[47] Lewis, B., *Islam in Crisis* (London: Weidenfeld and Nicolson, 2003).

[48] See for instance Sheikh Abdullah bin Bayyah, 'Muslims Living in Non-Muslim Lands' (1999), available at http://www.witnesspioneer.org/vil/Articles/shariah/muslims_in_non_muslim_land.htm.

[49] For instance, see Bowen, J., 'Does French Islam have Borders? Dilemmas of Domestication in a Global Religious Field', *American Anthropologist*, Vol. 106, No. 4, 2004.

[50] Sullivan, K., and Partlow, J., 'Young Muslim Rage takes Root in Britain', *Washington Post*, 13 August 2006.

[51] *New York Review of Books*, Vol. 50, No. 11, 3 July 2003.

The stakes involved in understanding the origins and drivers of the transformation described above are very high. The essential backdrop to integration and community cohesion strategies has changed fundamentally. According to Gilles Kepel:[52]

The militant Islamic movement is a phenomenon whose emergence was as spectacular as it was unforeseen.

Muslims in Western, secular societies face a range of obligations from both internal and external sources, including racial and ethnic lines of loyalty that can trample on aspirations for religious unity.[53] Relatively little work has been done to examine the Muslim conception (or conceptions) of citizenship in these circumstances.[54] For example, a recurring and often fraught argument is sustained on the question of whether, and in what circumstances, a Muslim can and should give allegiance to a non-Muslim. Tariq Ramadan, a leading scholar of Islam and citizenship, points to three aspects of this dilemma:[55]

- Citizenship—implying that Muslims everywhere are members of organized, structured systems that lead to both duties and rights.
- Belonging—accepting that, although emotional in nature, feeling a part of a society has to be genuine; by the same token, having to show this for external consumption can devalue the meaning of belonging.
- Patriotism—the open awareness that Muslims must contribute to the society they live in or have adopted in a collective manner.

This analysis leads to a more pluralistic account of Islam than has been seen hitherto. In particular, it creates the preconditions for a notion, as Ramadan puts it, of 'good' or enlightened Islamic citizenship that plays a healthy and vibrant role in Western liberal societies with four main elements:

- A strong denunciation of dictatorship by Muslims and an implied stance of resistance to such a dictatorship.
- Opposition to causes that give weight to specific, sectional interests over the interests of all in a society.

[52] Kepel, G., *Jihad: The Trail of Political Islam* (Cambridge, MA: Harvard University Press, 2003).

[53] Elliot, A., 'Between Black and Immigrant Muslims: An Uneasy Alliance', *New York Times*, 11 March 2007.

[54] An important exception, limited to the case of France, is Laurence, J., and Vaisse, J., *Integrating Islam: Political and Religious Challenges in Contemporary France* (Washington, DC: Brookings Institution, 2006). Another source of wide-ranging discussion of this question can be found in Hunter, S. (ed.), *Islam, Europe's Second Religion: The New Social, Cultural and Political Landscape* (Westport, CT: Praeger, 2002).

[55] Ramadan, T., 'Islam, Citizenship and Social Justice', keynote address to a conference on Islam and Social Justice, British Council/Citizen Organising Foundation/Islamic Foundation, June 2003.

- The capacity and knowledge to promote a critical, pluralistic debate within a framework that gives credibility to low religious and spiritual commitment and activism.

- Framing and adoption of clear ethical principles and teaching to guide Muslims—and non-Muslims—in their thoughts and their lives.

The significance of this position is that it reopens the question of what lies in the public and private spheres. Indeed, it stresses the distinction between these spheres, highlights the very considerable grey areas for interpretation and potential dispute, and concludes that distinction does indeed mean divorce. The objective, according to Ramadan, is to introduce 'a source of nourishment based on Islamic values'[56] in both spheres.

Cohesion, Foreign Affairs, and Terror

Obviously serious threats to security are the mainstay of most understandings of Islamist terrorism in Western countries. However, this is but one side of the question and this study is unusual in seeking to look beyond such a familiar frame of reference. The argument presented in this book is principally about seeking to shift the conceptual lens of security to examine underlying causes and wrinkles while simultaneously shifting the focus of integration to look more thoroughly at a variety of breakdowns of belonging and cohesion.

The greater concern, at this stage, is the degree to which such exceptional behaviour is tacitly condoned or accepted within parts of Western Muslim communities. Not surprisingly, there is only limited hard data on these tacit, undeclared sympathies.[57] Anecdotal evidence fills this vacuum although there is further analysis and discussion of limited data sources in Chapter 6 later in this book.

The involvement of young British men in a suicide attack in Tel Aviv in May 2003 led to the following kind of widely reported sentiment 'on the street':[58]

'In a way, I sympathize,' said Mohammed Zahid, 23, an automobile-plant inspector with a broad Midlands accent, who was strolling down Normanton Road, near where Mr. Sharif lived with his wife and two daughters. 'When you see what's happening in Israel, something comes into your mind, something just goes.'

---

[56] Ramadan, T., 'Islam, Citizenship and Social Justice', keynote address to a conference on Islam and Social Justice, British Council/Citizen Organising Foundation/Islamic Foundation, June 2003; see also Ramadan, T., *Western Muslims and the Future of Islam* (New York: Oxford University Press, 2004).

[57] Swain, S., 'Protective Security: New Challenges', presentation to a conference on 'Countering Suicide Terrorism', Royal United Services Institute, 6 March 2007.

[58] Quoted in 'What Drove 2 Britons to Bomb a Club in Tel Aviv?', *New York Times*, 12 May 2003.

Not surprisingly events in the past few years linking British Muslims to a range of conflicts have affected the shape of opinion and attitudes within this community. The outlook of younger members of the Muslim communities is revealing in that there is a deep scepticism about radical voices and the intertwining of Islam and political objectives.[59] A large survey of British Muslim youth in 2001 looked beyond reactions to 9/11 and probed aspects of positive and negative sentiment about Britain and Western societies. The findings are summarized in Box 5.1.

Evidence such as the survey quoted above suggests that academic understanding of social attitudes among British and Western Muslims towards foreign affairs is rather poorly developed.[60] This in turn signifies a larger difficulty in social science research in identifying the degree to which domestic public attitudes in general can be linked to, or be described as shaping, the foreign policy priorities of national governments. Studies in this area are remarkably scarce in number and in the detail they provide. Some exceptions can be identified, and these point to a number of conditioning effects.

One topical example from German politics illustrates this well. Survey research shows strong and persistent levels of oppositional feeling among German voters towards the Bush-led US administration generally and towards American foreign policy specifically. This feature of German public sentiment, more than any factors, appears to be the single largest obstacle to the ability of Chancellor Merkel to realign German foreign policy to bring it closer to the position of the US government. Elsewhere, more detailed studies of British Muslim opinion repeatedly point to the stronger salience of foreign policy issues among this group relative to the population at large.[61] Moreover, Muslims are regularly more likely to cite British and US policy in the Middle East—and specifically the US alliance with Israel—as a key factor in accounting for Muslim antagonism towards Western governments.

The underlying point of contention here is the extent to which modern Western liberal democracies view their foreign policies as subject to mass political legitimacy. An eighteenth- and nineteenth-century-inspired understanding of foreign affairs would take a sceptical view of such a claim, not least because of prevailing notions of the involvement and dominance of elites in shaping the foreign policies of such states. The contemporary efforts of several liberal democracies to modernize their approach to foreign affairs at least

[59] Roy, O., *Globalised Islam: The Search for a New Umma* (New York: Columbia University Press, 2004).

[60] See for example Zogby International, 'American Muslim Poll 2004', conducted by Zogby International for Muslims in the American Public Square (MAPS); available at www.projectmaps.com/AMP2004report.pdf.

[61] 'Gallup World Poll: Muslims' (Princeton, NJ: Gallup Organisation, 2007).

Box 5.1 British Muslim Youth Survey, December 2001

Conclusions from the September 11 attacks
- Strong feelings of outrage and shock on hearing of the attacks
- More importantly the majority believed that Islam either prohibited or discouraged such attacks

Best aspect of living in Britain—boys
- Being able to practice your religion freely and freedom of speech
- Freedom of action and of speech, freedom to criticize the government, freedom taken for granted
- Freedom to practice Islam, through your own views and opinions (and to a greater extent than in a Muslim country)
- Freedom to practice any religion
- Tolerance and opportunities
- No fear of being persecuted
- Good standard of living
- Freedom of speech better than most Arab and Muslim countries
- Understanding and support of the government
- Education and technology (the opportunities that are available; good technology; strong educational system)
- Muslim networks and facilities (Muslims living in the UK are much better off than Muslims around the world; lots of mosques around Britain; the right to practice religion; opportunities to learn more about own religion; global aspects of Islam)

Best aspect of living in Britain—girls
- Good education and career opportunities; absence of poverty
- Feeling that most non-Muslims are tolerant of Muslims
- Multicultural climate (people are more open-minded, and the media is fairer than in other places; people can start to accept Islam because it is a multicultural country; freedom to practice Islam; freedom of speech, education, facilities (Internet, television, etc.); some people really making the effort to make you fit in; can tell people about Islam)
- More freedom towards women
- Better environment (reliable security; cleaner areas; fresh/clean food and water; very little fighting; better healthcare; availability of Halal food)
- Muslim networks (family live here and it is the only place ever lived; talking to people about Islam and learning more about it in Islamic circles; being around other Muslims; seeing how Muslim families live together)

Most difficult aspects of living in Britain—boys
- Religious insults, discrimination, and fear of persecution
- Value of Muslims undermined greatly and not helped by the equation of Islam with terror

- Baggage of those Muslims who support Bin Laden or the Taleban
- Under constant pressure and scrutiny for being an Asian Muslim living in Britain
- Racism (racial tensions created by the BNP, NF, etc.)
- Not having enough awareness about other religions
- Having to contend with pseudo-freedom promoted in Britain and constant need explain that Islam is a comprehensive and ideal system that has real freedom
- People think you are different but you are not
- Non-Muslim lack of acceptance of Muslims with status in Britain
- Fear of being stereotyped
- Distraction of Western society (Muslims becoming Westernized; living as a Muslim life with restrictions, e.g. drinking, smoking; trying to keep Islam in a Western non-Muslim world; drugs, violence, sex, corruption; twisted morality of society; non-Halal food at parties/in restaurants)
- Bad weather, constant darkness

Most difficult aspects of living in Britain—girls

- Religious aspects (wearing a head scarf at school; not having prayer rooms in the workplace, in schools/universities; rude comments about choice of dress; wearing the *hijab*; lack of understanding of others for own acts of worship)
- Media coverage (misinformation about Islam promoted in the media; slanted coverage of Muslim communities)
- Racism, lack of respect and understanding (being constantly viewed as a foreigner; always feeling that Muslims are not accepted and not wanted; lack of respect for all people)
- Lack of interest in religion
- Dominance of Christian values in a Christian society
- Willingness of others to blame all Muslims for actions of small minority
- Belief of others that Britain at war makes it impossible for Muslims to be treated as if Britain is their country too
- Trying to be a good Muslim—there are too many distractions that weaken the faith
- Coping with different people and different lifestyles
- Britain becoming too 'Americanised' materialistic country where wealth, property, and power are put before people

Source: 'British Muslim Youth Survey', Muslim Council of Britain, 2001.

partly speaks to an appetite to acquire and maintain popular legitimacy.[62] Public diplomacy initiatives, in Britain, Canada, Australia, France, Germany, and elsewhere, are illustrations of this, where concerted efforts have been made to develop a consultative dialogue with members and representatives of disaffected sectional groups.

[62] Roy, O., *Globalised Islam: The Search for a New Ummah* (New York: C. Hurst, 2004).

The question of Muslim attitudes on foreign affairs must of course be set within an appropriate context. For one thing, it is important to remember that increasingly transnational Muslim communities in Western societies will often have quite legitimate concerns about foreign affairs that stem from personal and group links that go beyond local settlement and integration issues. This represents a case in point of the tensions arising from the foreign affairs aspects of mass migration policies.[63] In addition, the bigger contextual feature has to do with a growing sense of victimhood and alienation within Western societies, a point raised and discussed earlier in this chapter. However, victimhood and the nurturing of a wider suspicion of Western society and cultural influences can easily extend into the viewing of Western governments' interactions with the Muslim-majority world, particularly in Arab societies.[64] This essential point has been raised on a number of occasions and in a number of ways by Bernard Lewis in his analyses of leaders of countries in the Muslim world and the politics of grievance over several centuries.[65] The counter-point to this type of sentiment within Western Muslim communities has been the emergence of a strong anti-Islamic critique and political expressions in several Western countries in recent years. One prominent national German politician summed up this counter-position in 2004 and this outlook has done much to remind Muslim leaders of the fragility of the latter's concerns about foreign policy:[66]

This is not an Islamic country. It is a Christian country, and we should not be forced to accommodate Islam.

The question of underlying patterns of sympathy and support for Islamist extremism and political violence is brought up more fully and substantially in Chapter 6. At that point, the reasons behind forms of implicit identification with the grievances of terror are examined and related to wider implications for policymakers and others charged with providing a credible response. But first this chapter turns to consider some of details behind claims of religious discrimination and exclusion and how these have fuelled links to other grievances that lie more firmly in Western relations with global Islamic identities.

[63] An example in this literature can be accessed in relation to the tensions and paradoxes in US foreign policy towards Central and South America; see for example Martin, S., 'Migration and Foreign Policy: Emerging Bilateral and Regional Approaches in the Americas', in Weiner, M., and Staton Russell, S. (eds.), *Demography and National Security* (New York: Berghahn, 2001).

[64] Rubin, B., 'The Real Roots of Arab Anti-Americanism', *Foreign Affairs*, Vol. 81, No. 6, November/December 2002, pp. 73–85.

[65] Lewis, B., 'The Roots of Muslim Rage', *Atlantic Monthly*, September, 1990.

[66] As quoted by Andreas Tzortzis in *Deutsche Welle*, 21 April 2004; see www.dw-world-de.

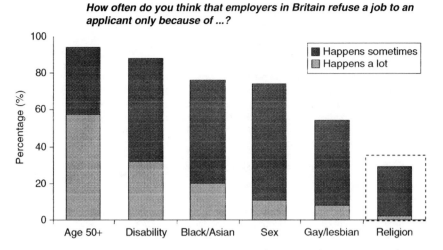

Figure 5.5. Prevalence of discrimination in the workplace

Source: Centre for Research into Election and Social Trends (CREST), based on British Social Attitudes data, 2002.

Religious Discrimination and Exclusion

Discrimination and harassment—based on racial, ethnic, cultural, or religious difference, or elements of each—persist for several reasons. It is often intertwined with different elements of racial, ethnic, or cultural exclusion— Box 5.2 sets out a number of important and familiar aspects of group-based discrimination founded on an ascribed identity.

A striking majority of people in the UK acknowledge the fact of religious discrimination and accept that it is wrong. Evidence to show this is provided in Figures 5.5 and 5.6 below. This is arguably not just incisive as a finding in social attitudes research but also runs counter to a number of generalizations that regularly punctuate public debate about religious tolerance and intolerance. Recent evidence from public attitudes surveys points to a widespread and little noted acknowledgement of the fact of different forms of discrimination in the workplace. Only around one in four adults believe that religious discrimination exists in the workplace, and only a tiny proportion of these believe that its prevalence is widespread. An important element of this is generational: younger generations are more likely than their older counterparts to acknowledge the existence of all kinds of workplace discrimination.

The response to this picture is striking. Approximately four-fifths of adults report that religious discrimination in the workplace is wrong, three times as

---

Box 5.2 The causes of the Persistence of Discrimination and Harassment in the Case of Employment

---

Human and learned behaviour

To make sense of the onslaught of people and objects we deal with daily, we must identify patterns in the world.[67] This can often result in reducing individuals to categories and lead to stereotyping and prejudice. Socialization in the home, at school, or through the media can lead people to notice certain patterns and to attach certain values to them, sometimes negative. Discrimination occurs when these stereotypes and prejudices start to influence the way in which people act.

Lack of understanding, information, and awareness

Friends, colleagues, schools, employers, and others may lack awareness of how discrimination happens indirectly, as an unforeseen result of the policies and practices of institutions. This is often known as the phenomenon of indirect discrimination whereby discriminatory outcomes occur and can be detected without any intentional act of discrimination. Thus, for example, in the workplace, employees may not know what to do if they have been discriminated against.[68]

Lack of leadership: for example, in the workplace

A key component in tackling discrimination in a workplace is commitment at the top of the organization, matched by commitment at other levels of management, to ensure that equality is a priority and that changes are effectively implemented.

Intolerant workplace and other cultures

There is growing recognition of the extent to which organizational culture can contribute to the exclusion of, and discrimination against, employees from a religious minority even if formal equal opportunity policies and procedures exist.[69]

An unbalanced, or even non-existent, enforcement regime

The enforcement regime in Britain can be criticized as being too reliant on a strategy of responding to failure, with legal and non-legal standards being coupled with enforcement mechanisms, such as investigations and legal proceedings.[70] This has been mitigated by the 2000 amendment to the 1976 Race Relations Act that emphasizes more active measures for the public sector to tackle discrimination.

The challenge of providing political leadership to combat religious and racial discrimination and intolerance

Government has historically been cautious about race equality and anti-discrimination legislation and policies because public attitudes have not always been supportive.

---

[67] For example, the work of the Facing History project notes that such patterns are fundamentally understood through the prism of people's understandings of the past. See *Facing History and Ourselves: the Holocaust and Human Behaviour* (Massachusetts: National Foundation, 1994).

[68] Metcalf, H., and Forth, J., *Business Benefits of Race Equality at Work*, 2000.

[69] Tackey, N. D., et al., *The Problem of Minority Performance in Organisations* (Brighton: Institute for Employment Studies, 2001).

[70] Hepple, B., Coussey, M., and Choudhury, T., *Equality: A New Framework* (Oxford: Hart, 2000).

> Tackling religious discrimination requires political leadership that highlights equal oppor-
> tunities as being central to the economic and social well-being of British society.
>
> ### Societal discrimination and harassment
>
> Discrimination and harassment in the workplace cannot be treated in isolation from the
> discrimination, social exclusion, and distance between communities that exists in British
> society more broadly.

many who state that such discrimination actually exists. Around half can be
described as core believers, in that their reaction to such discrimination is that
it is 'always wrong'. When compared with those who think that discrimination 'happens a lot', this points to an important norm about racial and other
forms of discrimination. Several times as many people are unconditional in
their reaction as the proportion who think that religious discrimination is a
commonplace problem. More specifically, the survey shows that barely a third
acknowledge the existence of religious discrimination in the workplace, and
the vast bulk of these comprise those who feel that this was sometimes, rather
commonly, the case. This finding overall places the question of religious discrimination in the workplace in a rather different location to other potential
kinds of discrimination that are considerably more likely to be confirmed,
at least through public attitudes survey research. Of course, one of the most
vocal counter-points to this type of finding which has emerged from parts of
the leadership of Muslim communities has been to refute the finding. This

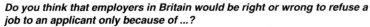

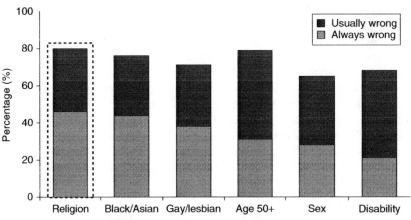

Figure 5.6. The acceptability of discrimination in the workplace

Source: Centre for Research into Election and Social Trends (CREST), based on British Social Attitudes
data, 2002.

has mainly centred on the case that anti-Muslim discrimination and bias goes unnoticed and that this is so routine and normal in the workplace that it is not obvious to bystanders that it is taking place.

A further criticism is that anti-Muslim prejudice can be and is so deeply embedded in the wider society that even fair-minded, moderate members of the public are unaware of the depth of the problem and barriers facing Muslims not just in the workplace but beyond it as well.[71] Survey research of this kind, in other words, can successfully tap attitudes on issues of discrimination within a moderate range but, the argument goes, this approach is redundant in the case of anti-Muslim bias. The grain of this argument is fuelled by the development of the concept of 'Islamophobia', a more pernicious and all-embracing idea, and was discussed earlier in this chapter in relation to evidence of Muslim communities' perceptions of the reputation of themselves and Islam in Western societies.

The continuing impact of discrimination is confirmed not only by statistical analysis but also by 'blind' discrimination tests, the outcomes of employment tribunals where religion is cited as a contributory (though not primary) factor, and personal testimonies. There are powerful norms about the acceptability of discrimination on a variety of grounds in employment at least.[72] They also speak, to a degree, to the potential reservoir of tolerance and inclusion in public sentiment to which government can appeal if it so chooses.

Social Capital and Social Networks

Complex social capital issues may lie behind headline yardsticks of immigrant integration. Similar factors can also be operating in respect of integration into the mainstream economy of all disadvantaged groups or subgroups.[73] In the case, for example, of labour market experiences and achievements in Britain, the evidence shown in Chapter 2 and earlier in this chapter shows that these vary considerably across and within ethnic groups. For instance, Pakistani and Bangladeshi men record considerably lower earnings and higher unemployment risks than do Indian, Chinese, or white men. Worryingly, this gap persists even after carrying out a like-for-like analysis that accounts for the poor human capital and other resources that particular minority groups bring to the labour market. Between two-thirds and three-quarters of the earnings

---

[71] Leiken, R., 'Europe's Angry Muslims', *Foreign Affairs*, July–August 2005.

[72] Rothon, C., and Heath, A., 'Trends in Racial Prejudice', in Park, A., et al. (eds.), *British Social Attitudes. The 20th Report: Continuity and Change Over Two Decades* (Oxford: Sage, 2003).

[73] European Commission, *Social Precarity and Social Integration: Report for the European Commission based on Eurobarometer 56.1* (Brussels: European Commission, 2002); see http://europa.eu.int/comm/public opinion/archives/special.htm.

'gap' that Pakistani and Bangladeshi men experience is not accounted for by the usual factors that explain labour market outcomes.[74]

Such a large, persistent gap is arguably strong circumstantial evidence for the impact of discrimination. It does not, of course, 'prove' that discrimination exists or its scale. However, the 'net gap'—also known as the residual or ethnic penalty—is partly shaped by the role of the employment-related social networks of different groups. Social capital matters in this case because there may be doubts about the ability, effectiveness, or possibly even willingness of certain groups to penetrate social networks—both formal and informal—that have a bearing on job opportunities and horizons.[75]

Large and complex bonding and bridging social capital issues underpin the trajectories of both 'successful' and 'unsuccessful' immigrant groups in Britain and elsewhere.[76] For example, the case of the Turkish-origin Muslim community in Amsterdam shows the positive correlation between bonding and bridging practices in action, and also highlights the subtle and nuanced role that government has to play in this outcome.[77] Similar trajectories have also been noted in relation to Japanese-American and Chinese-American communities in the Bay Area in California and also in relation to the Jewish and Indian communities of London.[78]

There is a basic proposition underlying the wider debate concerning ethnic diversity and social solidarity. In the UK, this proposition was initially aired by the publication of an essay entitled 'Too Diverse?' by David Goodhart in *Prospect* magazine. The argument advanced here was that there was a tension embedded in both seeking to extend ethno-cultural diversity, chiefly through immigration but also through domestic cultural and social policies, while simultaneously promoting the need to maintain a social consensus based on social welfare. This was dubbed the progressive dilemma in that Goodhart suggested that progressives had failed to appreciate the difficulties of attaining two equally desirable goals. In the case of ethnic diversity, it was, he contended, quite possible to see evidence aplenty that UK society viewed a lack of sameness and homogeneity as a real or potential threat to common ties and values. Similar patterns could be identified across a range of Western democracies that had been touched by immigration and stood likely to become more diverse in their future ethnic composition. The stakes, moreover, appeared

[74] Prime Minister's Strategy Unit, *Ethnic Minorities and the Labour Market: Final Report* (London: Cabinet Office, 2003).

[75] Performance and Innovation Unit, *Social Capital, A Discussion Paper* (London: Cabinet Office, 2002).

[76] Putnam, R., 'Ethnic Diversity and Social Capital', lecture to the British Academy, 24 June 2003.

[77] Jacobs, J., and Tillie, J., 'Introduction: Social Capital and Political Integration of Migrants', *Journal of Ethnic and Migration Studies*, Vol. 30, No. 3, May 2004, pp. 419–27.

[78] Favell, A., 'Games Without Frontiers? Questioning the Transnational Social Power of Migrants in Europe', *Archives Européennes de Sociologie*, Winter 2003, XLIV, 3, pp. 106–36.

greater in those Western societies that had prided themselves on inclusive social welfare traditions. In these places, it was suggested, we might see greatest pressures placed on those traditions since it was unlikely that funding for public services and backing for income maintenance programmes would become less attractive in the context of cross-ethnic public support.

In any case, this proposition sparked off numerous debates and controversies. The most critical of these was the question of how far identities and communities of interest could, in reality, extend across often sharply divergent ethnic boundaries.[79] Certainly, policymakers might predict that such common ties and interests would begin to wane in the face of tough choices about pooling and distributing public resources. At its heart, therefore, the debate was about with whom different communities could, and would want to, share.[80] Relationships of reciprocity have been slow, steady achievements that are found in many welfare state democracies. They have not been developed overnight, although their implicit understandings of the limits of sharing may be rapidly undermined by the appearance of not just ethnic diversity but also, more specifically, inter-ethnic and religious political differences and lines of potential conflicts.[81]

The basic difficulty with the argument to date has been the juxtapositioning of two variables, namely, solidarity and diversity. This is a basic conceptual limitation at heart since the argument hinges on a two-way, inverse relationship between solidarity and diversity.[82] Robert Putnam's examination of the USA has certainly challenged this formulation, suggesting that lines of causation may be more complex than thought.[83] Moreover, a number of environmental factors may also be at play that corrode both intra- and inter-group trust at one and the same time.[84] The implication appears to be that there is no simple, linear link that drives social solidarity and trust downwards

[79] Saggar, S., 'Solidarity, Diversity and Equality: Reading History's Lessons', response to David Goodhart, *Prospect* online, February 2004; available at http://www.prospect-magazine.co.uk/archives.

[80] Giddens, A., 'Diversity and Trust', *Foreign Policy*, November/December 2007; also published in *Prospect* November 2007.

[81] Letki, N., 'Does Diversity Erode Social Cohesion? Social Capital and Race in British Neighbourhoods', *Political Studies*, November 2007; also available at http://www.nuffield.ox.ac.uk/Politics/papers/2005/NLetki_social%20capital%20and%20diversity_final.pdf.

[82] Saggar, S., 'Labour Market Integration in the UK: Some Analytical and Policy Lessons Regarding Social Capital', paper presented to Opportunity and Challenge of Diversity: A Role for Social Capital? (Plenary 6: Role of Government and Stakeholders), OECD/Government of Canada/PRI, Montreal, Canada, 23–5 November 2003; the paper can be read at http://policyresearch.gc.ca/page.asp?pagenm = OECD_Background#session6.

[83] Putnam R., and Feldstein, L. (with Cohen, D.), *Better Together: Restoring the American Community* (New York: Simon and Schuster, 2003).

[84] Helliwell, J., 'Immigration and Social Capital: An Issue Paper', paper presented to the *2003 International Conference on The Opportunity and Challenge of Diversity: A Role For Social Capital* (Montreal Nov. 23–5, 2003); the paper can be read at http://policyresearch.gc.ca/page.asp?pagenm = OECD_Background#session6.

in the face of growing ethnic or religious pluralism. Pointedly, some of the least ethnically diverse places in the USA are near all African American or Hispanic neighbourhoods, in which levels of reported trust within the dominant group are exceptionally low.[85] The fact that trust across ethnic lines is also very low in these places appears to be an extension of a single theme of inward-facing, vulnerable, and sceptical communities. These are also, typically, characterized by exceptionally poor levels of socio-economic activity and engagement. Deprivation, in these circumstances, not so much feeds an untrusting environment as reflects a general lack of hope and support. A basic lack of community might be a better way to describe the situation since lines of trust, accountability, and reciprocity are scarce to begin with.

This observation has led some commentators to posit that solidarity and diversity are conceptually misleading in terms of the analytical light that can be shed on the relationship.[86] It has specifically prompted the criticism that the relationship is one that is three-way in nature, in which the experience and perception of ethnic inequality or equality fundamentally conditions the capacity of distinctive groups to trust and reciprocate across ethnic and religious lines.

Solidarity and diversity, in other words, are set in the context of equality across ethnic lines. The risks of seeing this as a straightforward two-way relationship are apparent and have coloured public debate about the consequences of mass immigration involving 'alien stock' in several Western societies. In Britain, the diversity versus community debate has, in one sense, been around for a long time. It was the Little Englanders, spurred on by Powell, who brought the argument into the open in the late 1960s. Britain's rapid absorption of large numbers of black and brown immigrants was opposed because of two fears. The first was the fear of undermining the underlying integrity of a distinctive ethno-cultural Britishness. Such identity was largely founded on an attachment to the unique sense of island identity formed through the four nations of Britain. The second held that the strangers, who had not, and, by extension, could not share in that development of identity, would detract from common, shared values as the basis of a national community. Both arguments were mistaken empirically in the long run, as the record of British integration policy and practice shows, although that is not to say that significant groups of immigrants and their descendents still lie outside the mainstream of British national identity and cohesion.

That a British national identity has been inexplicitly projected, if at all, is not in question. Bernard Crick was among the first to observe and comment on the effective vacuum that had developed in the post-war era when mass

[85] Social Capital Community Benchmark Survey; see http://www.ksg.harvard.edu/saguaro/communitysurvey/results.html.

[86] Helliwell, J., 'Maintaining Social Ties: Social Capital in a Global Information Age', Tilburg conference on Social Capital and Economic Development, 2003.

immigration, he argued, more than ever called for the successful projection of values and feelings of cross-ethnic togetherness and solidarity.[87] The larger issue has been the extent to which nationhood itself is dependent on ethnic and cultural homogeneity. Social and moral conservatives such as Casey and Scruton have often protested vehemently about this concern. However, as the US and Canadian cases amply demonstrate, the viability of the nation and its politics is not obviously conditional on a sense of unified ethnic identity.[88] A common attachment to the nation—something that many immigrant groups often excel at—is certainly desirable. In any case, it is highly questionable to think that post-war immigrants to Britain have been unable or unwilling to develop a sense of shared national identity with locals. Evidence from the British Election Study and the British Citizenship Survey highlight a clear pattern of black and Asian Britons declaring as strong (or even stronger) an attachment to broadly conceived British identity as their white counterparts.[89] An extensive MORI survey, carried out for the Commission for Racial Equality in 2002, further underlined the tendency among minority respondents to sign up to the badge of Britishness, although, naturally, much was still left up in the air as to what such an identity represented, or indeed implicitly excluded.[90]

Shared Values

Shared values are a trickier matter to understand properly. Goodhart's essay is effective in raising the profile of this elusive societal glue. But it is here that a sharper reading of contemporary immigration politics and history is most sorely needed. One distinction is between the major political parties in the UK, acknowledging the Conservatives' past magic in speaking to, and mobilizing the votes of, people in terms of latent ties, even kinship. David Willets, a long-standing Tory front-bencher, describes this as the Tories' 'ability to reach the hearts of the electors and evoke instincts and emotions which were a closed book to the rationalist progressives.'[91] Such an ability has been feared by their electoral opponents, in part because of the left's ambiguity in speaking openly about common values in cultural terms. It was Andrew Marr, in 1992, who spotted John Major's potential in building a broader British 'family' of belonging that was, unlike the narrative of most Labour and Tory leaders that preceded him, conspicuously inclusive

---

[87] *The New and the Old*, report of the 'Life in the United Kingdom' Advisory Group (London: HMSO, 2003).

[88] Rodney, R., 'Social Capital and Racial Inequality in America', *Perspectives on Politics*, (Vol. 1, No. 1, March 2003).

[89] Home Office, *Active Communities: Initial Findings from the 2001 Home Office Citizenship Survey* (London: Home Office, 2002).

[90] See www.mori.com/polls/2002/cre.shtml.

[91] Quoted in Goodhart, D., 'Too Diverse?', *Prospect*, February 2004.

towards New Commonwealth immigrants and their children. Major's unique strength was nothing more than his generational capacity to address New Commonwealth immigration in a way that did not stick in the throat. He and his generation, according to this perspective, were emotionally at home in pragmatically building commonness in a way that Margaret Thatcher's generation had not, and could not have, been. Indeed as a child and young man in Brixton, in south London, his generation would have been swept along by the demographic changes of that era. He and his contemporaries may not have wholly supported such change but, Marr argued, quite accurately, they would *not* have gone against the grain. It is also true that commentators have been confused by Mr Major as a personality—after all he did run *away* from the circus to become an accountant!

If there is a hidden lesson here, it is that political leaders—or would-be leaders—who are comfortable with the projection of religious identity into the political sphere are yet to emerge. It is by no means obvious that such religiously sensitized leadership will necessarily emerge in European politics since there are strong counter-pressures involved. Nevertheless, strong, religious, and political leadership and mobilization among European Muslim communities remains a new and unfamiliar phenomenon. It is rarely greeted in political and policy circles with ease or comfort. In fact, it is something that often leads to some antagonisms. Mainstream political leaders who have grown up on a diet of antagonistic religious identity politics are arguably consuming, if not feeding, such a diet at present. Some are actively engaged in repelling political identity and forces based on Islam in their countries.[92] Others are more engaged in nurturing the opposite effects. In both cases, there are few who are both intellectually and emotionally at ease with this setting and who are capable of transmitting this framework and its attending values to society at large.[93]

The greatest influences in this area are probably under way at present. These are most probably embodied in the generation that will come of political age one or two decades after 9/11. This generation will also be subject to many other cross-cutting and unsettling influences, including, most likely, growing internationalism, the emergence of a fairness and accountability agenda, the widespread presence of women in the workplace and in senior roles, a greater awareness of stewardship of the natural environment, and some systematic questioning of the need for spirituality (if not faith) in a post-material society.[94]

[92] Maher, S., 'The Diaspora Effect', *Prospect*, January 2008.

[93] See also Park, A., and Surridge, P., 'Charting Change in British Values', British Social Attitudes', in Park, A., et al. (eds.), *British Social Attitudes. The 20th Report: Continuity and Change Over Two Decades* (Oxford: Sage, 2003).

[94] Porritt, J., 'Securing the Future: Action is Needed Now to Tackle the Big Issues', *Ethos*, Issue 3, Autumn 2007.

Contemporary social attitudes further unpack the social history of post-war mass immigration, and popular reactions to it. By measuring sentiment on social distance, it is possible to show that the white majority has, overall, softened its previous hard-line stance towards black and Asian immigrants and their offspring. The British Social Attitudes survey shows that opposition to these groups as workplace colleagues, neighbours, bosses, friends, and even in-laws has generally declined considerably over the past twenty years. Equally, four-fifths of the (mainly white) public freely acknowledge the 'fact' of racial discrimination in employment, with a similar proportion reporting that this was 'always wrong' as a matter of principle. These changes have been much greater among the young, and it is likely that large parts of Britain are slowly filling up with new generations who are not only more comfortable with ethnic pluralism but are also keen for more of it. A slim majority state, according to the British Election Study (BES), that black and Asian immigration has turned out to be 'good or very good' for Britain.

Plainly, this sentiment is challenged in many other quarters, but the fact of moderation and growing conditional support for the changes that ethnic diversity has brought is worth dwelling on for a moment. There are two reasons why. First, it is not known how far or deep such sentiment runs. The absence of overt conflict may obviously shape liberal sentiment, in which case the test is to examine these beliefs in the context of the growth of religious and political extremism linked to Muslim communities. The roots of liberal backing for an inclusive diverse society may turn out to be shallow, so it is feared. Second, the greater, detailed description of liberal opinion and sentiment runs counter to political elites' own representation and understanding. All too often, public attitudes on related issues have been portrayed in bleak terms, and these may be somewhat bleaker than is actually supported by evidence. Offering some balance in this environment is important, not least because this can draw out more clearly the circumstances and contextual factors that stand in the way of better and sustained public understanding and support for issues of religious and political grievance.[95]

As for the reluctance of immigrant minorities to share or participate, the evidence is terribly mixed to say the least. Contrary to predictions, inter-marriage rates among South Asian groups in the UK are currently running between 12 and 15 per cent of all unions; twenty years ago it barely registered 1 per cent.[96] Concentrations within their own communities are chiefly seen among left-behind groups of Pakistani-origin Britons in northern former mill towns. But even here, the evidence points to concentrated poverty as a more

[95] Hansen, R., 'The Danish Cartoon Controversy: A Defence of Liberal Freedom', *EUSA Review*, Vol. 19, No. 2, Spring 2006.

[96] Saggar, S., 'The 1984 Labour Force Survey and Britain's "Asian" Population', *New Community*, 13, pp. 395–411, 1987.

likely obstacle to interaction and participation—for both South Asians and poorer whites in these places. Social and ethnic isolation is, therefore, as likely to be a symptom as a cause. The alternative is to focus on voluntary, co-ethnic concentrations and, to be sure, few political commentators and policymakers are about to condemn the relative success stories of towns such as Leicester in the East Midlands or Harrow in suburban north-west London.

If Britain is characterized by an unwillingness to live and share with strangers, there is really only patchy evidence to back this outlook. But patchiness is not to say that evidence cannot be found for the extent and depth of such feeling. Such an unwillingness is increasingly apparent in the case of the reputation enjoyed by British Muslim communities. Little Englanders, ironically, were right in drawing attention to kith and kinship as a factor in the transition process but one that is frequently misread and extended inappropriately. Membership of a community, national or otherwise, implies a sharing both in values and codes of conduct and in distributional concerns.[97]

Goodhart's discussion of a trade-off between diversity and community ends up obscuring a three-way relationship in which equality represents the missing link. As communities experience greater inequality—or at least continuing perceptions of inequality of opportunity and access affecting second-generation offspring than they have previously known—it is probable that this will impact on social cohesion and solidarity. The relationship works both ways, and cohesion can be destabilized by more than growing ethnic diversity. Putnam has pointed to this broader account in the USA where evidence suggests declining trust not just across, but also within, ethnic groups.[98]

With ethnic pluralism set to grow in every large-scale industrial democracy in the next decade and beyond, it is vital to develop a clear and practical understanding of these interplays.[99] In the first two decades on the twentieth century, public intellectuals and political leaders concluded that the USA was not so much full as already approaching its absorptive capacity of ethnic and religious difference, as brought by alien immigrants who shared little in common and who, it was feared, would threaten Americans' sense of 'we'.[100] Later chapters in this book will argue that this conclusion was flawed for

[97] Interestingly, this is accepted for instance in the argument put forward by Goodhart in *Progressive Nationalism: Citizenship and the Left* (London: Demos, 2006).

[98] Putnam, R. D., 'E Pluribus Unum: Diversity and Community in the Twenty-first Century: The 2006 Johan Skytte Prize Lecture', *Scandinavian Political Studies*, 30.2, June 2007, pp. 137–74.

[99] Lloyd, J., 'Harvard Study Paints Bleak Picture of Ethnic Diversity', *Financial Times*, 9 October 2006.

[100] Kaufman, E., *The Rise and Fall of Anglo-America* (Cambridge, MA: Harvard University Press, 2004).

reasons that are now readily apparent, and suggest that Western democracies today can learn profitably from that legacy.

Islam as a Political Constituency

Islamic leaders and followers are perceived to have a keen sense of *Ummah*, or community, which can be a source of cohesiveness on one hand and, on the other, can sometimes serve as a force for relative isolation and controversy. The common bonds and loyalties among British Muslims can act as an additional latent resource in negotiating the challenges of migration, settlement, and discrimination. Indeed, the common ties that bind together a number of immigrant groups have been commented upon for their influence in assisting groups in the face of a rocky and often uncertain path of upheaval and starting new lives. Sociological interest in such bonding social capital has also noted that migration can also have a devastating impact on existing social ties, and that it is not so surprising, therefore, that many immigrant groups emphasize internal ties initially over those outside their communities.[101]

Collective Muslim identity forged through a Muslim community provides both internal strength and a common form of external identity. However, alongside these two high-level effects, a number of difficulties can arise. In particular, the all-encompassing nature of internal community identity can emerge as in conflict with other, external sources of influence and identity. And there can be various unpredictable risks as well:

- Muslim collective identity can be distorted by radical Islamist influences, especially new leaderships seeking to promote a global interpretation of Muslims in conflict with Western secular societies.

- Overwhelming adherence to the Muslim *Ummah* can result in Western Muslims looking for guidance and leadership (beyond the spiritual) from overseas sources that cannot be easily influenced by Western governments.

- More controversially, the practice of viewing British society entirely through the prism of a collective Muslim consciousness, frequently tinged with deep-seated political grievance, can lead to patterns of self-isolation and an inward-looking, non-pluralist culture.

The latter of these is obviously of gravest concern since the by-product of such an identity prism can be to encourage gaping ideological divides where

[101] Vertovec, S., and Peach, C. (eds.), *Islam in Europe: The Politics of Religion and Community* (New York: St Martin's Press, 1997).

previously manageable political difference may have existed.[102] Western and Muslim identity can be pitted against one another, fuelling a zero-sum politics of conflict and hatred. For example, speaking of British and American policy in Iraq, one individual in Beeston, Leeds (home of three of four of the London bombers), stated in July 2006:[103]

You don't get anywhere with the dirty kuffar (infidels)... In order for America and Britain to go to Iraq they have to have reasons and sometimes, I'm afraid, if you haven't got a reason, you make up that reason.

However, the more significant aspect of *Ummah* being interpreted in such a fashion has to do not with the influence this may have on those already supportive of extreme, possibly violent action. The key impact is upon moderate, even conservative Muslim sentiment which can all too easily find it hard to speak in opposition to such a position within Muslim communities. In each case, Western Muslims who are opposed to religious and political extremism may face difficulties in asserting their position.

The question of developing or shaping a political constituency from within Western Muslim communities is an issue that is examined more thoroughly in Chapters 7 and 8. For the moment, the debate revolves around first, developing a better informed understanding of Islamic and Muslim identity in a Western setting and second, as the previous section noted, a way of specifying the degree to which such identity or identities contribute to a unique outlook to the political and non-political world.

As far as the former is concerned, social researchers have relied heavily on broad-brush approaches to examine the shape and composition of identity. Difficulties and arguments surrounding the degree to which anti-Muslim discrimination is detected in large survey research is just one pertinent example of the shortcomings of such an approach.

Muslims in Western, secular societies face a range of obligations from both internal and external sources. Relatively little robust work has been done to examine the Muslim conception of citizenship in these circumstances.[104] There is meanwhile no shortage of academic and quasi-academic accounts of the challenges placed on various national traditions of citizenship by aspects of Muslim political thought and aspiration.[105]

---

[102] Vertovec, S., 'Islamophobia and Muslim Recognition in Britain', in Haddad, Y. (ed.), *Muslims in the West: From Sojourners to Citizens* (New York: Oxford University Press, 2002), pp. 19–35.

[103] Quoted in 'Undercover on Planet Beeston', *The Sunday Times*, Focus investigation, 2 July 2006.

[104] Malik, I. H., *Islam and Modernity: Muslims in Europe and the United States* (London: Pluto Press, 2004).

[105] Seddon, M., Hussain, D., and Malik, N., *British Muslims: Loyalty and Belonging* (Leicester: Islamic Foundation, 2003).

An important exception has been the contribution of Sean McLoughlin who has pointed out the rare examples of key Muslim organizations that have called upon Western Pakistani and Muslim communities to 'move beyond religious group identity in a narrow sense to embrace a new identity based on a notion of the common good'.[106] This path is associated, in part, he notes, with the efforts of the Islamic Foundation and the Citizen Organising Foundation in Britain, and there are hints at this form of mobilization among a number of lesser known bodies and movements.

[106] Examples includes McLoughlin, I., 'Islam, Citizenship and Civil Society: "New" Muslim Leaderships in the UK', in Cersari, D. (ed.), *European Muslims and the Secular State in a Comparative Perspective: Final Symposium Report*, Network on Comparative Research on Islam and Muslims in Europe (Brussels: European Commission DG Research, 2005).

6

Extremism and Reputational Politics

On 22 July, on a bus, my heart started racing uncontrollably and sweat began pouring out as I sat down next to an Asian-looking man holding a rucksack. I thought of getting off, or of asking the man to show me what was in his bag. I decided I was overreacting, and that he would rightly be offended by my behaviour. I said nothing, sat tight and wondered whether I was about to die.

Philippe Legrain[1]

There is a pool of Britons lurking within our sizeable Muslim community who will joyfully commit suicide and mass murder. Each terror plot increases pressure on the Muslim minorities in western countries. It would be illogical and dangerous if our counter-terror efforts did not focus on those communities. But as we intensify those activities we make new enemies within our population. Those tensions offer Al-Qaeda a route to bring down the democracies that represent the antithesis of its world view.

Michael Portillo[2]

Mapping Extremism

Islamist-inspired religious extremism is often described as a comparatively rare phenomenon. This characterization is broadly supported by whatever patchy evidence has been gathered on this subject. Much of these insights are grounded not so much in its frequency of incidence but rather the underlying factors that are thought to be responsible for its largely undetected rise and apparent embeddedness. Extremism can in fact be mapped in terms of its background circumstances and its primary triggers for engagement. Such extremism is often discussed in anecdotal terms, so at first glance it is difficult to see this phenomenon more systematically. The fact that it can have, and

[1] Legrain, P., *Immigrants: Your Country Needs Them* (London: Little, Brown, 2006), p. 306.
[2] Portillo, M., 'Divided Britain Makes a Tempting Terrorist Target', *The Sunday Times*, 13 August 2006, p. 17.

has had, grave consequences on one hand reinforces the need to dig more deeply behind headlines and news reports about plots and conspiracies. On the other hand, the event-driven nature of public interest in Islamic religious extremism, or Islamist actions and behaviours, as this is often dubbed, means that there is relatively little scope to get properly behind one caricature before it is swiftly displaced by the next.

For example, the social background of the nineteen participants in the 9/11 attacks led many commentators to suggest that an atypical educational background, particularly involving Western educational institutions, had played a significant part in the conspiracy. Meanwhile, others have sought to place attention on the promotion of extremist and violent ideology at grassroots level, often via unwitting religious establishments, to younger men in Western Muslim communities. In August 2006, leaders of High Wycombe's mosque were placed under considerable media pressure to explain the degree of their knowledge of the operation of radicals promoting violence in their rank and file.[3] Both examples threw up vastly contrasting pictures of the nature of Islamic religious extremism within just one Western country.

To start with, there is a tendency to focus on small, self-contained groups or cells that are self-consciously determined to distance themselves from the larger community. The other tendency, by contrast, emphasizes the importance of the large community reservoir within which extremism is fuelled and possibly indirectly condoned. Both offer useful summaries but it is the latter pattern—involving knowing and unknowing backing for confrontation perhaps through violence—that this book in mostly interested in disentangling and tackling.

There are various estimates of the scale and potential impact of religious extremism linked to British Muslim communities. Pinning down the parameters of what constitutes extremism and what falls outside this phenomenon is the subject of enormous disputation. One arguably controversial perspective has been put forward by John Esposito who has underlined the need to define, if at all possible, the terms 'extremism' and 'terrorism'. Citing the importance of historically shaped doctrines of legitimate struggle, using violent means, he points out that much of the debate in fact sits within Islam and Islamic communities. He states:[4]

It is often rather difficult to distinguish between the legitimate and illegitimate use of violence, and between protest, resistance, and liberation movements and terrorist organizations....The acts of Osama bin Laden and al-Qaeda and similar extremist organisations that have terrorised Muslim and non-Muslim societies present a clear

---

[3] See www.news.bbc.co.uk/1/hi/uk/4780815.stm.

[4] Esposito, J., *What Everyone Needs to Know About Islam* (New York: Oxford University Press, 2002), pp. 129–30.

example of terrorism. The difference between aggression and self-defence, between resistance and terrorism, often depends on where one stands.

A standard, if slightly cynical, response to the above comment might be to note that it was always thus. However, the larger issue at stake arises from the controversial presentation, potentially underscored by reality, of a greater propensity towards violent engagement by Islamic political and religious leaders in the modern world. This characterization is widely acknowledged in implicit terms and underscores a lot of supposedly neutral reporting and interpretation of Islamic politics and political thought. It affects the manner in which political debate concerning Western Muslim communities is framed. For instance, the issue, however ill-deserved, of a group's presumed underlying tendency towards violence sits just below the surface of much mainstream debate. Furthermore, the violent 'propensity thesis' informs the wider characterization of radical political demands and grievances by many Muslims themselves. Once such contributions are thought to be guided by a weak appetite for non-violent engagement, it is something of a self-fulfilling prophecy that results in a perceived growth in religious and political extremism accompanied by an appetite for violent means.

In other words, the spectrum within which political Islam operates is often sufficiently narrow to mean that it is mostly and predictably associated with direct, violent action of one kind or another. This association, as already said, is frequently undeserved and harsh in the extreme. But the key point here is not the merits or demerits of such a characterization. It is, rather, to note as simply as possible the massive reputational damage that this entails.

Not only does this massively impact on the reputation of Western Muslim communities (something that is discussed more fully in the next chapter), but it also means that there is widespread conflation of legitimate political demands and aspirations with illegitimate mechanisms to attain political attention and outcomes. In this context, estimating the scale of religious extremism becomes highly elastic in that the general perception of political Islam, especially in Western settings, is, rightly or wrongly, with a violent propensity.[5] To be sure, a private media poll in 2005 (involving the author) revealed that while three-quarters of the British public fully backed the view that 'Most Muslims are not terrorists', worryingly two-thirds of the same sample nevertheless were happy to report that, to their minds, 'Most terrorists are Muslims'.[6]

A further variant on the dispute over terminology has been the protest voiced over the use of 'Islamic' and 'terror' adjectively in relation to each other. The argument, widely rehearsed, is that there is little, if anything, about Islam that colours modern understanding of terrorism, and that this

---

[5] Burke, J., *Al-Qaeda: The True Story of Radical Islam* (London: Penguin, 2003).
[6] Private polling, April–May 2005.

demonstrates a form of double standards since other religiously linked civil conflicts, such as in Northern Ireland, have not led to terms such as Christian or Catholic being presented alongside terror. In one poorly timely counter-blast in summer 2006, Sir Iqbal Sachranie, former general secretary of the Muslim Council of Britain, publicly argued that 'Muslim' and 'terrorist' were semantically incompatible. The larger point underpinning this protest goes beyond the usual rider that determining who or what qualifies as a terrorist is a difficult philosophical issue. In this case, even if there is general agreement about terrorism being hallmarked by the illegitimate use or endorsement of violence, the concern is that the popular perception of Islam and of Muslims has become noticeably pot-marked by the spectre of political violence. Thus, the territory at stake is the degree to which the ability and willingness of Muslim communities to engage in the mainstream political process has been eroded by the association with terror. Few serious commentators in Western countries credibly deny the association. What is in dispute is the impact, if any, this has had, and is having, on wider public perceptions of and engagement with Muslims' political priorities. Taking a particularly pessimistic view of this question entails adopting a virtual prohibition on using the terms Muslim and terrorist concomitantly, never mind interchangeably. The hope might be that, by disentangling these terms, there is enhanced scope to consider dispassionately Muslims and their views in public life.

But taking such an approach is, among other things, notoriously hard in practical terms. The BBC, following the failed transatlantic airliner terror plot of August 2006, sought to use a range of partially effective proxies to describe factually the background of the individuals alleged to have been involved. This policy not only suffered practical limitations but also attracted criticism for being brave to the point of incredulous and even manipulative. Presenting editorially the plotters as being 'British-born' added no light to the news coverage of the matter, for instance. One strident critic denounced the tactic because of its overriding desire to cushion Muslims from public perceptions of religiously inspired terrorism. He questioned:[7]

Wasn't there something else the BBC could have told us that might have better informed us as to who these people were and what their purpose was? Some common bond shared between them, an ideology, or a common creed?

Episodes such as the above are revealing because they show that there is probably diminishing common ground as to what forms of behaviour and thought constitute extremism. The emergence in the 1980s and 1990s in Muslim-majority countries (and elsewhere later on) of political Islam, or

[7] Liddle, R., 'An Ugly Cop-out on the Words Muslim and Terror', *The Sunday Times*, 13 August 2006, p. 27.

Islamism and Islamists, has been a very significant element in the weakening of previous common ground. The development of Islamism in this sense has inspired and emboldened countless individuals and grassroots movements within Muslim communities in the West and elsewhere to challenge standing assumptions about the distinction between faith and the public realm. By challenging in this way, and also by probing and experimenting with the limits of Western traditions of thinking about the public and private domain, it is apparent that many Western Muslims have run up against various unanticipated counter-reactions.[8] The most prominent of these has taken a strong secular, statist flavour and has reacted to political Islam uncompromisingly. The underlying aspirations, even the spirit, of political Islam have been taken to task for their inherent wish to push against secular patterns of organizing public life and moderating public policy. This wish, in many ways, has been the source of greatest difference and has often led directly to anger in the way in which it has been expressed and criticized. Extremism, according to this critique, comes essentially from a challenge to post-Enlightenment traditions of secularism. Indeed, it is often argued that the expression of political will to challenge secularism is itself characteristic of extremist thought, let alone behaviour.

The terms of this exchange are not always so elegantly stated, and there is no shortage of everyday reminders of anger and worse. The common ground of understanding is both thin and no less argumentative. A good example can be seen in the actions of demonstrators against the Danish embassy in London at the height of cartoons controversy in February 2006. The symbolism used by a small handful of the demonstrators was clearly designed to gain attention and spread further the notoriety of political Islam's attraction to indiscriminate violence. The bigger impact, however, came through the blunt reminder that Muslim anger and mainstream political channels were not remotely in alignment and could not realistically hope to meet. In this context, not only was this display widely described as constituting extremism, but it also fell into a category equally widely denounced as unacceptable. Partially as a result, the Danish cartoons episode served to move attention away from such graphic public displays of anger and towards its effects and interactions with anger among Western Muslim communities more generally.

The discussion thus far has been about setting a context for mapping and assessing religious extremism among Western Muslims. It is a contextual background that affects profoundly the understanding of the causes of such extremism. It also impacts on understanding the main strategic challenges that arise for governments and others. The next part of this chapter moves on

---

[8] Wiktoronwicz, Q., *Radical Islam Rising: Muslims Extremism in the West* (Lanham, MD: Rowman and Littlefield, 2005).

to examine particular patterns of radicalization and the most significant flash-points for anger that have arisen in relation to Western Muslim communities.[9]

Building and Fuelling Radical Political Islam

Perhaps the privotal source of tension between political Islam and Western societies is the question of the moral assumptions underpinning each. This question has been widely aired though there is little obvious sign of an informed debate taking place. Indeed, for the most part, attention has been swayed by sweeping generalizations and claims made about the moral superiority of one set of values as against the other. Khaled Abou El Fadl has touched on this tendency when discussing the relationship and interplay between Muslims and Western democratic principles. He notes with some dismay the mutually exclusive terms of the debate:[10]

I fear the willingness of some to assume that there is an inextricable convergence between the moral assumptions at the heart and core of a democratic system and the West betrays a cultural centrism that tends to void universal human values. While the West might appropriately claim the pride of authorship over the institutional and procedural system that we call democracy, this does not mean that the moral and ethical values that inform such a system are exclusively Western in origin or nature.

This lament goes to the essence of the greatest intellectual disagreements that have broken out in recent years in the relationship between political Islam and Western societies. This is partially as a consequence of Islamic scholarship that has drawn attention to the ethical and balanced aspects of Islamic rule in earlier historic epochs. According to this body of thought, there has been much about the application of Islamic principles in the past to remind modern societies of the faith's humanitarian face as well as its true moral compass. In this light, it is argued, it is unjustified to describe modern Islam as morally inferior either to other faiths or indeed to the moral values that are associated with Western democracy. Indeed, the comparison itself is deeply wounding to many Muslims themselves who draw their entire moral outlook from their faith. Thus, El Fadl's critique is justified in the sense that he wishes, like many Muslim intellectuals, to recall the traditions of personal freedom, tolerance, and religious coexistence that have been found in many earlier periods in Islam. Politically speaking, to present these values as principles that uniquely underpin Western democracy is at the very least highly biased and liable to cause offence on a systematic scale. In fact, it would be fairer

[9] McCants, W. (ed.), *Militant Ideology Atlas* (West Point, NY: Combating Terrorism Centre, 2006).
[10] El Fadl, K. A., 'Reply', in El Fadl, K. A. et al. (eds.), *Islam and the Challenge of Democracy* (Princeton, NJ: Princeton University Press), pp. 111–12.

to say that this is a recipe for widespread alienation from Western society by Muslims. Political Islam has noted this source of tension and in many cases has exploited Western democracy's own rather self-centred view of its moral underpinnings and purpose. Radical, oppositional sentiment has been an inevitable by-product.

What, for instance, is the scale of Muslim religious extremism, including violence, in Britain today? Some of the assessments are drawn chiefly from intelligence gathering efforts, while others are grounded in an examination of the socio-cultural and community context within which extremism is built.[11] A secondary question is how should government and others respond to this challenge? These questions, in short, are the theme of the final two chapters but are touched on here. Incidentally, it is worth clarifying that there are, inevitably, many myths attaching to the scale of extremism, the bulk of which are the result of seeing extremism of this kind out of historical and ideological context.[12] The purpose here is to tie together evidence concerning the facts of religious extremism among Western Muslim communities on one hand with a wider discussion of the fluidity of extremist beliefs and behaviour.

There is some evidence to suggest that the cultural foundations of radical, oppositional Islamic groups have been critical to their success.[13] These groups have been especially pronounced among Arabic-speaking Muslim communities both within and beyond the Middle East, although it is less well known how far their influence extends to the settled Muslim communities in Western Europe and North America.[14] Jyette Klausen's account of European Muslim leaders and mosque politics has noted the widespread presence of Arabic background and speaking clerics.[15] In many cases, this feature of European-based imams meant that there were significant linguistic and cultural barriers separating the senior hierarchy of mosques from second- and third-generation Western Muslims. Elsewhere in countries such the Netherlands, Germany, Sweden, and Belgium, there has been a propensity towards Turkish origin clerics acting as official and unofficial Imams. Again, where this pattern has cross-sected with Muslim communities in those countries who have not been of Turkish background, the result has been a yawning gap in communication and credibility. However, beyond these sorts of issues, it is not clear that the Arab or Turkish dimension has made any significant contribution to

---

[11] Sivan, E., 'The Enclave Culture', in Marty, M. E., and Appleby, R. S. (eds.), *Fundamentalism Comprehended* (Chicago: University of Chicago Press, 1995), pp. 11–63.

[12] Esposito, J., *The Islamic Threat: Myth or Reality* (New York: Oxford University Press, 1999).

[13] Sivan, E., 'Why Radical Muslims aren't Taking Over Governments', *Middle East Review of International Affairs Journal*, Vol. 2, No. 2, May 1998.

[14] Smith, J., *Islam in America* (New York: Columbia University Press, 2000).

[15] Klausen, J., 'Moral Panic: The European Imam Crisis', *Axess*; Klausen, J., *The Islamic Challenge: Politics and Religion in Western European States* (New York: Oxford University Press, 2005).

radicalization of political outlooks among Western Muslim communities at large.

The dynamics of the Arab–Israeli conflict meanwhile has certainly become a central political bone of contention and rallying cry for such radical groups. The Israeli–Lebanese conflict of summer 2006 brought it into sharp relief. The object of a considerable amount of anger and disillusionment in recent years has been the claim of a lack of even-handedness in Western nations' policies towards the Middle East at large. The Lebanese incursion specifically sparked off a fresh round of criticism with six prominent Muslim British MPs and members of the House of Lords publishing an open letter claiming that British policy towards Israel had become a prime factor in motivating the radicalization of young British Muslims.[16] One of the six, Lord Nazir Ahmed, was especially keen to pronounce that these criticisms seemed to chime with larger public disquiet over Britain's role in Iraq and its distanced stance towards the cessation of conflict in southern Lebanon.[17]

Within the Arab world, however, the real impact of this issue has been dependent on radical groups with an existing presence that is rooted in existing structures, norms, and institutions. The rallying call of Israel, as a regional object of hatred, has been largely usurped into the grain of existing local political ideas and movement. Moreover, the appeal of radical political Islam within the Arab world has been further based on factors such as the sharp delineation of gender roles, high fertility rates, and consumption habits, as well as a range of subordinate factors such as the marginalization of local Christian communities and the censorship of films, plays, and books.

The cultural success of radical political Islam resides, above all, in the strength of voluntary Islamic associations, a number of which are based on strong transnational linkages with Muslim communities in Western societies. Theologically, there is a deep well from which this form of organization and action is drawn. The purpose of Sharia law itself, according to Islamic jurisprudence, is to make provision for the welfare of the people—known as *tahqiq masalih al-'ibad*.[18] These are further subdivided according to necessity, need, and luxury, but nevertheless Islamic legal scholars have been robust in asserting the basic welfarist traditions with the faith.

Radical Muslims in European countries and North America have gone a degree further and achieved something else: improved coordination between the Islamist movements of various countries. For example, migrant workers recruited for their inherent sympathy with the objectives of Islamists frequently shuttle across the Mediterranean between North Africa and southern

---

[16] Ahmed, N., 'Islamophobia, Terrorism and Fragmented Immigrant Communities', Wardheernews.com, 18 October 2006.

[17] 'Miles Apart', *Economist*, 19 August 2006, p. 24.

[18] El Fadl, K. A., 'Islam and the Challenge of Democracy' in El Fadl, K. A., et al. (eds.), *Islam and the Challenge of Democracy* (Princeton, NJ: Princeton University Press), p. 23.

Europe along with family gifts, used cars, and electrical equipment, and carry propaganda material produced in the West as well as funds. The traffic between the Mediterranean Spanish coast and Algeria, as well as several other North African states, has been a particularly active area for radical Islamists to develop and propagate.[19]

The task of strengthening domestic Muslim voluntary organizations and reducing dependency on transnational networks can be exploited by extremists in order to create greater local roots for anger and its outlet.[20] For this reason, this has emerged as an apparent key priority for Western governments seeking to curb extremism among settled Muslim communities. The difficulty arises from the relevance of this general risk factor in specific contexts and cases. For example, the Pakistani dimension between Europe and South Asia has emerged as a disproportionately large part of the transnational networks that now underpin the effectiveness of extremist groups and subgroups. Thus, although many European governments and intelligence agencies have invested resources in monitoring these networks involving North Africa, the Middle East, South Asia, and South East Asia, the reality has been that some legs have carried much greater security risks than others. Referring to the most notorious and secretive movement of all, Al-Qaeda, Oliver Roy, a veteran French observer of Islamic politics, has stressed the extensive Pakistani connections that this network has maintained despite efforts to disrupt its activities by Pakistan's government led by President Pervez Musharraf.[21] Regardless of this dominance of Pakistani transnationalism, it is important to extract a larger lesson, namely, an appreciation of the ways in which radical Islamic groups have built and sustained popularity based on voluntary associations. Counter-measures to this success may appear an obvious starting point but are likely to be hard to deliver with credibility in the eyes of Muslim communities used to the regular participation of Islamists in social welfare provision.

The spectre of religious and political extremism among Western and non-Western Muslims dominates the popular mindset. This is a representation that is difficult to escape or understate. A central element of this popular perception has been the question of jihad, loosely speaking a conceptual category within Islamic traditions that refers to personal and communal struggle to a more worthy goal. Inevitably, there is little consensus within or beyond Muslims about the meaning or interpretation of this term, and it has been variously contested from the period of the Prophet Mohammed. The debates

[19] Saggar, S., 'The Challenge of Economic Integration: Labour Market Achievements of Immigrants', HMI World Congress Human Movements and Immigration, Barcelona, 4 September 2004.

[20] Sivan, E., 'Eavesdropping on Radical Islam', *Middle East Quarterly*, March 1995, pp. 13–24.

[21] 'School of Terror', *Economist*, 19 August 2006, p. 25.

197

and disputes over jihad amount to a symptom of a wider set of concerns about the degree to which doctrines of religiously sanctioned violence can be identified in contemporary Islamic thought and teaching. Behind this, it should be noted, stands a larger intellectual debate regarding the capacity of scholarship to describe credibly a religiously related theory of political consciousness and behaviour. This was a theme previously identified towards the end of Chapter 5, and is revisited again in this chapter.

But the starting point remains the impression, arguably ill-deserved yet widely reinforced and deeply ingrained, that modern Islam is both political and supportive of violence. According to Humayan Ansari:[22]

Recent global events, some undoubtedly dramatic, have deepened popular perceptions in the West that there is something in Islam, more than other faiths, which condones political violence. Exploring this question historically, there have been many instances when Islamic ideas have been drawn upon to justify violent activity. On the other hand, ideas…have been invoked that have stressed peaceful co-existence and toleration between Muslims and non-Muslims. Indeed, as religions go, violence is not unique to Islam.

Ansari's description undoubtedly meets usual conventions of even-handedness. However, it also exposes, through just four brief words, the crux of popular interest in and concern about modern Islam: 'more than other faiths'. In other words, the argument is less about the co-option of violence as a means in Islamic ideas and practices, but rather more, one that focuses on the extent to which such a relationship especially characterizes one faith more than others. Sadly, the reputation of Western Muslim communities, according to this argument, contains a point of departure by which Islam and political violence are already heavily interwoven.[23]

A secondary battleground that has emerged has been over the compatibility between democratic and Islamic principles of government and individual freedom and state authority.[24] As has already been noted, the polarization of this argument has been unmistakable. Bernard Lewis, for example, a long-standing observer of the dynamics of Islamic and world politics, has described these two traditions as fundamentally in collision with one another.[25] Muslims, to his mind, will find it unavoidable to choose between a modernist versus a fantasist path. This outlook has inevitably stirred up ill-feeling among mainstream

---

[22] Ansari, H., 'Attitudes to Jihad, Martyrdom and Terrorism among British Muslims', in Abbas, T. (ed.), *Muslims in Britain: Communities Under Pressure* (London: Zed Books, 2005).

[23] This is a link that is sadly missing from many recent in-depth surveys of the causes of terror networks. See for instance Sageman, M., *Understanding Terror Networks* (Philadelphia: University of Pennsylvania Press, 2004).

[24] Baran, Z. (ed.), *The Challenge of Hizb ut-Tahrir: Deciphering and Combating Radical Islamist Ideology* (Washington, DC: Nixon Centre, 2004).

[25] Lewis, B., *The Crisis of Islam: Holy War and Unholy Terror* (New York: Random House, 2004).

Muslim communities who see little purpose in juxtaposing traditions and values in such a way. More importantly still, this viewpoint leaves no room for consideration of liberal Islamic thought that first establishes the authenticity of concepts of liberty, freedom, and accountability within Islamic thought and second draws on and is inspired by the Western democratic tradition.

This leaves stark choices. El Fadl, for instance, places democracy at the heart of the collective challenge facing both Muslims and non-Muslims: 'Democracy is a moral and ideological institution that is to be sought after out of a normative commitment.'[26]

The focus of the next part of this chapter is to examine this link with violence and democracy in practice and how it impacts on Muslims and non-Muslims. A secondary purpose is to draw out the extent to which a social and political culture may have emerged within Western Muslim communities that serves to provide, however unintentionally, tacit backing for violent means to attain political objectives. And a final purpose—flagged here but returned to in the next chapter—is to assess the implications of these patterns for better informed security and community cohesion policies in Western democracies.

Tacit Support for Extremism

There are various responses on both the estimate and the definition of extremism. The analytical gap in understanding has become a serious matter in both scholarship and the framing of public and security policies. The seriousness of this gap matters because it affects the way in which the scale, nature, and growth of religious extremism is understood and internalized. At one end of the spectrum, the gap in understanding can contribute to a misreading and misidentification of risks facing Western societies, governments, and publics. This risk calculus requires a degree of iteration and revisiting if public credibility is to be maintained. However, any serious and long-running miscalibration of this calculus is likely to result in the research and policy communities collectively working to an ill-conceived model, with potentially damaging results for all. This model has the consequence of creating and nurturing an atmosphere of benign neglect (at best) and/or a pattern of looking exclusively for a security solution to a security problem (at worst). Such a solution, the evidence and arguments presented in this study suggest, is improbable.

The supply of public estimates of the scale of radical extremism within British Muslim communities has become commonplace in the aftermath of the July 2005 London bombings. Shortly after the attacks, Lord Stevens (previously Sir John Stevens), formerly London's policing chief, stated that, based on

---

[26] El Fadl, K. A., 'Reply', in El Fadl, K. A. et al. (eds.), *Islam and the Challenge of Democracy* (Princeton, NJ: Princeton University Press), p. 112.

his period at the helm of counter-terrorist policing in the capital city, about 1 per cent of Britain's Muslims were tied up with genuine forms of religious and political extremism. With a total population size of 1.6 million, the inference is that the public policy and intelligence communities should focus upon around 16,000 individuals—in short, the outer limits of the security problem. This was most likely an ill-informed estimate, for reasons outlined below, but its greater inaccuracy lies in assuming that the remaining members of British Muslim communities were and remained distant from extremism and violence. That is to say, Steven's interjection made sense only to the extent that it viewed British Muslims as all falling into one of two clear categories: mainstream moderate Muslims as against radical extremist ones. A peaceful, non-violent majority set alongside a violent, minority fringe. The lines are, in reality, not so sharp, as will be argued. Moreover, the concentration on a binary model, regardless of the estimates of each category, was misconceived.

There are some practical illustrations for questioning the estimates offered by Stevens. For example, a Populus poll of attitudes among British Muslims, carried out for *The Times*, at the height of the Danish cartoons controversy in February 2006, reported some alarming findings.[27] Some 7 per cent of the weighted sample signed up to the statement that: 'There are circumstances in which I would condone suicide bombings on UK soil.' This approximates to well over 100,000 British Muslims and overshoots massively the numbers intimated in the Stevens' assessment. An NOP survey commissioned by Channel 4 News in July 2006 revealed that a fifth of British Muslims 'respected' Osama bin Laden, although the poll did not shed any light on the reasons that lay behind such sentiment.[28] An official enemy of the British state, it seems, was not recognized in such terms by more than 300,000 British Muslims. A less generous interpretation might invert causation by noting that Osama bin Laden's considerable wave of grassroots support may have been the product of his enemy status. A poll of British Muslims undertaken by Populus in June 2005 reported that 13 per cent of respondents saw the London suicide bombers as martyrs. Again the poll did not delve into sentiment about the legitimacy or efficacy of their martyrdom, but it is reasonable to infer that this subgroup presumably saw the bombers' actions as both morally justified and politically effective.[29]

Another example is taken from an ICM poll of British Muslims, again against the backdrop of the controversial cartoons. Alarmingly, this survey showed that fully a fifth of respondents had 'some sympathy with the feelings and motives of those who carried out the London attacks'. Arithmetically speaking, this proportion yields a raw number of a little below a third of a

---

[27] Populus/*The Times*, Poll of British Muslims, 6 February 2006.

[28] www.ukpollingreport.co.uk/blog/archives/291.

[29] Populus/*The Times*, ITV News, Poll of British Muslims, 1–16 June 2006.

Attitudes towards extremism

■ Do you condemn the London attacks?

Yes   85%
No   4%
No response 11%

■ Would you tell the police if you found out that a fellow Muslim was planning an attack?

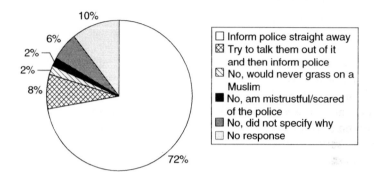

Figure 6.1. Fence-sitters: some evidence

Source: Populus/*The Times*, Poll of British Muslims, 6 February 2006; www.ukpollingreport.co.uk/ blog/archives/291; Populus/*The Times*, ITV News, Poll of British Muslims, 1–16 June 2006; Federation of Student Islamic Societies, 'The voice of Muslim students: a report into the perceptions and attitudes of Muslim students following the July 7th London attacks', London: FOSIS, 2005.

million people, a figure that was described by Sadiq Khan, the Labour MP for Tooting,[30] as 'alarming'.[31] This alludes not so much a fringe element but a considerable minority measured in hundreds rather than tens of thousands. The same poll showed, encouragingly, that only 1 per cent stated that the 7/7 and 21/7 bombings were 'right' in their aims and actions. More worryingly, another 10 per cent refused to say whether the bombings were right or wrong, implying that some degree of rightness could be seen in their violent behaviour (Figure 6.1).

A survey carried out in autumn 2005 of Muslim students by the Federation of Student Islamic Societies (FOSIS) contains an even larger concern.[32] Remembering that this poll took account only of those participating in higher or further education, its findings basically described sentiment among

[30] Khan was subsequently appointed to a junior ministerial post in the Whips Office following the Prime Minister's transition in June 2007. Khan was more recently appointed as Parliamentary Under Secretary of State in the Department of Communities and Local Government in the October 2008.

[31] Quoted in *The Telegraph* online, 19 February 2006.

[32] Federation of Student Islamic Societies, 'The voice of Muslim students: a report into the perceptions and attitudes of Muslim students following the July 7th London attacks' (London: FOSIS, 2005).

a better-educated, human-capital-rich subgroup within British Muslims. In other words, hardened views among those at the sharp end of social disadvantage, isolated in ghettos of oppositional culture, were *not* the scope of FOSIS survey.[33] Nevertheless, 4 per cent of Muslim students felt unable to condemn the London attacks, while a further 11 per cent refused to back or condemn such actions, again implying some positive value in such behaviour. But the more revealing aspect lies in attitudes about how individuals might hypothetically deal with a suicide bomber in their ranks. The encouraging findings were that 72 per cent of respondents stated that they would contact law enforcement agencies immediately, while a related 8 per cent thought they would attempt personally to talk a would-be bomber out of his or her plans, but would nevertheless do so in the understanding that they would call the police if persuasion failed. In aggregate, therefore, 80 per cent, it seems, were conscious of a line involving law enforcement, irrespective of their decision to involve the police at a primary or secondary level.

The less encouraging findings were that the remaining fifth were divided between various categories of equivocation. A hardcore 2 per cent would 'never grass on a fellow Muslim'; a further 2 per cent would not call the police since they were 'scared or mistrustful' of them; while a further 16 per cent said that they would not inform the police but were unable, or unwilling, to say why. Mapping such sentiment onto population numbers is tricky methodologically and can convey inferences that may betray the nuanced emotions and behaviours that such a scenario would typically entail. But, with this caveat accepted, using the FOSIS's own calculations indicates that the one-fifth who would not take pre-emptive action using the police could be as high as 18,000 students. This raw number would incidentally fill a large UK regional university and is a colossal figure by any reckoning.

The sample of Muslim students in the FOSIS study was not naive, it must be said. Some 43 per cent accepted that, in general, society's perceptions about Islam had worsened after the London attacks; and 90 per cent reported a worsening of perceptions of Muslim students. Given sentiment about calling the police to avert a bomber, such a deterioration is perhaps not so surprising.

Of course context is everything, and we need to keep in mind the reasoning behind such grassroots sympathy for violence. The most prominent of the public reasons attached to terrorism in Western nations has been the issue of foreign policy, and Anglo-US policy in Iraq has stood out conspicuously in this landscape. Survey after survey reveals that deeply held resentment over British and American policy in Iraq stands out in a long list of grievances. For example, the FOSIS survey showed that some 30 per cent of Muslim students

[33] Federation of Student Islamic Societies, 'The voice of Muslim students: a report into the perceptions and attitudes of Muslim students following the July 7th London attacks' (London: FOSIS, 2005).

believed that the war in Iraq was the single biggest cause of extremism, and 38 per cent attributed this to misunderstanding of Islam in the West.[34] It should be added that the West's involvement in Iraq was, of course, the resounding centrepiece of the martyrdom video recorded by Mohammed Sidique Khan, widely believed to be the ringleader of the London bombers. In his infamous video, first aired by al-Jazeera television in September 2005, Khan described himself as a 'solider of war' pitted against British forces occupying Iraq.[35] He said, in words delivered from his grave:[36]

Until we feel security, you will be our targets. Until you stop the bombing, gassing, imprisonment and torture of my people we will not stop this fight. We are at war and I am a soldier. Now you too will taste the reality of this situation.

In that sense, the words of a notorious terror conspirator appear to chime with the sentiments displayed in successive surveys of British Muslim attitudes towards Iraq and the causes of terrorism. The FOSIS survey did not only concentrate on supposed foreign policy causes of extremism, but also reported a litany of other grievances believed to lie behind extremism. Media and judicial bias against Muslims ranked just behind in the poll. For instance, a quarter of British Muslim students believed that the radical cleric Abu Hamza had not received a fair trial.

Thinking of the above in more theological terms results in having to revisit the question of Islam and Islamists' association with violence, or at least, as previously noted, of a greater propensity for such an association to take root in Western popular perceptions of Muslims. The *Quran*, for example, includes a number of detailed extracts concerning the proper and legitimate deployment of violence in the context of wartime.[37] These extend to sensitive and relevant issues such as the proportionality of violent responses to violent aggression.[38] Any fair-minded reading of Muslim public attitudes regarding the legitimacy of terrorism and violence must presumably take account of the role of scripture and religious teachings in shaping such attitudes. Most controversially, if the West's actions in Afghanistan and Iraq can be presented as an intrinsic act of aggression of war—itself naturally a highly contentious claim—then it is not so hard to read the thoughts and actions of radical Islamists in such a context. Mohammed Sidique Khan's loud assertion that he and his cell were operating in the context of war cannot be dismissed

---

[34] Federation of Student Islamic Societies, 'The voice of Muslim students: a report into the perceptions and attitudes of Muslim students following the July 7th London attacks' (London: FOSIS, 2005).

[35] BBC News, 'Experts Scrutinise Bomber Video', 2 September 2005.

[36] BBC News, 'Experts Scrutinise Bomber Video', 2 September 2005.

[37] Verses 48:17 and 9:91 provide fairly specific guidance on who is *not* exempt from fighting in war, for example.

[38] The doctrine of proportionality in these circumstances can be traced to Verses 2:294 that calls for responses 'in kind'.

entirely. For one thing, this claim represents a position which it is suggested is held, though not always vocally articulated, within several Muslim communities.[39] For another, it is a link that, others suggest, can be exploited within a very short timeframe by those seeking to incite others ordinarily embroiled in low-level, casual crime of kind or another.[40]

Thus, at its crudest level, Khan's message of war potentially reveals a huge chasm between general public views of the Iraqi invasion on one hand (a major intelligence and foreign policy failure for instance), versus a widespread view among British Muslims of the conflict (part of a pattern of systematic Western aggression towards Muslims and Muslim countries). A gap in perceptions of this kind is not especially in dispute since there has been, after all, an ongoing fierce debate about Western reponses to militant Islamists in the post-9/11 world. The significance rather lies in the enormous degree of difference in perceptions about the Iraqi conflict. In that sense, the conflict exemplifies a religiously related way of thinking about—and acting on—Western foreign policies that has been conceptually underestimated on a massive scale. Alternatively, it has been suggested that the religious prism through which such foreign policy has been perceived as something has been not so much understated as not seriously thought about to begin with. The judicial implications, for instance, have only begun to be aired more widely in public policy debates.[41] Either way, the example demonstrates a very serious contrast in beliefs and sentiment, and with serious consequences. The argument that is being pursued here is not so much one that seeks to adjudicate in any serious manner between contrasting views, but rather one that observes the potential extent of the contrast and attempts some precision in identifying its underlying causes. Hitherto there has been no shortage of research and comment on differences between radicals and others about the nature of the Iraq war. There has been somewhat less, if any, sustained attention paid to how such difference has arisen and the mechanisms through which it has shaped a coherent world view of terrorism and its supporters. The discussion below explores this terrain in relation to Britain and the emergence of a sizeable degree of popular indirect backing for terror within Muslim communities.

One tangible way to examine this phenomenon is to look at forces within and around Muslim communities that influence an equivocal response to violence. To what degree would such an equivocating population subgroup be willing to support violent behaviour, albeit indirectly? A number of detailed

---

[39] Gibb, F., 'Cherie Says Torture Confessions Can be Used to Save Lives', *The Times*, 2 March 2006.

[40] Cavendish, C., 'From Drug Dealer to Bomber in Weeks', *The Times*, 12 July 2007.

[41] This observation has also been made by the former President of the Supreme Court of Israel; see Barak, A., 'Human Rights and the Battle on Terror: The Judicial Point of View', The Second Leslie Scarman Lecture, The Great Hall, Lincoln's Inn, 13 February 2008.

studies have tried to probe this point, many of which end up grinding to a messy halt of imprecision by noting that there are some circumstances in which radical, violent Islam can been seen and not overtly condemned. The imprecision attaches to these circumstances and describing how they might create a different context for the interplay between faith, political goals, and violent means.[42] For instance, while it is apparent that an important context has been the proximity of international, generalized grievances such as the Iraq war, Israel–Palestine, Chechnya, or Kashmir, it is also the case that some of the grievances and conflicts pre-date acts and conspiracies of terror among Western Muslim communities, while others follow afterwards. Cause and effect, in other words, are heavily interwoven and not easy to isolate. Equally, if the international dimension drives the context as closely as is claimed, it is not obvious how the rapid absorption of collective grievance has taken place. For instance, do the events of 9/11 play a centrally important role or is that the result of the invasion of Iraq? Specifically, collective grievance appears to have been distilled on the basis of a common bond of faith in the face of international conflict, but it is not so clear that those bonds have played a central part in the conflicts to begin with. As previously said, to note the claim that the West is at odds with the Islamic world is not to accept as such the validity of a claim.[43]

The evidence does point, however, to a long tail of soft, unintentional acts of omission within and across Muslim communities in relation to violence carried out in the name of defending Muslims from Western dominance and aggression. This, crucially, can serve to support men of violence, although the link is surprisingly underplayed in the literature on political Islam and its relationship to democratic principles and traditions.[44] A key initial conclusion, then, is that the policy and research communities have focused too heavily on violence and conspiracies of violence, and have consequently neglected examination and explanation of Western Muslims who surround, and tacitly support, violence.

Western Muslim communities may not be unique in this characterization, historically and comparatively speaking. There have been other examples of anti-state violence committed on behalf of a group—typically ethno-national in nature—that can be used to inform and explain the position of Western Muslims. An informed reading of the literature and evidence about Irish, Basque, and Quebec nationalism and violence shows that hardcore minorities bent on confrontation are usually surrounded by some form of support

---

[42] Ramadan, T., keynote comments made to the Association of Muslim Lawyers 12th Annual Dinner and Muslim Lawyers Awards Ceremony, 17 November 2007.

[43] See Terms of Reference of the High-Level Group, United Nations Alliance of Civilisations Mandate, 25 August 2005; available at www.unAoC.org.

[44] 'The Practice—and the Theory', *Economist*, 12 January 2008.

mechanism.[45] In other words, Lord Stevens' belief in a binary distinction between violent and peaceful British Muslims is simplistic to the point of wishful thinking. The support systems will vary, from practical assistance finance, transport, housing, and the like. They will typically involve a safe house or houses, or access to laundered funds, part of an inner ring of logistical help. However, the support that they provide that is of most value to those engaged in or planning violence is the collective failure to speak out and pass information to the police and security agencies.

Security agencies in Britain have been well aware of this kind of tacit backing for a long time and have been on the front foot in trying to dismantle or disrupt such support. The monitoring, investigating, and event raiding of the Finsbury Park mosque is a well-known example. This was just the physical location for an array of support for violent jihadis. By taking away the practical support, the hope was that the opportunity costs of violence would become higher, and thus violence less probable. The main drawback with this strategy is that higher opportunity costs can, of course, be a perverse incentive to those who basically wish to demonstrate their commitment to a cause perceived as under suppression. Evading detection in their practical support for violence becomes just another challenge to conquer.[46] Once word gets out that places of worship or equivalent are unsuitable places to whip up excitement and draw new recruits, soft supporters quickly displace their efforts to gyms, bookshops, cafes, kebab restaurants, private homes, and, of course, the Internet. Even the latter now cannot escape detection. The response has been as imaginative as it has been sinister. One observer, Kevin O'Brien of the Centre for Intelligence Research and Analysis, has argued that private Internet networks that bypass servers and hubs are now the rage among conspirators.[47] Neil Doyle, author of *Terror Base UK*, has made a similar point illustrated with graphic evidence of filmed suicide missions in Iraq, Israel, and beyond.[48] Both note a larger point, namely, that technical ingenuity and political determination have combined to yield an ever-adapting network of radical Islamists who see as one of the main tasks the need to connect their brethren to the narrative of anti-Muslim oppression.[49] Such a cause can be constantly replenished with video footage of armed conflict from a number

[45] See for example Irwin, C., *Militant Nationalism: Between Movement and Party in Ireland and the Basque Country* (Minneapolis University of Minnesota Press, 1999); Newman, S., 'Nationalism in Post-industrial Societies: Why States Still Matter', *Comparative Politics*, Vol. 33, No. 1, Oct. 2000, pp. 21–41.

[46] 'Tube Bomber's Uncle Attacks Radical Imam', *The Sunday Times*, 19 February 2006.

[47] O'Brien, Kevin, 'Networks, Netwar and Information-age Terrorism', in Andrew Tan and Kumar Ramakrishna (eds.), *The New Terrorism: Anatomy, Trends, and Counter-Strategies* (Singapore: Eastern Universities Press, 2002), pp. 73–106.

[48] Doyle, N., *Terror Base UK* (London: Mainstream, 2006).

[49] Saggar, S., 'British Muslim Communities: The Politics of Social Exclusion and Religious Extremism', RUSI terrorism and politics conference, London, February 2006.

of parts of the world. Connecting Muslim communities in Western countries to this material allows a form of co-responsibility to emerge, whereby even those far removed from particular local disputes become prepared to identify with a form of globalized grievance.

Looking at support infrastructure abroad, the former Pakistani High Commissioner in London, HE Dr. Maleena Lodhi, has also drawn attention to the difficulty of pinning down the dynamics of who is supporting whom.[50] In a volatile and highly armed country such as Pakistan, the relevance of this insight cannot be understated. Pakistan has emerged as the key foreign source of radicalization for disaffected British Muslims and has also faced intense pressures of its own as a result of President Musharraf's own war against terror. The support mechanisms that have played a part here have included intensive training and preparation for cohorts of British-born Muslims drawn to Afghanistan and Pakistan post-9/11. These have also clearly extended to assessing the capacity of such recruits to fight a 'war against Islam' on British or Western soil. Such a scenario lay at the centre of the conspiracy behind the London attacks in July 2005, with at least two of the group known to have been present in Pakistan just months beforehand. The campaign led by the government against militants in Pakistan has been massively complicated by territorial autonomy and weak state authority in many parts of the country. In this context, conspiracies to train Western jihadists and thwart the national government sit on top of myriad complex alliances and counter-alliances involving drugs, arms smuggling, and heavily armed local militias. Breaking up one training camp has often proved to be little more than a drop in an ocean. In any case, the practical support these activities provide to men of violence is clearly considerable and, for that reason, can and will be regularly displaced into the next convenient arena or location.

The four 7/7 suicide bombers preparing to execute their mission in London did not operate in a vacuum. The intelligence and security communities accepted openly six months into the investigation that progress in unlocking their support network or networks had been patchy. On the first anniversary of the attacks, there were media reports of minimal communication between investigators and members of the Muslim communities of Beeston, the Leeds suburb where three of the four bombers had grown up.[51] The words of a neighbour of one of the bombers, surprisingly quoted on the record, successfully describe the gap between cooperation sought by, and given to, the police investigation:[52]

---

[50] Informal opening address comments by HE Maleena Lodhi, RUSI 'Terrorism and Politics' conference, London, February 2006.

[51] 'Bradford Muslims Warn New 7–7 "Inevitable" ', BBC News website, 7 July 2006.

[52] 'Bradford Muslims Warn New 7–7 "Inevitable" ', BBC News website, 7 July 2006.

I still believe there are people who know what went on but they are not coming forward and helping the police. They should be coming forward, not hiding. How do we stop this happening again when we know we could be next?

Echoing the same prophecy, Shabbir Dastgir, a member of the Muslim Public Affairs Committee (MPAC), went on to note the lack of engagement in the inner city neighbourhood:[53]

From where we are standing the last year has seen no change whatsoever in the actions of the Muslim community. Where the failure has been is that the Muslim community has not sat down and looked at itself and said Where did we go wrong and how do we take responsibility for what we do to make sure that something like that does not happen again?

And that community education and awareness-raising, bounded by clear markers about engagement in a democratic process, were the only credible ways forward:[54]

We [MPAC] are pushing one major agenda and that is every mosque, every Muslim organisation, every community group must develop a syllabus of education about the UK political system. Every single Muslim must be taught that it is perfectly fine to have views of what the British government is doing in Iraq or Afghanistan, but what you must do is learn to channel that in a constructive way. There are policymakers who represent your views; it is critical you hold these people, your MPs, to account. If you are not happy with what is happening make sure the people in power get that signal by not voting for them. It's only by engaging with politics in Britain that your voice can be heard.

There has been widespread unease, in some quarters, about the possibility of a fifth member of the team.[55] A late substitute in the composition of the final cohort appears to be a viable possibility, although the identity of the missing man has been elusive. Furthermore, the circumstances of the bombers' parked, loaded car at Luton railway station points to a larger series of attacks, possibly sequentially timed; this element, in common with others, has not been fully understood or explained. Scarcely anything is known for certain about the meeters-and-greeters for the two members of the team who spent time, and plotted in detail, in Pakistan beforehand. The link to the failed attackers of 21/7 is yet another Rumsfeldian known-unknown.

This series of serious gaps in knowledge about the bombing mission and the conspiracy that underpinned it so successfully continues to alarm senior figures in and surrounding the investigation. According to one:[56]

[53] 'Bradford Muslims Warn New 7–7 "Inevitable" ', BBC News website, 7 July 2006.
[54] 'Bradford Muslims Warn New 7–7 "Inevitable" ', BBC News website, 7 July 2006.
[55] Author's unattributed conversation with senior member of the 7/7 investigation team, February 2006.
[56] Author's unattributed source, June 2006.

It is as if these young men were transported from Mars to carry out these horrific attacks. Almost all their movements and conversations in the months before are shrouded in mystery. We have got lots of odd glimpses at what they were up to but nothing that looks like the big picture. But a number of people have got sight of that picture, and they are not coming anywhere near us. And a fair number have got a better picture than us, and they are keeping their heads down.

With rare exceptions, the final suicide mission team is presented as reasonably ordinary individuals with a dark side that virtually no one knew about. This is very, very unlikely.

The evidence illuminating such individuals and small, closed groups certainly is not rich in detail or texture.[57] However, it is useful in refuting claims that participants were completely unknown to others, such as families and friends. It paints a more nuanced picture of conspirators and in particular the interplay between those within an organized conspiracy and those at its fringes. In the case of would-be suicide missions, there is strong grounds for describing participants not so much as lonely, desperate individuals craving martyrdom at all costs, but rather as tactical and rational instruments of those fighting a much weightier conventional enemy.[58] One commentator, Hoffman, has pointed out that the universal attraction of suicide bombings has been because they are 'inexpensive and effective'.[59] But this level of analysis focuses mainly on the individuals concerned, and from their personal perspectives. A more informed understanding comes from the work of, for instance, Kalyvas and Sanchez-Cuena, who point to the need to explain suicide missions in the context of 'political repression and economic misery rather than belief in the afterlife'.[60] This kind of contextual analysis surrounding the individual is helpful in better situating and explaining the outlook and behaviour of supporting individuals and structures. In general, these reveal a motivation that is poorly connected, if at all, to an irrational nihilism or desire for random destruction.[61] Instead, supporters and instigators come in a range of categories stretching from loose associates who turn a proverbial blind eye to violent conspiracies through to those who actively plan and coordinate

---

[57] Neumann, P., 'Suicide Terrorism and Terrorist Strategy', Workshop on 'Understanding Suicide Terrorism', RUSI, London, 3 November 2006.

[58] North, R., 'As a 7/7 Survivor I Know Brown is Wrong on Terror', *The Sunday Times*, 18 November 2007, p. 9.

[59] Hoffman, B., 'The Logic of Suicide Terrorism', *Atlantic Monthly*, 291.5, pp. 40–7, June 2003; available at RAND 'Infrastructure, Safety and the Environment', http://www.terrormedicine.com/publications_files/RAND_2608.pdf.

[60] Kalyvas, S., and Sanchez-Cuenca, I., 'Killing Without Dying: The Absence of Suicide Missions', in Gambetta, D. (ed.), *Making Sense of Suicide Missions* (Oxford: Oxford University Press, 2005).

[61] Clutterbuck, L., 'Violent Jihad and the UK: Suicide Terrorism in Context', Workshop on 'Understanding Suicide Terrorism', RUSI, London, 3 November 2006.

missions.[62] For example, the estranged wife of one member of the 7/7 bombing team from Aylesbury has suggested that many tell-tale signs of violent conspiracy were in evidence beforehand but, crucially, these were not sufficiently clear to be acted upon by herself or anyone else.[63] The parents of one of the 21/7 team declared that their sustained lack of contact with their son had been a notable barrier—but not an insurmountable one—to acting on their informed suspicions about his movements and plans.[64] Similarly in relation to Saajid Badat, the Gloucester grammar school would-be shoe-bomber, who lost his courage just as he was detected.[65] Once indicted, a surprisingly large circle around him have admitted their suspicions. Finally, a host of co-worshippers in the Al-Madina mosque in Beeston, Leeds, have revealed an insight into the radical comments of preachers there that preceded (and persist after) the London attacks.[66]

The support network is, in fact, rarely completely unknown within these communities. Its purpose, effectiveness, and membership may vary over time, but its existence is not much in doubt. The awkwardness for researchers and security professionals is the task of interpreting the mixed emotions and behaviours of those within and around these support networks.[67] A passive, casual non-response to the known or suspected actions of others is difficult, by its very nature, to document, let alone draw firm conclusions from. Selective interview techniques involving the perceptions and recollections of third parties can assist in this task but are nevertheless subject to considerable caveats in terms of reliability. However, the failure in research terms to confirm the existence of a support network as a result of an absence of tangible evidence may also be unrealistic and distorting in the circumstances. Ultimately of course analytical research has to rely on a sufficiently deep evidence base while also taking into account that supporters and support networks lie mainly in the domain of support for common thinking and values.[68] Religiously shaped motivation bonds can be traced easily enough in the realm of non-violent sentiment and behaviour. The context being discussed here is very different and much more challenging for the researcher, to say the least.

---

[62] 'Police Question 7 July Suspects', BBC News website, 23 March 2007.

[63] 'Widow of Bomber "Abhors" Attack', 23 September 2005, BBC News website.

[64] Tumelty, P., 'Reassessing the July 21 London Bombings', *Terrorism Monitor*, 3.17, September 2005; available at http://www.jamestown.org/terrorism/news/article.php?issue_id=345.

[65] Dodd, V., 'Former Grammar School Boy gets 13 Years for shoe Bomb Plot', *Guardian*, 23 April 2005.

[66] www.business.timesonline.co.uk/article/0,13129–2047389,00.html.

[67] Corera, G., 'Don't Look Now, Britain's Real Spooks are Right Behind You', *The Sunday Times*, 2 December 2007, p. 7.

[68] Berman, P, 'The Philosopher of Islamic Terror', *New York Times Magazine*, 23 March 2003.

Shared Bonds, Common Cause

The problem, unfortunately, is bigger and deeper than identifying and evaluating the role of logistical networks that support terrorism operations. It extends to support conveyed through shared ideas and values that have the effect of turning a blind eye to, and implicitly issuing approval for, those engaged directly in the organization and delivery of violence. Whole swathes of such communities may be characterized by an ambivalence towards the use of violent means to pursue shared goals. The support is essentially tacit in nature, articulated publicly only in moments of severe crisis, and responsible for weak and indifferent engagement with law enforcement agencies. Meanwhile, those involved in or close to violent conspiracies are able to operate reasonably freely, safe in the knowledge—sometimes exaggerated— that their communities back them in both ends and means. Such knowledge can amount to a considerable source of emotional sustenance in the face of evading law enforcement agencies. It can be more than a residual endorsement and, arguably, may be tantamount to a mandate from community to individual that forces the latter to battle against the odds to deliver an outcome demanded by the former.[69] This is a powerful motivator by any reckoning.

The revealing aspect of the British public debate over religious extremism and terror has been to observe how the focus has shifted in the period after July 2005 to examining the attitudes of the wider community. In particular, an early turning point resulted from the broadcasting of a BBC documentary on the relationship between the Muslim Council of Britain (MCB), a largely moderate umbrella federal organization, and extremist politics in the immediate aftermath of the July 2005 bombings. In this broadcast, a number of damaging claims were made against MCB in relation to its indirect backing for violent actions undertaken in Israel and elsewhere.[70] The subsequent period has been filled by a number of eclectic probes into the attitudinal outlook of British Muslim communities and the recurring ability of mainstream, moderate organizations representing such communities to condemn some, but not all, examples of political violence. Typically, the argument has centred on how far identification with, and explanation for, political violence comes close to its justification.[71] The MCB/*Panorama* controversy led to the Council's lead

[69] 'Sparkhill Muslims "live in peace"', BBC News website, 1 February 2007.

[70] MCB's backing for the comments of Dr Yusuf Qaradawi in relation to Israel as a military society was a key point of controversy, since this argument allowed a derogation from the organization's condemnation of violence directed at civilian targets. See BBC *Panorama*, broadcast 14 July 2005; see also BBC News Politics 'Transcript: John Ware on Muslim Council of Britain', http://news.bbc.co.uk/1/hi/programmes/panorama/4171950.stm; see also Ware, J., 'MCB in the Dock', *Prospect*, 129, December 2006.

[71] Ivens, M., 'Cameron's Secret Weapon', *The Sunday Times*, 8 July 2007, p. 5.

spokesman, somewhat rashly, to remind the media and public alike that the blurred distinction also affected mainstream political leaders:[72]

We always condemn the taking of innocent life anywhere...But many of our own columnists, even members of parliament, have said that if they were Palestinians, if they were living under those conditions, if they were seeing their children humiliated in the way the Israelis humiliate their children, if they saw their children being blown to pieces, they would consider doing what the Palestinians do. Our own parliamentarians have said that. If they can say that, then of course Muslims will feel a greater affinity for the Palestinians...The Koran says you cannot take innocent life. But, again, to explain is not to justify. When we try and explain why the Palestinians are being driven to what they are doing it is not to justify it. It's trying to explain why they are doing what they are doing.

This kind of long-winded tacit support does not involve providing a safe house or weapons necessarily. Such backing can only be provided by those with a close stake in the project. Rather, it is a form of support that causes ordinary people—neighbours next door, so-to-speak—to keep their distance from law enforcement agencies that issue public appeals for relevant information. Switch between television channels when a grainy black-and-white CCTV photograph is shown on the late evening news is not, therefore, an unfounded caricature. Turning in one of their own, especially when they represent, however misguidedly, a common cause, is too great a sacrifice. Too great in the sense that the law enforcement agencies do not carry sufficient trust and credibility within particular communities that already feel under pressure. The Forest Gate raid, in East London, and arrests in April 2006, for example, created a substantial short-term backlash among Muslim opinion against the police. The conspicuous failure to convert arrests into charges in June 2006 not only reinforced scepticism against counter-terrorism efforts but also led to a number of vocal calls for British Muslims to withdraw cooperation with the security agencies.[73] Cooperating with law enforcers who are pursuing suspects requires Muslims to break ranks at a time when press stories, many believe, have been pre-written about Islamic terrorism in our midst. Their help to pursue suspects, they may reluctantly, or even indifferently, conclude, can probably wait. In any case, it is not the only factor they must weigh up. Internal consequences, namely, dividing Muslims when overt solidarity is sought, are also considerations in balancing cooperation against silence.

A number of commentators have noted that this configuration is deeply damaging for the reputation of Muslims in Britain.[74] This cannot be disregarded as an unhelpful coincidence or by-product of poor relations between

---

[72] Quoted on BBC Radio 4, 'The Today Programme', broadcast 14 July 2005.

[73] 'Opinion divided as brothers freed', BBC News website, 9 June 2005.

[74] 'British Exceptionalism: What To Do (and What Not To Do) about the Radicalisation of British Muslims', *Economist*, 17 August 2006.

the bulk of Muslims and law enforcement. It is a grade-A risk to all sects, factions, national groups, generations, theological followings, social classes, and political orientations. But it also gives credence to many Muslims, who despite not being linked to extremism or violence, worry that they are up against a self-fulfilling prophecy. Michael Portillo, a former senior Tory frontbencher, argued in July 2006:[75]

Although there has been no anti-Islamic backlash it seems that many British Muslims feel victimised by the authorities' response to terror. They think they face discrimination when stopped and searched. The bungled police operation in Forest Gate has become an emblem of supposed repression. Even peace-loving Muslim spokesmen feel obliged to give credence to the perception that their community is being unfairly harassed. It causes some Muslim men to withdraw further from a British society claimed to be hostile.

And, the long-run outcomes of this downward spiral of mistrust were alarming, he concluded.

At best that surrounds the terrorists with a penumbra of disaffected Muslims who may not condemn their crimes or denounce their murderous plots. At worst it enlarges the pool from which new bombers can be recruited.

This interpretation has begun to receive a wider appreciation following the 7/7 attacks and the fallout from the Danish cartoons controversy. It is a perspective that clearly does not equate perceived repression with a cause of extremism.[76] Rather, it strikes a needed balance between tackling terrorism using hard security measures and the consequences of such a course where the precision of intelligence-based measures will always contain flaws.[77] Moreover, although the Portillo extract above does not address this point, it is important to acknowledge the invidious position of British Muslims, facing moral and practical dilemmas on an enormous scale. It is arguably part of the human condition to feel and act on loyalty to kith and kin, even in the face of evidence about the substantial external costs of doing so.

Figure 6.2 illustrates two rather different conceptions of the role of religious extremists and their relationship with moderate members of a religious group. The left-hand set of concentric circles indicates that there is a large gulf between these subgroups that is impermeable. Radical and violent interpretations of the faith exists alongside more conventional peaceful interpretations as well as those who hold a limited cultural, though not especially theological, affinity with the religious group. Significantly, the potential for extremists to recruit more broadly is highly limited since they are essentially isolated.

---

[75] Portillo, M., 'No Offence, Imam, but We Must Call it Islamic Terror', *The Sunday Times*, 9 July 2006, p. 17.

[76] See for instance 'Culture Clash', *Economist*, 15 July 2006, p. 46.

[77] 'Case Unproven for 56 Days', *The Sunday Times* (leader), 18 November 2007, p. 16.

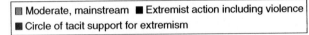

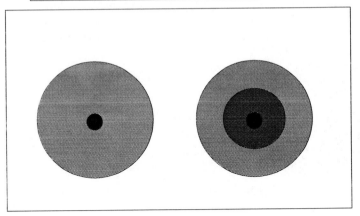

Figure 6.2. The circle of tacit support

The right-hand-describes a different dynamic. In this case, extremists are sheltered by and recruit from an inner core of sympathizers. Moreover, the hardcore and those who act as the supportive buffer around them are further strengthened by the presence of a level of tacit backing—or lack of condemnation—among a wider membership within the religious group. Their tacit backing not only fuels the potential for extremists to pursue political causes in the name of religion, but also ensures that any wider disapproval or rejection of these methods is relatively muted within the religion's rank-and-file moderate membership. The outer–inner ring, in other words, promotes ambiguity and uncertainty about the interplay between religion and politics as well as in relation to the use of violence to attain social and political objectives. This represents an obvious opportunity for religious extremism of any kind, and from a range of religions. Radical, militant Islamists, able and willing to take direct violent action, are just a case in point.

It is important to have a clear definition of who you want to support, and to be useful this needs to be more detailed than 'everyone who does not commit violence'. How can we be sure that the entire silent Muslim majority rejects terrorist acts of violence? And what about tacit support? For the purposes of moving ahead with the discussion, a working assumption can be made that moderation is defined relatively, but in this case would be defined as those who reject terrorism as a tool to achieve their ends. This still leaves sympathizers who supply, however unwittingly and passively, the crucial moral oxygen for those committed to and involved in violent confrontation. They are sometimes referred to as 'fence-sitters'. In Northern Ireland, at the height of the 'Troubles', they were dubbed locally in the nationalist community as the 'sneaking regarders'[78] who, according to non-violent political leaders, could not ultimately be relied on to turn their backs on men of violence in their communities. It is of little value to debate why or how far the rhetoric of Osama Bin Laden is popular, and it is far more profitable to accept that it has backing, overt and covert, in many quarters. While this does not mean that those people who like or are drawn in some way towards the rhetoric will execute violence, we need to be concerned with two distinct groups: perpetrators of terrorist acts and those that sympathize with them.

What is the relationship between passive and active violence? The thesis of this book posits that the circle of tacit support is the key problem. In terms of what we might do to increase or decrease them, it is important to understand how the small minority of terrorists impacts the fence-sitters, and how the fence-sitters impact the wider group of moderate Muslims. The priority must be for influence to be exerted outside-in, rather than from the centre out.

Therefore, the second conclusion of this chapter is that, in truth, we are describing what can be dubbed fence-sitters. Fence-sitters will normally identify with leaders in their ranks who are notably moderate and committed to tackling violence. But, as fence-sitters, they will also empathize with the frustrations and objectives of alienated members within their communities. So despite feeling that they want to see moderate solutions prevail, fence-sitters are probably poorly placed to judge the consequences of their failure to condemn violence. Such non-condemnation is arguably seen as an irrelevance cooked up by a hostile media and political elite. It may even be dismissed as a free good, the burden of which can fall on the next member of the group—who, not surprisingly, passes personal responsibility yet again, and so on.

These are all human reactions, as previously noted, and not the behaviour of an indelibly mistrustful or irresponsible minority. Similar fence-sitting prevailed for decades in Northern Ireland. British security policy there very rarely managed to drag tacit supporters of violent nationalism or unionism off their broad perches. In fact, the evidence suggests that tacit backers were only moved to act when the costs of misguided action by others became all too apparent. In spring 2005, the McCartney sisters became an international cause célèbre when they led a spontaneous campaign against the culture of silence among Catholic communities about the role of the IRA. Their obvious and immediate success has had far-reaching consequences by showing that tacit backing for violent behaviour had shrunk to a tiny rump where, before, it had been commonplace.[79] The circumstances of the killing of their sibling by

[78] Remarks of Lord Alderdice, in conversation with the author, London, February 2007.
[79] 'Bush Gives 100% Backing to McCartney Sisters', www.guardian.co.uk/Northern_Ireland/Story/0,2763,1440591,00.html?gusrc=rss.

the IRA served to illustrate a dramatic tipping point in wider attitudes towards violence within the nationalist community. The costs of fence-sitting in the context of a fragile peace process and tentative disarming process appeared vastly excessive not just to the sisters but to the vast majority of members of a group that had previously tacitly backed the IRA.

Other examples can be shown of the same changes in the calculus of fence-sitting. The most striking example arises in the aftermath of violent conflict, when, typically, the interim phases of confidence-building measures require a leap of faith. The absence of a fully-fledged, reliable peace means, by its very nature, that the wider community must make a revised and less risk-averse assessment of the situation. Renouncing or condemning violence previously committed in their name is one early challenge. Taking steps to bring about restorative justice is a harder task. Doing so while memories remain fresh can be even harder, but the capacity to carry on externalizing the costs of violence perpetrated in their name may have diminished.

Tipping points can be further accelerated if measures to internalize the costs are transparent, freely entered into, and based on symmetrical arrangements for former enemy groups. During the early spring of 2006, the supporters of General Ratko Mladic began to realize that evading law enforcement in Serbia came with a cost to ordinary members of the nationalist community. Mladic, nevertheless, continued to be a perfect hero in the remote mountains of north-west Montenegro, close to his birthplace, where no one would dream of turning him in. But, several hundred metres lower down, in the populated valleys of Serbia, realpolitik had begun to bite. For a new generation of Serbs, persisting with tacit support for suspects in cases of ethnic cleansing, had now to be balanced against the forces of transparency, democratic accountability, and externally induced peace-keeping and reconciliation. Post-Apartheid South Africans, white and black, experienced a similar dilemma. Support for one's kith and kin, in the face of closure and accountability about unspeakable horror, was obtained at a price. Lowering that price by creating incentives to turn against men of violence may have been difficult but, nevertheless, has proven to be possible.

Parallels exist all around. A substantial literature on the social pathology of gangs reveals the enormous grip of internal loyalty.[80] There is, crucially, also plenty of evidence to show that brothers, sisters, neighbours, and others act to provide a soft Praetorian Guard around gang members and leaders. The Metropolitan Police's long-running campaign—Operation Trident—to tackle gun crime in London is a tangible example. It has relied not so much on a belief that hardened gangsters are about to turn in their arsenals, but rather in a well-placed effort to incentivize tacit networks of support to draw away from

[80] See for example Horowitz, R., 'Community Tolerance of Gang Violence', *Social Problems*, Vol. 34, No. 5, December 1987, pp. 437–50.

gun culture. Anonymous tip-off lines, among other things, have produced results to penetrate the circle of silence.

This chapter has previously noted that risks of religious and political extremism can be mapped from two main sources. The first has to do with the proximity and transportability of international Islamic political grievance. The international dimension of this means that there has been a rapid absorption of collective grievance, in turn distilled into a common bond of faith. Thus, conflict in Israel/Palestine is linked to Kashmir, and to Aceh, Chechnya, Bosnia, and beyond, all-too-often in a click of a mouse. The other main source, as described here, has been the circle of tacit support, where extremist behaviour is condoned or accepted in some way. For example, after the May 2003 suicide attacks at Mike's Place, a Tel Aviv seaside bar, the *New York Times* ran the following quote from a 23-year-old British Muslim man from the Midlands, who said: 'When you see what's going on in Israel, something comes into your mind, something just goes.'

However, the role of bystanders, complicit or otherwise, has been difficult for the legal process to deal with. Members of the family of Omar Sharif, one of the Tel Aviv bombers, were cleared in late 2005 of charges of knowing about his mission and failing to alert law enforcement authorities before the attack.[81] Fears about such a trial amounting to collective punishment, that would further alienate fellow Muslims, arguably played a major part in the final verdict of the jury. To some critics, this is a curious logic whereby the potential, intangible reactions of others tomorrow was equated by the court with the facts about the actions, or inactions, of individuals yesterday. In addition, intelligence leads have since emerged purporting to link a member of the 7/7 attack team with the April 2003 attack in Tel Aviv involving Omar Sharif.[82]

In 2004, Jenny Tonge, then a Liberal Democrat MP for Richmond, found herself dismissed from her party's front bench for appearing to condone such attacks. Her precise words have often been disputed. She has also been cited, not least by MCB in its confrontation with the BBC *Panorama* investigation mentioned previously. She said:[83]

I was just trying to say how, having seen the violence and the humiliation and the provocation that the Palestinian people live under every day and have done since their land was occupied by Israel, I could understand and was trying to understand where [suicide bombers] were coming from.

And, cryptically, she added:

If I had to live in that situation—and I say that advisedly—I might just consider becoming one myself.

---

[81] Maher, S., 'Campus Radicals' *Prospect*, 126, September 2006.
[82] 'Bombers "Met Chief Plotter" in Karachi', *Timesonline*, 19 July 2005.
[83] http://news.bbc.co.uk/1/hi/talking_point/3422683.stm.

For many commentators, these remarks crossed a line, or at the very least graphically reminded all sides in the debate that such a line existed, something that Tonge and others may previously have avoided admitting to a public audience. Sometimes, however, unknowing interventions can also be controversial. For example, in 2002, Cherie Blair, spouse of the former British Prime Minister, caused offence with the following words:[84]

As long as young people feel they have no hope but to blow themselves up, we're never going to make progress, are we?

Perhaps unintentionally, the PM's spouse risked crossing the 'dangerously narrow line' between suggesting there could be some sort of rational explanation for targeting civilians in such attacks and justifying them. More recently in 2006, she suggested that intelligence derived from torture not only saved lives but also that it should be deployed to fulfil this objective.

This intervention, arguably as controversial as the first in 2002, undoubtedly furthered a reputation for even-handedness on the interplay between state power and terror. A more balanced interpretation might be that Cherie Blair's remarks showed that prominent figures continue to make contributions to a disaggregated debate, without much discernible interest or regard for the bigger picture that necessarily involves them assessing how their thoughts will be received in some circles. The signal sent cannot be guaranteed to be the signal received, in other words. It is also a big risk, where the consequences of misjudgement can easily escalate massively. However, more fundamentally, the notion that the pursuit of martyrdom is the consequence of hatred born of despair, is one that is not known or shown to be accepted by the vast majority of British people.

The Politics of Muslim Grievance

The discussion thus far has dwelt on the relationship between extremism and moderate opinion among British Muslim communities. It has only touched on the nature of underlying disquiet and disillusionment within these communities. The remainder of this chapter returns to the nature of perceived grievances held among members of these communities. It also tries to place these concerns in some context by examining the evidence to support much bigger claims about the systematic exclusion of Muslims from the opportunity structures of British society.

It is important first to say a word about the magnitude of potential grievances held by British Muslims and their various leaders and would-be leaders. This is important for two reasons. First, as this and the following chapter

---

[84] 'Blair Backs Cherie Terror Views', http://news.bbc.co.uk/1/hi/uk_politics/4721599.stm.

observe, there can be a significant gap between the perceptions of Muslim communities and the population at large on the question of systematic exclusion. This is indeed frequently the case and its significance lies not just in documenting the perception gap but also in accounting for this outcome in terms of deeper conceptual and ideological debates, frequently turning into disputes, about the nature of inclusion and exclusion. The conceptual lens through which political claims are made and analytical evidence understood is, therefore, a key part of the explanation in this case. Second, the nature of Muslim grievances can be as much the consequence as the cause of alienation. Thus, it is important to differentiate between British Muslim communities to appreciate better the source of the grievance and the extent of wider generalizibility. There may be disjunctures between what is said about and supposedly on behalf of British Muslims, as a single religio-political bloc, and what resonates in some quarters more than others.

There is, regrettably, plenty of scope for stereotypes to take root on all sides. A clash of civilizations, Huntingtonian style, can be detected in perceptions held by Muslims and non-Muslims in many Western countries. It would not be too much of an exaggeration to suggest that British Muslims are rapidly emerging as a new, national pariah group.[85] The deterioration in the relationship between Muslim and non-Muslim Britain is something that had previously been described as caused by and impacting on the small fringe within both groups that hold uncompromising views of the global reputation of Islam. In other words, so far as British Muslims were concerned, the difficulty stemmed from an extremist minority. A counter-view has been expressed that implies that the depth of anger and frustration is felt across Muslim communities as a whole and that, controversially, this has spawned sympathy for the methods previously espoused by radical extremists. A critique of this counter-view is that it places wider support for extremism on a pedestal of legitimacy. Indeed, it can be argued that Muslims' grievances are in danger of allowing Muslim leaders to have it both ways: working within mainstream legitimate channels to address concerns while hinting that involvement in or backing for illegitimate channels is both unsurprising and virtually inevitable.

Politically, this amounts to the charge of lobbying in favour of a carve-out for one particular embittered group and doing so on the basis of dramatically reduced public accountability. This is undoubtedly worrying since the broader credibility given to grievances can be easily undermined. However, an even bigger worry results from the spread of perceptions about such grievances and potential remedies from the fringe into the mainstream of these communities.[86] Indeed it has been argued that underlying support for radical extremism

[85] Saggar, S., 'Left Out', *Guardian*, 24 November 2004.
[86] Glynn, S., 'Bengali Muslims: The New East End Radicals?', *Ethnic and Racial Studies*, 25, 6, pp. 969–99.

is no longer something that requires a process of radicalization at the level of the individual.[87] This kind of sentiment, it is suggested, is widespread to begin with as a result of constant reinforcement by the media and other sources. Extremism, in that sense, has become mainstream to a far greater degree than previously imagined.

This is a difficult position for Muslim leaders and their concerns to occupy. For one thing, it creates unrealistic expectations from both sides, to say nothing of a draining of credibility in leadership that can span such widely diverging interests. Additionally, there is an increased likelihood that all grievances, whatever their nature, are left unheard, or worse are casually dismissed, in the wider public arena. Christine Fair and Husain Haqqani have commented on this risk:[88]

There is tremendous hesitance to admit that Muslim populations, on whose behalf terrorists claim to operate, have grievances or concerns that need to be addressed as a means to minimizing public support for terrorism. For some, this is the moral equivalent of negotiating with terrorism. This is unfortunate, because these grievances matter.

And, looking beyond Britain and other Western settings, they observe a hardening of sentiment about the perilous position of Islam:

In some countries, including Indonesia, Jordan, Lebanon, Nigeria, Pakistan, more than 70 percent of the population believes that Islam is under threat. Support for terrorism feeds on the belief that large segments of the Muslim world are victims of ongoing injustice. Some experts argue, with justification, that the perception of threats to Islam is deliberately cultivated by Islamist political groups and authoritarian Muslim governments to generate support for their agenda. But support for terrorism is unlikely to decline without addressing that perception, whether the perception is the product of propaganda or the result of legitimate political grievance.

The basic proposition that is being advanced is that grievance and a sense of victimhood have become sufficiently deeply ingrained among Western and non-Western Muslims that all responses must take this as a starting point. At one level, this is an entirely coherent argument and can be supported by evidence about the degree and nature of alienation. However, it is worth pointing out that such a starting point necessarily requires political systems and traditions to acknowledge fully a religious-based view of social cohesion and the public policy tools needed to achieve such goals.

It is doubtful whether this assumption can be safely made in the case of all, even most, Western countries. A more moderate assumption might be to assess the components of collective grievance in terms of social inclusion

---

[87] Akhtar, N., 'Integration into British society Will Not Stop Muslim Anger', *The Sunday Times*, 13 August 2006, p. 13.

[88] Fair, C., and Haqqani, H., 'Think Again: Islamist Terrorism', *Foreign Policy*, January 2006.

in education, employment, and other similar opportunity structures. The assumption, in other words, involves taking widely perceived religious griev-ances and treating elements in terms of existing and familiar paradigms for social inclusion.[89] This approach is likely to have traction in some Western democracies more than others, naturally. However, the possibility of some traction at all is arguably the more important point.

Closing Remarks

There are three basic complaints that are regularly advanced by and on behalf of the political constituency of British Muslims. Each has received detailed coverage earlier in this book. First, that British Muslims experience such high levels of social disadvantage that their plight goes beyond that of other excluded groups. In evidential terms, there are mixed findings in relation to this concern, although it is an area that clearly requires further analyt-ical investigation.[90] The fact that policymakers are informed by a detailed and nuanced understanding of ethnic disadvantage, impacting certain ethnic groups much more than others, speaks to the long tradition of understanding and responding to ethnic diversity by the research and policy communities.[91] Equally, a similar tradition with respect to a better appreciation of religious diversity is something that a number of moderate Muslim organizations and leaders have argued in favour of. The nature of such an appreciation is returned to in the final chapter, but for the moment it is sufficient to record that there is little reason to believe that such a moderate goal could not, in essence, be attainable. Difficulties arise in organizing and agreeing demarca-tion lines between a wider appreciation of religious pluralism in this sense on one hand, and an appetite for a more explicit role for Islam exclusively in conditioning society on the other hand. Presumably, the 40 per cent of British Muslim respondents who reported in an ICM survey in February 2006 that they favoured Sharia law in Muslim-dominated parts of Britain are a tangible reminder of this appetite.[92]

Second, it is frequently charged that anti-Muslim bias in the media, and in elite and mass attitudes, warps public policy and the attitudinal mindset of

[89] Ahmed, A., and Donnan, H., *Islam, Globalisation and Postmodernity* (London: Routledge, 1994).

[90] Malik, M., 'Law, Social Policy and Social Exclusion', Policy Network conference on 'Inequalities of integration: the British experience in comparative European perspective', London, 27 November 2007. This is also noted in Kyambi, S., 'Migrants and Social Inclusion: What Would a Progressive Approach Look Like?, in Flynn, D., and Williams, Z. (eds.), *Towards a Progressive Immigration Policy* (London: Compass, 2007).

[91] Saggar, S., 'Ethnic Minorities and the Labour Market', in Griffith, P., and Leonard, M. (eds.), *Reclaiming Britishness* (London: Foreign Policy Centre, 2002), pp. 78–90.

[92] ICM/*Sunday Telegraph*, Poll of Muslim public attitudes, 19 February 2006.

the public. This is also dubbed as 'Islamophobia' in short hand. It is also often interspersed with casual anti-immigrant sentiment as well as a soft link being cast between migration policy challenges and security concerns.[93] At first glance, it is hard to address this complaint systematically through analytical research. This is because the parameters of the complaint are not clearly set out. For instance, the widespread debate over the mass media's handling of the Israel–Palestine conflict is an issue that is regularly dragged into the Islamophobia question.[94] Evidence to show systematic bias in this case would not, in itself, allow any penetrating insights to be drawn about the positive or negative portrayal of Muslims in the British media. Another complication arises from the lack of consensus about the term Islamophobia to begin with. This definitional point was picked up in an earlier chapter, and it was argued that its widespread adoption by British Muslim leaders and others had not necessarily increased the resonance of the constituent issues subsumed into the term.

Overall, however, the portrayal of Muslims and of Islam contains a very large range of settings and outlets. Indeed, recent years have seen a proliferation of new forms of coverage of Muslims and of Islam, including the delivery of innovative services and markets that are linked to Islamic identities among British Muslims. For example, the *Economist* newspaper has described these changes in welcome terms, and contrasts them with the misguided defensive political changes witnessed during the same period:[95]

There are signs of British institutions and Muslims interacting in creative ways: from the willingness of banks of offer Sharia-compliant financial services to the establishment of Muslim 'chaplains' in prisons and hospitals, and the emergence of a lively Muslim press, with women journalists in the lead.

If the negative portrayal of Muslims in Britain is a serious concern within British Muslim communities, it is reasonable to note that the explanation for this may be linked to the nature of public disquiet about this group to begin with. For instance, complaints that excessive coverage is given to the involvement of Muslims in terrorism somewhat misses the point that almost all such cases of terrorism today comprise radical Muslims taking their collective grievances to a higher and more serious level. Moreover, it is impossible to imagine either a diminished media or public appetite for coverage of this phenomenon, or an outcome that did not taint the wider Muslim population negatively. By its very nature, the pariah characterization of British Muslims

[93] See Flynn, D., 'Progressivism and its Immigration Dilemma', and Lawson, N., 'The Wrong Dilemma', in Flynn, D., and Williams, Z. (eds.), *Towards a Progressive Immigration Policy* (London: Compass, 2007). See also 'BBC Series Will Focus on Whites' Fear of Migrants', *The Times*, 21 November 2007, p. 11.

[94] Zunes, S., *Political Islam: Revealing the Roots of Extremism* (Washington DC: Centre for Policy Analysis on Palestine, 2005).

[95] 'Miles Apart', *Economist*, 19 August 2006, p. 24.

depends on a sustained supply of information about the tendency of members of this group, however small in number, to engage in illegitimate and illegal activities. Sadly, there has been no shortage of such information in recent times and it is this source that then unavoidably feeds the coverage that some object to. Sceptics might conclude that their protests were too loud, and too grating, given the reality of the situation.

Of course, complaints about the negative coverage of Muslims are not the same thing as negative portrayals. The former, as noted above, is largely factually driven and cannot stray too greatly from the raw picture of Muslims' actual or potential involvement in violent action. The latter differs in that it describes the editorial stance of the media and of political elites in shaping public debate about British or Western Muslim communities. The grievance here is potentially more serious in the sense that it alludes to the underlying ideological and historical characterization of Islam in Western society. Such a characterization, in turn, depends considerably on the past and present interaction of the Islamic and non-Islamic worlds. British Muslims, therefore, appear to be concerned that past anti-Muslim bias has seeped casually into current outlooks and patterns of behaviour. Indeed, the involvement of some Muslims in violence, so the argument goes, can and has been linked to stereotypes about the violent nature of the faith and its followers through history. Historically speaking, Christian-oriented Europe's past encounters with Islam provide a guide, according to this neo-Huntingtonian perspective, and concerns about negative portrayal are hardly surprising.

The third and final leg of Muslim grievance politics is that the volatile dynamics of global Islam produce a steady stream of causes that sustain feelings of victimhood. Elements of the tensions surrounding global Islam have been reviewed in earlier chapters in some detail. It is more useful here to draw out two tentative conclusions that arise from this material. The first has to do with the degree to which second- and third-generation Western Muslims identify with a transnational, even globalized, view of Islam and the community of Muslims. The interpretations and significance of the Muslim *Ummah* were rehearsed in Chapter 5 in particular. The evidence for a collective religious consciousness is as striking as it was unpredicted. Growth in identity along these lines has been considerable in recent years, and in many cases combines with some kind of diasporic or Western immigrant-descended identity or identities. This much is clear and not overtly controversial. The controversy stems from the absorption of a defensive victimhood into global Islam. Presentation of the latter as subjected by and in conflict with Western secular society has given rise to the most aggression of all. A number of influential commentators have addressed themselves to the tendency towards political victimhood and its likely by-products of alienation and aggression. Many have concluded that while the goal of liberating collective Islamic identity from this weight may be desirable, the tools to achieve such an outcome are not present. Some of these tools are to be found within a liberal-humanitarian tradition within Islam, and elements of this can already be traced. Other tools are not so plentiful including patterns of governance through popular consent in the modern Muslim world. Furthermore, other essential tools are especially unlikely to be forthcoming in the context of current Western involvement in conflicts such as in Iraq and Afghanistan, to say nothing of rhetorical plots against Iran.

The secondary conclusion is that much of what is portrayed as global-Islam-in-conflict ought not to be taken at face value alone. This is because many of the regional conflicts have a long and well-documented ethno-national character, and have been subsumed into the construction of contemporary global Islam. For example, the conflict over Kashmir between India and Pakistan has simmered for almost three generations on the basis of regional security issues that have divided these two rivals. The religious dimension has transformed part of this conflict into a narrative of a struggle for theological liberation. A similar point can be made in relation to Aceh, Chechnya, and Bosnia. And, for some, it is probably most resonant and controversial in relation to the reputation of contemporary US foreign policy.[96]

Political victimhood is not to be underestimated when assessing the weight and future trajectory of global Muslim grievance. Historic parallels are limited in relevance, although there is considerable appetite to equate perceptions of Western hostility towards Islam with anti-Semitism suffered by Western Jews. Key organizations in particular have been responsible for promoting a brand of Islamic identity that is couched in these terms. Meanwhile, others have softened this identity, at least in part, by focusing on a range of growing lifestyle choices and value-led debates and differences among Muslim communities and within Muslim-majority states.[97] Influencing and affecting those organizations is a plausible way of encouraging a less victim-oriented view of Islam taking further root. Addressing and resolving particular regional and hemispheric conflicts that are drawn into this identity is another path. Incentivizing Islamic scholarship and political leadership to build a less distressed Islamic identity is yet another.

[96] Zunes, S., *Tinderbox: US Foreign Policy and the Roots of Terrorism* (Monroe, ME: Common Courage Press, 2003).

[97] Thomas, L., 'Sex and the Saudi Girl', *The Sunday Times*, 8 July 2007, p. 7.

7

Strategic Responses

The British government has used a variety of strategies to contain terrorism—military, political and diplomatic. There are some conditions working in its favour. It has a high level of control over Northern Ireland. Europe is a zone of peace. The governments of neighbouring states have been cooperative. Partly because of these factors, counter-terrorism has achieved some notable successes. Nevertheless terrorism has not be eradicated. The problems in dealing with Al Qaeda are vastly greater.

John Gray[1]

You can't just make token gestures towards European or American Muslims—i.e. 'take a Muslim to lunch'. Rather, there needs to be greater recognition of that the fact that 'it's the policy, stupid'. The worldview and the moral geography that seems to emanating out of Washington is... even more dangerous in terms of the effect it has on how Muslims, or the extent to which Muslims, are given space to have a voice with regard to foreign policy issues. And it's summed up and contained within the administration's famous post-9/11 'With us or against us' moment, where a very stark moral geography was painted in black and white: 'You're with us or you're against us'... leaving very little room for a Muslim to state that 'I totally renounce the violence of a Bin Laden, but I also have a few complaints about the way the United States conducts itself in other parts of the world.' In other words, you immediately become an object of suspicion if your critique of Bin Laden continues on to a critique of Washington D.C. So although there was much being said about 'Well, we must reassure Muslims that this is not a war on Islam in anyway,' the very terms of debate, the terms of engagement with the world emanating out of foreign policy making circles had the effect of setting up a world in which it becomes... very difficult for Muslims to articulate a sense of self without being trapped in some kind of securitisation dilemma.

Peter Mandaville[2]

---

[1] Gray, J., *Al Qaeda and What it Means to be Modern* (London: Faber, 2003).
[2] Mandaville, P., 'The Foreign Policy Impact in European Countries', Comments to an international St Anthony's–Princeton conference on 'Muslims in Europe post 9/11', April 2003; available at http://www.sant.ox.ac.uk/princeton/pap_mandaville.shtml.

Introduction

The study thus far has examined various aspects of the emerging problem of Muslim religious and political extremism in Western societies. The problem has been viewed from a range of perspectives and approaches. For example, in Chapter 3, we examined the nature of religious identity in a largely secular environment and the areas of tension that this threw up in relation to Western Muslim communities. In Chapter 4, our attention turned to theories and practices to build integration across ethnic and religious lines in Western immigration societies. And the concern of Chapter 5 was to pin down with as much detail as possible the nature and extent of radicalism and extremism within Western Muslim communities. In this chapter, we will draw on these findings and emerging conclusions to inform understanding not just of a bigger picture of the central issue. The central purpose of this chapter is to assess the task or tasks facing government or governments across the Western family of nations. This, as previously noted, is the main objective of this book, namely, to describe a story and assess responses as viewed from the perspective of government itself.

Different governments have dwelt and concentrated on slightly different aspects of the problem before them. This chapter seeks to bring their perspectives together in a single place and to identify the most—and least—promising ways to build social integration and cohesion, and bear down on extremism, while also fostering a more valued role for religion in public policy and society generally. These objectives, it must be said, are by no means modest and success in any aspects of these objectives would be counted as measurable progress in many quarters. The overarching objectives are just that: a way of thinking about the general direction in which governments would wish to steer change so as to not just reduce or remove threats of terror but also impact on the underlying causes of radicalism and latent appetites for confrontation and violence.

This chapter is organized into three main parts. To begin with, the chapter looks at a number of immediate stumbling blocks that have been placed before, or happen to lie in the way of, governments that are trying to tackle threats of terrorism. This is a story heavily laden with examples of unintended consequences of well-balanced policy measures. It is also a narrative concerning the adoption of better or worse intellectual models to explain the attraction of and support for Western Islamist-inspired terrorism.

The second part of this chapter is concerned with identifying the main priorities for governments. This section argues that although bearing down on extremism is one such priority, it is, significantly, nested in a set of closely related priorities to do with, first, identifying and combating long-term, settled disadvantage and, second, promoting radical recasts of opportunity structures to deliver social cohesion. The task of building greater inclusion across ethnic and religious lines is not new by any means.[3] The expression of this priority in the context of a small number of left-behind, alienated subgroups, is not so familiar.[4] A further, linked priority, in the case of a country such as Britain certainly, is the need to foster a more credible language of common bonds and shared values. This question is also picked up in the second section.

The final part of this chapter examines the main drivers of future change. This, in part, is achieved by identifying the main factors that are likely to affect such change. It is also unpacked further via discussion of a series of scenarios that describe and evaluate change in terms of religious tension and conflict[5] and settled patterns of inequality and exclusion.[6]

Facing Extremism and Violence

Starting in 2003, the UK government adopted a comprehensive counter-terrorism strategy in response to the emergence of radical Muslim terrorism threats.[7] The strategy has been much criticized in the period since and was substantially overhauled in 2006–7 in the face of operational difficulties and learning feedback loops. But it nevertheless purports to address the problem from a wide perspective. There are four main components of the strategy, namely, Prevention, Pursuit, Protection, and Preparedness. A report by the Joseph Rowntree Reform Trust (JRRT) published three years later in November 2006 sought to re-examine the objectives of the government's strategy and also to probe those areas either where progress had been difficult or where the strategy had potentially become unbalanced in its overall scope and purpose. The authors summarized the elements of the strategy as follows:[8]

- *Prevention* takes in long-term goals, such as working to reduce tendencies leading to 'radicalization', for instance, through helping resolve inter-national disputes which encourage terrorism (a prominent part of the FCO's duties); ensuring that all citizens in the UK 'feel fully part of our

---

[3] *Fairness and Freedom: The Final Report of the Equalities Review, Final Report of the Equalities Review* (London: Cabinet Office, 2007).

[4] 'Issue Paper on Future Trends', Equalities Review, Cabinet Office, January 2007.

[5] Nielsen, J., 'Scenarios for Likely Future Evolution and Direction of Radical Islam in Europe', unpublished Discussion Paper prepared by the National Intelligence Council/Oxford Analytica, June 2005.

[6] Saggar, S., 'A Vision of 2026', presentation to the Equalities Review: Future Trends Seminar, Cabinet Office, November 2006.

[7] The strategy documents and related supporting papers can be accessed at http://security. homeoffice.gov.uk/counter-terrorism-strategy/counter-terrorism-strategy/.

[8] Quoted from Blick, A., Choudhary, T., and Weir, S., *Rules of the Game: Terrorism, Community and Human Rights* (York: Joseph Rowntree Reform Trust, 2006).

society'; fighting the 'battle of ideas'; and introducing legislation to deter terrorism.

- *Pursuit* goes wider than actually seeking to prevent terrorist attacks and apprehending those involved to the disruption of terrorist organizations, through better understanding of their capabilities and intentions; prosecutions, deportations, control orders, and proscriptions of organizations; working with communities; making it harder for terrorists to operate domestically and abroad; and targeting their funds.

- *Protection* entails working to safeguard critical national infrastructure and other sites at risk and maintaining border security.

- *Preparedness* means ensuring that effective contingency arrangements are in place.

At the time of its publication, the JRRT report succeeded in bringing together a number of previously diverse and diffuse commentaries on strategic approaches to counter-terrorism. For example, Sir David Omand, Britain's own former Homeland Security supremo (as dubbed by the press), contributed by outlining the central objective of a strategic response to: 'reduce the risk from international terrorism so that our people can go about their daily lives freely and with confidence'.[9] The emphasis, he argued, lay in obtaining lower risk without paying too great a price in terms of daily freedoms whilst also retaining public confidence.

It is important to pause and consider this simple statement that has been repeated endlessly in public debate. One implication that it raises is that otherwise successful policy interventions that manifestly failed to uphold basic and familiar freedoms amount to a Pyrrhic victory. Political debate in Britain (and elsewhere) is now regularly punctuated with heated arguments about extent to which central freedoms are, or are not, being eroded by policy measures designed to combat terrorism. Fresh legal powers for security agencies have typically attracted the greatest controversy. For example, writing about a fresh proposal to establish a 'terrorist offenders register', a vocal London-based lawyer recently argued that:[10]

Given that one can be convicted of a terrorist offence without even having a terrorist intention, a considerable degree of caution should be exercised before placing a person on a [terrorist offender] register where he or she is then subject to notification requirements and possible travel restrictions... There is a currently too much emphasis on this type of 'thought crime' as opposed to dealing with genuine terrorist threats.

[9] Quoted in Blick, A., Choudhary, T., and Weir, S., *Rules of the Game: Terrorism, Community and Human Rights* (York: Joseph Rowntree Reform Trust, 2006).

[10] Qureshi, T., '1984 in 2008 (Comment)', *Law Society Gazette*, 31 January 2008, p. 14.

If nothing else, some comfort can be taken from the existence of this debate since it reminds us that certain freedoms are sufficiently cherished to deter ill-informed executive government. The other main plank of the Omand account of strategic purpose is to place it in some kind of time frame. Omand himself described the initial time frame (five years) as insufficient because it mitigated against effective planning that often required a ten-year time horizon.[11] The timescale argument is not just limited to noting the mismatch between politicians' time frames (short) against those of policy-makers and implementers (longer). It is also about better appreciation of the longer-term effects of revised policy measures to address social exclusion. In some cases such as compulsory education, it is both true and helpful that dramatic improvements in educational qualifications among low-attaining subgroups have been achieved (e.g. as noted in an earlier chapter, the significant recent improvement in the record of Bangladeshi girls in compulsory schooling stands out). However, policy measures designed to tackle educational underachievement normally operate on a much longer time frame (in the case of black Caribbean boys, for example, a government report first highlighted an apparent large gap in attainment as long ago as 1964, and, more than a generation later, improvement remains as elusive as ever). Time frames, and our sense and expectations of them, therefore, are a key discussion point informing policy and strategy to combat extremism and violence.

Just one step below setting and agreeing overarching strategy is the task of identifying the main factors that are driving the behaviours that governments are trying to influence. The UK government's post-2003 strategy (known as 'Contest') has without doubt been open to the argument that alienation and disengagement have been long-term factors driving rising levels of radicalization among BMCs. Inequalities and discrimination based on ethnic and religious background are, for example, squarely within this frame of reference, although plenty of care has been taken to ensure that this message is not misread as 'disadvantage causes radicalization'.

This book has concluded that the politics of radicalization are deeply embedded in a wave of religious and political extremism that largely cut across all sections of Western Muslim communities. Notwithstanding important national, linguistic, and cultural variations among Western Muslims, religious and political extremists ideas, movements, and networks are today capable of unifying Muslim opinion to a much larger extent than has previously been imagined.[12] In no particular order of priority, this study has argued

[11] Omand, D., 'Security Dilemmas', *Prospect*, 129, December 2006.

[12] Council of the European Union (Nov. 24, 2005) 14781/1/05, The European Union Strategy for Combating Radicalisation and Recruitment to Terrorism Council of The European Union (Nov. 15, 2005) 14469/05, The European Union Counter-Terrorism Strategy.

that the base causes of extremism of this all-embracing kind have been fourfold:[13]

- Social and economic patterns of disadvantage that have left significant Muslim communities cut adrift from mainstream employment and economic opportunity structures.

- Increasingly inward-facing social networks that vastly increase the chances of separation, isolation, and the creation of a parallel, embittered society.

- The effects of weak, single-issue political leadership that has nurtured a culture of victimhood and a grievance-centred political agenda located in a sea of oppositional cultures.

- The rise of globalized Islamic grievance politics that has sought to unify Muslim populations as the perpetual targets of Western, Judeo-Christian-driven foreign policies, to say nothing of various domestic policies.

The above fourfold characterization involves a number of behaviours within and beyond Western Muslim communities that are hard to address directly through policy measures. For instance, aligning EU enlargement policy with the expectations of successive Turkish governments is an example, although in this case a fifteen-year time frame can at least be sketched. And merely reversing US foreign policy towards either Iraq specifically, or towards the Middle East generally, is obviously no small matter. However, any hypothetical policy reversal, or even recalibration, in itself cannot reasonably be described as directly linked to changed behaviour in relation to globalized Islamic grievance.[14] This behavioural change may possibly result, of course, but it is also closely interwoven with a number of quite separate causal factors such as state policies among Middle Eastern nations, civil society relationships in the Arab world, economic development and modernization, the changing nature and role of international organizations, the proliferation of media, and democratic reform among Muslim-majority countries.[15]

Therefore, the reading of radicalization taken by Western governments has to be wide-ranging and sophisticated as well as tangible and realistic if it is to be credible. Equally, it is important to recognize as early as possible that a significant proportion of policy interventions designed to counter religious and political radicalization are likely to have some degree of unintended consequences. This recognition then has a bearing on trying to find fresh ways

[13] Quoted from Blick, A., Choudhary, T., and Weir, S., *Rules of the Game: Terrorism, Community and Human Rights* (York: Joseph Rowntree Reform Trust, 2006).

[14] Mandaville, P., *Global Political Islam: International Relations of the Muslim World* (London: Routledge, 2007).

[15] Hossain, K., 'Initiatives to Promote Mutual Understanding and Respect among All Faiths and Communities in the Commonwealth: Some Suggestions', unpublished submission to the Commonwealth Commission on Respect and Understanding, February 2007.

to join up existing policy measures to allow a better chance for the effects of a package of measures, rather than excessive attention being paid to any single measure, not least if it is linked to a short-term rise in hidden—and not so hidden—support for extremism itself.

Above all, however, getting the strategic balance right, or at least better than before, requires governments to develop a better understanding of the relationship between political violence on one hand and the well of support and backing for extremism on the other. This was, in essence, the feature of Chapter 6 of this book. The key aspect of such an understanding is that it is not realistic or credible to view Western Muslim communities as containing tiny elements of extremism—in a larger sea of moderation.[16] This kind of outlook has characterized earlier misreadings of political terrorism in places such as Northern Ireland, the Basque territory, and Quebec nationalism. A better informed reading has observed the role played by the relatively large circle of tacit supporters of political violence, that is, those among these groups who provide material and ideological support through their failure, sometimes unknowingly, to condemn terrorism.

And this is ultimately the pivotal group that matters most in combating terror. Its implicit loyalties may sit with a small, highly motivated violent fringe. However, this pivot group—or fence-sitters as they were dubbed in Chapter 6—is certainly not directly involved in or supportive of extremist methods. But, crucially, their underlying sense of sympathy for the goals of the men of violence means that they can, even unknowingly, provide succour for those committed to violent confrontation.

If it is important for governments to develop a more realistic understanding of the existence and importance of fence-sitting Muslims, it is, arguably, even more critical that a more balanced understanding is shared with and reflected in public opinion. This is exceptionally difficult to achieve in practice since the shapers of public opinion are numerous and often lie outside the direct influence of governments. Seeking condemnation can all too easily slip into a sense of a one-sided demand. The message can easily be misread or misinterpreted to be that Muslim fellow citizens are in some way 'not one of us'. All Muslims can be viewed as potential harbourers of terrorists if this point of nuance is deliberately or even unknowingly mistaken.[17] And it is only one small step then, if only by neglect and accident, to suggest that all Muslims are potential terrorists. This seemingly obvious danger may appear easy to avoid at one level, but in practice it is a risk that affects a wide array of measures to counter terrorism in Muslim communities.

[16] Klausen, J. 'Marginalized in the Middle: Moderate Muslims', unpublished Discussion Paper prepared by the National Intelligence Council, Oxford Analytica, June 2005.
[17] 'Analysis: Taking on Extremists', BBC News website, 14 August 2006.

A basic imperative, therefore, is to pursue a strategic response that is not easily blown off course by the pressure of events, some of which have all too often polarized communities into 'us' (i.e. non-Muslims committed to peaceful resolution of conflict) and 'them' (i.e. Muslims who are prepared to tolerate violent means to tackle goals shared across a religious community). The role of the intelligentsia in Muslim communities is one example of trying to stimulate a debate in relation to the recognition of violent extremism and Islam's own responses to fragmentation and discord.[18] Operation 'Contest', the previously mentioned Home Office-inspired initiative in 2004, sought to pursue this approach. Its particular objective was to create a reservoir of undeclared support among better-educated British Muslims for otherwise unpopular counter-terrorism surveillance measures. This example sits alongside a number of others that collectively aim to move hearts and minds, partly through greater exposure given to contestable claims, and partly through expanding the capacity among and across Western Muslims to engage in such debate themselves.

Boomerangs and Catapults

But the issue that lies to the fore is the tendency towards 'boomerang' effects and away from 'catapult' effects. That is to say, the unintended consequences of policy interventions can—and often do—make the strategic challenge even greater. A recurring feature of counter-terrorism policies has been their tendency to spawn alienation and soft support for political violence while tackling immediate threats. Even the most surgically precise intervention to act to remove a known and present threat of terrorism carries with it a small chance of imprecision in its implementation. For example, a covert surveillance operation can be derailed by even the smallest human error in target identification.

A terrorist conspiracy, typically, will involve not just gathering intelligence about those directly involved but also sweeping up information about a range of tacit backers who may not fully know about their own involvement in such a conspiracy. An operational decision to remove a threat via such a raid, or to aggregate existing evidence in support of an alleged conspiracy, depends on a high level of precision in its execution. Such a raid can easily pick up casual acquaintances of conspirators, and this can present genuine difficulties in trying to assess the graduated risk posed by individual as against the next. Worse still, as the case of the Walthamstow raid in Forest Gate, in East London in May 2006 showed, the quality of intelligence can be called into question at a point after the damage has been done to the reputation of intelligence.[19] One single miscalculated raid, regardless of the attendant

[18] *The Sunday Times*, 30 May, 2004.
[19] 'Two Held in Terror Raid Released', BBC News website, 10 June 2006.

levels of press speculation and unattributed briefing, can serve to create the worst possible outcome. The result is not merely a failed operation that leaves a neighbourhood in dismay. Its costs are also felt in terms of the recruiting sergeant effects such a scenario can have on future waves of terrorists. But the greatest negative impact that such a failure has is in the way in which, silently, attitudes towards mainstream policing and security harden within Muslim communities.

In other words, the effect is that word quickly spreads that counter-terrorism operations are managed and controlled by a mindset that, despite protestations, sees all young Muslim men as de facto threats.[20] In such circumstances, the result is something of a self-fulfilling prophecy by which the rhetoric shifts: 'If we are to be treated as moral pariahs, it is little wonder that some of us start behaving as if this is true.' And a close variation of this rhetoric becomes: 'Young Muslim men start with a high degree of scepticism towards the police and security services, and this only intensifies as a result of faulty operational policy.'

This is precisely the most pressing concern arising from current strategic attempts to engage Western Muslims. A number of CT policies are implicated in this concern but so too are aspects of the unplanned outcomes of other public policies. Both are explored more fully in the next part of this chapter, but we start by looking at the strategies for creating equality and opportunity as a route to harmony and trust.

Strategic Priorities for Cohesion

The discussion and evidence presented in this book indicate that a trade-off between diversity and community ends up obscuring a three-way relationship in which equality (and the perception of equality) is a crucial missing link. As communities experience greater inequality than they have previously known, or are willing to endure, or existing inequalities do not reduce substantially over time, it is probable that this will impact negatively on social cohesion and solidarity.[21] The relationship works both ways, and cohesion can be destabilized by more than growing ethnic diversity. Robert Putnam and colleagues have pointed to this broader account in the USA where evidence suggests declining trust not just across, but also within, ethnic groups.[22]

---

[20] Mamdani, M., *Good Muslim, Bad Muslim: America, the Cold War and the Roots of Terror* (Doubleday, NY: Three Leaves Press, 2004).

[21] Premdas, R., 'Multiculturalism as a Policy of Tolerance in the Face of Diversity', unpublished submission to the Commonwealth Commission on Respect and Understanding, January 2007.

[22] Putnam, R., and Feldstein, L., with Cohen, D., *Better Together: Restoring the American Community* (New York: Simon and Schuster, 2003).

These are high-level nuanced arguments but nevertheless ones that serve to impact both the policy debate and the choices generated by policymakers. It is obviously vital, therefore, to have a better shared understanding of the argument. The largest risks confronting policymakers in this area are threefold and each is mutually reinforcing in its nature and effects.

Settled Disadvantage

First, prioritizing left-behind groups: tackling settled disadvantage among ethnic groups who have been left behind, especially in terms of human capital assets and labour market participation. The evidence is clear that these groups include parts of the black, Pakistani, and Bangladeshi communities but also comprise elements of white, working-class communities. Better and more innovative use of the labour market and education is a plausible means of achieving improved outcomes. In any case, there is a strong case for using economic levers to do more of the heavy lifting for the economic integration of these groups.

In terms of practical measures to address socio-economic disadvantage, policymakers might focus on areas such as active labour market policies, the compulsory schooling system, and intermediate stepping stones into employment. Examples can be shown in each of these areas that are worth building upon. For example, the use of school and LEA floor targets has been associated with improved attainment records at GCSE level. This is an area where innovation has the advantage of building on existing strategy and measures. For example, in March 2003, *Aiming High: Raising Achievement of Minority Ethnic Pupils* was launched as part of the ethnic minority attainment strategy of DfES. The Cabinet Office final report on *Ethnic Minorities and the Labour Market*, published at the same time, welcomed the existing DfES approach and recommended that, in future, a greater appetite to bear down on underachievement should be the priority. This would mean a more critical examination of the risk that prevailing educational floor targets can sometimes have the unintended consequence of allowing disproportionate numbers of particular ethnic groups to 'slip between the cracks'. In practical terms, the case was made for adopting ethnic group-specific floor targets at school and LEA level. The trigger for this additional measure might, typically, be sustained evidence to show that a particular low performing ethnic group's average attainment had fallen farther behind that of children from all ethnic backgrounds. A similar approach might be taken in relation to the target regime established for personal advisers in the Jobcentre Plus network. Equally, New Deal for Communities, Young People, and Single Parents programmes could also assess the value of adding such an 'ethnic twist' to pre-existing targets.

Second, addressing tacit support for extremism: addressing alienation and extremism, particularly among small cores within the left-behind groups.

Young black men in several Western democracies are typically subject to a pariah status in employment, education, criminal justice, and so on. In countries such as Britain, this status is long-standing and has led to long-term alienation and hostility. The emergence of oppositional cultures, embedded in violence, gangs, firearms, and weaponry, has been just one noticeable aspect of this picture. A lack of trust and respect across ethnic and racial lines, and the adoption of identities of hatred in literature and music, has been another. There is a danger of the most alienated parts of British Muslim communities also adopting a similar oppositional outlook. Part of the engagement will also involve finding means to bear down on tacit support from extremism and violence among these communities.

Third, using the right glue to promote cohesion and interconnectedness— and wisely: building greater social cohesion, partly by emphasizing the genuine barriers to cross-community trust, and also by identifying the most suitable levers, some of which may not be in the hands of government to begin with. It is vital that policymakers identify correctly and use appropriately the chosen glue in this exercise.

Membership of a community, national or otherwise, implies sharing values and codes of conduct as well as in distributional concerns. With ethnic and religious pluralism set to grow in every large-scale industrial democracy in the next decade and beyond, it is vital to develop a clear and practical understanding of these interplays. In the first two decades of the twentieth century, public intellectuals, political leaders, and practical policymakers concluded that the USA was not so much full as already approaching its absorptive capacity of difference. These differences had been brought by alien immigrants who shared little in common with the existing society and who, it was feared, would threaten Americans' sense of 'we'. This conclusion was flawed for reasons that are now readily apparent and discussed earlier in this book. Britain's policymakers today can learn profitably from this legacy. Western governments can also learn from the general lesson that this presents, namely, to avoid policies whose language and substance needlessly essentializes Muslim identity.

Respect, Violence, and Cohesion

At a more prosaic level, building cohesion and interconnectedness across religious and ethnic lines involves the nurturing of respectful and nurturing relationships. These can be subject to severe strains and pressures, particularly where fault lines of economic and historical injustice overlap with highly defined single dimensions of identity. Breakdown can be gradual as well as sudden, but many of the warning signs are usually present a long time ahead of controversy or conflict, let alone violence.

Respect tends to break down, and violence most frequently occurs, when a strong sense of injustice is experienced along the fault lines of identity.[23] This can be the case even when the sense of injustice has been exaggerated and moulded into a victim culture that also suppresses internal debate and external criticism.[24] Experience across the world suggests that ethnicity, race, tribe, and religion are powerful identity markers in today's conflicts. The markers of the breakdown of normal forms of respect and understanding are apparent when:[25]

- Groups of people are ignored, slighted, or discriminated against because of their identity (e.g. because they are women, or from a particular country, ethnic group, or religion). This includes situations where inequalities are endemic or have become institutionalized so that unfair treatment of particular groups becomes part of the normal order or social structure.

- There is ongoing or occasional violence perpetrated by one or more groups defined in terms of a specific identity. There is no respect and no understanding in any manifestation of violence, physical or verbal, whether this occurs within the home, in the streets, between nations, or when it involves an act of international terrorism.

A sense of injustice may be experienced economically, politically, and culturally. Feelings of economic inequality are often paramount—the group in question feel that they have been discriminated against in terms of their ability to own land, gain employment, make a decent living, and access services. Political disempowerment may be an additional grievance if the system of governance allows them no power and no effective voice. If their very identity is questioned or ridiculed, this will tend to intensify the sense of group cohesion and exacerbate a group sense of injustice. Where economic inequality, lack of effective political voice, and a strong sense of discrimination on the basis of cultural identity overlap, violence is more likely. The spark for mobilization is often the appeal of an ideology or the charisma of a leader, or more likely, an interplay between ideas and personalities.

At a global level, and particularly with regard to the relationship between 'the West' and 'Islam', the sense of injustice has an additional element. This is a feeling, only partly documented but tangible nevertheless, that the world's superpowers, those assuming positions of economic, political, and moral leadership, are acting with impunity.[26] The foreign policy decisions of these

---

[23] Murad, A.-H., 'Muslim Loyalty and Belonging: Some Reflections on the Psychosocial Background', January 2003; available at http://65.39.144.73/ISLAM/ahm/loyalty.htm.

[24] Malik, K., 'Islamophobia Myth', *Prospect*, issue 107, February 2005.

[25] Material in this section is drawn from 'Towards Respect and Understanding: The Causes of Violence', unpublished paper presented to the Commonwealth Commission on Respect and Understanding, November 2006.

[26] Desai, M., *Rethinking Islamism: The Ideology of the New Terror* (London: I. B. Tauris, 2006).

powers has led to a sense that they are not being governed by international agreements but are acting on their own interests. For instance, the 'war on terror' is perceived, in many circles, as being waged without concomitant effort by Western countries to understand the deep sense of grievance within some parts of the Islamic world.[27] There is evidence that this is radicalizing the middle ground—those who would never normally condone violence or support terrorism. According to Sanneh:[28]

The West [...] has sought comfort in the convenient thought that it is only a renegade breakaway group of Muslim fundamentalists who have struck out in violence. Most Muslims do not share that view.

This lack of self-reflection on the part of some Western countries is detrimental to the underlying principles of respect that involve listening, talking, and a commitment to understand the point of view of the other, even if it means fundamentally disagreeing with them.[29]

In terms of strategically driven responses, it is sensible to note that not all aspects of the problem can be addressed in a single, unified strategy. Priorities have to be set, and bearing down more effectively on the various underlying causes of political violence must be the starting point. Five findings have particular policy relevance for this discussion and the particular need to identify policy interventions that allow greater resilience to the risks of confrontation turning to violence:

- Violent conflict is more likely in situations of multiple and sustained inequality, where there is no hope of change through the political system.

- Violence is more likely if root grievances are not addressed through peaceful mechanisms, and widely perceived to be unlikely to be addressed in these terms.

- Violence might be anticipated if affirmative action policies, however well-intentioned, so completely reverse the fortunes of the once-privileged group that they feel disempowered and disrespected. Alternatively, negative perceptions about religious or ethnic carve-outs can have the effect of fuelling antagonism towards the minority group.

- Violence can be sparked by the form democracy takes—democracy alone is no guarantor that different population groups will feel included and respected, and so much hangs on the inclusive effects of particular local democratic processes and practices.

---

[27] Ahmed, A., *After Terror: Promoting Dialogue Among Civilizations* (Oxford: Blackwell, 2005).

[28] Sanneh, L., 'Sacred and Secular in Islam', *ISIM Newsletter*, 10 (July, 2002) p. 6.

[29] Guelke, A., *Terrorism and Global Disorder: Political Violence in the Contemporary World* (London: I. B. Tauris, 2006).

- An active civil society does not by itself assure respectful relationships—the way civil society participates in decision-making is key to avoiding civil society organizations merely exacerbating inter-group tensions.

Building and Sustaining Inclusive Communities

What are the building blocks of more equal and inclusive relationships? What can be used to support a process of building inclusive and successful communities? And what are the key lessons for policymakers keen to embed Muslim grievances in a peaceful mechanism for change?

A large part of the answer comes from examining the idea of a *community* itself. A genuinely founded *community* is one that straddles a potentially fraught distinction. On one hand, there is a need to recognize fully the human value and respect of different members of a community who may have important differences in terms of ethnic or religious background. On the other hand, the community needs to have certain minimum things that bring it together. These are, typically, some basic, shared norms and assumptions that go across traditional boundaries and allow all members to have a stake in a shared outcome. There are numerous examples of shared norms and behaviour that go unnoticed every day and which are important ingredients in shaping wider social and public benefits. The textbook example is that of a range of unconnected individuals who individually choose not to park in a designated disabled parking space in a car park. Alternatively, there may be an unwritten 'rule' about eating habits whereby older generations eat before or alongside (but not after) younger ones. Elsewhere the shared norm in a traditional faith society may take the form of dress codes, dietary practices, or reminders of modesty between men and women especially in public places. Long-standing conventions (unwritten rules that have the effect of codified practices) about the political system can be further examples of shared norms. In a number of cases, almost all members of society understand these norms and, as importantly, operate on the basis that the largely unwritten rule is known—and will be followed—by everyone else. These simple cases centre on the idea of reciprocity, that is, that one will do something or give up something at one moment in favour of someone else (or another group or interest) and that this will be indirectly rewarded via benefits that either materialize later on or accrue to the society as a whole. This is an important point because it makes the case for individuals or groups *not* always operating in their own immediate interests.

In other words, what is needed, or may be lacking, is the powerful political articulation of the case for *why and how everyone is affected by everyone else*. Thus, the idea that interconnectedness cannot easily be sidelined, if indeed it can be ignored at all. This is a positive ideal and requires a great deal of support in terms of the messages of leaders and those in authority. It also requires regular nourishment through everyday practices, implicit public feelings of support and value, and, wherever possible, tangible examples of reaffirmation.

The specific difficulty is that people can only exchange things, ideas, and beliefs successfully if there is an underlying assumption that they are equal, at least in terms of their status. This might also apply to their particular opportunity structures. This assumption can and often is written down as a codified rule. It can, in addition, be a description of a shared, unwritten norm that is followed unknowingly. Both have a part to play, but the latter is likely to be the mark of real success for a cohesive community.

Governments' cohesion and integration policies emphasize the importance of building and sustaining genuine communities. These communities will often be plural in their ethnic or religious composition. In some countries, mere recognition of such pluralism may be a difficult stumbling block, and while this may be an everyday reality, it does not always follow that members of different groups enjoy recognition in an equal and fair way. So, for example, the right to believe in a distinct body of ideas of religious doctrine can easily be compromised. For instance, equality before the law is taken as read at one level, but it is challenged if one particular faith is formally established as the church of the state. That said, there have been many practical attempts to grant comparable status and recognition to non-established faiths: for example, the exemption in Britain, under the Road Traffic Act 1972, given to Sikhs in relation to compulsion in wearing motor cycle helmets.

Respecting Belief or, Rather, the Right of Belief

An especially difficult contextual question is the extent to which respect can, and should, be afforded to individuals and human beings, that is, directly as ends in themselves. The common identity of humanity provides a clear platform. So, related to this, is the question of respecting the beliefs held by groups of individuals and held on the basis of group identity. Greater effort can be made to promote recognition of the right of groups to hold distinctive beliefs and belief ideologies. The inability of some groups to enjoy this right has often been responsible for their grievances. However, there is a paradox of pluralism that needs to be aired in this context. This has to do with the limits and effects of greater respect. For instance, is the right to believe in an alternative or dissenting position an absolute one or one that is conditional? For instance:

- The counter-belief system may contain, as a central tenet, an idea that threatens the position of already powerful or dominant groups. This may even matter among groups of equivalent strength and influence. Sharing power with, or even granting a voice to, the source of the threat is the basic challenge. It is made harder if the belief system is couched in deterministic terms that tackle perceived past injustice. Of course, harder may not mean that it is invalid, and addressing the past in an even-handed way can be a prerequisite to making progress.

• The counter-belief system might contain an explicit rejection of the legitimacy of existing political and economic institutions and arrangements. A claim to secede based on these grounds would be a particular example. It is not obvious that granting recognition for this position would result in a self-fulfilling prophecy. Equally, choosing not to recognize this—and thus choosing not to respect its validity for some in a society—can become a powerful marker of greater alienation.

• The counter-belief system can call into question the basis and nature of a community to begin with. It is not always easy to respect a viewpoint that wishes *not* to live in and belong to a plural community, particularly if the heterogeneity of that community has been long established. The challenge is either to negotiate and nurture support for common belonging, in the hope that this reduces the appeal of rejection, or alternatively to reinforce the community basis of any solutions or responses to grievance.

Social Capital: Cohesion's Glue

A key aim is to create communities in which there are high and resilient levels of trust between individuals and groups. Trust is reflected in many things and ways, but certainly includes an open acceptance of difference between groups in society. In other words, trust is about (and is found when) ethnic or religious difference is not only tolerated but actively supported. Support in this sense involves three elements. First, the value of such difference requires some overt recognition as being integral to the nature and character of a society.[30] The role of policymakers and others in this context is to deliver interventions that are in the mainstream of building a cohesive and integrated society.[31]

Second, barriers to cohesion can be identified in a way that balances a range of causal factors, ranging from asymmetric economic relations through to simmering grievance and the effects of social isolation. This is important since many countries find it challenging to identify and tackle such barriers in a way that is not crudely identified as promoting one sectional interest or another. Barriers, in other words, are defined not simply as those facing one

---

[30] Home Secretary's speech to the IPPR, 'New Challenges for Race Equality and Community Cohesion' conference, London, 7 July 2004.

[31] Saggar, S., 'Ethnic Pluralism and Social Cohesion: Strategic Challenges for Policy' presentation to the IPPR, 'New Challenges for Race Equality and Community Cohesion' conference, London, 7 July 2004.

group or another from enjoying greater benefits, but rather those preventing social cohesion across the board and affecting all in some manner.

Third, active support is also required to build forward-looking narratives that accept complexity in the relationship between causes and effects. One of the biggest dangers for the design of any intervention is that these can be projected in misleading and unhelpfully simplistic narratives, for example in the link between poverty and extremism. The evidence base far from supports this picture, and therefore needs to be layered and nuanced. Ultimately, it needs to build a counter-narrative that sees various interconnected reasons for the breakdown of normal trusting and respectful relationships.

This is an important bone of contention in many societies where the basis of ethnic and religious diversity has been growing, or where the tensions associated with such diversity are felt to be more pronounced than they were in the past. The forceful argument has been made that social interaction may be harder and more elusive in societies that are ethnically and religiously diverse than in relatively homogeneous ones. That is to say, fears have been expressed about 'too much' diversity, the effects of which are thought to be placing existing trusting relationships under strain. This argument, of course, begs the questions as to whether, or how far, the cohesiveness of societies is itself shaped by their ethnic or religious diversity. Specifically, the question is whether—and not how far—diversity and cohesion are inversely related to begin with.

For instance, Goodhart has extended this argument to assert that a common Britishness has been threatened, in part by a reluctance to pin down the sources of shared identity and co-responsibility. Historical and geographical development, he argues, has been a large yet neglected source, and that changes brought about through post-war immigration have been underestimated in their impacts on such gradual development. He states:[32]

... talk about the 'British people' refer[s] not just to a set of individuals with specific rights and duties but to a group of people with a special commitment to one another. Membership in such a community implies acceptance of moral rules, however fuzzy, which underpin the laws and welfare systems of the state.

The example of Britain can be generalized to many other countries in order to recognize the underlying point, namely, the loose, uncodified ways in which belonging is achieved and recognized in a particular society. The point at issue is twofold. First, is there any evidence to suggest that special commitments to one another have been especially difficult to generate across ethnic and religious lines? And, second, is there a particular reason to believe that the acceptance of such binding rules has failed among particular groups or countries? Clearly, the example of Muslim communities in Western societies and

---

[32] Goodhart, D., 'Too Diverse?' *Prospect*, February 2004.

Muslim countries in the international security order are areas that regularly cause controversy and can become self-fulfilling prophecies.

The link between diversity and cohesion may be a small aspect of a much wider phenomenon. Some aspects of diversity are the results of lifestyle and voluntary changes, while others are the products of large-scale social transformations such as the role of women particularly in the workforce or the products of large-scale immigration or even internal migration. The drivers can be numerous and interwoven. It is therefore sensible to remember that both stocks and flows of social capital have been subject to change and continuity.

Drivers of Future Change

The main drivers of change are varied but are disproportionately influenced by factors that are capable of radicalizing young British Muslims There are a number of obvious and less apparent drivers of social, cultural, economic, and political change affecting British Muslim communities. Some of these drivers are common to other immigrant and immigrant-descended groups and are already well mapped by government (e.g. English language as a barrier to achievement and a source of accelerated integration into the labour market, in housing patterns, in healthcare services, etc.). Other drivers are less well understood or even acknowledged.

The range of key drivers that need to be considered and fed into the development of a coherent and credible strategy includes the following:

- *Demographic patterns of British Muslims relative to others.* The existing evidence shows for example that British Pakistanis and Bangladeshis have a considerably younger age structure than their white, or indeed British Indian, counterparts. Age structures of this kind are linked to a number of policy implications such as the need to build human capital through education and training, through to exposure to higher levels of particular kinds of crime (both as victims and as perpetrators). A further example is that of second- and third-generation British-born Muslim girls and women. Disproportionately large numbers of such girls are currently entering and progressing through the compulsory education system. In many cases, these trends involve leaving behind or even breaking down traditional cultural norms. Such development can be associated with rapidly changing cultural and social attitudes, both among British Muslims and in society generally.

- *Transnational patterns of family and community formation.* British Muslim communities vary enormously in terms of linkages to countries of origin and in use of religious institutions to support collective identity.

British-born and -educated Muslims whose backgrounds stem from middle-class urban parts of South Asia may retain elements of these links to reinforce pride in their own cultural heritage. Music, film, and literature are likely conduits. Other Muslims, whose origins may lie in rural, less-educated agrarian communities, may be more likely to rely on transnational bonds and ties to, for example, support family members through international remittances and to locate marriage partners. As a driver of change, such transnational linkages are generally under-researched and poorly documented. As a consequence, their scope, scale, and significance are also poorly understood by government.[33] Gaining greater purchase on transnational drivers of change is an important gap in knowledge and understanding still to be filled. Moreover, there is some evidence to show that greater levels of social, economic, and political integration among particular groups are not always inversely related to the maintenance of transnational relationships. In some cases, these may even be mutually reinforcing, particularly in the sphere of commerce where the development and exploitation of new markets has been closely associated with transnational business networks.

- *Larger societal attitudes towards British Muslims and Islam.* Current polling evidence is fairly patchy on the question of general societal attitudes towards Muslim communities in Britain. The bulk of empirical data in this area has focused fairly directly on issues of conflict and the perceived ingredients of severe alienation. Where attitudes relate to broad issues of cultural traditions and differences in values and behaviour, it is possible to rely on survey evidence geared to looking at ethnic and racial diversity. This evidence shows that only small minorities within the general public are supportive unconditionally of the customs and traditions of immigrant and immigrant-descended groups being retained indefinitely.[34]

A much larger question is that of tolerance and understanding of Islam as a religion. This is important since Muslim community and religious leaders are often at pains to stress that the role of Islam is not that of an external influence upon British citizens in a largely secular environment. The role that is emphasized by contrast is one that sees religion as integral to all aspects of life and society, from the domestic involving family relationships to wider norms governing social equity and welfare. There is a need to gather better and more sophisticated data that reflects the degree to which such a holistic view of religion is held either among British Muslims or among the public at large. Certainly, social attitudes data on questions of religiosity suggest that,

---

[33] Young, David R., 'The Peril of the Dominant Culture and the Idea of America', speech to the Congressional Institute/Senate Republican Planning Conference, Washington, DC, 7 February 2003.
[34] British Election Study 1997.

with the partial exception of women among older generations, sharp declines in religious orientation have been seen in British society in the recent years.[35]

- *Unpredictable levels of Muslim group consciousness.* There is very limited evidence to show that British Muslims are disproportionately more likely than non-Muslims to derive a sense of collective identity and consciousness from their religion. It is probably the case that such consciousness varies considerably with age, education levels, and residential and employment patterns.

Nevertheless, one of the challenges that emerges from British Muslim identity is that it can coexist with, and be mutually supportive of, a variety of other characteristics and sources of group identity. For example, socio-economic advancement into white-collar, middle-class employment and social status is not necessarily in conflict with Muslim consciousness. Group consciousness and identity among British Muslims is shaped by a variety of factors, some of which are reactive and the product of perceived threats (e.g. fears of anti-Muslim backlash during crises such as war), while others are more self-generating (e.g. voluntary and charitable work within and across religious communities). A potentially interesting test of the ability to translate such religious consciousness into concrete forms of behaviour might be the level of demands for Islamic mortgage products. These are currently at a rather embryonic stage of development with few products formally launched at the time of writing. However, it is likely that major financial institutions such as Royal Bank of Scotland and HSBC will come forward with significant marketing campaigns in the course of the next eighteen to twenty-four months, capitalizing on regulatory reform of such financial services in 2004–5. Evidence to show awareness and take-up rates among the targeted population will be helpful in assessing the extent of group consciousness. However, linked evidence on the motives of those who take advantage of this kind of opportunity will help to shed light on the depth and nature of such consciousness. This example implies that Muslim collective consciousness can also be nurtured and developed by the influence of lifestyle and commercial choices. Islamic mortgages and sources of credit finance are a specific current example but, if successful, suggest that there may be a larger untapped market that can cater explicitly for groups with particular religious principles. These products are now beginning to enter a more mature market phase, and reflect both greater awareness among providers of religious and commercial sensitivities and a fresh impetus among consumers to seek out tailored solutions.

Overall, it is increasingly important to know what factor or factors cause or impede the development of a collective, corporate Muslim identity in Britain.

[35] De Graaf, N. D., and Need, A., 'Losing Faith: Is Britain Alone?', *British Social Attitudes: The 17th Report* (London: Sage, 2000).

In addition, if it is possible to identify these factors, it is then vital to isolate the factors most likely to radicalize such identity. The rise of oppositional identities and movements is a clear possibility in certain circumstances but, as yet, not enough is known about these circumstances and what, if anything, can be done to influence them. There may be international or transnational factors that are linked with radicalizing Muslim collective identity, and there will be lessons to be read across to aspects of British foreign trade, development, and security policy. Equally, some crucial contributory factors may be entirely shaped by domestic social and economic policy.

Knowing what factors are most likely to increase collective radical consciousness, and whether these are present or not in Britain, amounts to a critical gap that needs to be filled. This should be a top priority for further work in this area, irrespective of whether it is pursued by the academic or policy communities, or a combination of both.[36]

Evidence shows that growing religious and spiritual consciousness exists in segments of British society. The level of religious awareness found among a single religious group—Muslims—therefore should not be seen in complete isolation. British Hindus, Sikhs, and Buddhists are also linked to growing semi-formal religious and spiritual organizations aspects of which build on transnational and international networks. For example, the *Shri Sathya Sai Baba* sect, drawing on a number of faiths but principally Hindu in reputation, has developed a strong following among British Asians of Indian and East African origin.[37]

Some such groups have been very successful in building dynamic networks for exchange and promotion of common values and norms regarding the role of spirituality in Western secular societies. The Prem Rawat Foundation, for instance, has been notable in identifying the interaction between spiritual self-awareness and wider social and economic objectives pursued by its members.[38] The ability of British Muslim organizations to appeal to the demand for greater spiritual and religious consciousness among notional members is therefore part of a wider picture about the nature of less conventional religiosity in British society.

- *Patterns of socio-economic change notably in building human capital.* A lot is already known about changing levels and forms of human capital and the relationship with wider aspects of social and economic change. Analytical work on social mobility[39] adds considerable insight. However, the reliance on pre-existing ethnic group classifications means that at best

---

[36] 'New Security Challenges: "Radicalisation" and Violence—a Critical Reassessment', Economic and Social Research Council/Arts and Humanities Research Council/Foreign and Commonwealth Office, January 2007.

[37] www.kheper.net/topics/gurus/Sai_Baba.htm.   [38] http://www.tprf.org.

[39] http://www.strategy.gov.uk/papers/socialmobility.shtml#ANNEX%20A.

there are limitations because of the use of proxies to capture the position of just over half the British Muslim population.

However, as previously noted in Chapters 2 and 4, there are conflicting messages contained within the evidence base on the labour market performance of the largest Muslim groups emanating from Pakistan, Bangladesh, and India. While the achievements of the former two groups lag considerably behind those of Indians generally, it is striking that Indian-origin Muslims record rather better achievements than their Muslim counterparts from Pakistan and Bangladesh. This points to a country-of-origin effect linked to the self-selecting nature of immigration from these different countries. The strategic issue at stake is the degree to which Muslims from these two low-achieving groups are able to close the gap with both Muslims and non-Muslims from Indian backgrounds. A prolonged failure to make progress among these two particular groups is likely to be associated with further alienation and an increased potential for political and religious extremism.

- *Social capital factors and their wider recognition.* Detailed work to understand the significance of and roles played by social capital in shaping access to opportunity structures among religious and ethnic minorities is relatively underdeveloped. Expertise in this area in government[40] could be easily exploited, partly to develop new insights for policy priorities, and partly in order to give greater recognition to social capital–related drivers of change.

However, the rise of Muslim collective consciousness is seen in the context of particular patterns of social capital and their relationship with wider feelings about integration into British society and culture. A 2002 poll found that while a clear majority felt that British Muslims were already well integrated or needed to be further integrated into 'mainstream British culture', a third reported that such integration had gone too far. The flip side of this argument is the extent to which the general population shows anxiety about the articulation of a distinct Muslim identity in Britain. The same survey revealed that seven in ten British Muslims believed that non-Muslims rejected the idea that Islam could be a part of British identity.[41]

- *The role of leadership and government itself.* Finally, the role of government itself can sometimes be an important variable in shaping and driving change. In one respect, this is already the case in terms of the general mood and tone of debate that ministers promote and/or intervene in. Providing helpful mood music is one thing, but following a strategic step, that both explains the long-term direction of travel and anticipates the buffering effects of event-driven criticisms, is another.

[40] http://www.strategy.gov.uk/reports/reports.shtml.   [41] *Guardian*, 17 June 2002.

Thus, there are other opportunities through activities such as:

- raising the profile of discrete religious groups such as British Muslims in the general work of government departments;
- greater commitment to religious sensitivity in drawing up fresh policy proposals;
- better dialogue with Muslim communities, both through existing community leaderships and with emerging voices; and
- ministerial speeches, visits, publications, and examples of personal interest-led initiatives.

Each of these kinds of interaction was highlighted in an unpublished 2002 Home Office discussion paper.[42] However, these were not integrated with government's wider policies on education, health, crime, and so on. Moreover, the basic question of which bodies have credibility with and purchase on social attitudes and values among British Muslims is conspicuously absent in this now dated government paper. One reason for this omission or ambiguity is that the differentiation within British Muslim communities—not least in term of achievement, participation, and mobility—is very poorly understood. The considerable progress made by British Ismailis, for instance, ranks alongside the record of Hindu and Sikh South Asian communities. The tendency towards forms of social isolation and self-driving forms of exclusion is another prime causal driver that is not addressed in the paper.

The profile of mainstream, moderate Muslim leaders could be further highlighted and affirmed by different parts of government. Obvious tools to do so might include more imaginative use of the public honours and public appointment systems. However, against this should be set the constraints of creating—or appearing to create—anything that smacked of a backdoor quota system that could stir further hostility against British Muslims.

The Foreign Office adopted an initial formal strategy paper in 2003 entitled 'Building Bridges with Mainstream Islam'.[43] This represented a more fine-grained approach to the task of engagement and which was ambitious in its understanding and scope. Three of its features stand out and represent important strategic opportunities:

- entering the *Ummah* loop—by which it is proposed that promoting mainstream Islam among British Muslims will have a ripple effect in other countries;
- laying down clear and principled challenges to British Muslims on substantive foreign policy questions as a way of better identifying solutions to present problems as well as limits on acceptable behaviour; and

---

[42] 'Engaging British Muslims', Home Office unpublished paper, December 2002.
[43] 'Strategy for Building Bridges with Mainstream Islam', FCO Board paper, April 2003.

- pinpointing those elements of mainstream Islamic thinking that is renowned for its compatibility with democratic norms and values—partly as a means of isolating groups and issues that lie beyond this parameter.[44]

Emerging strategic challenges and choices

An understated conclusion from the discussion thus far would be that British Muslim communities are not generally well understood by the public, the press, or government. By this is meant not how well these communities are understood factually but rather that issues of internal differences and divisions, and the turbulence created by the 'war on terror', are often skimmed over by external eyes. At the same time, the high profile of elements of the Muslim population is often projected in highly negative terms. This combination of insufficient understanding and such a high profile contributes to a sensitivity about government's role to begin with. The sensitivity can combine with confusion when it is sometimes claimed that government should do more *and* less to tackle extremism and radicalization. Government's role is already quite far-ranging and broad in its potential reach. This includes:

- isolating and removing direct causes of religious intolerance and exclusion;
- identifying and tackling indirect obstacles to achievement faced by certain Muslim groups in areas such as education and employment;
- seeking to sensitize public policy design and implementation to the diversity of needs including those of particular religious minorities;
- addressing the specifically religious aspects (where these exist and are robustly evidenced) of need and under-achievement that go beyond those faced by ethnic minority and/or immigrant groups;
- addressing (though sometimes only to reacting) the specifically Islamic aspects of the above; and
- leading public understanding through education about and familiarity with Islam, especially in the context of western secular societies.

Given such a broad scope, there is often very little that is coherent or consistent within government's current understanding of the issue. Although rarely expressed explicitly, there can, understandably, be a tendency to address issues relating to British Muslims in an ad hoc, reactive manner. In certain

---

[44] The FCO work was later further strengthened through the results of a series of focus group exercises on foreign policy issues. These assessed understanding and outlook based on ethnic group and religion, and provided greater insight into the influence of mainstream Islam in shaping viewpoints.

areas, government has developed an ongoing dialogue with British Muslim leadership. However, it is not obvious whether such dialogue is a part of a general dialogue with religious bodies and faith communities at large. It also represents difficulties for interpreting the policy relevance of these contacts, particularly with respect to the unpopular aspects of counter-terrorism within and among British Muslim communities.[45]

The current received wisdom (and thus partial understanding) of British Muslim communities in much of government is that the ethnic, not religious, background of these groups represents severe challenges for public policy. For example, looking specifically at the opportunity structure faced and utilized by British Muslims (and other marginalized groups), these challenges are principally about:

- *Ethnic minority disadvantage.* For example, in tackling disproportionate barriers and needs faced by ethnic minority groups such as British Pakistanis and Bangladeshis in jobs, education, training, health, criminal justice, and so on. These disproportionate barriers have historically been interpreted in relation to the white population. However, the traditional picture of white advantage and ethnic minority disadvantage no longer holds true in areas such as education and employment. The progress made by groups such as Indians and Chinese is now acknowledged and suggests that those 'left behind' groups such as Pakistanis and Bangladeshis (alongside black Caribbeans) are priorities for reformulation of existing strategy and policy.[46]
- *Circumstantial and/or latent barriers to access and achievement.* Government strategy is increasingly willing to address the range of obstacles that can arise from the geographic, household, or age profile of particular groups. Other barriers may be less overt but can have large effects on access and achievement such as family structure and size, household formation, basic literacy and numeracy, cultural preferences, and so on.[47]

There are, consequently, a number of further possible objectives that can be pursued at a strategic, objective-setting level. The most pressing (and it must be said, controversial) involves the systematic mainstreaming of religion in anti-discrimination policy.

The British system for protection against discrimination is based on measures of ethnicity which, while considering some religious aspects of different groups, does not currently fully classify British Muslims as a distinct ethnic

---

[45] Briggs, R., 'After the War on Terror', *Fabian Review*, winter 2007–8, pp. 12–13.

[46] For a lengthier discussion of the factors that shape such disadvantage, see *Ethnic Minorities and the Labour Market: Final Report* (London: Cabinet Office, 2003).

[47] For a deeper review of the interplay between different kinds of factors behind reduced chances of participation and mobility, see *Narrowing the Gap: Final Report of the Life Chances Commission* (London: Fabian Society, 2007).

minority subject to the same legal protections as other 'recognized' ethnic groups. The criteria for assessment are based on two essential characteristics and five relevant but non-essential characteristics:

- Essential characteristics:
  - A long-shared history, of which the group is conscious as distinguishing it from other groups; and the memory of which it keeps alive.
  - A cultural tradition of its own, including family and social customs and manners, often but not necessarily associated with religious observance.
- Relevant but non-essential characteristics:
  - Either a common geographical origin, or a descent from a small number of common ancestors.
  - A common literature, peculiar to that group.
  - A common language, not necessarily peculiar to that group.
  - A common religion, different from that of neighbouring groups or from the general community surrounding it.
  - Finally, being a minority or being an oppressed or dominant group within a larger community.

Under the above, criteria shaped by the House of Lords ruled that Jewish and Sikh communities constitute ethnic groups, but Muslims, Jehovah's Witnesses, and Rastafarians do not. There may be scope to revisit this approach in order to provide greater rights for Muslim groups under current anti-discrimination laws, but, meanwhile, protections for Muslims have been afforded through the incorporation into domestic law and policy rights originally cast by EU laws.

The theme of greater engagement between government and Muslim communities is a recurring feature of reassessments of strategy. Component elements include developing programmes of ministerial visits; engaging with MPs whose constituencies include significant faith communities drawn from the minority ethnic communities; spreading good practice around departments on engaging with Muslim communities to help develop and implement policies and programmes; requiring government departments to review their involvement with Muslims and Muslim communities; and so on. All of these suggestions are based on elements of existing practice in parts of government. The degree to which these should be brought together in a way that could be described as a formal policy is open to dispute. Some of the evidence points to a variety of experiences and outlooks among British Muslims that may not be well suited to treatment as a homogeneous, unified group. That said, since 2005, the restructured Department of Communities and Local Government (among several Whitehall departments) has undertaken various consultative exercises with Muslims and Muslim organizations at grassroots level that effectively avoid homogenization.

There are a number of policy options that might be explored in order to improve economic and social outcomes for, and enhance social cohesion with, Muslim communities. This could include a number of central policy areas such as the education system, urban regeneration, family law, the criminal justice system, and the implications of international conventions for UK domestic policy.

Exploring Policy Options: Education Policy

Within the education system, there may be a strategic trade-off between encouraging the development of Muslim schools versus integration within the wider education system. At present, there are only a small handful faith-based Muslim schools operating within the state system in England and Wales. Further development of such schools could allay the concerns many Muslim parents have over the state education system. Among a list of policy options, several stand higher in rank order in terms of their likely sensitization effects and their practicability. These include:[48]

- preference for single sex education, especially for girls;
- modesty in dress, especially during physical education activities;
- prayer times and religious holidays in the school timetable and calendar;
- provision of halal food in school cafeterias;
- recruitment of more staff members and governors of schools from Muslim communities; and
- options to learn Arabic, as well as about Arab cultures and civilization, within the school curriculum.

However, such a move may further alienate Muslim children from wider society and, it is feared, prevent them from forming the bridging social capital relationships between communities that can be important in labour market and social outcomes. Conversely, it is certainly more politically acceptable to address many of the concerns of Muslim parents within the state education system and thus promote a more socially integrated system of learning.

Exploring Policy Options: Community and Economic Regeneration

A number of regeneration initiatives have found it relevant and helpful to make full use of community outreach programmes to build better links with

[48] See Vertovec, S., 'Islamophobia and Muslim Recognition in Britain' in Haddad, Y. Y., *Muslims in the West: From Sojourners to Citizens* (Oxford: Oxford University Press, 2002).

all segments of local affected communities. The basic building blocks of this approach have been based on two related relationships. First, the traditionally isolated and under-represented have found it hard to participate in a range of civic engagement and regeneration initiatives. Therefore, it is important to build new opportunities for participation that are more explicitly oriented to the outlook and characteristics of these groups. Second, the needs of particular discrete groups can all too easily be obscured by regeneration policies that are not sufficiently culturally sensitized. Specific religious groups such as Muslim women may have needs that can be captured by efforts to target their experiences and priorities. The opportunity costs of such efforts for regeneration agencies, social landlords, and others may be quite modest and proportionate to the likely outcomes.[49]

Exploring Policy Options: Family Law Policy

Family law is another area where important and interesting trade-offs in policy options exist. In general, the liberal principles of the English legal system, in contrast to more prescriptive legal codes elsewhere in Europe, in which 'everything is permitted except what is expressly forbidden' provides a great deal of flexibility for all minority communities. Despite this, elements of Muslim family law have come into conflict with English law in the recent past. These include matters such as polygamy, 'forced' marriages, and *Talaq*, a form of Islamic divorce initiated by both men and women. This is partly reflected in the nature of the Divorce (Religious Marriages) Act 2002, which was implemented from 2003, although its impact has been most widely noted in relation to Jewish couples.

The majority of Muslims have found little difficulty in living within the structures of English law. This is in part because there is little consensus between Muslim groups on such issues, and many are not considered obligatory from a religious point of view. However, there may be the potential to develop a more systematic framework to deal with issues around marriage, divorce, custody, inheritance and investments, and professional conduct which could replace the many informal arrangements which currently exist between Muslim families in these matters.

Exploring Policy Options: Criminal Justice Policy

Within the criminal justice system, there are a range of options which could be explored to promote greater integration for Muslim communities. Although available data are weak in this area, it may be tentatively concluded

[49] The Peabody Trust is just one example: it employs a community development worker at its Sundial programme based at Darwin Court in order to build links with a local Muslim Women's Group who are keen to establish a swimming pool in the local community.

that Muslim representation in the police and prison service is extremely low.[50] Measures to increase recruitment and retention from Muslim groups could be considered in line with the recommendations to tackle 'institutional racism' following the Stephen Lawrence enquiry. In recent years, Muslim organizations have also highlighted fears of 'being looked upon suspiciously' by the courts and that the court service had 'in-built prejudices' against Muslims.[51] The treatment of Muslims within the criminal justice system could potentially be reviewed in order to ascertain whether there was any conclusive evidence of differential treatment for Muslim people. A concrete illustration of this is the training and awareness provided to court ushers in allowing witnesses to take an oath using a range of religious texts. Very little evaluation exists of this type of sensitizing of policy change, although it is probably rather easier to audit change and effect at this practical level than in terms of social attitudes or contested identity.

Finally, some Muslim groups have also expressed concern over treatment within the prison system,[52] including prisoners being unable to perform prayers on time, the regulation of meals during Ramadan (the Muslim month of fasting based on the lunar calendar), and provision of halal food. A review of practices within prisons with regard to different religious practices may be able to deal with many of these complaints.

Exploring Policy Options: Religious Observance (The Case of Animal Slaughter)

The question of the particular opportunities to religious groups to maintain methods of animal sacrifice has been the subject of considerable argument over many years. The halal method practised by Muslims and the shechita method practised by Jews both rely on religiously trained slaughter by men at dedicated abattoirs using sharp knives to cut the throat of an animal in a single stroke and allowing the animal to bleed to death thereafter. In particular, the religious principles underpinning both methods of slaughter forbid the pre-stunning of animals (typically using electronic interventions prior to slaughter). These practices have received exemption from existing laws governing animal slaughter. The exemption is kept under regular review by an advisory body, the Farm Animal Welfare Council. The Council concluded a four-year study in 2003 on the extent to which animals were being humanely slaughtered using Muslim and Jewish traditional methods of slaughter, concluding that exemption for Jewish and Muslim sacrifice was

---

[50] Ansari, H., *Muslims in Britain* (London: Minority Rights Group International 2002).
[51] Ibid.
[52] *Religious Discrimination in England and Wales* (London: Home Office, 2001).

no longer commensurate with ensuring humane animal welfare.[53] Any moves to remove the exemption enjoyed by Muslims and Jews would undoubtedly be met with strong objections by religious leaders in both communities.[54] Equally, the animal slaughter practices of these communities have been the subject of regular condemnation by members of the animal welfare community as well as by some press commentators.

Exploring Policy Options: Protection of Religious Minorities

A strategic assessment of the interface between domestic legislation and international conventions on the protection of minorities and religious discrimination may also help to shape the direction of future policies. There are a wide range of existing international instruments, including among others:

- Declaration on the Rights of Persons Belonging to National or Ethnic, Religious and Linguistic Minorities (UN General Assembly; Resolution 47/135 18 December 1992, UN Doc. A/RES/47/135).
- International Covenant on Civil and Political Rights (UN General Assembly; Resolution 2200A (XXI), 16 December 1966).
- Framework Convention for the Protection of National Minorities (Strasbourg, 1 November 1995).

Assessing current UK provision against the existing frameworks and conventions would allow clearer strategic development of domestic policy and could be used to guide UK planning for future international agreements on this issue. Until 2006, Northern Ireland was the only part of the UK to have a clear anti-discrimination law that prohibits discrimination on the grounds of religious belief or background. Public bodies and private sector providers of goods, services, and facilities are prevented by law from discriminating on these grounds.[55] In addition, a separate promotional duty is placed on public bodies only to carry out their functions while having 'due regard to the need to promote equality of opportunity between persons of different religious belief'. This is further accompanied by requiring public bodies to 'have regard to the desirability for promoting good relations between persons of different religious belief, political opinion or racial group'. The latter aspect of these public sector duties demonstrates the degree to which the legislation is alive to the peculiar sectarian issues found in Northern Ireland. Broadly

[53] Report on the Welfare of Farmed Animals at Slaughter or Killing (London: Farm Animal Welfare Council, June 2003); available at http://www.fawc.org.uk/reports/pb8347.pdf.

[54] See for instance The Muslim Council of Britain (10 June 2003), Press Release—'British Muslims Oppose FAWC Recommendation to Repeal the Current Religious Exemption for Slaughter Without Pre-stunning'.

[55] Northern Ireland Act 1998, Section 76—see http://www.hmso.gov.uk/acts/acts1998/80047-j.htm#76.

speaking, such issues have been highly sectarian in Northern Ireland and are not so prevalent in relation to Muslim groups in Britain at large, though there are occasional, isolated examples of sectarian attitudes and behaviours among some communities. The adoption of an anti-discrimination law to address the threat of religious discrimination in the absence of widespread sectarianism is therefore questionable.

Institutional Capacity

There are a number of small-scale initiatives taking place within and by government that relate fairly explicitly to British Muslim groups and/or the wider Muslim diaspora. Some of these are rather inward-facing within government, while others have a strong external dimension. It is instructive to review three such exercises that took place in the earlier part of the present decade.

The work of the FCO has been most advanced in that it has been agreed and adopted internally as long ago as 2003, although the immediacy of the Iraq war added urgency to the FCO's policy initiatives. A paper entitled 'Strategy for Building Bridges with Mainstream Islam' was prepared in April 2003 and adopted internally. Its main elements were threefold: that the FCO was keen to be focused on Muslim concerns where there was a real suggestion that these had gone unheard; that actively working on solutions, with a receptiveness to new ideas, was called for; and that seeking to be fully engaged with Muslim communities in Britain would require genuine short-term effort but would reap dividends in the longer run. The strategy paper contained thirteen specific action points under three thematic headings: promoting mainstream Islam, engagement with British Muslims on foreign policy questions, and demonstrating activism on the part of officials.

Elsewhere, and significantly, a paper entitled 'Engaging British Muslims' was drawn up by the Home Office in late 2002. This was in effect a discussion paper, highlighting interim policy conclusions, and had a wide scope across many different aspects of the work of government. For example, it contained discussion and suggestions under a range of areas including promoting dialogue, participation in civic life, protecting communities and building confidence, and tackling barriers to inclusion (in family policy, education, employment, etc.). Accompanying this paper, the Home Office established an informal seminar series to examine more deeply and better understand the position of Muslims in Britain. These covered a range of policy areas (education, criminal justice, employment, etc.) and were geared towards identifying practical solutions or ways forward. Linked to these events, and in part to address the problem of religious hatred and hate crime, the Home Office examined whether it should support—and therefore fund—the inclusion of a religious group item in the British Crime Survey. The Home Office also commissioned the Inter-Faith Network to map the degree to which faith organizations from a range of religious groups are active at local level across the country. This exercise was commissioned as part of the Home Office's then Community Cohesion Unit's work on local experiences and the potential for inter-faith activity and contact to bolster local community cohesion.

In addition, the Home Office in 2003 took forward a consultative exercise with Muslim leaders and representatives and Muslim organizations at grassroots level. This was led by then Minister of State, Lord Filkin[56]—with input from the Foreign Secretary—and comprised engagement with three key groups: Mosque officials, Muslim youth, and Muslim women. A series of consultative dialogue events were held both preceding and following the spring 2003 Iraq war; each of these events attracted around 150 attendees and was staged in prominent areas of Muslim settlement (Bradford, East London, Birmingham, and so on). This anticipated developing a more private dialogue through an informal policy discussion group centred on engagement with British Muslims.

There was, in addition, ongoing work within Home Office on these issues, leaving open the possibility that they could be synthesized at some stage into a formal strategy paper—although the machinery of government changes in May 2005 fundamentally altered the lead-departmental responsibility for race, faith, and cohesion matters to the reconfigured Department of Communities and Local Government (DCLG). The result has been a steady increase in the knowledge base and related capacity to debate and test fresh insights.[57]

There have been a number of initiatives taken forward first by the Office of the Deputy Prime Minister (ODPM) and, after spring 2005, DCLG, that come under the broad umbrella of better community engagement and regeneration policies. These have been extensive and varied, and have included:

- The New Deal for Communities Faith Communities Pilot Project— examining the role and potential of faith communities and organizations to play an active part in the NDC programme. There are currently three pilots in the field (Bradford, Wolverhampton, and Tower Hamlets). This kind of initiative appeared to come closest to examining the religious aspects of social exclusion in the context of a pre-existing community

[56] Filkin's lead responsibility within the Home Office transferred to Fiona Mctaggert MP, Minister of State for Race Equality, in June 2003.

[57] In addition, of course, expertise and understanding of British Muslim communities exists in the research community and also in parts of the NGO and policy advocacy communities. The main locations for expertise on a range of contemporary issues relating to BMCs (involving the author in one capacity or another) have included: the British Muslim Research Centre, the Islamic Foundation, the British Council Connecting Futures programme, the Citizen Organising Foundation, the Foreign Policy Centre's Global Britons Programme, the Demos programme on security, the Royal United Services Institute's programme on security and resilience, the Policy Network's programme on the inequalities of integration, and the Fabian Society's programme on Muslim integration.

development and labour market programme. It therefore has relevance for some of the options discussed earlier in this chapter.

• Internal departmental faith awareness workshops—these cover a range of religious faiths and have been convened chiefly for internal staff awareness purposes. Similar programmes exist in other departments. Early results indicated that demand for such workshops has been substantial, with the greatest demand for the workshop on Islam.

The political and public will to take forward strategic work on British Muslim communities needs to be judged very carefully. In the short run, there appears to be significant political will to address the challenges in this issue. External factors, not least current events in Iraq, Afghanistan, and the Middle East peace process, mainly drive this, but the dynamics of extremism and violence within Britain are now also a substantial locomotive for enhanced interest and concern. The other principal locomotive, of course, has been the steady supply of failed or partially successful criminal investigations into terrorist plots. These factors are further conditioned by political worries over links between fringe and extremist British Muslims and terrorism (both in Britain and abroad).[58]

There are also a number of partially voiced political anxieties about links to illegal immigration networks. However, in addressing these short-term concerns, it is important to avoid creating an unstoppable tide of expectations. Such expectations can easily lead to the issue becoming more salient than it already is, or indeed should be. In addition, expectations can be raised that it is the responsibility of government to have a single, unbending (and thus un-learning) policy towards British Muslim communities. Press commentators who have been hostile to British Muslim communities may equally interpret action based on short-run pressures as evidence that government can be shifted—not merely rhetorically in tone but also substantively in terms of strategic policy objectives. Neither of these kinds of outcomes appears particularly attractive from the perspective of strategically minded reviews of policy by government.

Managing Cohesion

Forty years ago, Britain was characterized by a single dominant ethnic group. It was a country in which most citizens were white and characterized themselves as belonging to, or drawn from, one overarching ethnic stock. Although significant differences of social class and region identity were present, these usually managed to touch only the outer edges of a sense of single

---

[58] See for instance 'Islamic Fanatic Who Plotted to Kidnap Soldier and Broadcast His Execution', *The Times*, 30 January 2008, p. 12.

ethno-national identity. A generation or two later, Britain has been transformed in terms of its ethnic composition. In the first decade of the twenty-first century, the numbers of visible ethnic minorities in Britain comprise between 4 and 5 million. The largest groups are those with migratory histories that stem from South Asia, the Caribbean, and parts of East and West Africa. Furthermore, newer waves of immigrants also make up a significant and growing part of the minority communities. It is conservatively estimated that Eastern European-born groups—partly fuelled by EU expansion and labour market integration patterns in recent years—constitute around 600,000 people. This figure is likely to be an underestimate once circular patterns of migration, settlement, and family reunification are accounted for.

The immigration of the post-war period has involved considerable cultural pluralism. Taking South Asians, for instance, traditional patterns of family and household formation have often contrasted with those of the white, indigenous population. In addition, significant linguistic and religious variations have resulted. These social changes have led to substantial challenges for policymakers and politicians. These have tended to centre on questions of reconciling the expectations and norms of different parts of society. They have also involved an element of majority group reassurance in the face of large-scale immigration and also legal protection of basic rights for minority groups.

Alongside these central concerns, it is possible to detect a further, deeper policy challenge. This challenge has usually been subtler in tone and character and has not always been accompanied by a shared understanding of its terms of reference. In brief terms, the challenge has been to ensure that growing ethnic diversity does not undermine—either indirectly or inadvertently—social cohesion. This is a crude simplification certainly, but it is designed to isolate a sensitive concern that is regularly aired.

It is therefore useful here to break down this high-level concern into a series of related problems and dilemmas.[59] Several of these clearly resonate in contemporary policy debates. Others, meanwhile, stem from longer-standing anxieties over national and social cohesiveness in the face of rapid social and economic change. And others still are linked to traditionalist opposition to greater sub-national identity and forms of government. Some fairly typical policy problems that have been associated with growing ethnic and religious diversity can be specified:

- Welfare legitimacy. The degree to which collective welfare institutions and programmes are underpinned by shared values and a sense of shared legitimacy. Some have argued that a full welfare state cannot take for granted that sufficiently deep solidarity is present in the values and outlook of a population that is more differentiated on ethnic grounds than in

---

[59] Mulgan, G., 'Talk Your Way Out of Conflict and Misery', *Guardian*, 21 January 2005.

the past. Indeed, the argument goes, there are real doubts that a successful national system of collective welfare provision can be sustained across ethnic lines that are unfamiliar and possibly resented.

- Bridging social networks. The capacity of certain ethnic minority groups to attain educational and labour market success may be hampered by a relative lack of networks that bridge into mainstream society. While discrimination and poor schooling play a big part, it is likely that insufficient connectedness with knowledge and opportunities outside the particular ethnic group are also important factors. This question was amply discussed previously in Chapter 6.

- Social isolation and alienation. The ties of trust and recognition within ethnic groups, but not across them, remain prominent, particularly among some second-generation minority groups. Again there is a risk of devaluing bridging relationships with members of other ethnic groups including the dominant white group. There is, additionally, a risk of social isolation and alienation setting in that is hard to penetrate through public policy. Finally, the risks these patterns present to the creation of oppositional culture and extremism should not be underestimated.

- Ethnically segmented services. In local public services, there are increasingly hard choices in creating and sustaining services that are shared across ethnic lines in an atmosphere of mutual trust and recognition. These tensions can be particularly stark in local schooling organized at the neighbourhood or community level. Equally, promoting housing patterns that comprise ethnic diversity can be hard to achieve.

- Threats of backlash. Persistent inequalities across ethnic boundaries mean that it is that much harder to sustain a dialogue about shared values and norms. White and minority groups characterized by settled disadvantage often find it impossible to engage the relevance of barriers faced by others to participation and opportunity. A zero-sum logic results in the politics of resentment and even backlash. The nature of disadvantage that is so settled and seemingly difficult to address can be illustrated by the example of the poor educational attainment levels of particular minority groups, again something that was rehearsed extensively in earlier chapters where detailed evidence of the extent of such gaps in attainment was presented. However, it is worth recalling that the first occasion on which the potential for serious attainment gaps to exist was first documented in a government report published as long ago as 1962. This implies, to the casual observer at least, that a forty-year legacy of such attainment gaps has become embedded. In realistic terms, this also suggests that the young black Caribbean children (often boys rather than girls) who are currently in crisis in the compulsory schooling system are arguably the children of black parents who themselves left school with very poor qualifications. Today, similar low attainment levels are becoming associated with Pakistani boys with similar risks of becoming embedded. The human capital disadvantage that this has created cannot be dismissed. For one thing, school and educational professionals today are facing considerable motivational barriers among such communities where strong educational attainment has not been widely seen for more than two generations.

- Corporate recruitment and leadership. Firms today pay a great deal of attention to securing the best combination of talent and experience to fill senior managerial positions. However, access to this search and competition often takes place via intermediaries, and this in turn implies that recruitment networks are open and flexible. There is a premium in knowing that they are and, if they are not, to findings tools to either sidestep their importance or to bring about reform.

This study has looked at these concerns from a strategic and evidence-based perspective. This examination has been underscored by a discussion of the central relationship between ethnic pluralism and social cohesion. The debate stems from the degree to which it is realistic to rely on a two-way relationship between these two variables. This book has argued that it is not satisfactory to isolate the degree to which ethnic homogeneity lies at the centre of the proposition regarding social solidarity and cohesion. Therefore, a more powerful third aspect to this relationship, namely, the presence of patterns of ethnic inequality. The argument pursued is that this factor needs to be examined in order to add a sense of context. Moreover, it is necessary to place concerns about ethnic diversity into a properly informed historical context. These concerns are not particularly new or even especially interesting or critical, and there are some clear lessons that can be drawn from contemporary history. This chapter in particular has focused on the strategic choices that arise in managing the main policy challenges of ethnic diversity, and concluded that priorities can be identified and potential remedies can be better specified.

It is apparent that a much larger difficulty exists. This is that growing diversity does not influence cohesion in a direct fashion but rather that it is conditioned by the facts and perception of equality. In particular, patterns of ethnic inequality may give rise to a lack of trust and reciprocity across ethnic lines. There are two further risks that arise in arguing too narrowly in favour of common ethnic ties as a precursor of common, shared values. First, this claim, if forcefully pursued, can switch from a background promotional message into a prescriptive answer placed in the foreground. Thus, minority groups with putatively distinctive cultural backgrounds may believe that they must rapidly shed their cultural heritage in order, purely, to get ahead or to fit in. At a local neighbourhood level, there may be a premium in keeping a low profile by being effectively forced to abandon any semblance of distinctiveness. 'Behaving white' (or shedding the obvious visible attributes Muslim culture and identity) becomes something of a survival strategy in these circumstances. At a societal level, there may be incentives to those who are seen to discard prominent aspects of a 'foreign' culture.

Second, the evidence for a common, shared identity and values may span traditional ethnic differences. Indeed, the argument appears to imply that members of different ethnic groups will find it hard, even impossible, to relate to one another and the position of those beyond their own ethnic bloc. This may capture sentiment at a particular moment or among a specific group.[60] However, it is the generalization that matters, namely, that inter-ethnic ties of common outlook and shared experiences are unlikely.

The narrow link between diversity and solidarity may be a small aspect of a much wider phenomenon. There are growing elements of a diverse society in Britain today. Some aspects of diversity are the results of lifestyle, voluntary changes, while others are the products of large-scale social transformations such as the role of women particularly in the workforce. It is therefore sensible to remember that both stocks and flows of social capital in Britain have been subject to both change and continuity. For example, there is evidence to suggest that general levels of cohesion and connectedness between individuals may have been declining gradually over a long period. This implies that there are dangers in shaping our current outlook on a mythical golden age of homogeneity said to have produced social trust.

One firm conclusion can be drawn for the purposes of the wider policy community: that overly prescriptive solutions should, in the end, be treated with caution. These may only contain highly artificial ties and unsustainable forms of bonding between different ethnic and religious communities. There is also a risk that small misreadings in public mood by government can in fact stifle the kinds of diversity that are valued, particularly in terms of business environments, commercial competition, and social innovation. Furthermore, a narrow agenda for building cross-community trust, say in terms of discouraging mother tongue languages in the home, may only serve to threaten marginal groups.

The focus thus far has been on breaking down the key elements of the relationships between diversity and solidarity. An important way in which this has been done has been to consider the possibility that exclusionary barriers—both actual and perceptional—faced by certain minority groups have acted to impede a strong sense of trust and cohesion across different communities.

---

[60] Garton Ash, T., 'A False Metaphor Has Been Written out in Blood. We Need to Think Again', *Guardian*, 2 November 2006.

This has been examined using evidence from a variety of areas. Another, complementary approach to the debate may be to review its hallmarks and parallels in contemporary history. Certainly, during the period of rapid mass immigration from South Asia and the Caribbean in the 1960s and 1970s, there were numerous echoes of a very similar debate. It is useful, then, to re-examine this debate and to have a suitable framework to evaluate the lessons for today.

In the past, what was so striking about this debate was the way in which diversity was pitted in opposition to solidarity and community cohesion. It was the Little Englanders, spurred on by neo-Powellites, who brought the argument into the open in the late 1960s. Britain's rapid absorption of large numbers of immigrants was opposed because of two fears. The first was that the fear of undermining the underlying integrity of a distinctive, cultural Britishness. The second held that the strangers in our midst would detract from common, shared values as the basis of our national community. Both arguments were largely mistaken in the long-run, as the general record of British integration policy and practice shows.

That a British national identity has been inexplicitly projected, if at all, is not in question. The larger issue has been the extent to which nationhood itself is dependent on ethnic and cultural homogeneity. Social and moral conservatives have often protested vehemently about this. However, as the US, Canadian, and even Australian cases amply demonstrate, the viability of the nation and its politics is not conditional on a sense of unified ethnic identity. A common attachment to the nation—something that immigrants often excel at—is certainly desirable. In any case, it is highly questionable to believe that post-war immigrants to Britain have been unable or unwilling to develop a sense of shared national identity with locals. Evidence from the British Election Study and the British Citizenship Survey, for example, highlight a clear pattern of the great bulk of black and Asian Britons declaring a stronger attachment to British identity than their white counterparts. The odds of such patterns were largely unimaginable and casually dismissed a generation ago. It is for this reason that they are noteworthy here when reviewing the future prospects for similar bonds across currently strained faith lines.

One important conclusion, then, is that shared values across different ethnic groups are a more subtle outcome of, among other things, a society in which all groups are not resentful of one another and do not suspect the hidden hand of discrimination, favouritism, or bias. This applies equally to all groups, whether constructed by ascribed identity or developed via described forms of identity. The ingredients that allow such a spirit of fairness are always hard to spot let alone quantify. Political leadership is undoubtedly one important ingredient in setting the right tone to begin with, and here the passage of time cannot be understated.

Contemporary social attitudes further unpack the social history of immigration and suggest important changes compared with the hard-line reactions of the past. By measuring sentiment on social distance, it is possible to show that the white majority has, overall, softened its previous hard-line stance towards black and Asian immigrants and their offspring. Several examples can be cited. The British Social Attitudes survey shows that opposition to these groups as workplace colleagues, neighbours, bosses, friends, and even in-laws has declined considerably over the past twenty years. The BSA evidence also indicates that four-fifths of the (mainly white) public freely acknowledge the 'fact' of racial discrimination in employment, with a similar proportion reporting that this was 'always wrong' as a matter of principle. Similar patterns are reported in relation to religious discrimination. These changes have been much greater among the young, affluent, educated, and mobile. Parents, women, and Labour voters have been especially likely to hold tolerant attitudes to a raft of diversity questions. This is potentially critical evidence since it amply shows that the white (and largely nominally Christian) majority are indeed capable and indeed willing to think and identify beyond their own experiences and preferences. A central ingredient in building trust and legitimacy across ethnic lines is such a willingness to operate—at least in terms of social attitudes—outside one's own group. The reasons for this reservoir of support are not clear though factors such as youth, gender, and exposure to higher education are linked as key drivers. Whatever the causes, the results are clearer as these include a public culture of support for a 'fair play' society. Backing for proactive measures that deliver such a collective preference is also likely to be present but much depends on the context and circumstances in which these may operate specifically. A slim majority of Britons state that black and Asian immigration has turned out to be 'good or very good' for Britain, according to the British Election Study. Finally, inter-marriage rates have risen significantly, albeit starting from a very low base in the case of Asian communities. Among Asians as a whole, the average rate of 'out' marriage is today 17 per cent of all marriages, whereas in the mid-1980s this stood at less than 2 per cent.

On the downside, there is obviously evidence of social isolation. Heavy concentrations within their 'own-group' communities are chiefly seen among left-behind groups of Pakistani-origin Britons in northern regions. But even here, the evidence points to concentrated poverty as a more likely obstacle to interaction and participation—for Asians as well as poorer whites in these places. Social and ethnic isolation is more likely a symptom than a cause. Certainly, voluntary, co-ethnic concentrations do not represent problems as such either to achievement or to wider social cohesion: the examples of the success stories of Leicester, in Britain's Midlands, or Harrow, in suburban north-west London, amply demonstrate this.

If Britain is characterized by an unwillingness to live and share with strangers, there is, in truth, only patchy evidence to back this outlook. Little Englanders, ironically, have been right in drawing attention to kith and kinship as a factor in the transitional process. But inferring from this that birds of a feather are only able to flock together is one obvious example of misreading the nature of human—as opposed to ornithological—migration and the various pluralisms that it has brought. As this chapter has sought to show, issues of kinship are in fact frequently misread, extended inappropriately, and exaggerated in terms of their real, long-term significance. The steers for better understanding and better public policy are therefore both clear and vital.

8

Concluding Thoughts and
Future Prospects

We acknowledge that there is radicalisation taking place in our community. This is a long-term problem. We are all affected, therefore we all have
a shared responsibility to denounce radicalism.

Daud Abdullah, Deputy Secretary-General, Muslim Council of Britain,
8 July 2007

The great majority of law-abiding Muslims feel understandably resentful
and fearful that a man or woman might be taken for a Muslim and a
terrorist. What is worse is the growing resentment among non-Muslims
about the terrible damage that Islamist terror does to us all and the failure
of Muslim families, congregations and so-called community leaders to do
much about it. Muslims who want this society to survive will have to take
on the distasteful duty of spying on other Muslims, where necessary.

Minette Marin, *The Sunday Times*, 8 July 2007

Imagination is more important than knowledge.

Albert Einstein[1]

Introduction

Considerable space and attention has previously been devoted in this book
to diagnosing aspects of the problem or problems at hand. Indeed, it is
striking that the shelves of volumes that have been published on this and
similar topics have become heavily congested with detailed and authoritative
diagnoses of one kind of another. In the case of Western Muslims and issues
of integration and security, there is no mistaking the fact that publisher,
reader, and even artistic interest, has swollen massively. A mighty avalanche
has been seen in the past half-dozen years, mainly involving either snappy

[1] http://rescomp.stanford.edu/~cheshire/EinsteinQuotes.html.

commentaries on particular controversies or noble accounts of specific pieces of evidence and their meaning. In both cases, the emphasis on analysing and dissecting the problem itself has been very sharp and has been at the expense, generally speaking, of equal attention being paid to the thorny question of plausible solutions and responses, to say nothing of the effectiveness of current interventions.

The purpose of this chapter is to rebalance things and to focus on two overriding points. The first is to look in a well-formed way at the issue of what is to be done and the essential elements of a strategic policy response. The second point, following on from this overarching assessment, looks again at how best to think about the issues discussed in this book and to direct this discussion—more explicitly than hitherto—towards the needs of the policy community. This chapter also contains a third and final section that ties together the above points and sketches a vision for change and long-term success.

But all of this has to be preceded with full review and discussion of the risks to social cohesion and security stemming from Muslim religious and political extremism. Indeed, the tone of this study has been to look at the nature and ingredients of such risks, and to link these more explicitly to a sense of how best to identify and deploy mitigators of risk. This is an intellectual approach that is not terribly common in the case of social change issues and identity politics, and no doubt one which probably has its limits in terms of assisting better understanding. That said, the risk calculus of the subject under discussion can be articulated in a way that supports intellectual scrutiny whilst also retaining high levels of practicability.

With these policy and operational imperatives in mind, the focus is really on three interlinked elements. The first is to identify more fully the risks involved, including the underlying causes and interactions that appear so hard to grasp when looking narrowly at religious identity and security. The second is to develop a better, more rounded view of the likely mitigators of these risks. In doing so, it is important to concentrate in particular both on ways to address roots causes of hatred and violence (hard by their very nature) and on the management of the unintended and unforeseen fallout from ongoing policy measures (something that has been deeply underestimated).[2] The final element involves trying to achieve a proper alignment between risks and responses, focusing particularly on the use of resource, and to do so in a way that is appropriately weighted with strategic ballast. In short, this means examining the overall balance of policy responses in relation to

---

[2] 'Human Rights and Terrorism', Speech by Lord Chancellor and Secretary of State for Constitutional Affairs, Lord Falconer of Thoroton, London, Royal United Services Institute (RUSI), 14 February 2007; available at http://www.dca.gov.uk/speeches/2007/sp070214.htm.

collective, intertwined, and changing risks. This last element has proven to be the hardest to grasp for the larger policy community, although the basic appetite for an enduring strategic response to Islamist terrorism remains as strong as ever.

Analysis Leading to Intervention

The analytical conclusions of this study are, in rough terms, threefold. To start with, the point of departure has been to look more critically at the nature and character of the security threats that have arisen among Western Muslim communities. Earlier chapters showed that the threats were multiple and driven by a variety of causes. However, the analysis also showed that we should be a little more concerned about attitudes and values among those *surrounding* the men of violence, whereas to date the emphasis has been squarely on preventing violent conspiracies from crystallizing. In one direct sense, this approach has been flawed because it has massively under-played the issue of where and how such conspiracies are sustained. The answer to this is the circle of tacit support for terrorism. This may be a circle comprising sometimes unintentional support but it is tacit support nonetheless, and it provides the essential moral oxygen for violent conspiracy and action.

Tacit Terror

The first and most arresting conclusion that this study draws from the evidence is that policy interventions that fail to tackle tacit supporters will hold very little prospect of long-term success. Indeed, these interventions may be worse than ineffective. They may inadvertently subdue the chances of moderate Muslims challenging conventional wisdoms that have turned a blind eye to extremism and radicalization.

Rebalancing strategy to grasp this mettle is therefore the single most important priority. It matters more than any other factor principally because of the lessons of political violence and terrorism from all over the modern world, and specifically from the Northern Irish, Basque, and Quebec cases. These, and other examples, drive home the folly of taking a narrow, security-driven response to what amounts, at best, to a security problem that is heavily embedded in and shaped by multiple non-security causes. So taking a community-based approach to tackling terrorism is just one obvious way of rebalancing strategy, although arguments endure over the precise interface between community and security policy levers. It is helpful, therefore, to accept the case to manage and lubricate this interface without necessarily getting carried away with the need to identify fully watertight definitions. Indeed, much of the evidence suggests that targeted community and security policy measures are—or can be become—flip sides of the same coin and that the currency of one side is heavily underscored by the other.

The more encouraging part is that strategic rebalancing is already under way, in part. It is neither partial nor complete, but it is well reflected in the strategic mindset of the larger policy world. Whilst presenting strategic advice as a government official in the years immediately following the 2001 New York City attacks, the author was struck by the very limited appetite of officials and ministers to look beyond the vague possibility of another 9/11 outrage. The notion of such an attack on European soil seemed remote to many, and the idea that Britain, more than others, might feature as a target was a novel, if anxious, suggestion. The events in, and effects of, Iraq clearly made this much more likely. So many things which once seemed hard to imagine have moved to the front burner of imagination and attention in the course of a half-decade. The author has been in a unique position to observe and judge these changes, and it is certainly true that the basic premise of Western Muslims representing a security threat is nowadays not far from anyone's powers of imagination.[3]

Two other pennies have been slower to drop, but have dropped nonetheless. The first has been the possibility that domestic Muslim communities could and would be the source of violence. Home-grown terrorism has been the most notable aspect of the reverberations from the July 2005 London attacks. This is curious from one standpoint since the author, and others, had begun focusing over several years on the potential, often thought to be very slim at most, for disengagement to turn to anger to turn to hatred and worse. But the largest penny that has landed, with something of a clunking din, has been the suggestion that peaceful, moderate Muslims may be inadvertently responsible for terrorism. This has been a deeply unsettling suggestion to many minds, and it is no exaggeration to say that even the intellectual and emotional building blocks of this idea have been resisted at all levels among Muslims and non-Muslims. In the case of the former, this has frequently taken the form of near-blanket denial, sometimes indignant at the affront to dignity that such a suggestion may—or perhaps may not—contain. In the case of the latter, resistance has been the product in part of political discomfort and in part of a lack of understanding about the complex politics of grievance. Whilst this book can do only very little to move levels of political comfort, it can, and should, do something to improve understanding of grievance and its sometimes unpredictable and unstable effects on Muslim collective consciousness.

[3] Prins, G., and Salisbury, R., 'Risk, Threat and Security', *RUSI Journal*, February 2008; available at http://www.rusi.org/downloads/assets/Prins_and_Salisbury_RUSI_Journal_FEB08.pdf.

Settled Disadvantage

A second analytical conclusion of this study has been to revisit the issue of disadvantage and exclusion. The argument pursued here is that settled disadvantage among many Western Muslims, notwithstanding some mixed evidence, now looks and feels like patterns of religious exclusion. It is felt and thought to be *about* religious exclusion, no matter how caveated and blurred the data on this may be. A faith divide involving Muslims and non-Muslims has become the overarching model of best-fit in most minds. This is a difficult point both conceptually and in evidence. The conceptual complication is just about the hardest to navigate for the purposes of consensus. To start with, it takes no time at all to realize that opinions about faith and exclusion are very deeply held and loudly voiced. This means that ingrained views, on all sides, are themselves important to unpick, and to do so by challenging analytical myths and policy stereotypes. For instance, a common position taken by many community and pressure groups is that anti-Islamic bias is the sole and sufficient reason behind the poor attainment of Muslim communities in education, housing, and employment markets. This perspective typically flies under the emblem of 'Islamophobia'. It is frequently held and articulated without rider or caveats, making dialogic approaches to common understanding that are much harder to achieve.

Set against this purist outlook are a number of counter-positions that not only deny the 'Islamophobia' thesis but also go on to challenge various other premises. One of these is that Muslims, alone, experience severe bias and prejudice, citing, for example, the negative portrayal of young, black men in many Western societies. The counter-positions also tend to question the evidence, some of which points to Muslim exceptionalism in terms of poor socio-economic trends and prospects, but most of which is either inconclusive or else suggests that faith is a mask for other causes of inequality and disadvantage.

This book has specifically examined the evidence base in considerable detail and has concluded that this is terribly inconclusive for the purposes of drawing firm conclusions. It certainly contains nuggets of evidence regarding the particularly precarious socio-economic position of certain (but not all) Muslim communities, but the fact remains that the gaps in evidence and knowledge far outweigh what is presently known. However, the biggest plank of counter-opinion rests on the claim that Muslim victimhood shapes both the outlook of many Muslims and also the approach of most non-Muslims alike. This serves to distort politics and policy, it is argued, because it starts from a decidedly questionable premise. Political victimhood and grievance can quickly become as much of an obstacle to solutions as a way of identifying them. (This is a line of thinking that the author has some sympathy for, but, as ever, qualifications are important. It is something that we will return to later in this chapter.)

Meanwhile, the conclusion that has emerged from this study is that Muslim settled disadvantage has attained a political dynamic of its own. This is the case even though the Muslim differential in explaining disadvantage is far from compelling and the factual reality is that patterns and forms of inequality are driven by numerous causes that have almost nothing to do with faith. Crudely, faith is not much of a cause or conditioner of opportunity structures and outcomes for Muslims any more than it is for Catholics, Jews, or Sikhs. That said, religious bias is, for sure, a recurring part of the picture portrayed and internalized by many, many Muslims (and a number of non-Muslims) and to a far greater extent than among other faith communities.

This makes for a highly charged outcome. The claims of religious exclusion generally and Muslim bias specifically have merged to create a powerful new narrative of grievance. This grievance has localized manifestations in areas such as schools and jobs. But, more critically, it is anchored in a much wider world view. It cites and takes umbrage from a wide range of examples and settings. Some are nested in everyday experiences for many Western Muslims in tangible areas such as employment and housing. Others are found in less common experiences such as criminal justice and welfare. And others are rather effectively anchored in global tensions, ranging from Palestine to Iraq to Kashmir, of which few Western Muslims typically have much direct experience or knowledge. However, the narrative of globalized grievance means that all of these things are internalized into a collective consciousness.

The simple point that needs to be made is that socio-economic disadvantage can and should be tackled more forcefully, not so much because it uniquely blights Western Muslims, but rather because it helps to remove an important plank in the narrative of grievance. This conclusion will no doubt be challenged by those who favour a more rigorous standard in evidence-based policy interventions. It is a fair challenge but two things should be borne in mind, however. One is that politics, as the cliché goes, is the art of the possible, and in this case, the load of carrying aggrieved opinion and sentiment is made considerably lighter by more effectively tackling economic disadvantage. The other is that, according to the wise policymaker's maxim, the absence of evidence is not to be confused with evidence of absence. That is to say, anti-Muslim bias and behaviour may not only exist on a larger scale than is currently evidenced, but it may also take forms and have impacts that are hard to understand. For one thing, it is more than likely that low levels of anti-Muslim public sentiment have an effect on many dark-skinned non-Muslims. Anecdotal evidence for this is already widespread, not least of all in and following security crises involving mass transit systems. In the future, we can expect to see more such naive policy sweeps that serve to alienate a number of non-Muslims. The likely impacts will be extremely hard to navigate among CT policymakers and operational leaders.

As previously mentioned, the evidence points to a number of factors beyond religious faith that shape and drive the socio-economics of opportunity and its absence. The analytical base supports the claim that many circumstantial (and even some cultural) factors are at play in shaping opportunity and achievement among Muslim communities. Some of these are in common with other non-Muslim communities sharing a South Asian ancestry and suggest that religious specificity claims are vastly over-made. And in some cases, the evidence also points to profound variations within and across Muslim communities, for example highlighting Ismaili and Middle Eastern Muslim experiences in education and employment as substantially more promising than, say, those of Pakistani and Bangladeshi Muslims in Britain. This implies that, at a minimum, it is hard and inadvisable to draw grand generalizations about the so-called Muslim experience, since there are many experiences and thus as many outlooks and perspectives.

The evidence also contains some important signposts about the role of circumstantial and cultural influences. The work, for example, of Ceri Peach has highlighted the role of hereditary and traditional norms about the role of girls and women in shaping collective values. This research suggests that the prospects for integration via educational and labour markets are especially poor in these settings. In the case of Pakistani and Bangladeshi Muslims in Britain, these factors serve to erode the odds of successful participation in opportunity structures even when and where they do exist. Such factors do not eliminate the prospects for participation and with it social change, but they do dampen the overall effects of policy interventions that rely on creating participation-based routes to tackling disadvantage.

This is an important layer of nuance that is all too often neglected in a lot of analysis on the subject of immigrant and minority integration. Moreover, the effects of such neglect can be even more serious. At one level, the poor participation rates of Muslim girls and women can be too simply and too quickly laid at the door of cultural explanations. This is frustrating because of the generally agreed principle that variation in the operational delivery of public policy may be the even greater barrier. At another level, full-bodied explanations and arguments have been constructed around the general willingness of Muslim communities to integrate and take advantage of ladders out of poverty exclusion. This element has been variously repeated and forms a generalized set of doubts about Muslims—and perhaps others—in fact turning their backs on integration as the shared long-term goal. One recent full-blooded criticism put it as follows:[4]

The United Kingdom presents itself as a target, as a fragmenting post-Christian society, increasingly divided about interpretations of its history, about its national aims, its

[4] Prins, G., and Salisbury, R., 'Risk, Threat and Security', *RUSI Journal*, February 2008; available at http://www.rusi.org/downloads/assets/Prins_and_Salisbury_RUSI_Journal_FEB08.pdf.

values and its political identity. That fragmentation is worsened by the firm self-image of those elements within it who refuse to integrate. This is a problem worsened by the lack of leadership . . . thus undercutting those . . . trying to fight extremism.

The above characterization has been seized on for contributing to a view of Britain's fight against terrorism as being 'soft touch' in nature. This is unfortunate since it tends to offset attention being given to changing behaviour, to say nothing of norms, among Muslims themselves. The onward march of large improvements in school attainment among Bangladeshi girls is testimony to the substantial scale of change that is already taking place. Much of this is fuelled by the availability and promotion of educational pathways to a kind of greater female emancipation that is largely organic and shaped by the Muslim (and other minority) communities themselves. This is helpful in many ways, not least because of the drift towards external prescriptive answers—often by ministers and narrowly focused security heavyweights—to integration and segregation concerns. In this case and others, the very best outcome would be that the supply of credible and timely solutions has genuinely had the impact of creating its own demand.

Hearts and Minds

The third and final main conclusion of the analysis contained in this study is about the interplay between objective and subjective worlds. This is perhaps the most critical one of all when looking at the link between cold analysis of causes against the chances of interventions gaining real traction in everyday lives and communities. The study shows that there are a number of inter-related problems at work, some of which operate at the level of objectively defined features of the positivist world, while others are situated more heavily in the subjectively perceived, imagined world. Not only are both of these dimensions rather different in tone and colour from one another, but it is vital to remember that they also inform and nourish the political choices of individuals and communities objectively and subjectively.

This makes for a delicate balancing act in terms of setting—and sticking to—strategic priorities. The conclusion is, therefore, to hold both thoughts at one and the same time.

Holding both thoughts simultaneously should, in principle, be possible but it involves some latent tensions. For instance, a lot of the material presented in earlier chapters leaned towards the public policy gaps and challenges facing governments on the long-term immigrant integration front. Many of the communities being examined are not immigrants as such, and birth rates in Western societies have soared in general over the past two to four decades. Nevertheless, the problems of integration are largely centred on housing patterns, educational and employment participation, and criminal justice, much as they were, and remain, for recent migrant groups. The policymaker's task often has to do with promoting interaction with the wider society and avoiding the slide into separate lives and identities. These tasks are, of course, much the same for all kinds of immigrant and immigrant-descended populations. They involve a range of policy tools that combine innovative application of existing policy measures and additional, better targeted measures. But, in the end, the task is very heavily anchored in altering, perhaps transforming, real-world objective experiences. Measures to extend educational participation and boost attainment, for example, are tangible policy objectives and the measures that are required will ordinarily be familiar and equally objectively defined.

Meanwhile, the tension with the subjectively perceived dimension cannot be ignored. This is because there is, at a minimum, no certainty about how such policy measures (particularly shortcomings in their successful attainment, relative to expectations) will be felt and interpreted. As mentioned previously, low, stagnant rates of economic activity among Muslim women can very easily be linked to all number of deeply held convictions about anti-Muslim bias and discrimination. The fact that these economic patterns are largely influenced by many other factors matters little in such a context. The wise response is certainly not to treat such claims seriously, the effect of which will almost certainly undermine existing measures to influence actual, not real, drivers of change. But it is nevertheless sensible to recognize that the larger barrier to integration in this case lies in the imagined world of intense, subjective feeling. This is something of a pattern when looking at the broad political challenges surrounding Muslim integration. It is something that we will return to later in this chapter.

The notion of influencing hearts and minds together involves nothing less than perfect synchronicity between the real and imagined worlds. That is not to say that policy measures are always required to achieve perfect outcomes separately and collectively, since that would be unrealistic and even unnecessary. The perfect outcome would really be the enemy of the good if the bar were to be set at such a height. But it does imply that any and all the positive benefits of successful policies (in promoting social participation, in improving material outcomes, in curbing extremism, and so on) are effectively used to support an appropriate political narrative. This narrative has been touched on previously and features some obvious critical nodes: avoiding Muslim exceptionalism, questioning historic determinism, championing organic change, criticizing unbalanced strategies, and, above all, rebutting Huntingtonian simplicity.

To move hearts implies policies and actions that have the effect of shifting sentiment and passion in a direction that is fundamentally compatible with the grain of Western societies. Anything that even remotely smacks of standalone treatment or exceptional carve-outs, however good the intentions that may lie behind, is bound to fail in these circumstances.[5] And failure may not be the end of it, since even the suggestion of political carve-outs can serve to undermine wider public faith in the political treatment afforded to Western Muslim communities. Such a loss of confidence, already fragile in many countries, is hardly advisable and certainly not desirable.

Meanwhile, to move minds implies, to start with, taking steps that impacts positively on the objective circumstances that surround Muslims. In order to be successful, these steps need to be grounded in everyday realities which, for a large proportion of Western Muslims, tend to be characterized by patchy socio-economic patterns and isolated and defensive mindsets. So, whilst effective measures may be designed and deployed, their real success hangs upon having a direct, credible link with everyday experience and perspectives. At present, these combine to produce a political outlook among many Muslims that is about being under siege. Virtually everything else that is experienced is experienced via that lens. And certainly political and policy efforts to curb extremism and radicalization involve sensitivities that all but guarantee the predominance of that particular lens.

Hearts and minds are, without doubt, an opportunity with all the potential to deliver a virtuous circle of success. But to do so necessarily requires synchronizing the real with the imagined so as to produce beneficial results that are both known and felt. The starting point of each can be at different points on the scale. The larger conundrum is not this difference but rather the possibility that they may be on separate dimensions altogether. Successful synchronization becomes that much harder as a result.

The Enemy of the Good

This constraint is a reminder that the ideal should never become the enemy of the good. It is a helpful maxim for policymakers and opinion-formers across the board, but it is especially pertinent in the case of tackling the politics of extremism among Western Muslim communities. The discussion above was devoted to the uncertain interplay between objectively defined problems and solutions on the one hand and the complexities of subjectively felt perceptions and sentiments on the other. These two dimensions, in was argued, in effect, need not clash with one another, but there is plenty of scope for tensions to develop. With this scope, the likelihood for further, consequential, and unintended grievances forming is increased, unless sensible precautions are taken further upstream.

Such precautionary steps may include looking more sceptically at, for example, the possibilities for so-called boomerang effects of CT measures. A number of well-designed CT policies have led to such negative outcomes that

---

[5] 'Defining the Limits of Exceptionalism', *Economist*, 16 February 2008.

have further eroded confidence and trust in the overall strategic approach taken.[6] Overall, however, the avoidance of clashes will be significantly aided by strategies that build in, and thus implicitly expect, a normal dose of unintended side-effects. What constitutes 'normal' may of course be subject to differences of opinion, but this does not detract from the larger point, namely, that failures of this kind will often be a fact of life that comes with long-term effective strategy.

Strategic success, in that sense, is no stranger to policy failure, no matter whether it is caused by external factors or unintentionally triggered by well-meaning policy measures. Sir David Omand, Britain's former Cabinet Office chief security coordinator, put this point well in late 2006 when he made the case for strategic CT policy machinery that was not deflected by various short-term setbacks, irrespective of where these came from. More recently in July 2007, Britain's domestic security minister, Admiral David West, reinforced the same general point by noting that the effort, led by government, to tackle Islamist political extremism and terrorism was likely to last for ten to fifteen years. This was probably no exaggeration and underscores not just the need to think and operate on a longer-term timeframe but also the need to expect and anticipate drawbacks from whatever source. By way of putting this challenge in perspective, it is worth noting that, as at summer 2007, as many as one in four British Muslims doubted that the 7/7 London attacks were executed by the four named members of the suicide mission. This, surely, is confirmation of the importance of the imagined-world dimension described earlier. And it is also a strong and compelling reason to conclude that the interactions between the objective and the subjective are much greater obstacles to effective solutions than has hitherto been appreciated. Strategic success, therefore, requires a longer, cannier game plan, accompanied by a shrewd reaction to setbacks and obstacles that does not undermine the real prize.

What particular steers does such an astute and wise strategy require? First of all, canniness should not be mistaken simply for clever cunning. If it is, it is likely to spawn behaviours that will be quickly perceived as superficial and 'too clever by half'. The initial response of security and policing agencies following the May 2006 Forest Gate debacle was to argue a defensive case that operational failure had been the result of faulty intelligence alone. Whilst this line may have persuaded some to accept that such CT operations could not and should not be conducted in a zero-failure context, it nevertheless prompted probing questions about the reliability of the underlying system of gathering and interpreting such intelligence. If faulty intelligence could best describe Forest Gate-style failure, it also rang true in the case of the Jean

[6] Briggs, R., Fieschi, C., and Lownsbrough, H., *Bringing it Home: Community-based Approaches to Counter-terrorism* (London: Demos, 2006).

Charles de Menezes killing in Stockwell in July 2005. Both were substantial failures without doubt. But the issue at stake was, and remains, the degree to which such examples illustrated systemic failures or weaknesses. Intelligence-based CT policy measures, by definition, require a level and type of support that include reliable and consistent filtering of weak and inconclusive information. Any direct actions that are not supported by such filters carry with them a substantially increased chance of error. The consequences of such error are clearly catastrophic both individually and politically. With this in mind, it is quite right that reactions to failure should seek to defend operational decisions and decision-makers. But it is not right or defensible that these reactions should shy away from the need to look for systemic failure and, if found, move rapidly to correct weaknesses that may only cause repeat failure. In other words, canniness and wisdom are steeped in the importance of taking a balanced approach to operational failure. Such failure is bad enough of its own accord; it is even worse if it is caused by systemic weakness. And it is politically barely possible—only just—to defend a strategy that is willing to bend and adapt to the uncovering of weakness of this kind. It is, by contrast, neither possible nor advisable to defend one that is not.

The second component of a wise and astute strategy is the need to look beyond cause and effect simplicities. Much of the earlier part of this book has made this general point, arguing that, for instance, there are multiple causes at work which require commensurate responses. However, the point that is pursued here is somewhat different. This is to suggest that the collective mental map of policy—typically held by the policy community—can contain some serious false premises. The most striking of these is that particular causal drivers of problems can be addressed through public policy that is self-contained, properly evidenced, and direct in its effects. All of these assumptions can be seductively entertained without being formally articulated. They can also betray an essentially Newtonian way of looking at the world and nature of public policy problems and remedies. And they can, therefore, act as a partial (at best) and distorting (at worst) guide to the rather more messy nature of the real world.

To make this observation here is not in any way to imply that policymakers are driven to oversimplification in a way that makes matters worse rather than better. That kind of criticism would be the preserve of a scholarly purism that this study has sought hard to avoid. Indeed, so intellectually pure are some academic contributions to this subject that they fall at the first hurdle of practical relevance, to say nothing of their intellectual relevance. For example, the following especially wordy academic abstract falls—sadly face first—at that basic hurdle and makes perfectly clear the seriousness of the credibility gap:[7]

---

[7] Hutnyk, J., 'Pantomime Terror: Media South Asia as Civil Society Green Zone', visiting speaker seminar presentation, University of Sussex, 18 January 2008.

With terror alerts and constant announcements at train stations and airports in the UK, where the Queen's subjects are called upon to 'report any suspicious baggage'; with stop and search security policing focused on Muslims (and an unarmed Brazilian shot on the London underground); and with restrictions on civil liberties and 'limits' to freedom proclaimed as necessary, it is now clear [sic] that spaces for critical debate are mortally threatened in contemporary, tolerant, civilised Britain.

This study has been encouraged by serious academic analytical rigour for sure, but not, it must be said, at the price of real-world relevance and usability.

Rather, the point is very much about building more timely readings of analytical insights. This is in order to take swift action to address real world problems in real time. Anything less runs the risk of being sound in an isolated way that impacts hardly anything at all, save the footnotes of contemporary history. That is not a reasonable risk to take in the case of the subject matter under discussion. Above all, this study is about shaping and changing thinking and behaviour in a way that is both intellectually and practically credible and sustainable.

The Newtonian world is, of course, essentially about fixed certainties regarding actions and reactions. It is a world that is all too familiar in collective mindsets, especially among the policy community, but is also widely shared in all manner of decision-making settings, including the corporate structures of the private sector and, increasingly, many parts of the corporatized public and not-for-profit sectors. However, when tackling the causes and symptoms of particular problems, it is generally the case that public policy suffers most from this kind of mindset. It is not a mindset that is especially produced by one set of decision-makers and nor is it something that, say, politicians more than officials are responsible for. Instead, Newtonian assumptions about the world and changing it are about trying to establish some broad degree of certainty in the face of complexity and flux.

The point that matters for our purposes is that this search is clearly laudable but necessarily carries significant risks in the case of tackling Islamist extremism. For one thing, as we have noted, many of the manifested problems are obviously distinguishable as causes as opposed to symptoms. Many are partially both causes and symptoms. Further, policy interventions that set out to tackle causal factors can often have important effects on symptoms (and vice versa), some of which then require fresh attention and remedies. For instance, programmes to support Muslim women's participation in employment training are predicated on the idea that low employment participation is caused chiefly by the absence of opportunities. The intervention can certainly reduce this opportunity gap. However, it may be less effective in supplying opportunities that are driven basically by the need to create options for such women that lie outside the domestic world of the home. A more sensitized intervention might therefore set out to create intermediate opportunities that ensure that it is possible and, in due course, acceptable (as a norm) for such women to be involved in activities beyond the home. These may, for example, be through mother-and-toddler groups or via sewing clubs and equivalents. These are arguably better starting points. Taking a more direct approach may set out to create opportunities where there are currently few. But the wrinkle comes from the relative absence of support for (preceded by the imagination to see) such women to have lives and identities that are not as mothers, wives, and daughters. Finding interventions to address this absence is a more challenging task than simply taking a direct route to stimulating demand. This is because there is arguably no shortage of latent demand for such opportunities. The policy problem instead lies in the familial, cultural, and community obstacles to releasing such demand. This is one solid example where a Newtonian mindset may, however well-intentioned, create interventions that act on the wrong targets. Put more simply, the obstacles and targets of wise policy measures are not the Muslim women in question but rather the Muslim men that so heavily and implicitly condition the opportunity calculus facing such women and girls.

Wise and astute public policy must, therefore, avoid selecting the wrong targets even for the right reasons. The benefits of astuteness come from this simple observation: supply, in this case at least, will not generate its own demand. It requires instead the perceptive promotion of a very different kind of demand.

What Should be Done?

The strategic credibility of the argument thus far cannot be taken for granted. It requires some testing, not least to gauge the tolerance levels of assumptions surrounding the judgements that have been built in by the author. And some test-track feedback is important in any case to assess the general saliency and relevance for others of this book.

The core question of 'what should be done?' is one that is embedded in the title of this study and, as mentioned at the outset of the first chapter, it is a study that seeks deliberately to examine the main issues from the perspective of those with executive duties and responsibilities. This involves some discussion of the application of ideas and conclusions in relation to the main causes of Muslim extremism and radicalization identified in this study. The four domains that this study's conclusions pinpoint are given below in no particular order:

- Patterns of social and economic exclusion that have created many of the hallmarks of a long-term, settled underclass.

- Tendencies towards social isolation that ensure that many Western Muslims live and think separately from mainstream society.

- The rise of strong and shrill oppositional politics and political leadership, wedded to grievance agendas, that have very little resonance in politics at large.

- The often-volatile dynamics of global Islam that, in the case of Western Muslim communities, serves as a damaging backdrop for anything that can be imagined, let alone achieved, in Britain.

Setting and Acting on Priorities

There are several major strategic choices facing government. At present, understandably enough, the focus has been on protection and preparedness, coupled with tentative forms of partnership with Muslim communities to help build resilience and preventative mindsets and measures. Behind this, current understanding within government about its role is fairly broad. This comprises at least four elements: first, isolating and removing the direct causes of religious intolerance, particularly those thought to create stereotypes of 'Muslims as pariahs'. Second, identifying and tackling indirect obstacles to achievement, especially in schools and jobs, and, by extension, addressing the specific, Islamic aspects, if any, of underachievement. Third, sensitizing public policy generally to the needs of religious groups, and Muslim concerns in particular. Finally, leading public understanding about Islam in Western society and promoting, where possible, tendencies towards pluralism in the projection of Islamic identity.

More generally, the integration debate has taken on new life, as indicated by the government's recent anti-discrimination legislation, the introduction of formal citizenship ceremonies, and its predilection for debates, sometimes circular it seems, about 'Britishness' and national identity. Since September 11, and now July 7, this debate has focused increasingly on Muslim communities and, specifically, on how to tackle radical elements within those communities.

These are all rather broad-brush ways to address the problem, or rather problems, identified in this study. Most are not obviously unhelpful and several are, at worst, examples of focusing too heavily on immediate demands and symptoms. Some, however, are characteristic of carts being placed before carriages in presuming, rather naively, that anti-Muslim public sentiment emanates from general, unknown sources, when in fact there is substantial evidence pointing to extreme patterns of behaviour among some Western Muslims as driving such negative sentiment. Aspects of the strategic narrative pushed by government are regrettably unrealistic in appreciating the scale of anger and hatred in parts of the Muslim communities, to say nothing of such feelings among others directed against Muslims as a whole. The upshot has been some wishful thinking combined with an unrealistic amount of hope being placed in the use of security policies alone to tackle what is no longer—and has not been for some while—merely a security threat.

In sum, penetrating the circle of tacit support has been the one obvious dimension where even well-informed public policy initiatives have been terribly slow out of the traps. The importance of this central focus cannot be understated, as this book has consistently argued, and the impact of absence has been felt on the effectiveness of many other parts of the overall strategy to curb extremism.[8]

The British government for once has, notably in the period since summer 2005, set itself the job of winning over British Muslims in a hearts-and-minds strategy. This is broadly appropriate by way of a high-level map and compass but one that nevertheless implies a great deal by way of illustrative, interlocking examples that provide a political signature. Persuading enough moderately minded Muslims to no longer tacitly back extremism and terror is a basic test of success against such a strategy. The issue that arises then is to identify and deploy the appropriate policy levers that, collectively, bring about behaviours that accelerate that basic outcome. To say that the combined levers have not been fully understood and measured is not to suggest that little has been achieved. In fact, much has been.[9] But the nature of the interactions between different strategic levers is an area of public policy that is still taking shape, and where feedback loops and combined learning are at their most critical stage. And the job is one that involves the growing of new policy neurological nodes between and across disciplines on a scale rarely seen before. Winning over hearts and minds in a way that compares with the titanic struggle of the Cold War is, therefore, an appropriate way of describing the essence of the task. Encouraging greater use of the experience of thinking and policy around winning hearts and minds during that long conflict would be especially innovative and helpful.

Averting a Muslim Underclass

The challenge of breaking free of a Muslim underclass is no small challenge. The scale of this challenge and its remedies have been rehearsed extensively in earlier chapters. The purpose here is to highlight hidden twists and undetected opportunities on this first front of strategic policy.

Arguably, the most valuable aspect of the response to this challenge is to recognize that the problem, as such, is by no means unique to Muslim

---

[8] Saggar, S., 'Extremism and Extremist Sympathisers: Better Understanding, Policy Responses', presentation to the conference on Policy Options for Britain II, Nuffield College, Oxford, 28 February 2008.

[9] Carroll, M., 'Diversity and Cohesion', presentation to the conference on Policy Options for Britain II, Nuffield College, Oxford, 28 February 2008.

communities and that therefore the solutions lie in the realm of existing efforts to tackle disadvantage. This recognition broadly matches the strategic approach of government but unfortunately this does not extend to all parts of the broad policy community. The latter includes some who have been determined to force the issue of a so-called Muslim penalty in education and employment outcomes. Such an approach is fairly widespread in public thinking and public policy, and suggests that anti-Muslim bias is the big, even biggest, factor at play. In fact, the evidence does not support such a claim. (The author—and others—have been steadfast in pointing this out whilst acknowledging that there remains widespread subjective support among Muslim communities for the opposite view. But this, then, speaks amply of the sharp disjuncture between objectively defined and subjectively felt aspects of the present challenges facing many Western Muslims.)

It does, rather, support the view that Muslims' low achievements, on average, are the product of human capital poverty (in common with some other minority groups), poor connectivity with workplace opportunity (again in common), circumstantial barriers such as transportation and housing (again in common), and finally, enduring discrimination against visible minorities in general (yet again in common). In other words, there is very little that is unique about Muslim disadvantage, and in the case of a quarter, perhaps one-third, of Muslims, there is precious little evidence of low achievement or disadvantage to begin with. This large minority within a minority represents a powerful counter-example and counter-narrative.

Again, it would be helpful if greater use were made of these valuable existing resources and specifically the political outlook of leaders who have helped create such a virtuous circle. The reputation of pariah-dom has been most damaging in this quarter. As this book has argued, the steps taken from within to tackle, reject, or replace such a reputation is probably the single most important step that can be taken. In jargonistic terms, it involves ending tendencies that have falsely externalized the costs of a negative reputation. Moreover, internalizing formerly externalized costs is both powerful and likely to be effective symbolically and substantively. There are few cases where self-ownership of group reputation has led to failure or half-heartedness. There are, by contrast, a rich number of cases where such self-ownership has greatly raised the odds of success. Such success is achieved not least by helpfully turning a virtuous wheel that others beyond the group are increasingly willing to push and gently accelerate.[10]

Muslim socio-economic disadvantage is, in overall terms, a significant policy problem but one that should be understood within the context of an existing strategy to tackle disadvantage. The drivers are largely in common

[10] Saggar, S., 'Circles, Wheels and Boomerangs: Successfully Tackling Muslim Extremism and Radicalisation', *Political Quarterly*, forthcoming.

with other, non-Muslim poorly performing groups, although the effects of disadvantage are often felt more deeply and extensively among Muslim communities. The policy response can adjust for this particular twist. It can also recognize that there are a number of more culturally embedded factors that operate to heighten the absence and take-up of opportunity structures.

In practical terms, the challenge placed on policymakers is to develop and adjust existing forms of intervention so as to ensure that the resulting effects are suitably sensitized to the needs of Muslim citizens. But it also needs to be nested within a general strategic framework of faith sensitization of public policy. To fail to do so would merely result in Muslim communities being (further) represented as solely aiming for a single group carve-out, something that it is terribly damaging in political and reputational terms. Such sensitization ought, in principle, to be consistent between Muslims as parents and school-children, job-seekers, residents, patients, and so on. That is to say, the nature and degree of adjustment should be fairly predictable from one domain to the next and, more importantly, should be consistent with the over-arching and pragmatically driven need to improve policy outcomes and citizens' experiences.

None of this, it should be stressed, implies a type or degree of adjustment that allows public policy to be specially designed or deployed for the needs of one faith group or another. This would be a severely retrograde step since, as previously mentioned, one easy rule of thumb for good policy is policy that avoids—and is seen to avoid—the mantle of special carve-outs for Muslims, or indeed any other faith group. A national Muslim policy, to be blunt, must be avoided at all costs.

The net result of adjustment and adaptation is such that it builds on Britain's long-standing tradition of pragmatism when addressing the challenges of ethno-religious pluralism. That tradition has fuelled and delivered a degree of ethnic sensitization of public policy over forty years that is now well established, if not always fully effective, in shaping particular aspects of policy design and implementation. Debate regularly rages on the definitive outcomes of that tradition, but what is less—if at all—contested is that such sensitization is now largely embedded in the basic framework for politics and public policy. The challenge, therefore, is to take this rough template as a way to think about and act to expand the sensitization around faith. Such an outcome is certainly attainable and indeed appropriate given the circumstances of large vessels of strong religious identity floating in a larger sea of secularism.

Ending Isolation and Building Connectivity

The problem of an apparent Muslim underclass, as noted above, is not an economic problem alone. If it were, the nature of the task facing the policy community would at least be a tangible enough, and warrant direct comparison with the problems of other severely disadvantaged social groups. Those comparisons exist and are helpful in one regard, namely, in reminding commentators and practitioners that the existing machinery to tackle socio-economic opportunity structures is widespread and well embedded. They are certainly associated with rather better results for some more than others, suggesting that differential outcomes remain a concern across the board in terms of social inclusion.

But what drives better or worse outcomes from group to group, or from place to place, is only partially understood. Sophisticated analyses have been assembled to highlight the relationship between educational attainment and labour market achievements for instance, reinforcing the centrality of the compulsory schooling system. However, variations in outcomes continue to persist that are shaped by factors that lie beyond these well-known relationships. For example, the conditioning effects of social networks, particularly in and around employment-related spheres, are sometimes highly influential in shaping eventual outcomes.

For example, the effects of rapid improvements in school performance among London's Bangladeshi girls are arguably more likely to crystallize into positive wider outcomes than similar changes among Pakistani boys in northern England. The variations are considerable. For one, the former example is largely actual where the latter is at most hypothetical. Second, the former enjoys very close proximity to one of the world's most dynamic and innovative labour markets, unlike the latter. Third, the former builds on existing successful patterns of educational success among girls whilst the latter only reinforces the troubles of many working class boys in compulsory schooling and employment. And finally, the social networks reinforcing an accelerated virtuous circle in the former are often marked different from the grievance-tinged alienation found among the latter's social networks. The importance of social capital factors of this kind affects a number of disadvantaged groups as a matter of course. Helpfully, when tackling social exclusion generally it is clear that policymakers have begun, albeit gingerly, to respond so as to minimize these influences and/or help to build counter-measures.

In the case of immigrant-descended communities (including but not exclusively Muslim communities), the relevance of social networks has usually been thought of in terms of bonding and bridging relationships. The two kinds of relationships are, of course, not necessarily in tension with one another. However, in some cases, the relative over-supply of bonding influences in relation to education, employment, and housing in particular cannot be understated. These have served, at best, to restrict choice and opportunity at the margin, and, at worst, have been implicated within particular communities in patterns of long-term social isolation and separation. The policy challenges to unpick and re-engineer these patterns among settled communities are substantial by any reckoning.

Among British Muslim communities specifically, the patterns of relative isolation and separation are largely found among South Asians, particularly those with Pakistani or Bangladeshi roots. In both cases, residential housing patterns have tended to fuel and reflect this tendency and, in the case of several large locations, have become acute. Places such as Bradford and Luton, to name just two obvious examples, are characterized overwhelmingly by socially isolated and separate Muslim communities that live largely in parallel with other ethnic and religious communities. For policymakers, this is a complex picture to understand, never mind tackle, in a proportionate way. To start with, creating incentives for Muslims—or indeed any other group—to be less likely than before to live alongside other co-ethnic or co-faith members is extremely difficult. It is also a startlingly crude solution. But it is one, to be sure, that is regularly hankered after and rhetorically celebrated by politicians and their officials. This can be especially unfortunate since it ignores, or is ignorant of, the reality that ethnic or faith concentrations, by themselves, are not particularly great problems. For instance, Anglo-Jewish communities, the most concentrated of all, are not associated with social concerns and nor are increasingly affluent British Indian-descended communities. In both cases, clusters are helpfully combined with often positive socio-economic patterns, suggesting that the problem of separate communities is, in fact, not a problem at all. However, in the case of many Muslim communities, the ethno-religious distinctiveness of these communities and the places where they are most concentrated, also tends to combine with bleak socio-economic patterns. It is this combination that defines the core problems to be tackled.

Greater precision in identifying problems does not necessarily bring with it any greater certainty in terms of suitable policy responses. This is not to be defeatist but rather to point out that even some of the better suited interventions carry with them a number of twists and risks of secondary effects. For instance, the policy intervention may seek to build improved awareness of, and connectivity with, wider societal influences and institutions. A textbook example might be in relation to political skills and capacity, where interventions tend to focus on party political participation. This is a sensible and helpful intervention without doubt. But the difficulty lies in the nature of party political organization and mobilization in many of the places in question. In far too many of these places, mainstream parties have given weight to crude machine-politics ways of operating. Machine politics, at most, has worked on increasing voter numbers and delivering vote banks by leaders. But, worst of all, it has massive incentives for isolated communities to remain isolated and disconnected from mainstream politics. Political participation-based potential routes to greater integration and connectivity with society at large have, as a result, often served to make isolation even greater than before.

This is surely one of the bigger and most tortuous stories of the unintended consequences of public policies that set out in good faith to drive political inclusion. That said, the lack of conscious intention is no alibi for the shortfall in accountability that has been widespread among individuals, communities, leaders, parties, and, it must be said, regulators and government itself.

The policymaker's challenge is further complicated by a limited understanding of Islamic-related political identity. This understanding has simply been too one-dimensional. It has given rise to the idea that Islam's influence on such political identity is either confrontational and seized by one-sided grievance—or not. This binary perspective serves to negate the spectrum upon which such identities—political Islam and Islamism generically—can and do exist. The impact of social distance and isolation from mainstream social institutions and influences can be crucial in narrowing down the point on that spectrum. For example, some strains of Islamist argument have stressed the importance of the allegedly corrupting nature of non-Muslim influences. Other strains of Islamism have singled out separate identity and isolation as more of a figurative way of thinking about how best to retain the purity and solemnity of Islamic ideals in a largely non-Muslim environment. And yet others have championed a strain that, whilst relaxed about objective patterns of isolation, urges a political Islamism that is in fact well versed in and connected with so-called outside forces. This latter strain is certainly one of the most exciting opportunities for examining the prospects for a critical, engaged Western Islamic identity. It is also, incidentally, not unimportant in shaping the context for a more dignified dialogue between and within Western Muslims themselves.

The issue that matters most in respect to isolation is the putative link with extremism and radicalism. The question-mark it creates towers above all others, to say the least. At one level, Muslims' isolation and separation has been singled out by some as a largely self-chosen preference. The inference is that the faith itself drives a form of self-identity that is suspicious and hostile towards the outside and outsiders. Of course, this viewpoint can also serve to bait Western Muslim communities in a particularly unhelpful way. It suggests that Muslim identity is both a singular and a juxtaposed identity, inferring that it is not like any other social or faith identity. Such thinking betrays a shallowness that is widespread and recurring, not least in some government circles. It fails to account for the possibility that isolation and separation may be the products of other divisive forces such as, but not only, discrimination and hatred towards Muslims as well as other migrant-descended groups. Communities that stick together in such hostile circumstances are not only to be expected but their behaviour may even be rational and normal as a way of coping with external pressures.

Shallowness of another kind is also displayed by the lack of historical awareness. The concerns expressed in the past about Jewish communities' isolation and separation were equally couched in terms of a perceived lack of a basic desire to mix and interact with others. This trait was presented (and frankly often projected) as inherent in the group, rather than symptomatic of other factors. But the possibility that it may be a little of both, in a self-fulfilling manner, was marginalized, much in the same way that the position of Muslims today is presented categorically as cause or consequence. The idea that it is both is really quite rarely heard in research and policy communities. That strikes the author—with a foot in both—as unreasonably unrealistic, inflexible, and unimaginative.

Isolation can be literal or psychological, or even both. It involves disconnection with surrounding influences and conditioners, either because they are absent or because they are countered and controlled by other forces. The radical Islamist viewpoint, or viewpoints, is keen to play on both routes to establishing a narrative around serial grievance based on unjust outcomes. In extremis, an individual or small group that is truly isolated—both in their physical space and in their imagined world—is likely to be more receptive than others to the strength of such a narrative and also to the unconditional way of presenting evidence of one-sided oppression against the group at large. These extreme scenarios may be very limited in scale but they nevertheless provide a way of demonstrating the critical interface between social isolation on the one hand and the influence of extremist ideas on the other.

The policy challenge that lies at the heart of this interface is essentially twofold. One is to generate fresh ways to disrupt the basic link between the isolated individual and community and the narrative of oppression. This involves creating or supporting counter-influences that try to build counter-narratives about the nature and causes of injustice. A further linked task involves highlighting, where appropriate, the non-Muslim aspects of these controversies or conflicts. For example, for a long period, the essential nature of the Kashmir conflict was that it was a territorial dispute before it was ever a religious one; its underlying link to religious identity and grievance has been intermittently stoked as a means to presenting the conflict in simplistic, bipolar terms. Equally, the Palestinian question has festered for many decades as a national-territorial conflict, albeit involving a quasi-Hobbesian state; only in recent times has this conflict been projected and understood in overtly religious terms.

What should be done? Most crucially, policymakers, ranging from foreign policy to urban policy through educational policy, can feed into a mitigating strategy by tackling and presenting problems that, whilst they may contain a Muslim dimension, are chiefly about other factors.

Another way to address the isolation–extremism challenge is to approach it from the other end of the telescope. This is can be done by re-examining the reasons for social isolation and the capacity of policy levers to affect change. In looking at physically and culturally isolated communities, this challenge is a return to the familiar territory of policy interventions that can best promote awareness and take-up of opportunity. Interventions cannot by themselves deliver the take-up of opportunity or better outcomes. This truth is rarely stated, never mind projected, by government and its stakeholders, most probably because various counter-assumptions are deeply culturally embedded in politics and public life. In Britain, for instance, the bulk of such opportunity structures exist in places that, by chance, are not close to areas of Pakistani and Bangladeshi settlement. In some cases, opportunities and communities are not always deep-frozen poles apart and can be grasped via transport, commuting, and some imagination and impetus.

However, for government, within the approach to social inclusion overall, there is a strong rationale to build the ingredients of mobility. Such mobility can ensure that opportunity structures that do exist are as fully exploited as possible. This maxim, moreover, is one that generally applies to any number of socially disadvantaged groups. Policy interventions that create mobility-cum-opportunity in one sense are not, and should not be, a by-word for the deliberate break-up of ethnic or faith communities of any kind. In fact, the rationale is the opposite. It is one that ensures that those members of traditionally isolated and impoverished communities who wish—or can be incentivized—to take advantage of wider opportunities are able to do so. And those who choose not (or do not respond to reasonable incentives) are nevertheless able to reverse or hedge their choices at a later stage.

Barriers to accessing opportunity can normally be tackled using normal policy measures, sometimes via delivery mechanisms that are effectively sensitized to local needs and circumstances. These kinds of obstacles are identified and tackled on an objective basis. They are not necessarily any different to barriers experienced by non-Muslim communities. And they are, of course, barriers that are best tackled by communities themselves, in which case the role of public policy is to facilitate, rather than synthetically create, change.

However, isolation that is bred and reinforced through the collective mind-set of Muslim communities is another matter altogether. This is also about imagined and imaginary isolation, rooted in a rationale of idealized and even fetishized victimhood—followed by a call to 'right a wrong'. Policy interventions to tackle isolation of this kind are much, much harder to identify, never mind the need to do so consensually. Therefore, the role of leadership is important for a whole host of reasons centred around the narrative of political Islam. Arguably, another useful thing that government can do is to look at leadership—its own and of Muslim communities—in a more sober and balanced way. Leadership cannot by itself deliver desirable change. But it can be encouraged, prodded, cajoled, even hectored when necessary, to make a contribution to overall credibility. Such credibility is defined by realism about the scale of the challenge, the extent of social isolation and related victimhood, and the degree of subjectively felt grievance. This will, over time, yield leadership which understands that misplaced pressure group politics alone can make today's existing problems bigger than they already are. A good start would be to use leadership among communities as a way of curbing imaginary isolation and grievance. A better start would be to deploy public leadership—including that of government—to do much the same.

Spawning Credible Political Leadership

The discussion in this and previous chapters has touched on the role of leadership in its widest sense, and concluded that the politics of grievance broadly dominates the landscape. Although critical in some respects, the role of leadership should not be overplayed, however. For one thing, it is useful to remember that to a very large extent community leadership serves to reflect and lead what already exists. That is to say, it is rather delegatory in its nature and tone, operating on the most simple axis of democratic and community accountability. In the case of the leadership of British Muslim communities, many have commented that these communities often get the leadership they deserve—rather than the leadership they profess to want. And distinguishing intelligently between the two is profoundly difficult, for sure.

Another impediment to the argument that effective leadership is vital to success is that leaders can ordinarily only make the best play of factors that already exist. There are no simple magic bullets that can deliver a turnaround in the reputation of Western Muslim communities. There are, as this book has argued, some elements that are more central to this turnaround task than others. But these elements can only have a positive impact in a cumulative way, ideally building strength upon strength. Leadership factors are one such element and can be pivotal in some instances without doubt.

The leadership of Western Muslims can only be evaluated by asking: how effective was it (or parts of it) in deploying the supportive factors that were available to be deployed? This is not so very different from the questions asked of political leadership in general and also of the cadre of corporate leaders. Both are regularly reminded of the task of effectively and efficiently managing resources so as to maximize the odds of favourable outcomes. That said, neither are left to deploy resources that are simply given, and must instead play a part in creating more or better resources which, if generated, need to be best deployed wisely. The leadership challenges facing Western Muslims are, in the end, not that different. Much can and should be achieved by playing given, known cards with greater sensitivity, balance, and even guile. Much but not everything can be achieved by doing so, however effectively and efficiently. To be more effective in building a better, or even transformed, reputation requires a large element of creating additional resources. And to be better assured of such a positive outcome involves the genuinely smart deployment of fresh resources alongside extant ones.

Providing leadership for an embattled, tarnished reputation is a task and responsibility that tends to suggest a particular kind of style. Taking hold (i.e. by taking ownership) of that reputation's failings and pinpointing the ingredients of building a better reputation suggests a different style. And embracing ambitious, defined action, rather than only taking modest steps gingerly, speaks of a very certain style of leadership. This style carries with it some unspoken self-confidence. It may be deployed for the purposes of demonstrating that proactive measures to shape a reputation are commensurate with the scale and urgency of the problem. Political leaders heading up electorally unpopular parties and facing the prospect of political wilderness can speak to this, for instance. It may also be reflected in some refreshing talk about the need to find solutions from within communities themselves. Community leaders facing daunting problems of crime against fragile targets within their communities have faced this challenge. And it may be set in a tone that is balanced, obviously not in denial, and, above all, conscious that bad things can and do take place in the name of a good faith, identity, or cause. This kind of responsibility fell, for instance, on Republican and Loyalist leaders in Northern Ireland after the Good Friday Agreement. Leadership for them involved addressing collective humiliation and worse but in way that fundamentally acknowledged suffering on all sides. Some Muslim leaders, for example, sought to highlight that the 7/7 attackers killed and hurt Muslims through their action. This may have been true but it was also remarkably unbalanced—and wrong-headed—by implying that the victims of terrorism could be differentiated in such a way. It was an example of well-guided but flawed leadership, precisely because it overlooked the indiscriminate, brutalizing nature of terrorism, Islamist-inspired or otherwise. The fact that some were Muslims, and many others were not, is little more than a reflection of demographic and transportation patterns. Rather unconvincing attempts have been made to suggest that the identity of victims of this outrage carried a political message about Muslims living among non-Muslims. But it has to be said that these are weak and misguided attempts, and that they also miss the larger central point about human suffering and trauma. In a city such as London (or Madrid), victims of mass transit terrorism could only ever be victims, each one as innocent as the next. Or they could be portrayed as guilty as one another, in the narrative of men of violence and their tacit supporters. Leadership that appeared—or perhaps sought—to qualify this is surely flawed leadership by any criterion.

Policy interventions operating to raise the game of leadership are, by their nature, vexed and uncertain. That is to say, there is no easy way to improve the calibre and judgement of those holding leading or leadership positions. Initiatives to improve the skills and effectiveness of the supply of potential leaders is something that has been valuable in some limited areas, and certainly several shadowing, mentoring, and coaching programmes have been associated with moderately beneficial outcomes.

The bigger prize, however, remains in coupling better-tuned, strategically aware leadership and persuasion skills with a fine-grained appreciation of the role of leadership in all kinds of organizations and settings in society. This point has been exemplified by leaders of Muslim backgrounds in areas as diverse as policing, finance, education, health, consumer markets, regulation, media, housing, community development, and so on. Few of these roles require any direct or detailed understanding of one or another faith community but they do all involve a degree of pragmatic sensitization to faith, ethnic, and other identities. Indeed, leadership generically may be not only defined by such sensitization but also measured by success along an axis of routine awareness of single and multiple identities. Whilst this may sound at first glance like an advertisement for identity politicians, its real value lies in seeking to ensure that faith and ethnicity are not sidelined as special considerations in the work and leadership of public institutions. The very worst outcome is one in which a limited pool of so-called Muslim leaders, and associated specialists in so-called Muslim affairs, are assigned full autonomy to mediate between Muslim communities on the one hand and all other communities on the other. This would be little more than a recipe for single issue politics and dysfunctional policy, at best. At worst, it would herald leadership-by-cabal, thereby neglecting important issues that would allow Muslims and others to share and be connected with each other. And it would fundamentally stymie the possibility of Muslims playing a full part in public policy for the benefit of all citizens.

Combating extremism is the most immediate tasks facing Muslim leaders. As an earlier part of this chapter noted, a key element to do so requires a fundamental shift in the politics of grievance. Muslim leaders, both heading Muslim organizations and also among other bodies, have tended to take a narrow view of the nature of grievances within Muslim communities. This view has been too one-sided to much of the outside world. It has also sometimes been shrill in voicing protest whilst appearing to be rather more silent on possible self-criticisms. In other words, it has been anything but balanced. That said, there are presently simply insufficient incentives for current and future Muslim leaders to change tack, given that existing patterns, many believe, have served their interests well. This collective assumption is somewhat naive because, as previously noted, it can only serve these interests well so long as the matter (i.e. damaging cost) of external reputation is ignored. In the longer run, such a matter cannot be ignored, perhaps not even minimized, however attractive it may be to try to do so.

As this study has contended, the principal case for change must be that the reputational damage incurred is neither modest nor without serious costs to Muslim communities themselves. That is to say, actions and behaviour that are designed to bring benefits to Muslim communities can also serve to dry up the well of support for Muslims among other communities. Others can, and have, taken an increasingly sceptical view of the wisdom of measures and initiatives that more and more appear to single out one troubled group for special consideration. In the eyes of some, this is a manifesto for preferential treatment. In the eyes of others, this is the absolute least that is needed to protect a besieged group. There is little point debating the merits of either viewpoint. Moreover, the contrasting characterizations reveal a great deal about the lack of a broad political consensus in relation to the position and future reputational trajectory of Muslim communities, in itself a deeply worrying sign.

The focus on the costs of a negative reputation, however caused, remains the most fruitful. These costs have historically tended to be externalized by Muslim leaders and many influential voices within Muslim communities. Both have been used for leading and representing a sectional minority that they perceive to be in conflict with others in Western society. It is a particular frame of mind that is not all that unusual given the circumstances of an often stand-apart, collective identity among Western Muslim communities.

The significance of any loss to Muslims is that it is solely understood and seen as a gain for non-Muslims, and vice versa. It is basically a zero-sum collective mindset. Indeed, it may be rational to many minds to view the representation of this sectional minority in strictly zero-sum terms. This betrays the outlook of the leaders of Jewish (and several other ethnic and faith) ghettos in many leading European cities in the eighteenth and nineteenth centuries. At that time, Jews were required, and expected, to live in separate, parallel communities to European gentiles. Their segregation was sometimes absolute, sometimes incidental. And their spiritual, emotional, and thus imagined sense of being apart (and not just living apart) was widespread. It was typically embedded in cultural norms, group assumptions, literary metaphors, political outlooks, and hidden poor appetites for change. Such communities were not part of the mainstream, and could not become as such, as a result of influences from outside and, crucially, also from within. Leadership in this ghettoized world, therefore, required essentially a one-dimensional mediating role. All Jews, it was held, had a similarity of interests to be represented and led. And these interests, moreover, had a universal relevance and appeal to all Jewish people. This did not involve a sectional, faith identity within and a part of a Western society. It was merely a Jewish world view and identity that was a stand-alone phenomenon with virtually nothing in common with the wider society. Many Muslim leaders today have unknowingly adopted a similar path. Their posture has had many of the same hallmarks of ghetto leadership and representation from the past, and in many ways the body language of grievance politics has barely moved at all.

291

Many Western Muslims may, of course, take the view that their position more closely resembles a nineteenth century ghetto community than a strand within a modern multi-faith, multi-ethnic society. The former model involves ghetto politics and with it a predictable dose of grievance. Yet it makes for an agenda that is much weaker and more vulnerable than might appear. The latter model is by contrast a leadership style that is altogether more engaged and self-confident. It is able easily and sensibly to disaggregate concerns and grievances appropriately. It is capable of swiftly separating issues that truly involve genuine group outrage requiring a proverbial federal case, from those that do not. And it is willing to take long-sought risks and initiatives to highlight severe problems that exist from within Muslim communities. It is, therefore, oriented towards putting its own house(s) in order before, and alongside, criticizing the architecture or appearance of others.

Something similar can be seen in the example of long-standing efforts to mobilize leadership among black British communities to tackle urban black-on-black violent crime. Decades passed in which the scale of this problem grew to a substantial scale. The idea of using leadership figures to bear down on the causes of the problem was widely and routinely mooted, often with little tangible success. More specifically, the thorny issue of personal and group responsibility was systematically and sometimes cynically side-stepped. Where it was not, it was couched in highly contingent terms. The role of leadership was broadly understood from within and from outside as a means to deflect criticism and responsibility. It was basically poor and ineffective leadership.

The impacts of such a minimalist approach are not difficult to read. Yet, over time, change has come about from two related sources. The first has been the supply of sensitive, tailored remedies. In terms of policing such criminal behaviour, the Metropolitan Police's designated policy measure, Operation Trident, has combined intelligence-led operational measures with an emphasis on black communities leading the search for solutions from within. In some circles, the latter has amounted to a policy of neglect and self-absolution. This is hardly credible given the long-standing controversial nature of policing measures that were condemned for their failure to consult and involve the communities in question. Moreover, past efforts came with little or no success in curbing such criminality. At the heart of Operation Trident's toolkit lie initiatives such a confidential hotline that members of affected communities can use to pass on both factual and circumstantial information. Although the reliability and overall effectiveness of such information will inevitably vary, there is no doubting the significance of the hotline itself. It marks, very simply, a readiness to confront a problem and its causes, and to do so using a unique advantage of a community knowing itself best. It is terribly unlikely that such an approach could have made it off the test-track without a genuine degree of support and sponsorship from relevant leaders.

This is confirmation of an appetite to grasp a thorn that would be easier to leave untouched. Grasping it comes with some costs of its own but costs that are proportionately modest in comparison with the other costs of inaction and indifference.

The three high-profile quotations that appear at the beginning of this chapter are apt in making this point. The question of sympathy for Islamist-inspired confrontation and terrorism has been well documented, and calls for appropriate behaviours among Muslims themselves in response have not been in short supply. However, very little attention has been given to difficulties that are involved in Muslims acting on this logic. Specifically, spelling out the case for Muslims informing on other Muslims is hardly the same thing as ensuring such a scenario, however strong the evidence to do so. In the end, such behaviour is fraught with difficulty because there always is a short-term reason not to do so as well as the effects of misplaced group loyalty. It is not impossible, by any means, but it is hard to attain at the best of times. But the qualification offered by Marin, the author of the second quotation, is the point that matters: cooperation, as opposed to denial, is required by Muslims 'however distasteful' that may be. The human condition itself often serves to prevent one member of a group informing on and betraying another member. It is, by its nature, distasteful. It is, however, appropriate and proportionate to the circumstances of Islamist-inspired extremism and terrorism. And, however distasteful, it is certainly wise and very much in the revealed, genuine interests of Western Muslim communities and their longer-run reputation in Western societies.

Challenging the Huntingtonian Mindset

The discussion in this chapter thus far has picked up on a small handful of prominent causes of the challenge. The evidence base surrounding each, whilst not comprehensive, certainly points to particular kinds of strategic change and choice. The research and policy community audience will need to take a broad view of the merits of the arguments that has been pursued here. Much of that operates at a high level, involving many of the usual hallmarks of genuinely strategic public policy. It necessarily speaks to the underlying assumptions that exist, but are rarely aired, in relation to Western Muslim communities and the prospects for peace and cohesion. After all, the case is one that involves numerous risks of severe polarization and sectarianism.

Arguably, the most powerful assumption of all is that the modern world comprises one or more sets of binary identities and resulting conflicts. Samuel Huntington's description of such identities and conflicts is just the most prominent of several such accounts. It is neither more nor less stark in its conclusions and nor are its basic building blocks any different, conceptually, from others that have prosecuted a similar line of argument. Moreover, it is important to recall that binary ways of thinking and behaving are by no means limited to religious or ethnic identity. The Deep South of the USA for many decades, even centuries, operated around a basic black/white dichotomy, transforming, somewhat abruptly, during the 1950s and 1960s into a black versus white narrative. South Africa during the Apartheid era was equally a racially ordered, binary way of looking at and organizing the world, albeit one that actually separated out 'mixed' categories. And, of course, beyond politics, there are many a literary, creative, and sporting narratives and mindsets: ranging from stories of cowboys versus Indians, to footballing tribes of Reds against Blues, and various allegorical tales of Good triumphing over Evil and the feeling of Love conquering that of Hatred.

Rather dishearteningly, the typical mental map of Western Muslims does little to challenge cosy binary assumptions. It might have been thought that claims about *The West* and/or against *The Muslim World*, and the tensions between them, may have weakened some, if not all, assumptions about Muslim communities located in Western societies. Something of the opposite has been the case, whereby Western Muslims can often be portrayed and portray themselves as proverbial permanent outsiders. This can swiftly lead to fears of Muslims as threats or fifth-column forces, analogous in large part to 'reds-under-the-beds' scares during the Cold War. In extremis, there are ample hints about the incompatibility of Muslims in (but not of) the West. And this line of thinking can and very often does descend into the posing of uncomfortable questions about the true loyalties and allegiances of Western Muslims.

In the case of the loyalties of Western Muslims, the arguments and evidence have been rehearsed in earlier chapters, and there is comparatively little that is conclusive by way of claims in either direction. Nevertheless, a number of rough conclusions are drawn on a daily basis, in spite, rather than because, of the existence of firm evidence and reasoning. The perceived threat is one that is set in the context of the appeal of the Muslim *Ummah*, or faith community. This is a pretty loose assumption by any standards when so little is known, or could ever be known, about the general and specific conditioning effects of such a claim to loyalty. Loyalty is open to wide interpretation and has been so in practice. If Muslims everywhere are subject to this influence, it is almost impossible to pin down what this actually means in practical terms with any degree of certainty or precision. For instance, it may amount to little more than a tautological assertion that has been used to both criticize and defend Western and non-Western Muslims. It may equally be a crude logic that is invented to shore up an occasional round of breast-beating by leaders of injured feelings. It can also be a spurious logic used to cloak a random episode of Muslim-baiting by populists in and outside government. The effects may be everywhere and nowhere at one and the same time, hardly a recipe for convincing strategic solutions of any kind.

The 'Outsider Within' syndrome is far from unique. Its presence in relation to Western Muslim communities represents a twist on a much older theme. It echoes the position of Roman Catholics in several Protestant-dominated societies during the seventeenth and eighteenth centuries. This is not an appropriate or necessary place to rehearse the historical record. What is relevant is to highlight parallel cases that illustrate the same difficulty. Jewish diasporas right across the Western world are familiar with the observation—most usually a criticism—that their undeclared loyalties rest first with the modern state of Israel. In some instances, this observation has had traction in that tangible resources and assistance have been gathered and transferred by Western Jewish communities to develop and defend Israel. And, in the context of the challenges Israel has experienced over half a century—some, no doubt, self-inflicted—it has not been especially hard to mobilize Jewish loyalties. The case of the Sikh diaspora involved a call to defend similar loyalties in respect of political efforts to found a faith-based homeland state, Khalistan, in the 1980s. East African Asian refugees in the 1960s and 1970s also faced (and those still in situ today still face) an undercurrent of criticism about the extent of their true loyalties to their adopted African homelands. And Roman Catholics over many centuries, and even in the post-war era, have endured a question-mark over loyalty to Rome and the Papacy. A US President in the 1960s broke new ground in quelling unsaid doubts, and largely succeeded in creating a less questioning legacy. A British Prime Minister serving in the 1990s and beyond is said to have held back his Catholicism in acknowledgement of a question-mark over his faith-based motives. An American presidential hopeful in 2007–8 sought, rather unsuccessfully, to portray his Mormon beliefs as not in conflict with his accountability under a secular federal constitution. And a Democratic contender for the presidency in 2008 deliberately tore up the old rulebook of black leadership in American politics. The doubts, if voiced, were not in relation to national-political loyalty but to the individual politician's rootedness—and presumed loyalty—to faith in a largely secular age.

Addressing Global Islam

The above observations, once again, contain rather little by way of causation or explanation. What matters is to establish to what degree there is alignment between a faith identity on the one hand and a political identity on the other. The alignment can be close or not, but it does not in itself reveal much that is useful to know about, let alone predict, behaviour. If it is not too disheartening to admit, sometimes it is tricky to say quite what causes what when discussing Western Muslim communities in general. It is rather trickier, and perhaps demoralizing, when focusing on the appeal of a globalized Muslim identity.

In terms of addressing risks of exclusion, alienation, and violence, it is important to pay enough regard to causes that are rooted in the dynamics of global Islam. That is, obviously, a tall order and can potentially suck in almost any aspects of misunderstanding and conflict almost anywhere in the modern world. That is too high a bar to expect to cross here. What is more realistic is to identify a small handful of prominent examples of global change and conflict that are closely linked to the current and future dynamics of global Islam. These examples can serve to illustrate the different trajectories of not just those cases but also the linked narrative around globalized Islamic politics and identity as a turbulent, revolutionary force (or in some cases, not) in the modern world.

The case of modern Turkey amply demonstrates the narrative at work. It is arguably the most prominent illustration of the cross-over between so-called Western and Islamic values and cultures, and has been in this role throughout much of the twentieth century up to the present. The story of Turkish secular society has been an abiding characteristic of the story of modern Turkey in any case. This story has been pot-marked with tensions and arguments over the correct balance between faith and secularism in public life and the role of the state in regulating Islam and Islamic institutions. The general election of summer 2007 reflected this theme and specifically the rising doubts of traditionally secularly minded Turks about the subtle growth of Islamic influence in public and political domains, and beyond. One commentator went so far as to describe the re-election of an Islamist-inspired government in 2007 as amounting to a virtual clerical *coup d'état*, whereby the centre of gravity had decisively shifted to clerics and their supporters.[11] The overall relationship between secular and faith-based forces continues to appear finely balanced in the case of modern Turkey.

But for Western nations the dynamics of political change within Turkey can have a larger significance. For one thing, attention is placed on even small indicators of the influence of Islamic faith in shaping political choices and behaviour. This is mainly because of long-standing Turkish aspirations to join the EU and, with it, the broad family of Western liberal-democratic states. Turkish ambitions to belong to the EU, in other words, create a powerful backdrop to almost every aspect of internal change and conflict within Turkey itself.

From a foreign policy perspective, the case for backing Turkish membership of the EU has been singled out as a potentially big lever to strengthen Turkey's secular habits. It is a lever that, not surprisingly, has divided existing EU countries and also split parties and politicians within and across national political systems. The dogmatic opposition to such a policy shown by, say, the early French presidency of Nicholas Sarkozy goes to the heart of a lot of the political scepticism across Western societies. It is largely founded on doubts

[11] Taheri, Amir, 'A Very Turkish coup? It May Already Be Under Way', *The Times*, July 2007, p. 15.

about the cultural roots of change and continuity in Turkey, arguing that the economic modernization that membership would bring would be ineffectual in the face of a very deep-seated role for Islam in everyday life.

In fact, it is a doubt that cannot be easily answered because it casts faith and identity at the heart of Turkish society. It is, therefore, very different in character from the position taken by other sceptics who call for internal economic, social, and cultural change within Turkey as a prerequisite to proper consideration being given to EU membership. This rival scepticism is analogous to the tough stance taken by some prior to the inclusion into the European family of Mediterranean countries such as Greece, Spain, and Portugal in the 1980s. It also does places impenetratable identity questions at the heart of equations for inclusion, and helpfully concentrates on improving existing social and economic development policies to deliver shared objectives.

These points are, however, all arguments that sit within a larger question regarding the capacity and appetite not of Turkey to change but rather of EU member states to accept and accommodate such a large Muslim country among its ranks. The appetite for Turkish membership across the EU is not particularly great. It tends to be rather stronger among younger EU citizens and among the better educated and more affluent. But it is, for instance, only minimally higher in countries with significant experience of Turkish migrants such as Germany. Public and elite backing is also modestly greater in Mediterranean countries that joined the European club in the 1980s.

That said, some governments have opted to take a more positive stance and have argued the case, sometimes even aggressively, for the principle of Turkish accession. The British government is a notable case in point. And it is the principle above all that is at stake. This is to relegate the importance of issues concerning the social and economic modernization of Turkish society, suggesting that these are chiefly outcomes of underlying change. It also suggests that the pace and shape of modernization can of course be significantly accelerated both by eventual EU membership and, equally, by the timetable towards accession. In other words, the issue of the principle, once successfully navigated, allows energy to be invested in creating the best combination of incentives to promote the degree and style of modernization.

The changes that result can be seen as both the outcomes of policies that precede accession as well as the causes of certain kinds of transformation that might become more embedded following accession. Membership of the EU, therefore, serves to consolidate a path of change that is already well rooted and central to Turkey's future. A form of path-dependency ensures that deviating options and risks are either directly mitigated or kept to a minimum.

But all of this hangs on grasping the mettle that is the principle of Turkish membership itself. It allows a number of policy options and combinations to be considered that would have the purpose of tightening and reinforcing change and modernization. The outcome would render a large and diverse country such as Turkey essentially unable to wander very far from the path of imperfect secularism, the line of travel that Turks already broadly committed to almost a century ago. Moreover, the wider effects of Turkey's full incorporation into the EU are not to be missed. These would presumably include the force of counter-Huntingtonian influence and example, to say nothing of economic strength, in neighbouring societies in the near Middle East and lower Central Asia. But the ripple effects might also be felt in a number of Islamic countries throughout—and even beyond—the greater Middle East. Many of these societies are openly grappling with the pressures of rapid population growth, economic stagnation, ineffective forms of accountability, and deepening cynicism and disillusionment towards the international order.

Turkey's singular accession to the EU, however speedily or successfully executed, may not significantly impact on any of these societies directly. A number of neoconservative voices have rather unhelpfully spoken of these impacts in exaggerated terms, inferring that the Turkish model alone might be deployed to large effect throughout the Islamic world. But to act as a model of any kind means that a wider relevance can be seen, and it is far from clear how widely the EU/Turkish story can and will be sensed and used in global Islam.

That said, attention remains consistently focused on the long-term inclusion of Turkey, as one large and prominent Muslim society, into the Judeo-Christian historic traditions of the European club. This is in many ways a compelling rationale for two reasons. The first is that the capacity of the EU and its predecessors to incorporate southern and eastern European countries into the EU mainstream was once widely doubted. These challenges were no less great in their own ways but were also met, largely successfully, as a result of comparatively early decisions to agree membership in principle. Those decisions were integral to the larger strategy of incorporation and inclusion, and in many cases enabled effective policies to be agreed and implemented to reduce the scale of difference that membership was designed to resolve.

The second reason is that Turkish membership of the EU would serve to question, perhaps shake, the Huntingtonian vision itself. This vision holds that successful accession of a Muslim-dominated society into a non-Muslim, and increasingly secularized, family is by definition improbable. Huntingtonians usually do not deny that it can be done, only that it is not a simple task and is probably an undesirable one. It is a viewpoint that is founded upon a one-dimensional and mostly deterministic understanding of human identity and patterns of behaviour and conflict. To agree upon Turkey's membership of the EU would, by itself, raise a gauntlet to the claim that Muslim and non-Muslim societies would not choose to live together in an integrated and cooperative manner. It is a powerful point of principle in that sense. The principle at stake matters greatly to all. Issues regarding how this objective should be achieved, and how its unintended consequences might be managed, tend to pale into insignificance. That is not to suggest that successful accession would be guaranteed by a decision based in principle. But it is to point out that the principle of accession in Turkey's case stands out very prominently because of what it might say about the integrative capacity and appetite of European societies. And it would also say a great deal about such appetites in Turkey itself, potentially setting off a virtuous cycle that rebuffs the Huntingtonian mindset from all sides.

The main caveat that accompanies such an approach is that even the most optimistic accounts would place Turkish EU membership on a fifteen-year (or longer) timescale. So the dividends, wherever they would accrue, would be felt over a relatively long time frame. In the context of those who have argued that counter-terrorism policies in Britain and elsewhere might have to operate on a thirty-year timescale, then this calculus may seem both realistic and acceptable. However, in terms of identifying policy measures that can have more immediate effects, foreign and trade policy levers such as this are likely to be less attractive.

The discussion in this chapter has been mainly about how best to respond to the problem or problems identified earlier in this book. In public policy terms, positive foreign policy levers clearly exist which serve to address the obstacle of a Huntingtonian outlook to world affairs. But the larger, related question is to establish the usefulness of such levers, their chances of delivering effective change, and the time frame within which these calculations are set.

For example, it could be argued, somewhat simplistically, that the absence of a credible peace between Israel and her neighbours in the Middle East has been a cause of Muslim grievance. To some degree, this is supported by the evidence certainly. However, the policy levers to respond to this obstacle come with two certainties. The first is that it is a peace that has eluded governments for more than half a century, implying that a comprehensive Israel–Arab settlement is something that is likely to take decades to attain, never mind bed down. Much the same can be said of the dispute between India and Pakistan over Kashmir which has dragged on, and sparked several near-wars, for more than half a century. Second, there is quite a lot of dissensus about the choice and effectiveness of the foreign policy levers themselves. Some have favoured policy interventions that focus on limiting arms and building confidence in alternative security measures. Others lean towards solutions that are grounded in resolving territorial disputes, including claims and counter-claims that must involve compromise of some kind. And yet others have poured scorn on the credibility of any of these kinds of measures, advocating in their place tough, balance of power measures designed to deter aggression.

The disputes over the choice of policy tools of course betray the lack of agreement about the nature of the problem to begin with. Nevertheless, all this dissensus makes for uncertainty and delay in the proposition that a comprehensive peace can be realized. The upshot of this is simple enough to see, namely, that there are no easy or swift ways to pull or tweak important foreign policy levers. The chances reduce, therefore, of influencing opinion and assumptions that are nested in Huntingtonian thinking about conflict.

Creating Trust and Dignity

Foreign policy levers to address global Islamic grievance are not just restricted to specific theatres of conflict such as Israel–Palestine, Bosnia, Chechnya, or Kashmir. These conflicts are certainly important in shaping the larger narrative around global Islam but they are not necessarily definitive. A bigger factor arguably stems from the way and manner in which powerful Western nations interact and engage with others. This has to do with Western leaders—political, economic, cultural, and others—taking stock of the underlying reputation of 'The West' in general across the world.

It is worth stating that aspects of such a broad reputation are certainly ill-deserved and wrongly attributed, to say nothing of being improperly informed. Nevertheless, it is possible to identify the threads of a counternarrative that increasingly afflicts the ability of Western societies to command confidence and credibility internationally. Some of that inability may also be felt in the attitudes and sentiments of minority, alienated populations within Western societies themselves. The views of many Western Muslim communities may only illustrate this lack of credibility, observing, as many of them believe, a growing gap between standards held up to praise 'at home' versus patterns of behaviour on the ground at home and abroad. Numerous public rows over moral codes, particularly in relation to women, are a good example. The perceived hypocrisy lies in using a grand narrative that speaks of the liberties of all women whilst sidestepping the evidence regarding the degradation and exploitation on some women in everyday Western societies. Equally, dress codes that set out to protect the modesty of women can be harshly criticized, even denounced, for being repressive or worse. And recent crises over cartoons and the depiction of religious icons have been roundly attacked as unqualified attacks on artistic and personal free expression.

Each of these cases, and others, flow from the well of perceived double-standards. The well can feed a number of loosely related concerns and has in practical terms fed the argument that various forms of hegemonic power underscore Western countries' relationships with the world. A similar logic can be applied to Muslims settled in Western countries, the bulk of whom are thrown together with a rudimentary sense of 'The Muslim World'. In any case, double-standards are at the heart of this general viewpoint and grievances based on these are detected in a number of areas. Some of these are linked to dominant economic relationship enjoyed by many Western countries, and sometimes resented in a wide range of less-developed societies.

Other forms of double-standards are sometimes seen in relation to tackling particular conflicts, most notably in the Middle East but also in several other global hotspots such as Chechnya and Indonesia. The same sort of logic also underpins the doubts held and expressed by a number of Asian—Southern, Eastern, and South-East Asian—leaders about the merits of so-called Asiatic versus Western models of economic and social development. And much the same thinking has often run through the international arguments over remedies for environmental protection and climate change.

These are, of course, very generalized sentiments about the reputation of Western society and civilization. Many are held at an extremely high level of abstraction, and can effectively be linked to almost any dispute or difference involving perceived and actual unfair advantage. These sentiments also magnify when linked to any number of more subjective assessments of imbalances in privilege or power. The net result can easily create a mushy soup of disaffection which, without intention, is in search of a collective banner of protest. Such protest banners may be useful in identifying underlying disaffection and generalized alienation by scale and nature. But these sentiments can also be unpicked in a helpful way that identifies critical nodes and priorities for policy, as well as for the communication of policy, by Western governments. For instance, many of these protests are underpinned by a recurring narrative of sorts compromising many of the following perceptions:

- opposition and anger at perceived acts of impunity carried out by strong Western powers and which ride roughshod over the concerns of local populations;

- sometimes linked to the above, political alienation created by the absence of properly accountable governments, especially in countries where citizen preferences are given only minimal attention;

- perceived tendencies among Western nations to favour—and impose— one-sided solutions to both high profile conflicts involving close Western allies (e.g. Israel–Palestine) and lower profile ones that cause Western powers to look the other way (e.g. Chechnya);

- apparent non- or insufficient availability of credible mechanisms to surface and to air issues of mounting grievance within the international order;

- linked to the above, the scarcity of recognized ways to achieve redress that are balanced, proportionate, and sensitized to widespread feelings of powerlessness and lack of hope;

- most controversially, in the era since 9/11, a widespread view that the USA, supported by its allies, is engaged in a battle against Islam and Muslim-majority countries; and finally,

- the sense that global Islam is under a grave assault that can only be rebuffed via an equally uncompromising approach based, if necessary, on hatred and violence meeting hatred and violence.

It almost goes without saying that many elements of the above narrative may only incidentally relate to the policies or actions of Western nations. Indeed, several elements may arise from disgruntlement with local governments, some of which may even share a sense of relative weakness and despair in shaping better outcomes. And, of course, these are all highly subjective assessments based on generalized concerns that are poorly grounded if at all, in objective evidence about the world and the reasons for comparative political, economic, and cultural strength and weakness.

Nevertheless, with these caveats aside, what matters is that the underlying reputation of Western powers for even-handedness is severely in doubt in many parts of the modern world. In many places, this poor reputation passes for anti-American sentiment. In other places, it takes the form of cautious admiration for Western societies, and American society in particular, combined with a deep disrespect for the specific policies or behaviour of Western governments. This distinction, incidentally, is helpful in pinpointing areas where changes in policy and/or presentation might assist in rebuilding a tarnished reputation. And elsewhere, there is mounting evidence of a semi-coherent ideological stance centred around opposition to the West. For instance, Iqbal Riza, the former special adviser to the UN Secretary-General, has described this phenomenon as a 'Westophobia'.[12] It is, he argues compellingly, the corollary of the sense of 'Islamophobia' that many Muslims feel and internalize. Moreover, it has become silently embedded in the mindset of leaders and mass populations alike throughout many Muslim-majority countries. As a consequence, it has not been checked or balanced by routine counter arguments or evidence. In fact, phobias towards Western countries, like so many phobias, have taken on a strongly irrational and exaggerated form. These seize on even the smallest scrap of unrelated evidence to confirm a familiar point, namely, that the globe has become a binary one, Huntingtonian in style, divided between the imagined Muslim and non-Muslim worlds. This is an intoxicating brew wherever it is supped.

Moreover, this observation provides an insight into the power of irrational belief that has become genuinely phobic, either towards Islam or towards the West. The insight is to note that the remedies are likely to involve a slice of desensitization to the source of the phobia, combined with measures jointly to construct a shared future. The former will tend to involve confidence building exercises that demystify the other, whilst the latter will involve several concrete steps to offer dignity and hope between and within both

[12] Iqbal Riza, opening comments to the Salzburg Seminar, 15 May 2007.

camps. Both serve to reinforce one another by creating a virtuous circle that first questions the irrational belief, then its underlying premise, and finally, the actions and behaviours that have previously been taken for granted.

In some respects, this approach is remedial in that it deals with a pair of belief systems that have already taken hold in the social psyches of many Muslims and non-Muslims. It might even be argued that the approach is distinguishable by its focus on the collective psychological aspects of mistrust, suspicion, and hatred. These sentiments are certainly collectively held and reinforced across many societies, and they are also not routinely subject to self-imposed checks and balances. Moreover, they may be the result of a subtle drift towards bias and deionization that is not overtly intended or choreographed. The upshot is that individuals themselves are especially unlikely to question the basis or nature of the anti-Western or anti-Islamic phobia. The remedies, therefore, lie in collectively weaning whole societies off diets that they have become accustomed to and may have little incentive to question or change.

This amounts to a very tall order by any reckoning. The obstacles to be traversed are essentially located in the imagined—rather than real—world. Nevertheless, the imagined dimension, to all intents and purposes, sits in the real world of and for many. It is a known—but not certain—truth that subtlety is rekindled every day. For example, in 2007, a television soap-drama produced and aired in Turkey, *Valley of the Wolves*, contains a story-line in which Jewish doctors, sponsored by American business, are paid to remove organs from deceased and living Muslims.[13] The levels of anti-Americanism and anti-Semitism in such a portrayal may be horrendously offensive. However, they are woven into a form of mass entertainment whose viewers have become desensitized to these and other similarly negative stereotypes. In such circumstances, it is not so surprising to observe much larger narratives of suspicion and hatred towards Western powers and their equally hated allies. Therefore, the issue is not so much that the reputation of the West has slipped so low but rather that it has not deteriorated even further.

The task, in essence, is about how best to rebuild a more positive and trusting reputation and relationship. This challenge is not strictly the remit of this study but it is possible to sketch the barest bones of the relationships that this would entail. These would comprise three basic, interlocking features and modes of engagement.

The first would be the better and greater use of public diplomacy efforts to highlight those elements of the reputation of the West that are most prized in Muslim-majority countries and also among Western Muslim communities. As noted previously, the poor reputation of the West in Muslim eyes is not

---

[13] Quoted in Taheri, Amir, 'A Very Turkish Coup? It May Already Be Under Way', *The Times*, July 2007, p. 15.

one that extends to all spheres on all occasions.[14] In fact, the evidence shows that it is rather selective, and therefore includes elements that are generally valued and supported. For instance, the relative openness of Western societies and their tendencies to encourage a wider ambit of personal freedom and discretion stands out. These elements appear to be valued in the Muslim world and are also singled out by Western Muslim communities as among the features they most like and admire in Western societies.

Public diplomacy can do a lot to project these features to a wider reach. For instance, free broadcast and print media continue to have a buoyant market. These influences are shown to matter in shaping outlooks and can be magnified in their scope and impact. In addition, Western higher education is also associated with these valued traits, and can therefore be better deployed through public policy as a mitigator against strong anti-Western sentiment.

Second, there is scope to use liberal education and awareness as a means to offset the worst effects of both anti-Western sentiment and also the larger narrative of hopelessness and despair. Eventually, education, broadly defined, amounts to one of the largest levers of all. The scale of attitudinal change that is needed should not be underestimated. This involves a recognition that young people are the inheritors of global change by placing them in an active role to shape solutions. This starts with affording dignity which, sometimes, is easier to do when dealing with younger cohorts who are not in positions of leadership or responsibility.

Education to rebuild reputations is not just about educational content. Positive measures are required in terms of access to education, particularly in less-developed societies, as well as in educational content. The objective is to prepare young people to live successfully in a world made up of differences of many kinds, not just ethnic or religious difference. The means to do so lie in harnessing the deliberative, dialogic, and preventative effects of education in its broadest sense. Specifically, challenging yet balanced forms of education involving young or younger minds has great potential in building alternative outlooks that are both better informed as also more respectful of others.

The rationale for action is to build and capitalize on an already-important factor, namely, the demography of Muslim populations worldwide. The vast bulk are young, and significantly younger than most Western populations. If it is compelling that education is a central instrument for understanding difference, then the potential benefits of success are that much greater when looking at the young age profiles in question. And building a counter-narrative for difference and conflict lies at the heart of what can be achieved. Many of the world's religious and ethnic differences have potential for conflict, although not all have done so. Thus, appropriate educational tools are

---

[14] Bulmer-Thomas, V., 'Living with Two Megapowers: The World in 2020' (The Director's Valedictory Lecture), December 2006.

a powerful way to understand identity and conflict, and to reflect on the fact that they are not the same, nor that one unavoidably leads to the other. The message for policymakers is therefore to build on one of the reliable available planks: education, broadly conceived, is one of the best ways that people, younger ones in particular, can best navigate an increasingly plural world so as to produce less, not more, conflict.

Third, perhaps partly via public diplomacy and education, some of the best remedies lie in greater connectivity both between Western societies and others, and between Muslim-majority societies and the West. By connectivity is meant a degree of routine and normalized familiarity with the realities of significantly different societies to one's own. For instance, aspects of such connectivity already exist, in part, among the internationally minded outlooks of younger, educated citizens of affluent Western countries. Many are reasonably well-informed about lifestyles, priorities, constraints, and opportunities is less-developed societies. Many are also aware of the indirect effects of these factors in shaping choice, aspiration, and life chances. Both information and awareness are reasonably grounded in spite of the general absence of direct, tangible experience of the lives of young people in rather different societies. This is largely as a result of mass communication and a user-led appetite to learn and share experiences across traditionally closed divides. Indeed, modern consumer culture in many more affluent settings has fuelled this appetite and, with it, the capacity to deliver information and knowledge that is actually demanded. The supply of such information ad knowledge has largely fuelled the demand for fresh insight and meaning.

Rather less of this is the case in poorer or socially restricted societies where, unsurprisingly, the desire to learn and share is often curbed by lack of opportunity structures. However, the underlying appetite to build connections between and across ordinary individuals remains an important opportunity. There are various ways to achieve this, including and beyond education, media, travel, entertainment, and youth culture such as music and sports. None of these elements operates in isolation. Indeed, many are growing forces as a result of new relationships and demands unleashed by globalized markets. Mobile telephony, once assumed to be the preserve of business communications and consumer lifestyles, has emerged in recent years as arguably the most powerful force connecting individuals and societies. Much the same can be said of lifestyle social networking. Not all of these forces are easily controlled or shaped by public policy and most may only be open to influence at the margins. Thoughts around building connectivity of a benign, liberal nature may, therefore, have to be scaled back by this constraint. But influencing and building on patterns of this kind that are already present and accelerating is the most plausible way forward for embedding liberal values and ideals.

In terms of building relationships, the emphasis remains on offsetting the worst aspects of the anti-Western reputations and on nurturing dialogue that is on an equal and mutually respectful basis. Either can have major positive impacts. Both are likely to have effects that are larger than their sum. For instance, effective redress mechanisms can be constructed via better balanced and more effective relationships. But it is better still to aim for jointly prized forms of redress that are designed to be used exceptionally rather than routinely. This is certainly more ambitious. But, in truth, it may not be so realistic against a backdrop in which there might be, and probably are, multiple, interwoven grievances against Western societies. However, the logic remains that those grievances certainly cannot all be aired, let alone resolved, in one go. They might just be so in the bizarre fantasy of some who speak privately about the appeal of a Western Muslim holocaust narrative. Beyond this fringe, however, there are usually well understood and reasonable limits to the politics of grievance and group-based redress.

Greater awareness through better connectivity is also designed to encourage heightened sensitivity among Western governments about the scale of disaffection. By being more aware of the perception that 'The West' is associated with naked acts of impunity to begin with, it is reasonable to believe that some of these actions can be reconsidered or avoided altogether.

They cannot, of course, even be reconsidered on the basis of a balance of power model. What is required, rather, is the growth of alternative ways to model and predict thinking and behaviour. One of the most promising is to understand global Islam, and other identity banners, in terms of common interests that span Muslims and non-Muslims alike. A more focused and ambitious approach to development and aid policy, emphasizing benefits that accrue to all sides, is one obvious example. This in itself is built on, and will build greater, routine connectivity of the kind that thwarts strident Westophobic and Islamophobic attitudes alike.

This way of approaching the rebuilding of positive reputations is sadly rather scarce at the present time. Very little is heard about the need to carry others' hearts and minds. And even less is said about the importance of common interests that jettison the Huntingtonian mindset. Perhaps this is not so astonishing given that so much of global Islamic identity is presently defined by what it is against, rather than what it is for. Equally, Western projections of hard power and determination to tackle radical Islamists in solely security terms have caused an already tenuous Western reputation to erode considerably over the past decade.

Despite this, the positive effects of even the most well-calibrated foreign and domestic policies will be reduced sharply without a sufficient consensus to highlight common interest. This is as much dependent on *how* things are done as *what* is done. Creating fresh hope and confidence, where there is presently hardly any, in fact requires real attention being given to the 'how' question. Even the smallest misjudgement on this axis can lead to massively greater odds of all sides reverting to worst-case stereotypes. Success thus becomes even harder to achieve, somewhat needlessly. The 'how' is grounded in offering dignity, irrespective of the nature and degree of differences over values, ideas, or goals. It builds trust among moderate opinion because it is willing to engage at a level of reality and credibility. Moreover, it carries genuine strength for not claiming sweeping grand solutions and by projecting a stylistic modesty. It also benefits from a willingness to start incrementally, not least to underpin confidence and recognize existing fragility.

But, above all, paying attention to how things are carried forward means that the chances of slipping back into a one-dimensional identity straitjacket is best averted. This suggests that the contextual surrounding are central to the textual core, an insight that is very commonly overlooked in addressing the socio-psychological aspects of historically laden conflicts. Dr. Kamal Hossain, a former foreign affairs minister of the young state of Bangladesh, has expressed the sentiment within this contextual task as follows: [15]

We need to build consensus and coalitions among the women and men, who make up the large majority, within nations and across nations, who yearn for peace and justice. We need to recapture a sense of history in which progress has been made by overcoming narrow minded concepts of 'us' and 'them'. Those who are enlightened and liberated may need to work together to develop and strengthen values of tolerance and respect for human rights in order to prevent the predatory few, who would sacrifice these common values and goals to secure their narrow self-serving special interests.

Final Thoughts, Future Prospects

This book has argued that qualitatively better strategic responses to the rise of religious and political radicalism among British Muslim communities are required. This is based on a growing reassessment of both the conceptual and practical shortcomings of existing strategy and policies. The conceptual gap stands out, by far, as the major priority in terms of addressing real credibility concerns. More specifically, and following the analysis contained in the study, greater credibility lies in a combination of, first, better ways of addressing underlying settled disadvantage and, second, rethinking religious sensitization for all religious groups, of whom British Muslims are just one large subset. In addition, solutions lie in nurturing more credible leadership

---

[15] 'Initiatives to promote mutual understanding and respect among all faiths and communities in the Commonwealth: some suggestions', unpublished communication, January 2007.

that is able to represent sectional interests in conjunction with the public interest. And finally, important solutions are also nested in foreign policies that are self-aware of the risk of one-sidedness.

These particular solutions involve, for instance, enlightened public diplomacy initiatives to address Britain's and the West's poor reputation in many parts of the modern world. They are designed as major solutions in their own right and as important supportive steps to help ensure that the chances of misreading Western motives—either towards Western Muslim populations or internationally—are minimized. With supportive measures such as these, there is a corresponding increased likelihood that the merits of a pragmatic, evidence-based approach to alienation and grievance are seen and judged without distortion. Public diplomacy in that sense can make a disproportionately large impact on how Western society and government is represented and seen. The how dimension, as noted earlier, can often be just as crucial as the what dimension of public policy.

There is an ever-present danger in studies such as this to arrive at strategic remedies that, however well-informed, may prove to be intellectually elegant at the expense of being sufficiently practical in tackling current threats. That danger, to be sure, is very acutely felt by the author having observed this kind of stumble on many occasions within the policy community. It is a risk that this study in fact sought to navigate in its original inception, and also something that this chapter in particular has set out to meet.

The immediate threat facing Britain and several other Western countries lies in the sharp imbalance between efforts to reduce the stock of extremism (and related sympathies) and the continuing flow of fresh hearts and minds to extremism (and related sympathies). So, in fairness, the solutions also lie in creating better incentives to fence-sitters to cooperate with law enforcement (by understanding and valuing the benefits of doing so) as a credible complementary means to prevent carnage. This necessarily means being explicit about costs of non-cooperation. These external costs matter (i.e. bombs targeting the public and causing real damage to lives and minds). But the message of this study has been that less publicized internal costs also exist and can be measured (i.e. reputation of Muslims in Western societies as peaceful citizens alongside others).

In terms of handling, there is a premium on avoiding what often appears to be a National Muslim Policy. Thus, the pursuit of the religious sensitization of public policy, if this is remotely attractive to a sometimes strongly secular-minded policy community, is something that must be justified in the name of religion, faith, and spirituality at large. It must not become the cynical rationale for stakeholder management of national Muslim lobbies and sectional interests.

It is worth adding that all of these possibilities are partly governed by what we can imagine as our future. Today, it may be difficult to sketch much beyond the discovery or prosecution of the next terrorism plot, or the next turning of the ratchet of mutual misunderstanding. However, a central argument of this book is that being able to describe a better future is a prerequisite to attaining one.

Therefore, learning from the experience of other historical de facto pariah groups may be instructive. A generation ago, it is no exaggeration to say that British society at large had nothing remotely good to say about East African Asian refugees. The Ugandan Asian influx represented a low watermark in a national inability and unwillingness to see new citizens as anything other than pariahs. The newcomers were described as intent on taking British jobs whilst also not wanting to work and claim public benefits. They were thought to be responsible for inflating as well as deflating property prices. Their children's presence in schools would, it was commonly believed, cause indigenous school age children to fall behind and yet concerns were expressed about their academic overachievement. In terms of national orientation and loyalty, it was felt that they would make for unlikely loyal subjects, although it was quickly apparent that their appetite for public displays of British identity was second to none. Most sensitive of all, a generation ago, it could be casually said that they would never really fit in, but the early evidence suggested that their fit could hardly have been better. Boasting assets such as English language fluency, an urban background, and significant white-collar experience in fact meant that the odds of a good fit were high to begin with. But seeing Ugandan Asians overwhelmingly through the lens of a public pariah group ensured that these and other key strengths were not seen, or even imagined.

Infamously, in autumn 1972, municipal leaders of Leicester in the East Midlands placed an advertisement in the Kampala press imploring the Asian refugees to stay away from Leicester. Many, as we now know, ignored this advice and subsequently Leicester went on to become a thriving home to many Asian refugees. And, as we also know, today this smallish group are commonly regarded as paragons of hard work, industry, resilience, commitment to social good, and, above all, loyalty to Britain. In short, public pariahs became notable public paragons in much less than a single generation, aided considerably by the self-created traits and extant advantages summarized previously. But, in addition to these factors, the apparent reputational turnaround was only possible by virtue of a readiness among the group's members to understand and take ownership of its original poor public reputation. This readiness has served to create a public perception of a group not only unhappy about its profile but also one with a astute willingness to take steps to bring about positive change. The composition of the East African Asians included many Muslims alongside other faith communities, and strongly suggests that such a willingness can easily span across particular identity groups.

This is an excellent synopsis of the CV of any immigrant or immigrant-descended group, especially since it was not predicted a generation previously. It would be a good benchmark to aim for among the next generation of British Muslims.

Achieving this is unlikely to happen by accident, or even via the effects of better public policy. It is often suggested that greater respect for Islam and for Muslims in Western society is itself a prerequisite for moderation and curbing extremism. For sure, this is a strongly held perception among many Muslims who complain of the twin burdens of internal extremism and of external hostility towards Muslims. There is, however, something of a flaw in this argument. For one thing, it muddles greater respect as a cause, when in fact it is chiefly an effect. There is no reason in principle to doubt that Western Muslims can be thought of in considerably more positive terms in the future. The difficulty lies in their current reputation which, however deserved or ill-deserved, sees all Western Muslims, with few exceptions, in a pretty poor light.

The bigger flaw in the argument, however, is linked to the previous depressing observation: it is important not to confuse respect with fear. That is to say, there is reason to think that the sense of respect that is shown in public towards Muslims and their leaders may in fact be not much more than a veneer. Its superficiality can be explained partly by public codes of political correctness towards any and all putatively unpopular minority groups. But it can also be the result of something very different to respect, namely, fear. Such fear might comprise a rational element that is roughly in line with what should be expected (i.e. that 'most Muslims are not terrorists'). The rub, however, is that fear can and probably does also carry an irrational element that equally cannot be shied away from (i.e. that 'most terrorists are Muslims'). It is the latter that really ignites and fuels suspicion, fear, and worse. Only the most naive or dogmatic would confuse this with the desperately misplaced demand for respect. As many wise sages have been minded to say, in the long run, respect of any kind is earned and never demanded.

Active Reputation Management

Western Muslims' faith identity currently commands minimal public support. Building a credible political consensus around the central job of the faith sensitization of public policy—and society broadly—therefore starts from a terribly weak position. And it probably makes it rather harder to sustain any legitimacy surrounding whatever consensus can be arrived at to begin with. That said, it is also the case that, regardless of adherence to faith, Muslim communities overall stand to be disproportionate winners of a moderate degree of faith-sensitization. Much the same is true of just about any other faith group, but particularly those with higher than average levels of faith self-awareness and identity. This would include most Hindus, Sikhs, Catholics, and Jews, and possibly some segments of traditionally minded Christian denominations and several new, evangelically oriented Christian movements. It follows, therefore, that the related task of building and maintaining the political consensus to move in this kind of direction is something that Muslims, and all faith groups, have a key interest in addressing. The politics of reputation management is a helpful step in doing so, thus producing the nucleus of a virtuous circle. Such a circle, as this study has argued, is very far from being grasped on present trends. But it remains graspable in an imagined, shared future.

There are various necessary and sufficient conditions that need to be met in order to allow even the possibility of a better, shared future. A genuinely credible assessment of the nature and causes of current trends and reputations is central. And with that, several other, equally crucial, steps can be taken. At the top of the list is a full and frank appreciation of the need to take ownership of a battered and bruised reputation. This is a need that exists irrespective of objective assessments of how deserved or ill-deserved such a reputation is in itself. It is equally required regardless of any subjective perceptions of the same.

The fact that many such subjective attitudes are deeply ingrained, and on a massive scale, is no reason to conclude that not taking ownership of the reputation is a viable option. It is, at most, a factor behind some prevarication. Whatever the delays and doubts, efforts to externalize the causes and the effects of the reputation only serve to entrench further the pariah reputation. It is, in other words, a recipe for a vicious, downward spiral to take hold. The spectacle of Western Muslim communities rejecting any reasonable ownership of extremism and radicalism would fail even the lowest test of public credibility. This would rapidly turn into a self-fulfilling prophecy of Muslims as perpetual outsiders and the casual demonization of Islam and all Muslims. The hurt and offence that this would bring would move the problem onto a new stage of permanent, deterministic conflict of a civilizational nature. This is essentially the binary Huntingtonian vision.

The scale of intergenerational suspicion and animosity cannot be dismissed lightly. In such circumstances, even the most enlightened and well-calibrated public policy may be able to moderate behaviours at the margins, and yet have almost no effect on underlying relationships and reputations. Most well-informed estimates agree that genuinely strategic remedies of any kind would have to operate over thirty or more years to have any real impact. And this may not be sufficient to reverse fully an already well-cast pariah reputation.

So taking radical steps now to own the reputation is more desirable than the alternative of either not doing so or doing so in a conditional or grudging way. The act of positive reputation ownership and management, to cite the jargon for a moment, has substantial symbolic value. This, in itself, would establish a fresh opportunity that has been scarce for so long. For instance, in the immediate aftermath of the 2005 London transit attacks, the leader of the Muslim Parliament, Dr. Ghayasuddin Siddique, counselled that British Muslims should respond in a way that was mindful of British public opinion. This advice came at a crisis-ridden time and went unheard for the most part. It was nevertheless the kind of behaviour that chimes with the message of proactive reputation management offered here. Such a strategy requires many more and bolder components, some of which are plainly beyond the appetite of the vast majority of Muslim leaders and would-be leaders. But the bold, radical thinking that this involves is not entirely beyond the imagination of many members of Muslim communities, to say nothing of the motives of non-Muslim friends and supporters of Western Muslim communities.

Muslim communities who resent their pariah status in Western societies are not, to be sure, sufficient reason for change to take place. But those who recognize, perhaps more tactically, that not all reputations are fully deserved, are likely to be well served by the instinct of creating positive change. Challenging stereotypes as exaggerated can and does assist in the general task, but so too does the acceptance publicly that not all of these negatives are the result of unfair impositions from outside. In fact, both things are likely to be true, to some extent, in one place or another. Suggesting this is clearly beyond the operational comfort zones of most—but not all—British Muslim communities and their putative leaders at present. Challenging and expanding that zone is certainly a priority, and in some cases and places such recalibration is already under way.

The instincts that drive change of this kind from within are neither bald grievance nor misguided accommodation. They are, in fact, drawn from a deep well of realism and optimism about what has been responsible for such a poor public reputation and what is involved in nurturing a better future. These are profoundly important and helpful instincts. They are certainly in short supply and may even be smothered where they exist. But they cannot be thwarted altogether.

This book's message above all is that reputations matter. The reputation of Western Muslims may lie somewhere between the one that they deserve and the one that they desire. The balance at present is sadly, and sometimes unfairly, skewed towards the former. This is a reputational position that, regardless of causation, cannot be ignored. To skim over this is tantamount to accepting a hostile, fractious world of Huntingtonian suspicion and conflict.

Tackling this reputational problem collectively is consistent with taking the opposite approach. British Muslims, along with others, must broadly want to achieve a better, more peaceful future. They must also been seen to want this future. The odds and incentives are possibly stacked against this path. But it is not closed definitively, merely heavily obstructed.

To bring about positive change means that many things must first happen. The most important, in conclusion, is that enough people must be willing to consider, and then embrace, a more hopeful trajectory. And imagining a better future is, surely, an essential prerequisite of attaining one.

Epilogue

This book has its origins in thinking about the long-term development of Western Muslim communities. That path has, over much of this decade, taken a perilous route. In many Western capitals, the levels of political anxiety over Islamist radicalization are now palpable and unlikely to diminish in the short run. The basic concern has thus embedded itself in many Western democracies, although it is clear that levels of risk vary enormously and understandably.

This book has linked together several high-level causes of extremism and radicalization and suggested that these cannot be tackled in isolation. And nor can they be addressed without proper examination of the number and effectiveness of policy levers at the disposal of government. This is a sombre message for policymakers, not least because of the regular expectation that policy responses can and should be found for all aspects of the problems at hand. They cannot; and doing something, rather than nothing, can be recipe for creating even greater difficulties. The conclusions here are of relevance to the public policy community at large.

That said, initial feedback to these arguments has tended to see this book as painting a broadly pessimistic account of current problems and future trends. It was thus in the company of various other titles that had questioned the capacity and likelihood of Western Islam to develop fruitfully. John Gray's 2003 *Al Qaeda and What it Means to be Modern,*[1] for instance, sketched a somewhat pessimistic account. Others have emphasized the relative dearth of genuine debate about values and ideas that might influence ordinary hearts and minds. And others have dwelled on the closed eyes and ears posture of governments and societies towards the root causes of conflict.

This study should not compare directly with such accounts since it has mainly sought to examine matters as seen by governments, not communities. The difference is that whatever trajectory can be painted for intra-community developments, it remains the case that the job of government will be to influence the full range of causal drivers irrespective of ideological considerations.

---

[1] Gray, J., *Al Qaeda and What it Means to be Modern* (London: Faber, 2003).

The initial impetus behind this book was, and remains, to put forward a broadly optimistic vision that is grounded in empirical realism. For instance, it focuses on four broad causal drivers and emphasizes the need for government to gauge not just settled disadvantage but also subjective feelings about exclusion and alienation. The latter by their nature are hard to square up to, but it would be naive and unrealistic to think that social exclusion can be tackled using existing policy levers alone. Exclusion can certainly be addressed in this way but it has also been approached in terms of the oppositional, grievance narrative that has been adopted in many quarters. It is, presumably, helpful to make this crucial distinction. The optimistic intent, if it can be dubbed as such, is to seek to influence both the objective and subjective elements of the issue at one and the same time. It is also surely positive to remind readers of the law of unintended consequences faced by government. And the optimistically minded spirit of the argument, above all, stands on the claim that a pariah reputation can be tackled and reversed. This scenario may in fact seem fetching and unduly upbeat to some observers. If it is, a key rider is attached to it. This is that group reputation matters above all else, whatever the merits and demerits involved.

So the potential for turnaround is highly limited to begin with. Such potential can be greatly, greatly increased, so long as the subject group shows sufficient willingness to take ownership for its reputation. This involves not just tackling factual misconceptions but, more seriously, accepting that negative reputational damage is done daily by casual jihadist talk. The costs here, this book has argued, simply cannot be externalized forever. The central, presumably optimistic, message is that Islamophobia and Westophobia cancel out one another. Progressive leadership can recognize this simple reality, and can seek to determine a better reputational future regardless of the short-term obstacles.

This book may also seem to some readers to see things too readily from the perspective of government. This is of course the basic rationale behind writing it to begin with, although in fairness this can expose certain limitations as well. So a late word is probably needed to explain this thought more fully. Government can certainly be expected to reflect properly on the faith and other identities of citizens and settlers. It cannot, for sure, take as granted that a consistent secular framework for public policy is matched in the contours of society and community. Radicalization and extremism have been partly fuelled by the sharp mismatch between secularist assumptions on one hand and the shrill language of faith-based oppression on the other. This tension has been spectacular in some cases, and it continues to be a regular feature of the brew of oppositional politics that feeds the appetite for confrontational and violent behaviour.

Such a picture has been described endlessly by other commentators. It is not so pivotal in this book, mainly because the task here has been to consider the appropriate role for government. Part of that role is to check which levers it owns and which it does not. The role is also to distinguish between direct policy interventions (in schools and employment) versus indirect policy influences (in communities and places of religious worship). And the role is to raise awareness about the so-called boomerang effects, principally in CT policy and the muddiness of grievance culture and politics. The latter of these necessarily requires this book to stand back from particular group dynamics and to see things from the angle of government. Government's angle includes assessing the resilience of society in the face of severe deteriorations in behaviour and reputation. This also includes the resilience of unpopular, demonized groups to such a climate.

In addition, it means looking, sometimes proactively, for ways to focus on policy questions that are soluble rather than those that are not. To achieve A, it is not enough to say that government should do X. This would be a pretence, given the multiple causes of and influences on problems identified in this study. It is much fairer to say that raising the odds of achieving A requires government to do Y and promote others to do Z. The Y and Z measures are often linked to B-type outcomes that are beneficial to A. In the end, this is an angle that is solely occupied by government although, with foresight, it can be viewed by all.

Therefore, the subtitle of this book deliberately identifies the proverbial 'what is to be done?' question. The answer is that quite a lot can be done to break down the overall challenge and to calibrate policy responses on an informed basis. But the biggest answer of all is that a preventative strategy is required. This represents a strategic direction of travel for government and a heavy strategic investment by society. Its constituent elements have been outlined in the preceding pages and some aspects are certainly more compelling for government than others. The really essential elements are likely to require patience, resilience, and determination. They also involve separating out the uniquely faith-based aspects of social problems from more general aspects that are shared by society. This implies the importance of avoiding essentializing Muslim identity and politics, a trap that is recurring and deeply damaging in equal measure.

But all of the responses that are needed are *absolutely* conditional on the power of imagination. If harnessed to good effect, this will allow a better, shared future to be described—by both Muslims and non-Muslims. This surely represents success of the highest order and it can be accelerated, retarded, or deflected by the actions of government. The odds are very sensitive to the picture seen and influence by government. This book has sought to draw such a picture accurately—and with an optimistic undercurrent to the message. If it has done so, it will have succeeded in meeting its original purpose.

Index

Abbas, T. 9 n., 31 n., 33 n., 45 n., 115 n., 198 n.
Abdullah, Daud 265
Abdullah bin Bayyah, Sheikh 168 n.
absorptive capacity 3, 185, 235
Abu Hamza 203
accommodation 127
  capacity to foster xvi
  difficult aspects of 6–7
  forced 174
  long-term 13
accountability 183
  community 288
  conflict with 295
  democratic 216, 288
  ineffective forms of 298
  public, dramatically reduced 219
  shortfall of 285
Aceh 166, 217, 224
achievement:
  barriers to 76, 117, 151, 242, 249, 261
  poorer records of 41
Adolino, Jessica 94 n.
advantages 83
  educational and linguistic 40
  key 34–5
  second-generation groups 40
  unfair 301
  white xiii, 249
affiliation 67, 82
  religious 32–3, 154, 157
Afghanistan 52, 54, 165
  British-born Muslims drawn to
    (post-9/11) 207
  British government in 208
  low-skilled jobs 56
  peace process 257
  West's actions in 203
Africa:
  immigrant cohorts 81
  Muslim countries 32
  potential conflicts between ethnic groups 79
  slavery 69
  temporary and permanent migrants from
    29

see also East Africa; North Africa; South
  Africa; West Africa
African-Americans 90, 180–1
age distribution 35–7
aggression 115, 191
  balance of power measures designed to
    deter 299
  by-products of 223
  reconciliation towards victims of 134
  systematic 204
  violent 203
agitation 110
agrarian communities 33, 110, 243
Ahmed, A. 221 n., 237 n.
Ahmed, N. 196 n.
airports 277
Akhtar, N. 220 n.
Alam, M. Y. 103 n.
Albright, Madeleine K. 109
Alderdice, John, Lord 15 n., 71, 72 n., 105 n.,
  215 n.
Alderman, G. 85 n.
al-Fayed, Dodi 73
Algeria 28, 197
  de facto civil war (1990s) 28
  Islamists operating on French soil 50
  political turmoil 153
  war of proxy against 50
Ali, T. 68 n.
Ali, Y. 89 n.
Alibhai-Brown, Y. 103 n.
"alien stock" 181
alienation 103, 115, 215, 217, 220, 227, 229,
    234, 240, 246, 251, 259, 270, 300
  addressing risks of 295
  by-products of 223
  consequence and cause of 219
  deep-seated concerns about 62
  generalized 301
  grievance-tinged 283
  growing 155–62, 174
  long-term 235
  political and social 94
  politics of 111

Index

Index

black people:
  Africans 32–3
  Christians 31
  large differences in earnings relative to white
    men 141
  pariah status of young men 235
  political behaviour 81
  young men 4
Blackstone, T. 87 n.
Blair, Cherie 204 n., 218
Blair, Tony xi, 100, 101, 103
blasphemy xiv, 5
Bleich, E. 7 n., 156 n.
Blick, A. 106 n., 227 n., 228 n., 230 n.
Boase, R. 163 n.
Bodi, F. 161 n.
Boroujerdi, M. 112 n.
Bosnia 217, 224, 300
Bosnia-Herzegovina 52
Boswell, C. 134
Bow 93
Bowen, J. 28 n., 168 n.
Bradford 207 n., 208 n., 256, 256, 284
breadwinners 45, 57, 146
Breton, J.-M. 34 n.
Briggs, R. 10 n., 249 n., 275 n.
British Academy 178 n.
British Black and Asian communities 81,
  262
British Citizenship Survey 262
British Council 169 n., 170 n.
  Connecting Futures programme 256 n.
British Crime Survey 255
British history 103–4
British identity 181, 246
  appetite for public displays of 309
  attachment to 182, 262
  inexplicitly projected 262
  public displays of 309
  strong backing for pride in 165
British media 157, 160, 222
British Muslim Research Centre 256 n.
British Muslim Youth Survey (2001) 172–3
British Muslims xvi, 26, 30–48, 119, 126, 217,
  256 n., 257, 275, 310, 312–13
  apparent unpopular case of 5
  Arab, Turkish, and Mauritian
    background 137
  attitudes towards Iraq and causes of
    terrorism 203
  benchmark for next generation of 310
  common bonds and loyalties among 186
  demographic patterns 22, 242
  disaffected 207
  distinctive and collective interests in
    politics 94–5
  Dutch Muslim communities and 54

  endemically part of a left-behind fringe 136
  especially sore issue among 117
  events linking them to conflicts 171
  experiences and preferences perceived as "not
    counting" 124–5
  foreign policy questions 255
  fringe and extremist 257
  government winning over of 280
  hostility against 247
  Indian country of origin 122
  integration of 22
  invidious position of 213
  isolation and separation 284
  job of winning over 280
  labour-market achievement 121, 136–7
  leaders of xiv, 288
  number of 27
  opportunities for advancement 102
  Osama bin Laden "respected" by 200
  overwhelmingly from South Asian origins
    61
  pariah politics of 150
  participation and progress 136
  percentage drawn from Indian country of
    origin 122
  political extremism 200
  political outlook and behaviour 107
  political radicalism 307
  poor outcomes for 139
  potential grievances 218
  press hostility to 257
  radical extremism 199
  radicalization of 212 n., 229, 242
  recruitment pool for extremist beliefs and
    violent action 165–6
  religion as a central part of identity 164
  religious extremism 190, 200, 307
  reputation enjoyed by 185
  second- and third-generation girls and
    women 242
  September 11 negative impact on 157
  singled out by the media 125
  social disadvantage 221
  social exclusion 124, 146
  stereotyping of 153
  transnational linkages 160, 242–3
  umbrella representative organizations 99
  understanding of position and reputation
    of 21
  unemployment rates 56
  well-integrated 246
  younger generations 97, 102, 152, 171,
    172–3, 196, 242
  see also Bangladeshis; England/England and
    Wales; MCB; Northern Ireland; Pakistanis;
    Scotland
British self-image 116

Index

Index

Rowntree, *see* JRRT
Roy, Oliver 171 n., 173 n., 197
Royal Bank of Scotland 244
Royal Commission of Population (1949)
47
Rubin, B. 8 n., 174 n.
Rubin, J. 8 n.
rules 67
 commonplace 66
 moral 150, 241
 unwritten 238
Rumsfeld, Donald 25, 208
Runnymede Trust 35 n., 86 n., 157 n.
Rushdie affair (1989) xxiv, 60, 99
RUSI (Royal United Services Institute) 170 n.,
 256 n., 266 n.
 terrorism and politics conference (London
 2006) 206 n., 207 n., 209 n.
RUSI Journal 268 n., 271 n.
Russia 166 n.

Sachranie, Sir Iqbal 192
safe houses 206, 212
Sageman, M. 15 n., 16 n., 198 n.
Saggar, S. xv n., xvii n., xxiv, 10 n., 19 n., 20 n.,
 47 n., 75 n., 79 n., 81 n., 87 n., 89 n., 94 n.,
 97 n., 98 n., 105 n., 111 n., 115 n., 135 n.,
 162 n., 180 n., 184 n., 197 n., 206 n.,
 219 n., 221 n., 227 n., 240 n., 280 n.,
 281 n.
Sahgal, G. 114 n.
Saikal, A. 110 n.
Salafist thinking/movements 114
Salisbury, R. 268 n., 271 n.
Salzburg Seminar, The (2007) xxii n., 16 n., 75,
 302 n.
Samad, Y. 89 n., 93 n., 113 n.
Sanchez-Cuenca, I. 209
Sanders, P. 87 n.
Sanneh, L. 237
Sardar, Z. 112 n., 164 n.
Sarkozy, Nicolas 296
Saward, M. 21 n.
Sayyid, B. 111 n.
Scheffer, Paul 59
Schmid, Alex P. xix n.
schools 52, 113
 accountability and funding
 arrangements 130
 attainment 25, 127, 130
 attendance and success in 53
 ban on overt display of religious symbols
 49
 dietary practices 98, 120
 faith-based 120, 251
 Islamic 124
 political and history teaching 135

political importance of 107
right to wear veils 50
underachievement in 6, 18, 34
Scotland 37, 39
Scruton, Roger 182
second-class citizens 117
Second World War 4
sectarian issues 68, 72, 254–5
secularism xviii, 8, 50, 167, 296
 Arab nationalism 28
 challenge to post-Enlightenment
 traditions 193
 difficulty of exploring the limits of xvii
 fervent 76
 imperfect 298
 in Islam and among Muslim communities
 112
 official 48
 Turkish traditions 29
 "unbelieving", harmful influence of 114
 widespread 96
secularization theories 164
security 207, 233
 border 228
 challenges created by Islamist terrorism 8
 crises involving mass transit systems 270
 democracy and 8–13
 employment 134
 energy xii
 intelligence agencies and xiv
 international 61, 242
 migration policy challenges and 222
 outer limits of the problem 200
 personal xiv
 regional 224
 stop and search policing 277
 threats to 9, 14
 worries over 105
security agencies 206
 fresh legal powers for 228
 vocal calls for British Muslims to withdraw
 cooperation with 212
security policy 10, 19, 75, 280
 better informed 199
 framing of 75, 199
 demographic and transnational aspects xxiv
Seddon, M. 187 n.
segregation 6, 62, 84, 272, 291
Seldon, A. 135 n.
self-employment 33, 56, 138
self-fulfilling prophecies xiii, 14, 76, 191, 213,
 233, 240, 242, 311
self-identity 164
self-interest 4, 15, 67
self-segregating communities 62
Sen, Amartya 63, 73, 74 n.
Senthilkumaran, A. 98 n., 102 n.

344